1 BOOK 1 DISC

W9-CPE-465

then-
rbert
their
ok,''
emp
op-
the
eye
the
ales
iley
ates
tzog
old
port
njoy

AUG 0 7.

At the Heart of Texas

*One Hundred Years of the
Texas State Historical Association, 1897–1997*

At the Heart of Texas

One Hundred Years of the
Texas State Historical Association, 1897–1997

By Richard B. McCaslin

Foreword by J. P. Bryan

Illustrated and with Captions and Sidebars by Janice Pinney

Texas State Historical Association
Austin

Library of Congress Cataloging-in-Publication Data

McCaslin, Richard B.

At the heart of Texas : one hundred years of the Texas State Historical Association, 1897–1997 / by Richard B. McCaslin ; foreword by J.P. Bryan. — 1st ed.

p. cm.

Published in cooperation with the Center for Studies in Texas History at the University of Texas at Austin. Includes bibliographical references and index. ISBN-13: 978-0-87611-216-8 (alk. paper)

ISBN 978-0-87611-216-8 (alk. paper)

1. Texas State Historical Association—History. I. Texas State Historical Association. II. University of Texas at Austin. Center for Studies in Texas History. III. Title.

F381.M38 2006

060'.9764—dc22

2006026754

5   4   3   2   1   07   08   09   10   11

Published by the Texas State Historical Association.

Design by David Timmons.

The paper used in this book meets the minimum requirements of the American National Standard for Permanence of Paper for Printed Library Materials, Z39.48–1984.

Walter Prescott Webb, TSHA director from 1939–1946, outside the Eugene C. Barker Texas History Center, the first real home of the Association.

Webb became director of the Association in its forty-second year, following George P. Garrison and Eugene C. Barker, and like them he was also a professor in the University of Texas Department of History. Although he served the shortest term of any of the permanent directors, he was one of the most influential leaders of the Association. During his tenure he expanded the scope of *Southwestern Historical Quarterly*, initiated the *Handbook of Texas* project, and established the Junior Historian program.

The Eugene C. Barker Center was housed in the Old Library Building on the main mall of the University of Texas campus. Designed by New York architect Cass Gilbert in 1910, the Old Library Building was the first separate library structure built at the University of Texas. From 1950 to 1971 it housed the Eugene C. Barker Texas History Center and the administrative offices of the Texas State Historical Association. It is today known as William J. Battle Hall. In 1971 the Association moved to its new quarters in Sid Richardson Hall, on the eastern edge of campus in the LBJ Library complex. *Photograph courtesy the Walter Prescott Webb Papers, DI 02272, CAH.*

Contents

To my Texas mentor, L. Tuffly Ellis, a Texian of the old stock.

Foreword

I T IS MY HONOR TO WRITE THIS FOREWORD to Richard McCaslin's *At the Heart of Texas*, the intriguing history of the Texas State Historical Association. McCaslin details the organization's service in the vanguard of Texas history and at the same time tells the story of the organization's own interesting history as it developed through a century of dedication from the many distinguished individuals who formed the personality and refined the purpose of the TSHA. The history of the Association, like the history of Texas, has a fair measure of conflict and color, but mostly it is about a rare 110 years of accomplishment.

I was nearly born into the TSHA. My Aunt Hally Bryan Perry, founder of the Daughters of the Republic of Texas, and her brother and my uncle, Guy M. Bryan, were founding members of the TSHA. My father was a president and shared a close relationship with H. Bailey Carroll and most especially with University of Texas president Harry Ransom, who was an activist in his support of the Association. My cousin Gervais Bell and my brother-in-law and closest companion in the search for Texas History, F. Lee Lawrence, were both TSHA presidents. I joined the TSHA in 1959, encouraged by H. Bailey Carroll, my history teacher at the University of Texas. I first distinguished myself in the work of the Association by not dropping books as an enlisted acolyte for its annual book auction. Some twenty years later I was fortunate to serve on the Executive Council and later as president.

Throughout my now nearly fifty years of connection, the one thing that has always impressed me is the talent and loyalty of the staff, those who served day to day, year to year, in the vineyard of Texas history. There are so many who could be named, but I mention only two people because they, more than anyone else, made my time with the TSHA special. They are Coral H. Tullis and Colleen T. Kain. Their service to the Association can only be described as extraordinary, and you will read more about them in the chapters that follow. I met them at very different times in my life, these exceptional women who served the TSHA with an uncommon dedication and ability. And I can say from my long years of working with them that their only insufficiency was in how little they asked for how much they gave to the TSHA. No one could have done it better.

I have served numerous causes in my lifetime, and on more than a few boards, but there is no organization for which I hold fonder memories or warmer affections than the Texas State Historical Association. This is because of the people the Association has attracted, all of us joined in our love for Texas and our commitment to its history. I count these remarkable people amongst my dearest friends and associates. The likes of most of them I know I shall never see again.

The TSHA had as its original mission the unique charge to preserve and promote the history of the state of Texas. University of Texas history professor George P. Garrison, the Association's first director (called secretary then), assembled some of the most respected names in Texas to serve the cause— John S. "Rip" Ford, famous Texas Ranger and Civil War hero; John H. Reagan, postmaster of the Confederacy and railroad commissioner; former governors O. M. Roberts and Francis R. Lubbock; and president of the University of Texas, George T. Winston. Garrison wisely suggested that the task was not to write a comprehensive narrative of the history of Texas, but rather to preserve the events of the past through the collecting of primary documents and the recording of the recollections and thoughts of still-living history makers. The journal created in 1897 for this cause was the *Quarterly of the Texas State Historical Association*, later renamed the *Southwestern Historical Quarterly*, a publication which for more than one hundred years has not missed an issue, featuring diaries, drawings, eyewitness accounts, and historical recollections about Texas and its history, these contemporaneous accounts supplemented with scholarly interpretations and analyses by both the professional and the nonacademic historian.

The self-appointed task has been both daunting and admirable. For more than a century now, the TSHA has stood as the guardian of a history that rivals that of any state in the Union, given Texas's early existence as a colony of Spain and then a province of Mexico, its Revolution and brief existence as an independent republic, and the challenges it faces in today's world, in which, again, the border with Mexico puts Texas in a salient position as the United States struggles with issues of immigration. More books have been published on the history of Texas than on any other state, and here again the Association has played a major role. In documenting the history of its state, the Association has evolved its own history, until, at the end of the organization's first century, it is recognized as one of the most successful historical associations in the country, or—we might say in a Texas-sized claim—the world.

The leadership of the TSHA—certainly in its formative years—answered to the drum roll of the best western historians of the day. Their names were a clarion call to those devoted to the history of the Southwest and particularly of Texas: George P. Garrison, Lester Gladstone Bugbee, Eugene C. Barker, Herbert E. Bolton, Walter Prescott Webb, and later J. Evetts Haley, H. Bailey Carroll, and Rupert N. Richardson.

The brilliance of George P. Garrison, founder of the Association, lay in following the model of the Wisconsin Historical Society and affiliating, financially and scholastically, with an established state educational institution. Garrison could not have chosen better than the emerging and, in time, powerful University of Texas. Where several previous attempts at forming a state historical organization in Texas had failed, the connection with the University of Texas proved to be the foundation for success, providing not only stability but a prestigious stage upon which to perform, invaluable to an association in need of the credibility and resources such a patron could provide. And, as time would reveal, this was not a one-way relationship. The Association's executive directors, as well as its other prominent historians and citizens of the state, gave stature to the fledgling history department at the University. Eugene C. Barker, Herbert E. Bolton, and Walter P. Webb began to take their rightful places among the recognized scholars of the time, and a Solomon's treasure of Texana material—books, documents, maps, papers—began to come pressing down. Due to the prudence of Association officers and members such as Garrison, Barker, Webb, J. Evetts Haley, and H. Bailey Carroll, this abundance would become a seed for the University's now renowned Texas collections. In addition, the generous donations of two early benefactors toward the development of the University's collections of Texas materials, George W. Littlefield and George W. Brackenridge, can be credited in large measure to George Garrison's work and encouragement.

The directors of the Association with the active participation of its Executive Council and its politically prominent presidents have done much more over the years than just preserve the state's history. They have promoted it with all the zeal of Texas wildcatters. The best effort to creatively expand the influence of the TSHA goes to Walter Prescott Webb. Webb founded the Association's Junior Historian program, inaugurated the seminal effort on the *Handbook of Texas*, expanded the book publications endeavor, and instituted the book auction at the annual meeting. He, like his predecessors, worked tirelessly to increase membership, unfazed by the often modest results.

Though there have been lapses into elitism, the TSHA has proven to be an inclusive organization which encourages participation by the nonacademician and the professional historian alike. This has been true not only of the annual meeting presentations, but of the books published and the articles selected for inclusion in the *Quarterly*. The rotation of the office of president between the lay business/professional person and the academician has also been an important component of the lay-academic balance, and the early selection of women to membership and the later embracing of historians with diverse ethnic backgrounds has further enriched the mix.

From 1946 to 1966 H. Bailey Carroll formed the bridge between the TSHA of the past and what it would become in the future. During its first fifty years the Association's leadership could claim to be among the elite of the professional historians of the Southwest. Its primary challenges were, first, survival of the organization and then preservation and publication of the history of Texas. After Carroll the leadership would embody a variety of distinguished talents in addition to academic scholarship, and the challenges to the organization in the new age of technology and diversity would be in maintaining the significance of the TSHA and passing on the importance of the history of Texas to a generation less devoted to regional history.

Carroll was a student under Webb and for years his close confidant and assistant. When Webb retired, Carroll followed as director and led the TSHA with a conservative rein. He looked the part of the quintessential Texan with his Stetson hat and a Trelles Triangle cigar firmly gripped between his teeth. His Texas history course was my favorite class at UT because of Carroll's commitment to teaching, which reinforced for me the notion that there is no such thing as bad history, just bad teachers of history.

Carroll did not always please the more liberal thinkers in the history community, especially his mentor Webb, but, with a leadership style that looked more to the past than to the future for its inspiration, he expanded all the traditional programs of the TSHA, especially the Junior Historian movement and the work toward completing the first *Handbook of Texas*; he also oversaw the occupation of the new Barker Texas History Center and was a critical force in the placement of historical markers across the broad landscape of Texas. After a contentious fight that extended over more than five years concerning for the most part unsupportable allegations and following several years of declining health, Carroll resigned. Two weeks later he died. With his death began a new era of endeavor and challenge for the TSHA under the successive tenures of Joe B. Frantz, L. Tuffy Ellis, and Ron Tyler.

Under the direction of the team of Joe Frantz and Tuffly Ellis there were numerous changes—some superficial, many significant. For the first time the *Quarterly* put on paint and powder, abandoning fifty years of a lifeless green cover and adding photographs and an expanded number of articles. Ellis, with the blessing of Frantz, clearly favored the academic historian, perhaps giving weight to a claim by amateur historians that these were wilderness years for their own historical efforts. Frantz, himself a distinguished historian with a streak of irreverence and a peripatetic nature, gave national importance to the Association through his connection to Lyndon Johnson, but the daily chores of maintaining and expanding the programs were the work of Ellis. The Junior Historian program grew to unprecedented size under the leadership of Kenneth B. Ragsdale, whose importance is finally properly documented here by Rick McCaslin. Ragsdale did much more than inspire young Texans to a passion for their history; he was also instrumental in forming the Walter Prescott Webb Historical Society, a college-level organization, and in developing history awareness workshops for the teachers of Texas history. Frantz oversaw the publication of the third volume of the *Handbook of Texas* and expanded the Association's publications program with both scholarly and more popular books. These years also brought peace in the valley, at least at the Barker Center. The end of the Carroll Era was a period of near civil war amongst Executive Council members, and Frantz's open style and humor brought a quiet unity to the Council and the TSHA as a whole. His reign could be called the Golden Age of the Association, whose programs grew to both local and national recognition under his leadership; relations with the University of Texas were solid and finances were sound and on the verge of significant improvement.

When Frantz resigned, L. Tuffly Ellis, long Frantz's second in command, stepped into his shoes as director. During Ellis's tenure, the TSHA finally addressed its most serious problem, one that had plagued every director since George Garrison—the need for a permanent endowment. Primarily through the generosity of the organization's nonacademic members, the 100-year financial drought was ended. West Texas rancher Clifton Caldwell; U.S. Ambassador Edward A. Clark; Fred H. Moore, former CEO of Mobil Oil; Fort Worth businessman Jenkins Garrett; and entrepreneur J. Conrad Dunagan of Monahans were the kindling that lit the fire of fundraising. An auction event in Houston in 1981 netted nearly $500,000 for the TSHA's first permanent endowment. Then Tuffly Ellis, through inspiration from the patron saint of historical societies or his own instincts, came up with an idea both brilliant and simple: the expansion of the long-popular *Handbook of Texas* to six volumes, funding the $2,400,000 project through grants and endowments. This heroic fundraising effort was successful due in large measure to the generosity of numerous foundations, individuals, and, early on, the special efforts of Fred Moore and Ed Clark, and later given continued impetus by University of Texas regents Jack S. Blanton and Jon P. Newton, and Houston attorney and civic leader A. Frank Smith.

When the printing dust finally settled in 1997 the *Handbook* project was an historic watershed for the TSHA. It not only produced the finest historical resource book in America, it also provided a permanent endowment of nearly 3,000,000 dollars. Certainly George Garrison, Eugene Barker, Walter Webb, and Bailey Carroll shared a moment of gratification in some heavenly place as the dream that lay always beyond their reach was finally realized. An objective analysis of this landmark achievement suggests that the final encore of appreciation for the feat belongs to Tuffly Ellis; though he resigned before its completion, without him it never would have begun.

Ron Tyler, who inherited from Ellis the finest staff in the Association's history, brought a new vision to the publication efforts of the TSHA. George B. Ward ably edited the *Quarterly* and directed the book publications program. He and Tyler can be credited with producing the best and most visually appealing books in the history of the Association. Most importantly, just as Carroll finished the original *Handbook* begun by Walter P. Webb, Tyler and Ward brought to completion the incredible six-volume cornucopia of Texas history, the *New Handbook of Texas* begun by Ellis. This was not merely a matter of stitching together a few remaining articles, but rather involved completing more than 90 percent of the articles—23,640 entries in total. And, in a move that would establish the *New Handbook*'s reputation with the public, the entire text was made available online at no cost, due in large measure to Tyler's insistence.

Under educational director David C. DeBoe's leadership, the Junior Historians, the Webb Society, and the History Day program blossomed like a field of wildflowers. For his incomparable success, DeBoe was selected an Outstanding History Educator for 1996. If there was anything awry in the Republic of the TSHA, it lay in the complacency with which it approached its relationship with the University of Texas; perhaps because the University's recognition of the Association's work had been so solid for so long, the significance of a continued nurturance of that recognition was underestimated. In many other important respects, the tenure of Ron Tyler and his boards of directors was largely an extension of the Golden Age of Frantz and Ellis.

For 110 years the TSHA has stood nobly as protector and promoter of the history of the state of Texas. Though now better funded, it faces critical challenges. Its relationship with its greatest benefactor is strained as the TSHA struggles to reestablish an awareness of its importance to the University of Texas and an appreciation of the longstanding mutual benefits conferred by a common bond between the two institutions. Many historians consider regional history parochial and romanticized, irrelevant to the broad march of history as it is now being taught. Texas is also experiencing an influx of new arrivals, many with little interest in the state's history; and there are those quick to censure with a revisionist's eye the history of Texas as understood by generations of Texans. The challenge to those of us who love the state and its history is to resist a simplistic polarization that too easily vilifies or glorifies our complex heroes of old and the times in which they lived. We must weave new threads with care into the beautiful old tapestry, and give the new citizens of the state a connection with place and a curiosity about what has come before them in making Texas what it is today.

For the better part of its first century, the TSHA drew on the finest historians of the Southwest and the best of the state's business leaders and politicians for inspiration and direction. In more recent times it has struggled to keep up with its history. It needs a new vigor and enlightened leadership that will carry the guidon of Texas history for the next one hundred years to the historic high ground it has occupied for most of its existence. Texas has potentially the most inspiring history of any state in the Union. It is the sacred trust of the Texas State Historical Association to ensure that this history is shared among our citizens as a revered reality, not an unheralded heirloom.

J. P. Bryan
January 2007

Author's Preface

I FIRST CAME TO TEXAS IN 1983 to be a graduate student in history at the University of Texas at Austin. My years there were difficult, and I found myself without a mentor. Someone told me about a Texas history professor by the name of Tuffly Ellis, who was the director of something called the Texas State Historical Association. I had no idea who he was, or what this organization was, but I soon discovered that I had been adopted by the perfect mentor, and he was connected to this great group of people who loved Texas as much I had come to love my adopted state. I enjoyed every meeting, met so many wonderful fellow historians, and was patiently guided to complete not only my dissertation but my first books on Texas history.

It broke my heart to leave Texas, but young scholars have to go where there are jobs. Tuffly never gave up on the dream that I would return to Texas, and I kept my ties strong by continuing to explore the history of Texas. I was honored to be asked to write a history of the Association, and my journey came full circle when I was employed by the University of North Texas to teach Texas history just a few years before the publication of this book. Today I am a Fellow of the Association and I teach the history of Texas in the Lone Star State. More than that, I have had a wonderful opportunity to give a little back to the mentor and the group who put a lost graduate student back on track.

There are so many people to thank for their assistance with this project. Ron Tyler and the Executive Council gave me the chance to write the book, and all of the Association staff assisted in its production. Downstairs, the long-suffering staff of the Center for American History brought me literally hundreds of boxes of papers—no one can ever say the Association has been lazy about keeping its own records! Tuffly and others offered documents found and copied elsewhere. Dozens of people offered me their time, memories, and memoirs to complete this work, and they have my heartfelt gratitude. Their names appear in the bibliography; after all, they are important sources.

My family as always provided patient support, especially my wife Jana, who was raised in Texas and is very happy to be back. With any luck at all, we will be writing Texas history and attending Association events for many more years to come.

Richard B. McCaslin
University of North Texas

At the Heart of Texas

One Hundred Years of the
Texas State Historical Association, 1897–1997

The Main Building (later referred to as Old Main) of the University of Texas, as it looked during the early decades of the Texas State Historical Association. The first two directors of the Association, George P. Garrison and Eugene C. Barker, had their offices in this building, and the Association's first "quarters" were here, in a corner of the University Library, where the archives of the Association were housed. And it was in this building that the first, unofficial, organizational meeting for the Association took place, on February 13, 1897. The West Wing of Old Main, designed by F. E. Ruffini, was formally opened in 1883; the central section and east wing were designed by Burt McDonald and completed in 1899. The building was demolished in 1934–1935 to make way for the current Main Building. *Courtesy of Prints and Photographs Collection, DI 02308, Center for American History, University of Texas at Austin (cited hereafter as CAH).*

ONE

Academic Alchemy

The Roots of the Association

EORGE P. GARRISON SCRIBBLED FRANTICALLY in the flickering
light of a kerosene lantern. He had worked hard to bring together
some of the most prominent historians in Texas, and he would not let
them leave without approving his scheme for a state historical association. Convincing the group to accept his plan that busy night was an impressive feat of academic alchemy that succeeded after many earlier attempts had
failed. It combined the zeal of the devoted amateurs that dominated previous
historical societies in the United States, including Texas, with the discipline of
the professionals who had established the American Historical Association.
That scholarly recipe would serve the Texas State Historical Association well
in the ensuing century as it grew far beyond the goals envisioned by Garrison
and his associates on that March evening in 1897.

Texans love their history. Unfortunately for many of those who wish to
preserve this history, Texans also cherish their independence. Ask anyone who
has tried to organize a historical society in Texas, and they will tell you that
getting a dozen Texans, much less several hundred or even thousands, to agree
on a historical project is just about impossible. Today there are over seven hundred historical organizations in Texas. When you consider also that of the millions of people who live in the state most have never joined any of these groups,
you begin to understand the difficulty of establishing a successful historical
society of substantial size. The Association has accomplished a miracle in this
large cantankerous population interested in preserving both history and their
own independence. Through a century of old-fashioned perseverance and
innovation, Garrison's Association has survived to become not only the oldest
scholarly organization in Texas, but also an historical organization that serves
as a model for other states.

None of the Association's success could have come without George Garrison's determination. His obituary in the *Quarterly of the Texas State Historical Association* explains that he "was the originator and inspiration and virtually the life" of both the Association and the *Quarterly*. Thirty years after the meeting at which his constitution for the nascent organization was adopted, charter member Bride N. Taylor, who herself had founded the venerable American History Club in Austin, declared that Garrison was "the inspiring force which had brought us together." More than that, as the Association struggled through its first years, Taylor remembered that Garrison served as a "true father" for the state organization, directing every aspect of operations and development.[1]

Like many nineteenth-century leaders of Texas, the man who established the first successful historical association and the oldest scholarly society in Texas was not a native of the state. Born in Georgia in 1853, Garrison came to east Texas in 1874 and taught school. After five years, he went to the University of Edinburgh in Scotland, where, by 1881, he completed certification in several academic fields. He returned to Texas, married, and settled in San Marcos, but tuberculosis forced his temporary retirement from teaching in 1882. Two years later the new University of Texas offered an irresistible opportunity, and he joined its faculty as an instructor in History and English, the two disciplines being then combined in one department.

Leslie Waggener Sr. outranked Garrison in title and seniority, having become a professor in the department in 1883. In 1888 History and English separated into two departments. Waggener focused on English, while Garrison abandoned early efforts to write poetry and became an assistant professor and chairman of the new Department of History. The title of chairman initially meant little because Garrison was in fact the only full-time member of the history faculty. He took his job seriously, joined the American Historical Association, became an associate professor in 1891, and completed his doctoral degree in history at the University of Chicago in 1896. His efforts were recognized with a promotion to full professor in 1897, and he continued to teach, write, and chair the department until his death in July 1910 at the age of 56. By that time, as his successor Eugene C. Barker recalled, Garrison had become "in everything save birth a Texan."[2]

The year that Garrison became a full professor, 1897, was also the year in which he established the Association. It was not the first state historical organization, nor even the first in Texas. In the United States, history organizations emerged quickly after the ratification of the Constitution in 1789. The first, founded in 1791, was the Massachusetts Historical Society, modeled on the London Society of Antiquaries, which had organized in 1572. The group in Massachusetts was greatly influenced as well by the Society of Antiquaries of Scotland, which formed in 1780 and included many faculty members from the University of Edinburgh, where Garrison later studied.

Like their predecessors, the men in Massachusetts hoped both to preserve the history of the country in which they lived and to promote proper writing about the past. The latter objective was twofold: they intended not only to tell the particular story of their own state, but also to demonstrate its importance to the nation. Other state historical associations pursued similar goals as they organized. The most important of the early ones that survived were the New-York Historical Society, which began in 1804, and a branch of the American Philosophical Society that was established in Philadelphia by 1815 and later evolved into the Historical Society of Pennsylvania.

The Massachusetts, New York, and Pennsylvania organizations experienced different degrees of success, but all became models for a flood of state societies in the decades prior to the Civil War. These were dominated by local historians with differing amounts of talent and training, but Congress actively encouraged their proliferation by distributing copies of official documents to incorporated historical organizations. Zealous residents of older states, both North and South, established more than sixty societies to preserve their history and status within the Union. As each new state emerged on the frontier, its settlers organized societies to record their history. Such organizations made it evident that a state had achieved cultural maturity, much like the presence of schools, churches, and fraternal orders. Sadly, most antebellum historical associations, especially those in the South and West, failed as the initial zeal of the founders faded, unlike other social organizations whose benefits were much more readily apparent.

Texans joined the antebellum rush to organize a scholarly society whose interests included history. In December 1837, during the early days of the Republic of Texas, a small but quite distinguished group of political and business leaders assembled in the rough village that was Houston to found the Philosophical Society of Texas. The purposes of the Society were not clearly defined, and the founders were all preoccupied with other matters and jealous of each other. Political rivalries, economic chaos, and removal of the capital of the Republic to an even rougher new community, Austin, made it difficult, if not impossible, to hold regular meetings. Within a few years the Society ceased to meet at all. Almost a century passed before it was revived, in 1936, by a small group that included William E. Wrather and Herbert P. Gambrell, the incumbent and a future president, respectively, of Garrison's Association.

Statehood for Texas in 1846 was followed by the publication of the first general history of Texas, written by Huntsville attorney Henderson K.

Ashbel Smith, physician, Democratic leader, former Confederate officer, and first chairman (1881–1886) of the Board of Regents for the University of Texas, was involved in several early attempts to establish a state historical organization. Smith was among the first to donate his books to the Association's archives collection, then housed in a corner of the Old Main Library. *Photograph from TSHA Files.*

Yoakum. Its appearance in 1855 coincided with at least two attempts to found a historical organization in Texas. In San Antonio, the *Ledger* published a call in early May 1854 for the organization of a state historical society before the first generation of Texans and their stories were lost. John S. "Rip" Ford, a colorful veteran of many military and political battles in and on behalf of Texas, was proprietor and editor of the *Texas State Times* in Austin. He enjoyed a lively and often mean-spirited competition with his cross-town rivals at the *Texas State Gazette* on many topics, not the least of which was public education. During the fall of 1856 Ford tried to revive the cause by calling for the establishment of a state historical society in his paper. Nothing came of the idea, perhaps because Ford was far too busy at that time with political and military agendas to devote much effort to history. He would return to that field much later, when age forced him to abandon war and politics and devote more time to recording his stories.

Texans made another effort to establish a historical society after the Civil War. The demand for reunification and the approach of the national centennial prompted more efforts throughout the country to create new state and regional historical societies. States wanted to preserve the history of their role in national events, and each section, especially the South, wanted to make certain that their story was told properly. By the beginning of the twentieth century, there were over four hundred historical organizations operating in the United States, according to a report of the American Historical Association, but there likely were many other groups whose work went unnoticed outside of local circles.

In late 1869 Ashbel Smith contacted Francis R. Lubbock, former Confederate governor of Texas and aide to Jefferson Davis, about the creation of the Southern Historical Society at New Orleans that year. Smith was a well-known Texas physician, but more importantly he was a Democratic leader and a former Confederate officer who had been a charter member of the Philosophical Society of Texas. He remained active in education, later serving as the first chairman of the Board of Regents of the University of Texas. The Southern Historical Society planned to have a chapter in every southern state and had appointed Smith as vice-president for Texas. He was in good company: among the appointees were Robert E. Lee, for Virginia, and other popular Confederates.

Smith asked Lubbock how their state would cooperate with the Southern Historical Society. They pragmatically decided to hold an organizational meeting in conjunction with the first annual state fair of the Agricultural, Mechanical, and Blood Stock Association at Houston in May 1870. While Smith won a prize at the fair for his winemaking, his efforts at organizing a history society proved to be less successful. The group he assembled included former governor Hardin R. Runnels among its officers, but the members came almost exclusively from the Houston area. They focused on preserving the records of early Texas leaders and apparently did collect some documents, but they soon faded into obscurity as the tasks of rebuilding the state and their careers absorbed much of their time and energy, as well as their money. Smith turned his attention to other matters of interest to him, such as farming, medicine, and railroad development, to name just a few.

Smith may not have been aware of it, but his was not the only historical organization in Texas by 1871. The Galveston Historical Society organized in about August 1871 and began its own effort to preserve Texas history by creating an archive. In a move that would trouble Garrison, the Galveston organization changed its name to the Texas Historical Society of Galveston, several years before Garrison founded the Texas State Historical Association. This led to friction between the two groups and began some confusion in the minds of many people concerning the various historical groups in the state. Correspondence intended for the 'Texas Historical Society' continued to arrive in the offices of the Association for many years after the Galveston organization was defunct. Much of it was harmless, though it certainly did not amuse Garrison that a letter to him from prominent historian Albert Bushnell Hart was innocently addressed to the Society. More alarming were the hucksters who used the name of the Society to defraud Texans by promising the publication of books containing family histories. Association staff often sent the victims' puzzled inquiries to federal authorities.

The activity of the Southern Historical Society and its satellites on the Texas coast may well have spurred Austin leaders into action. Chief Justice of the Texas Supreme Court Oran M. Roberts, the president of the Texas secession convention in 1861 and a former Confederate colonel, hosted a meeting in his office in 1874 to organize a state historical society. Eighteen men joined Roberts, including fellow Confederates John H. Reagan, Confederate postmaster general; Guy M. Bryan, a nephew of Stephen F. Austin who also enjoyed the distinction of being a former United States congressman; and John S. "Rip" Ford, the erstwhile Austin newspaperman and a soldier not only for the Confederacy but also for the Republic of Texas and in the United States war against Mexico. Among the others present for the meeting was one of their former political opponents, Unionist ex-governor Elisha M. Pease.

Despite this impressive array of talent, Roberts and his associates failed to establish an enduring organization in 1874. Part of the problem was a lack of funds. At the same time, many members of Roberts's group had political agendas that demanded much of their time. Roberts, for example, would be elected

Guy M. Bryan, charter member and fellow, was elected one of four vice-presidents of the Association at the March 2, 1897, organizational meeting. He was a nephew of Stephen F. Austin, "the Father of Texas," and had inherited his papers; at Bryan's death the papers were given to the Association's collection at the University of Texas. *Courtesy of Prints and Photographs Collection, DI 02584, CAH.*

governor in 1878, and Reagan was destined for the United States Senate. Ford had come to town from Brownsville, where he served as mayor, to assist in the ouster of Republican governor Edmund J. Davis, who futilely defied the Democrats who had defeated him, legally or not, at the polls in the fall of 1873.

Roberts served two terms as governor, and then joined the law faculty at the University of Texas, which had been established during his first term as governor, before another opportunity arose to take part in the creation of a state historical society. He was not present when the groundwork for this effort was laid. This ironically occurred in the home of an Austin carpetbagger, Ira H. Evans, a highly decorated Union officer from Vermont who served in Texas as an agent for the Freedmen's Bureau and the Internal Revenue Service, as well as being a very controversial Republican legislator. Evans had made a fortune in railroads, real estate, and banking, but retained an interest in history and education. About 1888 he hosted a group that included Garrison; geologist Robert T. Hill of the University and his wife Jennie R. Hill; Julia M. Pease, the daughter of Governor Pease and a well-known supporter of education; Zachary T. Fulmore, a judge who later wrote well-received works on the history and geography of Texas; and William Gaines.

The plans laid by the group at Evans's home in 1888 did not bear fruit until two years later and again were quickly derailed. Sectional animosity may have undermined this effort at unity in the cause of history. Hill later wrote that Evans and Pease were "damned" Yankees, and the former was an "awful damned jackass" as well.[3] Hill left the University to return to fieldwork, though, and cooler heads prevailed. In April 1890 an assembly of perhaps twenty-five people gathered in the office of Lafayette L. Foster, commissioner of insurance, statistics, and history, to organize what they christened the Texas State Historical Society. Roberts joined them, chaired their committee for writing a constitution, and was elected president of the new organization. Foster became a vice-president, and Lubbock was treasurer. Sebron G. Sneed Jr., the Travis County superintendent of public instruction and a longtime promoter of education, became the recording secretary. Unlike Roberts's 1874 meetings, this meeting included women, some of whom served as officers: Julia M. Pease was a vice-president, and Jennie R. Hill was corresponding secretary and librarian. Again, though, the organization did not survive, perhaps because the depression that wracked the nation after 1893 made it hard to continue without a source of funds or a strong institutional sponsor.

The failure of early efforts to create a state historical society left the task of preserving Texas history to other groups. The first of note was the Texas Veterans Association, established in 1873 at Houston. Ashbel Smith and Lubbock served as charter members with Guy M. Bryan, who struggled to sustain this organization as its president from 1892 until his death in 1901. The veterans met each year, published annual proceedings, and amassed an archive that was later donated to the University of Texas. After Bryan died, they lost their battle with time. Only six attended the 1906 meeting, and the Association disbanded in 1907. Bryan aided his daughter Hally Bryan Perry in founding the Daughters of the Republic of Texas, which met for the first time (in conjunction with the Texas Veterans Association) in 1892. They enjoyed more success than the Sons of the Republic of Texas, which lapsed after the demise of the

". . . a great lady in her own right. Cultured, highly intelligent and gracious, she had a charming personality and a warm humanity. She was vivacious and a sparkling conversationalist up to her eighties." Hally Bryan Perry was a great-granddaughter of Moses Austin, who laid the groundwork for the original Austin colony, and a grandniece of Stephen F. Austin. She and her brother, Beauregard Bryan, made the decision to give Austin's papers to the University of Texas after Garrison assured them that the collection would be put in a fireproof vault. In 1892, she helped found the Daughters of the Republic of Texas and for three-score years was a moving spirit in that organization. Quotation from *Houston Post*, June 29, 1955, quoted in H. Bailey Carroll, "Texas Collection," *SHQ*, 60 (Jan. 1956), 390. Photograph ca. 1892. *Courtesy of Prints and Photographs Collection, DI 02582, CAH.*

Texas Veterans Association and did not revive until 1922. Throughout this era, the United Confederate Veterans, created in 1889 from pre-existing organizations and new chapters, and their twin successors, the United Daughters of the Confederacy and the Sons of Confederate Veterans, begun in the 1890s, worked to ensure that their perspective on Texas was not forgotten.

Garrison did not look to earlier attempts in Texas for his model for a state historical association. Instead, he selected one of the most successful efforts in another state: Wisconsin. That state had solved the problem of faltering support for its historical organization by developing a close relationship between it and the state university. Lyman C. Draper had become secretary of the Wisconsin Historical Society in 1854, when the group was all but defunct and unable to pay his salary. He secured state funding, aggressively marketed memberships and publications, and flourished. Reuben G. Thwaites, his successor, convinced the legislature to deposit the state archives with the Society.

Old Main, the west wing, as it looked in 1897 when the Texas State Historical Association was founded. *Courtesy of Prints and Photographs Collection, DI 02570, CAH.*

The University of Texas Campus

On September 6, 1881, Austin was chosen as the site for the University of Texas, and an eight-member Board of Regents was chosen. The next year, on November 17, 1882, the cornerstone of the west wing of the first Main Building ("Old Main") was laid in a ceremony at which the main address was delivered by Ashbel Smith, president of the Board of Regents. The year after that, on September 15, 1883, the University was formally opened in the new building, though classes were held in the temporary Capitol as late as January 1884. In the first year, 1883–1884, the faculty consisted of eight professors, four assistants, and the proctor. Enrollment for the first long session was 221. Fourteen years later, in 1897, the Texas State Historical Association was formed. "Old Main" still consisted of only the west wing; the building was completed two years later in 1899.

"Most people who walk over the magnificent campus of the University of

Texas can little imagine the tribulations of the infant school of eighty years ago.... A co-ed who became a grandmother after leaving the University said her first recollection of the campus was 'a large area covered with grass, wild flowers and a scrubby mesquite and inhabited by horned toads, snakes and grasshoppers; bounded on the north by a church and her mother's house; on the east by woods and pastures; on the south by Rector Valentine Lee's house and more pasture; and on the west by the street car tracks.' ... She said her mother was champion chicken raiser of the neighborhood and raised hundreds of fryers that thrived and fattened on the pickings of the campus. She, with all the other children in the town, watched the first dirt turned up for the building of Old Main. Of course, when she started to school there at the University it consisted of one wing only, facing west....

"When the University moved out of the Temporary Capitol and into the new Main Building it ran into further difficulties. There had not been sufficient funds available to install steam heat so stoves had to be used. Imagine—a big building like the Old Main west wing heated with stoves! As a result, many of the students caught colds....

"When George T. Winston took over as first president he said the campus was used for grazing horses and cattle. Although the forty acres had been fenced, the fence, he said, was gone on one side and was about to fall down everywhere. Ironically enough, however, the regents did protect building and students from lightning as $400 was appropriated one year and $550 the next to install lightning rods....

The spacious entry foyer, Old Main. *Courtesy of Prints and Photographs Collection, DI 02596, CAH.*

Girls Study Hall, Old Main. *Courtesy of Prints and Photographs Collection, DI 02575, CAH.*

"Faculty and regents continually were comparing the generous budgets of the big northern schools and telling the legislature that the University must have more money if it was expected to be a 'University of the first class.' Those funds were slow in coming and for many long years the great University of Texas had to live by the old precept that 'Poor Folks must have Poor Ways'."

Handbook of Texas Online, s.v. "University of Texas at Austin," http://www.tsha. utexas.edu/handbook/online/articles/UU/kcu9.html (accessed Apr. 21, 2006); H. Bailey Carroll, "Texas Collection," *SHQ*, 69 (Oct. 1965), 231–235 (quotation).

A classroom in Old Main. *Courtesy of Prints and Photographs Collection, DI 02595, CAH.*

Of more interest to Garrison was Thwaites's decision to move beyond Draper's opposition to a consolidation with the state university. By 1897 an imposing building was being built on the campus of the University of Wisconsin to house the offices and archives of the State Historical Society. Wisconsin thus became the first to link its state history organization with its state university. Garrison would make Texas the second, and both would serve as models for others.

The Wisconsin Historical Society was not the only agency that influenced Garrison's organizational design. Many older state organizations, Wisconsin included, attracted sharp criticism from the emerging cadre of professional historians in the United States after the Civil War. Garrison was one of this new generation of historians, and like many others he joined the American Historical Association (AHA), organized in 1884 as the flagship organization for professional historians in the United States. Establishment of the AHA represented the culmination of over thirty years of effort to reform the teaching and writing of history in this country. Americans who had studied in Germany returned home determined to employ the methods of scientific inquiry for historical study and writing. New classes, including graduate seminars, were offered, doctorates were awarded, and more faculty members devoted themselves to history. Garrison did not attend the first meeting of the AHA in 1884 but he joined soon afterward and regularly attended the subsequent annual conventions.

The new AHA had much to offer academics such as Garrison who wanted to establish state historical societies, but the arrogance of its early leadership nearly undermined its potential for influence. This proud attitude probably developed in part from the fact that there were very few professional historians in the United States. When the AHA organized, there were only eighteen persons with doctoral degrees in history in the nation. In 1884, unaware of what the future would bring, the founders of the AHA were a "small band of zealous young scholars, fresh from German seminars and armed with the twin gospels of evolution and the scientific method." They believed that their emergence marked a watershed in the study of the history of their country, and they were both proud of that fact and jealous that others might more appreciate the efforts of previous writers, whom they bitterly derided as the "literary historians."[4] It was not until the turn of the century that the number of historians with doctorates exceeded a hundred, though during the next decade their ranks expanded rapidly.

The insecurity and zeal of the professional historians who dominated the AHA prompted them to display "withering contempt" for many state and local history organizations as well as amateur historians. J. Franklin Jameson, who would become editor of the *American Historical Review* and chief of the Manuscript Division of the Library of Congress, declared in 1891, "With but a few exceptions, the local history societies are not likely to be of great use" in the writing of new scientific history.[5] Ironically, in their campaign to create the new national history the professionals recognized the value of local archives and relied on the work of amateur historians in them. Despite their initial disdain, they combed local collections and courted both amateur historians and their wealthy friends. Herbert Baxter Adams, the most prominent early leader of the AHA, led the way in recanting his colleagues' aloofness, and in 1904 the AHA belatedly launched the Conference of Historical Societies as a way to bring local groups into the fold. Jameson in 1909 admitted that he had earlier been wrong to denounce local organizations, though he immodestly claimed that the fact they had doubled in number since 1884 was largely due to the work of the AHA!

George Garrison represented his own Association as a charter member of the Conference of Historical Societies in 1904 and remained active in the organization until his death six years later. He certainly did not share the contempt of historians such as Jameson for local history societies and amateur historians. Garrison copied what he thought was best from the AHA, but he also encouraged the high level of local involvement that made older organizations such as the Wisconsin Historical Society so successful. While he carefully linked his own Association with the University of Texas, thus placing control of the group in academic hands, he harnessed the love of Texans for their history by recruiting amateur historians as valuable allies in education and research. All had to embrace the new standards of academic history, which Garrison regarded as crucial to good scholarship. As Bride N. Taylor, herself an ardent amateur, recalled, the perception that history was a "science, calling for the cold, exact methods of scientific investigation, was a fact just beginning to percolate down from the specialists to the rest of us," but Garrison repeatedly stressed thorough investigation, objectivity, and preservation.[6]

In preparing to launch his effort at organizing a state historical association, Garrison carefully selected a partner. Lester G. Bugbee had received the first Master of Arts degree from the Department of History at the University of Texas in 1893. The Texas native had taken no graduate courses—there were none in the Department then—but he had taken classes from both Leslie Waggener and Garrison, who also directed his thesis on Austin's Colony. Impressed with Bugbee as a student, Garrison welcomed him back to the University as a tutor in 1895 after two years of graduate study at Columbia University. Bugbee enjoyed only six short years in Austin; he departed in July 1901 for a tuberculosis cure in El Paso, where he died the next March. While at the

University, he and Garrison worked together as a "well-matched team," though the observant Taylor remarked, "Bugbee did the drudgery which made the directing force effective."[7]

The Texas State Historical Association unofficially began with an organizational meeting of what Garrison described as "a number of gentlemen interested in Texas history."[8] There were ten of them and they met in the Old Main administration building on the campus of the University of Texas on February 13, 1897. The University was not yet fourteen years of age, and Old Main housed all of the classrooms and offices for the fledgling institution. Garrison shared his vision with an interesting and determined group that day. Bugbee of course was there, taking notes. Judge Fulmore, who had been at Evans's house in 1888, came to join again in the effort to establish a historical society in Texas. Also present were Robert L. Batts, a prominent jurist serving on the University of Texas law faculty; former Texas A&M University president John G. James; Martin M. Kenney, a colorful adventurer and erstwhile historian working as a translator in the Texas General Land Office; editor Robert E. McCleary of the *Texas Magazine*; Eugene Digges, whose title of historical clerk meant that he served as the state librarian; William Corner, author of a popular 1890 guide to the history of San Antonio; and Thomas Fitzhugh.

Unfortunately for the ten, their initial contribution was overshadowed by the list of names chosen by Garrison to endorse his new effort. Several who later wrote about the Texas State Historical Association have wrongly praised as founders the six men whom Garrison convinced to place their names alongside his on a pamphlet calling for members. Along with Oran Roberts, Garrison recruited Francis Lubbock and John Reagan from among the ranks of well-known Texas political leaders; perhaps more politic for Garrison was his inclusion of President George T. Winston of the University of Texas. Last but certainly not least among Garrison's politically savvy choices was the man tersely identified in later accounts only as an "Ardent Texas historian." His name was Archibald J. Rose, leader of the Grange in Texas, Grand Master of the Texas Masons (among whom was Garrison), and trustee for several schools including Texas A&M University. Since 1894 he had been Digges's boss as the Texas Commissioner of Agriculture, Insurance, Statistics, and History. Garrison's organization would assemble in Rose's office to adopt their constitution on March 2, 1897.[9]

To enhance popular and official support, Garrison completed his list by adding Dudley G. Wooten, a Dallas attorney with a master's degree from Princeton whose father, Thomas D. Wooten, was chairman of the University of Texas Board of Regents. Wooten was both a popular politician and a prolific author. In 1898 he would produce what a contemporary referred to as the

Thomas D. Wooten, chairman (1886–1899) of the University of Texas Board of Regents at the time the Association was founded, and father of Dudley G. Wooten, a charter member of the Association. *Courtesy of Prints and Photographs Collection, DI 02601, CAH.*

"first Comprehensive History of Texas," which included many chapters penned by his fellow charter members in Garrison's organization. Two years later he would be elected to Congress. Wooten did not care much for Judge Fulmore, one of his rivals in a growing host of amateur Texas historians, but Wooten had written to Rose in 1896 asking if something could not be done to create a state historical society. The opportunity had come, and Wooten would not let his rivalry with Fulmore interfere with the opportunity to found an enduring association. He replied to Garrison in mid-February, praising the idea of trying again to establish a state historical society and pointedly adding that it had been a "pet scheme of mine for several years."[10]

Garrison obviously respected the influence wielded by each of the six men who endorsed his membership appeal, but he had more ambitious plans for at least one. To Oran Roberts he wrote on February 15, 1897, jovially describing

UNIVERSITY OF TEXAS,
AUSTIN, TEXAS.

Feb. 15, 1897

Gov. O. M. Roberts,

Marble Falls, Tex.;

Dear Governor:—

A few men here in Austin whom you might perhaps call historical cranks, men like Judge Fulmore and myself, have held a meeting and decided to try to organize a state historical association Mar. 2. The object is to be the location, collection, preservation, and publication of the materials for Texas history. Our intention is to send circular invitations to a number of persons from whom we may hope for efficient cooperation throughout the state to be present, or, at any rate, to become members, and we wish to have the names of a few well-known citizens of Texas signed to the call. Are we at liberty to use yours in that way?

Along with the invitations will be sent a sketch of a proposed constitution. If you have any suggestions to make concerning it, please give them freely.

Can you not arrange to be with us and take part in the actual organization? We shall not, I fear, have many

UNIVERSITY OF TEXAS,
AUSTIN, TEXAS.

189

present, and you could help us greatly.

Please answer at your earliest convenience, as the time is short.

Very sincerely yours,

George P. Garrison.

P. S.
Would you not kindly enclose a list of names of those to whom you think invitations should be sent?

G. P. G.

Garrison's letter of February 15, 1897, to Oran Roberts, asking for Roberts's endorsement and asking him to attend the March 2 organizational meeting. *Courtesy of Oran Milo Roberts Papers, 1815–1897, DI 02581, a, b, CAH.*

Circular sent out

Dear Sir:

You are cordially invited to be present and take part in a meeting to be held in the rooms of the Commissioner of Insurance, Statistics and History at 8:30 p. m., March 2, 1897, for the purpose of organizing a State Historical Association. The general object of this association will be the promotion of historical studies; and its special object the discovery, collection, preservation and publication of the materials for the history of Texas. The proposed annual fee for membership is two dollars.

We feel the duty of immediate action in order that the sources of Texas history may be preserved, and we sincerely hope that you will be able to lend your aid.

If you are unable to attend the meeting, but wish to become a member, kindly signify the same on the attached blank, which you will please mail in the enclosed envelope.

> O. M. ROBERTS,
> F. R. LUBBOCK,
> JNO. H. REAGAN,
> GEO. T. WINSTON,
> DUDLEY G. WOOTEN,
> A. J. ROSE,
> GEORGE P. GARRISON.

George P. Garrison,
University of Texas, Austin:

Dear Sir:

I approve the object of the proposed Texas Historical Association as set forth in the attached circular, and wish to be enrolled as a member.

> Yours truly,

Garrison's endorsed circular sent out in 1897 to drum up membership in the new Association. *Courtesy of Oran Milo Roberts Papers, 1815–1897, DI 02582, CAH.*

the meeting almost two weeks earlier as a gathering of a few "historical cranks." He asked not only for his endorsement, but also for his presence at the organizational meeting to be held on March 2. Roberts had presided over the founding of two previous state historical organizations, and apparently Garrison wanted to give him another chance. Roberts, whom Garrison later described as "bluff and vigorous-minded," was a natural choice to be the first president of the Association. He was not only prominent in politics, both Federal and Confederate, but also a very popular writer of Texas history, a revered founder of the University of Texas, and a respected former member of its law faculty. In short, Roberts would be an effective spokesman for Garrison's Association in several Texas constituencies.[11]

As March 2, 1897, approached, Garrison worried that he would preside over the failure of yet another attempt to organize a historical association in Texas. He had deliberately chosen that date for its great significance in Texas history, but its legacy also portended a possible disaster. He well knew that the people of his adopted state revered March 2 as the day when independence from Mexico was proclaimed, and that they continued to cherish a stubborn streak of individualism. He quietly confessed to his handpicked presidential candidate, Roberts, "We shall not, I fear, have many present, and you could help us greatly."[12] What Garrison counted on, though, was the desire of Texans to preserve and retell their history, a task that was becoming increasingly difficult as old settlers passed away. If he could combine that zeal with the discipline of his comrades in the American Historical Association, his organization just might succeed where others had failed.

Two

We Will Not Fail

George P. Garrison, 1897–1910

T HE FIRST ISSUE OF THE *Quarterly of the Texas State Historical Association* began with a reprint of the June 17, 1897, presidential address of Oran M. Roberts, the first president of the Association. Roberts recalled that there had been "two such institutions in the city of Austin, in which I participated, that failed to be continued in operation," adding his hope that he would not preside over the demise of another such organization.[1] Even as Roberts spoke, George P. Garrison was working hard to make sure that his group would not fail. Ably supported by a small but capable group of associates who shared his vision of Texas history as a vital element in the nation's process of development, Garrison united amateurs and professionals in a successful effort to preserve, write, and teach the story of Texas.

The fact that Roberts's speech appeared in print indicated that the Association had more substance than its predecessors. Publication indicates the influence of Garrison, who well represented the professionals who dominated

George Pierce Garrison (1853–1910), director of the Association 1897–1910.

George P. Garrison, "the Professor of History" at the University of Texas, was the first director (then called recording secretary and librarian) of the Texas State Historical Association. Although there had been many previous attempts in Texas to found a state historical organization, it was Garrison who finally succeeded by following the example of Wisconsin, the first state to secure financial footing for its historical organization by linking it to its state university. Garrison joined the University of Texas faculty in 1884 and was chairman of its history department from 1888 to 1910. He offered the department's first courses in graduate study in 1897. In addition to being a founder of the Texas State Historical Association, Garrison helped win passage of legislation that established the Texas State Library, and helped the University acquire the Bexar Archives. He died on July 3, 1910, at the age of 56. *Photograph courtesy of Eugene C. Barker Papers, DI 02311, CAH.*

THE QUARTERLY

OF THE

TEXAS STATE HISTORICAL ASSOCIATION.

VOL. I.   JULY, 1897.   No. 1.

THE PROPER WORK OF THE ASSOCIATION.¹

O. M. ROBERTS.

The subject of my remarks upon this occasion is "The Uses of the Texas State Historical Association." There have been in the past two such associations instituted in the city of Austin, in which I participated, that failed to be continued in operation. It is to be hoped that this one has been organized under such circumstances as that it will be a permanent institution.

As declared in its constitution, "The objects of the Association shall be, in general, the promotion of historical studies; and, in particular, the discovery, collection, preservation, and publication of historical material, especially such as relates to Texas."

It is proper that the collection of the materials of history should not be confined exclusively to Texas, though they may be most important in forming a complete history of Texas. For being one of a number of associated States, in the same country, and under a common government, there will necessarily be subjects of a general character that will affect Texas in a way to become a part of its history, as well as those arising within its own territorial boundaries. Its objects are not so much to induce the writing of a connected and complete history as to furnish the facts for that object in the future. In a country like Texas, of a great diversity of con-

¹President's Address, read before the Association at its first annual meeting, June 17, 1897.

The opening page of the first issue of the *Quarterly of the Texas State Historical Association*, which began with the speech given by Oran M. Roberts, the first president, at the first annual meeting, June 17, 1897. From this beginning, the July issue came to be the first issue in each volume; the April issue of the subsequent year closes each volume. At the annual meeting on March 2, 1912, the Executive Council voted to change the name to the *Southwestern Historical Quarterly*. The July 1912 issue is the first to use the new name. *From QTSHA, I (July 1897), 1.*

the teaching and writing of history in the Progressive era. His major professor, Hermann E. Von Holst, had come from the University of Freiburg in Baden, Germany, to lend distinction to the University of Chicago. Like most of those who taught the new scientific history, Von Holst imparted a Darwinian belief in history as a social science that would reveal human activity to be a process inevitably moving forward. Historical Darwinists like Von Holst and his students focused on politics, institutions, and organizations as sources for their evidence of progress, earning the popular nickname of "Progressive" historians, not only for the era but also their attitude. Pouring forth not only from Chicago but also from many other prestigious universities, the Progressive historians produced publications that promoted a new scientific vision of historical progress.

Von Holst became best known for his constitutional history of the United States. Garrison followed in his footsteps with his own contribution to the crowning achievement of the first generation of scientific historians, the American Nation series. His volume on westward expansion, which focused primarily on politics, earned him a reputation as one of the few scholars in the West with an important impact on the study of United States history. Closer to home for most Texans was Garrison's history of Texas. Entitled *Texas: A Contest of Civilizations*, the book clearly revealed his belief in historical Darwinism. He noted how the conflicts among Indians, Spanish, French, and Anglo-Americans ultimately, and rightfully, ended with the triumphant conquest of Texas by the last-named group of settlers. Similar themes shaped a textbook he wrote on Texas and his compilation of a three-volume set of the diplomatic correspondence of the Republic of Texas.

GARRISON AND SCIENTIFIC HISTORY

"Dr. Garrison called the [organizational] meeting to order.... He made a very deep impression on me when he said that the first and most important work of the proposed organization would be the collection of material for the use of the future investigators and writers of the history of our State, material much of which, he warned us, had been lost beyond recall for want of such a body.... and when he mentioned such things as letters, circulars, old books, bills, lists of names, personal recollections, newspapers, pictures, etc., I had a realization of receiving something definitely educative in the ... entirely new field of historical science.

"This ignorance of mine as to what constitutes historical material must seem amusing to the company here before me this evening, but ... it was typical of the majority of educated persons, even of many present on that occasion. History was, to us, an art to be dearly loved and ardently enjoyed. That it was also a science, calling for the cold, exact methods of scientific investigation, was a fact just beginning to percolate down from the specialists to the rest of us. So what Dr. Garrison was saying struck the note most needed to arouse our immediate enthusiasm. It offered every one of us something tangible to work for at the outset, and end, too, with the added charm of novelty and thrill of patriotic feeling."

Bride Neill Taylor, "The Beginnings of the State Historical Association," *SHQ*, 33 (July 1929), 2.

Garrison had obvious scholarly biases, but fortunately for the future of the Association, Progressive study of America's past continually stressed not only greater precision but also wider perspectives as people of diverse social, geographic, and economic backgrounds entered the field. Garrison did not have a patrician upbringing and certainly did not limit his studies to economic elites. At the same time, he and many others embraced economics, sociology, geography, archaeology, anthropology, and other social sciences. Frederick Jackson Turner, whose seminal essay on "The Significance of the Frontier in American History" influenced generations of American historians, emerged as the most prominent writer blending these elements into a powerful argument. A graduate of the University of Wisconsin and Johns Hopkins University, Turner argued that social, geographic, and economic conditions on the Amer-

"Exhortation for the purpose of awakening interest in the work of the Association ought to be unnecessary. History like that of Texas is rare. In its color, its dramatic movement, and its instructiveness when viewed from the standpoint of political and social science, it has few parallels. These characteristics make it well worth preservation and study. To the genuine Texan, however, or the man that feels thoroughly identified with the State, one of the strongest motives to the cultivation of the subject will be found in his patriotism. Is it seeming, is it not discreditable to the people of Texas, that they should leave the collection of material for the history of the State to the great endowed Northern libraries, so that her own citizens, when they wish to learn of her past, must go to Boston, or New York, or Madison? Shall outsiders be permitted to lead in perpetuating the memory of the patient endurance and heroic deeds of those who builded the Republic? It is to be hoped that the neglect so long shown the graves of Houston and of Rusk will not be reflected in popular forgetfulness or disregard of their public services. Let Texas arouse herself for very shame, and begin at once the discharge of her filial duty."

George Garrison, "Affairs of the Association," *QTSHA*, 1 (Oct. 1897), 130–131.

ican frontier melded immigrants into a new race. Perhaps more than any other volume in the American Nation series, his entry, which focused on the West, fulfilled the true purpose of the series and moved beyond politics to discuss economics, religion, education, and literature.

Garrison's books usually did not reflect the influence of Turner and the wider perspectives of others, but his work with the Association demonstrated his acceptance of the frontier as a powerful force in shaping American history. For him, Texas was a key part of that greater national experience with conflict and expansion. In sum, Garrison "proved to be more American than Texan, and more nationalistic than provincial."[2] The *Quarterly of the Texas State Historical Association* became his principal forum for exploring broader facets of the story of Texas. His own books focused mostly on politics, but the journal included social and economic articles as well as political topics. Both primary and secondary materials could be found in each issue. The content sometimes suffered from cultural biases inherent in a people only a small step removed from the frontier themselves, but, in addition to the Anglo story, Garrison printed pieces on the Indians, the Spanish, and the French, during a time when many historians dismissed such material as irrelevant. His efforts to be inclusive led to a relatively rapid rise in membership, which made it easier to organize diverse programs for annual meetings. It may be that the Association survived where its predecessors had not because Garrison, who was as much a Progressive historian as any of his contemporaries, understood the value of inclusiveness.

Garrison and Lester G. Bugbee invited 250 individuals to join the new Association, and by early March 1897 they reported that about half of that number had agreed to enlist. Many wrote to express support, while twenty or thirty—no one kept a complete roll—attended the official organizational meeting on March 2 in the Capitol at Austin. They gathered in the office of Archibald J. Rose, the commissioner of Insurance, Statistics, and History. Among them were Garrison's comrades from February—Robert L. Batts, Bugbee, William Corner, Eugene Digges, Zachary T. Fulmore, John G. James, Thomas Fitzhugh, Martin M. Kenney, and Robert E. McCleary. Rose, Roberts, and Francis R. Lubbock were there, representing the six enlisted by Garrison to endorse his invitations, as well as John S. "Rip" Ford and the noted compiler of the laws of Texas, publisher and pioneer Texana dealer H. P. N. Gammel. Cadwell W. Raines, a Civil War veteran from Georgia who began the Texana collection at the Texas State Library, had been deposed as state librarian by Digges but was present (and would regain his post in 1899). The vice-president of the Texas Philatelic Association, railroad executive Henry G. Askew, attended, as did a young University of Texas law student, J. Morris Sheppard, who later became the state's longest-serving United States senator.

There were at least three women in the group, two of whom belonged to the American History Club in Austin. The club, which enrolled only women, continued to meet for decades and included many prominent members of the Association. Bride Neill Taylor, an influential journalist and teacher (and University of Texas graduate), had founded the club in 1893 and later joined the Texas Woman's Press Association. The other club member to attend the orga-

FIRST LIFE MEMBER

"The name of the first life member, Mr. D. M. O'Connor, of Anaqua, Victoria county, has been placed upon the rolls of the Association. In a modest but enthusiastic letter expressing his interest in the objects of the organization, Mr. O'Connor encloses a check for fifty dollars, and adds a promise to give as much or more annually while alive and able. May he live long and be always as rich as he is generous."

George Garrison, "Affairs of the Association," *QTSHA*, 1 (Oct. 1897), 129.

nizational meeting was Dora Fowler Arthur, whose husband James was also present. Arthur was a writer and served as an officer in the Daughters of the Republic of Texas. Julia Lee Sinks was the third woman. She was not an American History Club member, but her husband had served as the chief clerk of the post office of the Republic of Texas. She had assisted in reburying the remains of the Mier and Dawson expedition prisoners in 1848, and had joined the Texas Veterans Association. Like Taylor and Arthur, she was a published writer and continued to be active in the Association for many years. There may well have been other women present; Julia M. Pease, for example, appears on the first roll. Taylor, however, in her speech at the 1928 annual meeting, mentioned only herself, Arthur, and Sinks as the women present at that first meeting.

While Garrison hastily finished preparations for the business meeting, Roberts spoke "very entertainingly" and at length about Thomas J. Rusk, prominent soldier, politician, and jurist in early Texas. Garrison finally called the meeting to order, then accepted the job of secretary after Fulmore was elected chair. Fulmore's election proved largely honorary because Garrison already had a clear agenda. As Taylor recounted, he remained the "central figure" throughout the gathering because, as the "original promoter of the movement which had brought us together he best understood what should be done."[3] The primary task for the assembly was to adopt a constitution. Garrison, Corner, and Digges had been appointed as a committee at the February meeting and had already written the document, which Garrison intended to see adopted in short order.

The constitution set clear goals and established a simple framework for operations. Article II declared the Association would focus its efforts on the "promotion of historical studies" and the "discovery, collection, preservation, and publication of historical material, especially such as relates to Texas." The next article defined four categories of membership. Members were to be nominated by the Executive Council and elected by the other members. Fellows were to be selected by the Executive Council from among "Members who show, by published work, special aptitude for historical investigation." Life Members would be anyone who gave $50.00 in cash or historical material. Finally, Honorary Life Members were "Persons who rendered eminent service to Texas previous to annexation." This last group would be nominated by the Executive Council and elected by the members. For officers, there would be a president, four vice-presidents, a secretary, and a treasurer to be elected annually from among the Fellows, while the "Professor of History" at the University of Texas would serve as librarian. All of the officers together would make up the Executive Council, together with the state librarian, three Fellows, and four regular members.[4]

ANNUAL MEETING DATE

"Until this year the regular annual meetings of the Association have been held at the University on the day following Commencement. The time has been found very unsuitable, mainly for the reason that all those who attend the Commencement exercises—as most of the members in Austin do—have little energy left for the meeting of the Association. The Council will soon take up the selection of another date, and it is hoped that the time chosen will be satisfactory enough to become fixed permanently."

George Garrison, "Affairs of the Association," *QTSHA*, 5 (July 1901), 72.

Garrison's constitution was adopted with few changes, but there was one angry exchange during the meeting—when Ford objected to allowing women to have the same status as men in the organization. Garrison read aloud Article III of his constitution, defining the classes of membership, and Ford testily proposed an amendment to create the category of "lady members." This "disturbed" the genteel Garrison, who looked mutely around the room for anyone to oppose Ford. His pleading gaze included the women, who, given the tone of the times, sat silent. Ford pressed Fulmore, as the chair, to rule on his motion, and still no one spoke. Bride Taylor finally rose and said the article was acceptable as written. This provoked a hot condemnation of Taylor's "brass" from Ford, but, in the end, his proposal did not get a single vote of support.[5]

Ford had been repulsed in his first assault on Garrison's effort to include women as equals in the Association, but he had not yet quit the field. When Garrison continued and reached the section on Fellows, Ford again interrupted to ask, "how would it sound to call a lady a fellow?" This time Garrison defended himself, defined "Fellow" for Ford as an academic title, and continued reading. Thus rebuked, Ford "rose, grumbling his indignation audibly, and went stumping out of the room, the loud strokes of his big stick as it hit the tiled floor emphasizing his disapproval of us at every step down the long corridor outside." Those who remained in Rose's office sat in thunderstruck silence, listening to Ford's stick.[6]

Lubbock and two others rushed to speak with Ford in the hall before he left the Capitol, but he did not return to the meeting. Garrison and others visited Ford in his Austin hotel room the next day, but apparently the old Ranger was adamant. There was great concern that Garrison's fledgling Association would thus lose a valuable ally, and Roberts wrote a letter to try to smooth

"One of the names among the charter members of the Association which will always stand out is that of Mrs. Julia Lee Sinks. She was vice president of the Association under the first president, O. M. Roberts, and remained as vice president or as a member of the Executive Council until the time of her death on October 24, 1904." Sinks was one of three women mentioned by Bride N. Taylor as attending the March 2, 1897, organizational meeting. She was one of five women who were among the original Fellows, and one of seventeen women enrolled as members. Quotation from H. Bailey Carroll, "Texas Collection," *SHQ*, 64 (Jan. 1961), 398.

"Public meetings in those days were thought of as men's meetings. The only meetings where women properly belonged, as a matter of course, were church meetings. Each one of us had been invited to this [organizational] meeting [of March 2, 1897] for particular reasons: Mrs. Sinks because she was one of the most valued collectors and producers of historic material, herself a pioneer of pioneers; Mrs. Arthur and Mrs. Taylor because they had cooperated in founding a club which was designed to devote itself exclusively and forever to the study of American history . . . but primarily it might be said that we were there because Dr. Garrison was a forward-looking man and had sensed among the signs of the times that women were about to take their place in the intellectual and political world.

". . . . Receiving no help from other sources [when Rip Ford challenged women's equal status in the Association], Dr. Garrison finally glanced toward us women with pleading in his eye. Colonel Ford, in the meantime, was indignantly calling on the chair to put his motion to vote. Now, Dr. Garrison was the gentlest of men, the most considerate of age and dignity of anyone I have ever

Mrs. Julia Lee Sinks. *Courtesy Adina Emilia de Zavala Papers, DI 02309, CAH.*

known, even in that day, when it was the thing to honor age and dignity, but he simply could not stand for the proffered amendment. His silent appeal to us, however, put us in a position of embarrassment. An innovation indeed it would be for a woman to get up and speak in a man's meeting. So we sat immovable. We were seated together in a row a little to one side so as to give what moral support we could to one another. Colonel Ford was just opposite us, leaning forward on a big gold-headed stick with which he supported the evident weight of his years.... The secretary's [Garrison's] face grew desperate in its pleading. Mrs. Sinks nudged me on one side, whispering: 'Say something.' Mrs. Arthur, on the other side of me, did the same thing. 'No,' I whispered back, 'you do it, or you.'... I finally rose and with a timidity characteristic of the era, ventured with: 'Mr. Chairman, I believe that the section as it stands is all that is needed.'

"... No one here who is not over fifty at least can realize the attitude of that day toward the position of woman outside the home. Her appointed place was a very important one, one deeply revered

Col. John S. "Rip" Ford, ca. 1865, wearing the uniform of a Confederate colonel. Carte de visite by Louis de Planque. *Courtesy Lawrence T. Jones III collection.*

by men, but that place was not speaking before a man's meeting. For her to do so was something startling, but to speak in *contradiction*—well, that was nothing less than revolutionary. Looking back tonight from this meeting, where so many are women, also as a matter of course, I might say that we three women there that evening in 1897 were ourselves documents of history—flesh and blood documents.... I do not remember that I specially resented [Ford's] flinging the word 'brass' at me. I felt myself that I was brassy."

Bride Neill Taylor, "The Beginnings of the State Historical Association," *SHQ*, 33 (July 1929), 4–5.

Ford's ruffled feathers. Certainly little could be done to change the fact that women served in every level of the organization. Sinks was both a vice-president and a Fellow, Taylor and Arthur served along with her on the first Executive Council, four other women joined Sinks as original Fellows, and there were no fewer than seventeen women members on the rolls. Tensions finally eased when Ford sent a note to Roberts on March 20 assuring him that he would remain with the Association.

That Ford represented a distinctly minority view was apparent even before his amendment failed to be adopted on March 2. When Dudley G. Wooten wrote to Garrison in February 1897, offering ideas for the constitution then being written, he concluded, "I cannot close this without impressing upon you the importance of enlisting the ladies in this organization and support of this Society. The most intelligent, discriminating and active laborers in the collection and preservation of Texas historical memorials have been her noble women."[7] Wooten may be forgiven for his slight overstatement, but his point was sound. Texas women could not yet vote in national elections, but in the field of historical preservation they had contributed greatly as activists, writers, and members of such organizations as the Daughters of the Republic of Texas.

The adoption of a constitution was followed by a confused election of officers after the Capitol electric plant shut down for the evening, leaving the meeting room in utter darkness. Two lanterns were "procured from the janitor" to provide a feeble light.[8] Roberts had departed but was elected president in absentia. Sinks and Corner became vice-presidents along with two others who were absent: Guy M. Bryan and Dudley G. Wooten. The latter was among those who had written to Garrison endorsing the appointment of "the Professor of History in the State University" to serve as librarian and thus secure institutional support.[9] With such strong endorsements, Garrison was quickly installed in that post and was also elected secretary, while Bugbee became the treasurer. Nine others completed the first Executive Council: Arthur, Batts, Rufus C. Burleson (the popular but controversial president of Baylor University), Digges, Fulmore, Kenney, Lubbock, Raines, and Taylor.

Some adjustments had to be made in the hasty appointments of March 2. Bugbee's title was clarified in a few days, making him the corresponding secretary and treasurer, while Garrison became the librarian and permanent or recording secretary. Bugbee's title was later confirmed in 1901 with an amendment to the constitution. More juggling took place in the ranks of Fellows and Honorary Life Members before the list was published. As printed, there were nineteen Fellows. Garrison and Bugbee led the list, along with political stalwarts such as Bryan, Lubbock, Reagan, and Roberts. Ford, Fulmore, and

Four members of the first Executive Council: (left to right, top) Robert L. Batts, Governor Francis R. Lubbock, (bottom) Rufus Burleson, and C. W. Raines. Other members of the sixteen-member council were: George Garrison, recording secretary and librarian; Lester G. Bugbee, corresponding secretary and treasurer; Oran M. Roberts, president; the four vice presidents, Julia Lee Sinks, William Corner, Guy M. Bryan, and Dudley G. Wooten; Dora Fowler Arthur; Eugene Digges; Zachary T. Fulmore; Martin M. Kenney; and Bride Neill Taylor. *Courtesy of Prints and Photographs Collection, DI 02604, DI 02609, DI 02569, DI 02615, and DI 02612, CAH.*

An Early Sorrow:
Lester Gladstone Bugbee (1869–1902)

"In any study of the first years of the Association, two names stand out together—Garrison and Bugbee. Dr. Garrison was more than founder; he was a true father to the organization.... but he, overloaded as he was with his regular duties as head of the department of history, would have found himself bitterly handicapped in his efforts without the intelligent self-sacrificing helper so fortunately provided. Bugbee did the drudgery which made the directing force effective. Together the two were like a well-matched team pulling ahead with a single mind. The younger man, first as student and then as instructor in history, had imbibed to the full the spirit of the older, and the main business of the Association under these circumstances went straight ahead, straight but slowly, and painfully. Keeping up THE QUARTERLY was the main business. It was like the house that Jack built. In the spare time of the long term, and all of the time in the summer vacations, the faithful secretary-treasurer [Bugbee] went at his task systematically ... in order to get members, in order to get money, in order to get out THE QUARTERLY.... In addition, he bore also a part in editing, besides contributing

some of the best material which went into its make-up. To those of us who know all of this, those early numbers have a deep human interest."

Bugbee was born near Hillsboro, Texas, at the little settlement of Woodbury, on May 16, 1869. Named "L.G." by his parents; he later gave himself the name Lester Gladstone. He entered the University of Texas in January of 1887, and in 1893 he received his master's degree with a paper written on Stephen F. Austin's colony. This paper won him a fellowship to Columbia University, where he started but did not finish his doctorate. In 1895 Garrison brought Bugbee back to the University's history department as a tutor, and thus began Bugbee's short, but intense teaching career.

"I can describe some of the characteristics of Bugbee's teaching," wrote Eugene C. Barker, "but can convey only a faint idea of the impression that he made on freshman and sophomore classes. . . . He never sat at a desk, never lectured formally, but moved around the room asking questions and discussing the answers. . . . He had one mannerism that all who saw him in class will remember, the habit of playing with his watch chain, winding and unwinding it around the index finger of his right hand."

It was Bugbee who brought the Bexar Archives to the University, and by 1900 he had earned national recognition for his writings. "Though the total volume of Bugbee's publications was not large, their influence was significant," writes Barker. "They changed the tone of American historical writing concerning the colonization of Texas, the Texas revolution, the annexation of Texas, and, in a measure, the causes of the Mexican War."

The tuberculosis that would ultimately take Bugbee's life has an indistinct beginning, but Barker remembers that for some years Bugbee was medicating himself for chronic bronchitis. By the winter of 1900–1901, he was feeling bad enough to take a month off for a rest at Junction. He returned "sunburned to a finish," as he wrote, but by that summer he was in serious decline, and on July 27, 1901, he left Austin for a cure in El Paso. Before long the doctor there, his old friend Charles Norton, gave up on him and he turned to the medical officer at Fort Bliss. Bugbee described him as "a great talker; makes you think you'll get well tomorrow; exaggerates a great deal, but a good old soul." Bugbee wrote his friends at the University often and reminisced about his Austin days, writing, "It's all different here; as I pass along I hear—'There goes another lunger; El Paso ought to pass an ordinance to keep those fellows away from here'" He played with the idea of starting a chicken ranch. In October his friend Dr. Norton asked him if he'd ever thought seriously about not getting well, and said to him, "I don't think I'd start that poultry farm yet." On New Year's Day 1902, Bugbee made the decision to go home to the family farm, where he lived out his last two months, dying on March 17, 1902.

Memorial services were held two weeks later in the University auditorium on what would have been Bugbee's thirty-third birthday. In the April 1902 *Quarterly*, Garrison wrote: "The Association especially owes Professor Bugbee a great debt for his effective efforts in enlarging its membership, building up its revenues, and keeping its finances in order. Professor Bugbee. . . . had done much valuable work in Texas history, and his career was full of promise till disease began to paralyze his energies. His race was short, but he bore well the uplifted torch, and he has not run in vain."

Bride Neill Taylor, "The Beginnings of the State Historical Association," *SHQ*, 33 (July 1929), 13 (opening quotation); Eugene C. Barker, "Lester Gladstone Bugbee, Teacher and Historian," *SHQ*, 49 (July 1945), 15–16, 27–29 (Barker and Bugbee quotations); George Garrison, "Affairs of the Association," *QTSHA*, 5 (Apr. 1902), 357 (last quotation). *Photograph courtesy Prints and Photographs Collection, DI 02610, CAH.*

"The Executive Council has decided that the regular annual meeting of the Association shall be held hereafter on [Texas] Independence Day at the University of Texas. Since the exercises on the part of the University that have become customary for that day always include addresses befitting the occasion, there will be no address on the program of the Association, which will provide only for one or two historical papers in addition to the regular meeting for business."

George Garrison, "Affairs of the Association," *QTSHA*, 8 (Oct. 1904), 196.

Wooten were included, as were popular women historians such as Sinks, Fannie C. G. Iglehart, Anna J. H. Pennybacker, and Mary M. Brown, the widow of prominent soldier and historian John Henry Brown. Both Pennybacker, who became president of the American History Club in 1901, and Brown wrote popular textbooks. Those who had been instrumental in founding the Association, such as Corner and Raines, were not forgotten. Harry F. Estill, who later became president of Sam Houston State University, made the first list of Fellows, as did Chief Justice Reuben R. Gaines of the Texas Supreme Court and Allen C. Gray, owner and editor of the *Houston Telegraph*. Angelina V. Winkler, who, like her late husband, Col. Clinton M. Winkler of Hood's Texas Brigade, remained active in aiding Confederate veterans' organizations, completed the roll of Fellows.

Garrison and his associates obviously selected their first roster of Fellows with great care, paying attention not only to what those so chosen had done in the past, but also to what they could do in the future for the Association. Similar thought went into the selection of the initial roll of honorary members. Most of the twenty-five on the honorary list were veterans of the Texas Revolution, such as Bryan and Ford, but there were also two former governors, Roberts and Peter H. Bell. Again, a handful of women appeared on the roll, including Sinks; Mary J. Briscoe, the widow of prominent early Texas businessman and judge Andrew Briscoe; and Mary S. Jones, the widow of Anson Jones, last president of the Republic. Mary J. Briscoe had hosted the organizational meeting of the Daughters of the Republic of Texas, and Mary S. Jones was the president of that organization in 1897.

Garrison's careful arrangements drew sharp criticism from one he considered a reliable ally. Roberts wrote to protest his election as president. He appreciated the honor, he said, but remained certain that a younger man would be a better leader. Specifically, he insisted that the University of Texas president should serve ex officio as president of the Association. Bryan, who had also protested his election as vice-president on the same grounds of age,

endorsed this idea. Garrison apparently had no interest in sharing the leadership of the Association with anyone who outranked him at the University. In
addition, he considered the office of Association president to be a position in
which nonprofessionals could work effectively with University professors. He
stood his ground, and the practice he established of excluding academic professionals from serving as president would endure with few exceptions for
more than fifty years. By mid-March, Roberts wrote to Bryan that he would
serve as president solely to help Garrison and the Association, and that Bryan
should accept his election as vice-president with similar good grace.

Nor was this the only complaint that Garrison received. John H. Reagan
wrote to Bugbee on March 19 to protest that the Association's constitution
created "a sort of self-perpetuating closed corporation, which I cannot
approve." Reagan agreed that founding a durable "historical association for our
State" was "of the first importance," but believed the organization's honors and
titles were not "justly or wisely distributed."[10] He demanded that his name be
dropped from the rolls. Garrison guessed that the source of much of Reagan's
ire was that he had not been given an honor or title. After explaining that mis-
takes had been made in the haste to close the meeting after the lights had gone
out, Garrison assured Reagan that he was enrolled as an Honorary Life Member, and when the list of Fellows appeared, Reagan was included in that distinguished group as well.

Reagan's wounded pride had been soothed, but he gave voice to a concern
that would surface again. He believed that the organization was being operated by a small elite, who could be identified by their selection as Fellows. On
the other hand, no less a publication than the *Atlantic Monthly* praised Garrison for preventing his organization from becoming no more than a social club
by thus ensuring the "permanent dominance of the historical purpose in its
councils and composition." Garrison responded to Reagan that any amendments could easily be made, adding, "I have no doubt that if the fellowship can
be shown to be a dangerous feature it will be abolished." He wrote that he had
been concerned about geography in his choices for officers, implying that no
region that had shown interest was spurned. When Reagan withdrew his
request to cancel his membership, he did not address the issue of geography
but again asserted that the Fellows seemed to manage the Association, with
members "being made a mere tail of the kite."[11] Reagan became president of
the Association in 1899 and served until his death in 1905. In his second year,
he secured an amendment eliminating the requirement that all officers had to
be Fellows, and he graciously accepted a compromise from Garrison that
assigned former presidents to the Executive Council as ex officio members.

Challenges to the new Association came from outside as well as inside. The

Oran M. Roberts (1897–1898)

John H. Reagan (1899–1905)

Dudley G. Wooten
(1898–1899)

David F. Houston (1905–1907)

A. W. Terrell (1907–1912)

Five men served as president during Garrison's tenure as director. In the early decades of the Association, the presidential terms were varied, ranging anywhere from one year to, in one case, ten years (Adele B. Looscan). From 1949 to 1967, two-year terms were the norm, then in 1967 the one-year terms that have continued to the present were instituted. *The Wooten photograph is from TSHA Files; the other four are courtesy of Prints and Photographs Collection, DI 02604, DI 02583, DI 02563, and DI 02564, CAH.*

Memorial

"In this issue of the QUARTERLY appears a memorial page in commemoration of the services of John Files Tom. His death removes one of the last survivors of the battle of San Jacinto."

George Garrison, "Affairs of the Association," *QTSHA*, 9 (Apr. 1906), 289.

Texas State Historical Association was of course not the first such organization in the state, so it encountered opposition from others claiming a more distinguished pedigree. Garrison's invitations to membership brought a stinging response from Eldridge G. Littlejohn to Fulmore. As the secretary of the older Texas Historical Society in Galveston, Littlejohn scolded Fulmore, angrily asserting that his Society was "no mere local institution as you seem to think." Littlejohn added, "We would not think for a moment of giving up our name, nor would we be willing to 'co-operate as a member of the state organization'." Instead, Littlejohn invited Fulmore and his colleagues to join the Galveston group.[12]

Garrison probably realized that Littlejohn's bitter response had as much to do with personal rivalries as it did with concern for the proper telling of the history of Texas. If Garrison did not understand this, he quickly learned. Wooten certainly cared little for Fulmore, but he apparently thought even less of Fulmore's rivals in Galveston. In a letter to Garrison, Wooten dismissed the "attitude of the Galveston Society" as "unfortunate and wholly unwarranted, but not surprising." He explained tartly, "That little community has all the insular pretensions and prejudices of England without its civilization and culture, and I have never known any kind of convention in Texas that it did not assume the role of exclusive and arrogant leadership."[13]

Unfortunately, the 1900 hurricane resolved this problem by almost destroying Galveston and thus its Society. Phillip C. Tucker Jr. wrote to Eugene C. Barker in 1901 to suggest a merger. Tucker's father had blocked the sale of most of the Galveston archives in 1885, and father and son had kept their Society alive until they could secure a charter nine years later. Littlejohn, who heroically saved most of their archives from the hurricane, also endorsed consolidation. He admitted that his group had been in a "moribund condition" for years and had been "finished by the storm of last year which, in addition to the damage done to our archives, carried off some of our most active and energetic members and destroyed the enthusiasm of the rest."[14] As an incentive for the merger, Tucker and Littlejohn offered to give their archives to Garrison's

THE *Quarterly*

"In the printing of this number of the THE QUARTERLY an unusual number of annoying delays have been experienced. It is hoped that ere long the successive numbers can be issued at least within the month in which they are due. That this has not been so during the past year can hardly be considered the fault of either editors or printers."

George Garrison, "Affairs of the Association," *QTSHA*, 8 (Oct. 1904), 196.

Association, an idea that President Reagan happily accepted. Public outcry in Galveston, however, forced the pair to cancel their plans, and most of their papers eventually went to the Rosenberg Library in Galveston. Tucker later joined the Association and donated other materials to it.

The settlement or elimination of challenges from within and without left Garrison with the time to address more substantial issues. One of his first tasks was to recruit members. In the official report of the first meeting, the Association claimed to have "three or four hundred" enrolled.[15] This was far from true. Bugbee wrote to Roberts on March 12, 1897, that the total number of Fellows and regular members was only ninety-eight, including seventeen women. Within a few months, diligent effort filled the ranks to about the number originally claimed by Garrison. While it was a distinguished and fairly diverse list in that it included women as well as men, there were no blacks or Indians and very few Hispanic surnames. The first paid Life Member did join during the fall of 1897—Dennis M. O'Connor of Anaqua in Victoria County—but he may have blundered into the honor: he originally declined to join but sent fifty dollars to help the Association. In response, in accordance with the rules, Garrison informed O'Connor that he was now a Life Member because of his donation. O'Connor was so pleased that he sent another check for a hundred dollars.

Garrison's efforts to increase the number of Fellows unexpectedly ignited a brief conflict. When he nominated David F. Houston at the first Executive Council meeting in May 1897, Roberts asked if this was the same man recently investigated by the Texas legislature for opposing the "principles of the Confederacy" in his book about South Carolina nullification. Garrison admitted that he was but added that a committee had dropped the inquiry after being informed that Houston's source for the offending quotations was Founding Father James Madison. Roberts did not stand alone in defending the Lost Cause; Wooten wrote to Garrison in 1898, "The present war with Spain will in the end teach our people that all this parade about the removal of sectional differences is a hopeless piece of clap-trap. The differences are radical, racial and ineradicable."[16] Some worried that Houston's selection might harm the Association, but he and other nominees were elected unanimously by the Council. Houston did much to allay Texans' concerns when he and Garrison testified together before a legislative committee in June 1897, successfully denying that anti-Southern ideas were being taught at the University of Texas. In 1906, after serving as president of Texas A&M and then of the University of Texas, David Houston became president of the Association and delivered the address at its tenth anniversary meeting.

Such quarrels did not prevent Garrison from continuing his push for membership. The addition of members helped to offset the natural attrition among the longtime Texans recruited into the Association. The first obituary, for John Ford, appeared in the January 1898 issue of the *Quarterly*. Peter Bell died in March, then Oran Roberts in May. Acting President Dudley G. Wooten's speech to the second annual meeting of the Association in June 1898 was a eulogy for Roberts. Still, the membership increased to 710 by the fall of 1899. Most (132) came from Austin but a significant number came from San Antonio (63), Houston (40), and Dallas (33) as Garrison pressed for all regions to participate, focusing on the enlistment of rural leaders such as Floresvillle attorney Joseph B. Polley, president of the Texas Division of the United Confederate Veterans, and author of *A Soldier's Letters to Charming Nellie*. By 1899 the TSHA had at least one member from 178 towns, and could also boast of two dozen members from outside Texas.

Garrison understood the importance of using existing groups to boost recruiting efforts. While he continually begged his own members for lists of names to solicit, he also contacted leaders in other organizations. The Daughters of the Republic of Texas initially proved to be one of his best allies. At their annual meeting in 1900 the officers of that group asked their members to join Garrison's Association. Their motivation was twofold: they wanted to support the preservation of Texas history, and they considered the *Quarterly* to be a useful forum for publishing articles and reports. Adele B. Looscan, historian general of the Daughters and a charter member of Garrison's organization, reported in June 1901 that she was sending a letter to every chapter asking members to join the Association. Looscan's support was welcome because she was also a member of the United Daughters of the Confederacy and the Daughters of the American Revolution, and was the daughter of Mary J. Briscoe, Honorary Life Member of the Association. In December 1901 Garrison praised the Daughters of the Republic of Texas and the Texas Veterans Association for their support.

To Emily Cooley of the Daughters of the Republic of Texas, it appeared by early 1906 that "Texas is slowly wakening to the necessity of this work and I rejoice that our University (provided for by the men who made no small portion of her past history) is leading the way." Her optimism proved premature. Garrison's business manager Luther E. Widen admitted to another supporter that the Association was "almost at a standstill."[17] The Texas Veterans Association was slowly fading away as its members lost their fight with time, and the Sons of the Republic of Texas were winding down with them. To complicate matters, the Daughters of the Republic of Texas split in 1907 as Adina De Zavala, granddaughter of Lorenzo De Zavala and a charter member of the Association, battled with Clara Driscoll for control of the Alamo. De Zavala was expelled from the Daughters but remained a vital member of the Association, as did her ally, Looscan.

Zavala's battle with Driscoll created a schism between the Daughters and the Association that would last for three decades, significantly undermining Garrison's effort to boost enrollment. In spite of this, he no more tried to intervene than he had when a similar, if less dramatic, rift alienated a potential supporter just a few years earlier. Elisabet Ney, the colorful German sculptress who settled in Austin, sharply refused to join the Association. She would not enlist in the same organization as John H. Reagan, whom she had to sue to secure payment for her bust of him, and who later opposed the placing of Ney's statue of Sam Houston in the national Capitol. Ney had many prominent female friends, including Bride N. Taylor, but Garrison had not replied to her outburst and he did not confront Zavala or her opponents. He contented himself with a letter to Hally B. Perry, Bryan's daughter and the popular founder of the Daughters, remarking that their "breach" appeared "to be irreconcilable, and I fear the results will be most mischievous. I do not know what to expect from it, but I certainly deplore it greatly."[18] Garrison had a good reason to be unhappy. David Houston in his presidential address in 1908 claimed there were over two thousand members in the Association, but records indicated that the true number was not half that.

While struggling to recruit members, Garrison also had to contend with a miserly budget. Both he and Bugbee spent money from their own pockets to recruit members and pay the costs of producing the *Quarterly*. They constantly begged their fellow Texans to send not only materials but also money to support their cause. An early issue of the *Quarterly* declared, "History like that of Texas is rare . . . and has few parallels." Was it right that Texans had to "go to Boston, or New York, or Madison" to learn their state's history in the archives of other states' historical societies? Although "Affairs of the Association" was not a signed section of the *Quarterly*, the voice is unmistakably that of George Garrison himself, who goes on to repeat his question in a more inflammatory

ON THE PAYING OF DUES

"From the Treasurer's report it will be seen that there was a consider-able deficit for the year just ended. This was caused by the tardiness of members in paying their dues...."

George Garrison, "Affairs of the Association," *QTSHA*, 3 (July 1899), 71.

"It becomes necessary to purge the list of members to some extent. Those who are far in arrears with their dues, of whom there are fortu-nately not a great many, need not expect to receive the QUARTERLY after this number. The member that does not pay is as expensive as one that does; and the Association, for economy's sake, will be forced to exclude those who show a disposition to join permanently the class of non-payers."

Ibid., 3 (Apr. 1900), 882.

manner for emphasis: "Shall outsiders be permitted to lead in perpetuating the memory of the patient endurance and heroic deeds of those who builded [*sic*] the Republic?"[19]

The income of the Association showed little improvement during Garri-son's life, despite his chiding. Every penny was spent, and by the third year of operation Garrison was borrowing money to make ends meet. The problem was that many members did not pay their dues. They owed only $2.00 a year, or $5.00 for Fellows, but it proved difficult to make some of them pay. To com-pound the problem, Honorary Life Members did not pay dues, while ordinary Life Members could make their one-time payment of $50.00 by donating his-torical material. A solution, announced in 1899, was a fund drive to create an endowment of $2,500, but even that effort failed. The donation of an old state writ in 1901 brought a windfall of $297, but the Executive Council wisely vetoed Garrison's proposal to revive endowment efforts. They insisted instead that the money be used to repay their debt to Garrison and Lester Bugbee.

The adoption of a tougher policy toward deadbeats brought some financial relief for the Association. A system was created to draft bank accounts, and those who still refused to pay were dropped from the rolls under a constitu-tional amendment adopted in 1901. Garrison reported his first surplus the next year. This allowed some generosity in handling dues: Life Memberships were reduced to $30.00 in 1904. At the same time, Fellows were told that they had to pay $5.00 only once; thereafter they would pay $2.00 a year like the other members. Such changes did not indicate that the Association enjoyed an abundance of riches. Business manager Widen during the same period

Herbert Eugene Bolton (1870–1953), a student of Frederick Jackson Turner and John Bach McMaster, came to the University of Texas from Wisconsin in 1901 to teach medieval and European history in Garrison's history department, where he remained until 1909. While at the University Bolton served as associate editor of the *Quarterly*, and it was also during this time that he began to develop his interest in the Spanish expansion in North America. Beginning in 1902 he traveled many times to Mexico to study archival materials relating to the United States. Bolton left the University of Texas in 1909 to teach American history at Stanford University, and then in 1911 he accepted a teaching position at the University of California at Berkeley, where he was the chairman of the Department of History and director of the Bancroft Library until his retirement in 1940. Bolton's research resulted in 94 works, including approximately 24 books he wrote or edited, including works on Texas history, most notably *Athanase de Mézières and the Louisiana-Texas Frontier, 1768–1780* (1914) and *Texas in the Middle Eighteenth Century: Studies in Spanish Colonial History and Administration* (1915). Bolton's concept of the Spanish Borderlands as a field of study was an important addition to historical thought. He declined to succeed Garrison in the Department of History and in the Association when Garrison died in 1910, and he declined the presidency of the University of Texas in 1923, but throughout his career he retained a strong interest in Texas history and in the Texas State Historical Association. He died of a stroke at the age of 82 on January 30, 1953.

John Haskell Kemble, "Herbert Eugene Bolton," *New Handbook of Texas*, ed. Ron Tyler et al. (6 vols.; TSHA, 1996), I, 629. *Photograph from TSHA Files.*

reported that plans to expand the *Quarterly* were tabled because of "financial embarrassment."[20] Nonetheless, in April 1910 Garrison, in what would be his last report, proudly wrote that the Association had $3,097.75 in cash and interest-bearing bank accounts or notes after paying its bills for the year.

Persistent budget problems, compounded by tragedy, made it difficult for Garrison to keep good help. Lester Bugbee made himself indispensable not only as a secretary but also as a Progressive historian with his own solid reputation. After completing his master's degree under Garrison, he studied under the direction of prominent scholars Herbert L. Osgood and John Bassett Moore at Columbia University. Hired by Garrison before he completed his dissertation (which was never finished), Bugbee immersed himself in the colonial history of Texas. An 1898 article in the *Political Science Quarterly*, in which Bugbee corrected erroneous assertions about slavery and the Texas independence movement made by Von Holst, Garrison's mentor at Chicago, drew some attention to the younger scholar. Within a few years, he became a member of the Archives Commission for the American Historical Association. Bugbee left the University in 1901, but not for the better paying job he was always looking for. He had tuberculosis and went west, seeking a cure. Garrison, who had himself recovered from tuberculosis (in 1889), reported to Hally B. Perry that Bugbee was on leave and probably would not return. Bugbee died in 1902, at the tragically young age of thirty-two.

After Bugbee left Austin, Garrison hired Herbert E. Bolton, an alumnus of the University of Wisconsin (where he had studied under Frederick Jackson Turner), with a doctoral degree from the University of Pennsylvania. Schooled in medieval history and assigned to teach European courses, Bolton, with the encouragement of President David Houston, embraced the study of Spanish colonialism. Of course, Garrison, who would not share his responsibilities for United States history, allowed him to do this as it enhanced the study of the frontier, especially its Spanish era, emphasized by Garrison in his work with advanced undergraduate and graduate students. He surrendered all work in Spanish archives to Bolton, who soon became an associate editor of the *Quarterly*. Eugene Bolton, like Turner and Garrison, was a Progressive historian who regarded Texas history as a key part of the national settlement process, but he added a twist. He emphasized the influence of Spain, advancing into the Southwest not from the east, but from the south.

Bolton dug deep into Spanish records, producing articles on both colonial administration and Indians for the Association and for Frederick Hodge's handbook on North American Indians. His work attracted attention, and he departed in 1907 to work in the archives of Mexico under a grant provided by J. Franklin Jameson, director of the Carnegie Institution. After producing one of the first guides to the Mexican archives, Bolton returned to the University of Texas for a year, but no pay raises came and Garrison would not allow him to expand his research into areas Garrison claimed as his own. Bolton left in 1909 to teach at Stanford University, then accepted yet another position in 1911 at the University of California at Berkeley. His old comrades made several attempts during that period to lure him back to Austin, and Bolton wrote to Zachary Fulmore that "Texas is where I belong," but his wife liked the climate and he enjoyed the higher salary in California.[21] There he won renown for his distinguished scholarship on the Spanish in the Southwest, a research interest that had begun in Texas.

Bolton's constant search for a bigger paycheck left most of the daily tasks of the Association in the hands of his friend, Eugene C. Barker. A native of Comal County, Barker had studied under George Garrison and Lester Bugbee, earning his bachelor's degree in 1899 and his master's in 1900. Except for a year of study at Harvard University in 1906–1907, followed by a one-year fellowship to complete his doctorate at the University of Pennsylvania, Barker remained at the University of Texas as a member of the history faculty until his retirement in 1951. He served as associate editor for the *Quarterly*, alongside Bolton, then continued when the latter left for California. He followed closely in the footsteps of Garrison as a Progressive historian and, after Garrison's death, took charge of both the Association and the Department of History.

Barker in turn relied greatly on Charles W. Ramsdell, a Salado native who earned bachelor's and master's degrees from the University of Texas in 1903 and 1904 respectively, then completed work for a doctorate from Columbia University in 1910. Ramsdell inherited the titles of corresponding secretary and treasurer in 1907, and then, after completing his graduate studies, became an associate editor for the *Quarterly*. Ramsdell worked closely with Garrison and Barker on the task of explaining Texas's role in the development of the United States, though Ramsdell, as a student of William A. Dunning, tended to see events through the perspective of Southern, not Western, history. Dunning pushed his students into writing studies on Reconstruction that were distinctly sympathetic to the South and its resistance to rapid change at the hands of the Radical Republicans. Ramsdell wrote the first, and most influential, study of Reconstruction in Texas, and emphasized the role of Texas as a Southern, not Western, state throughout his life's work.

Garrison and his comrades at the University made important contributions in teaching Texas history, but perhaps not more than those made by many other Association members. Garrison began a graduate course on Texas history, the first graduate class in his department, in the fall of 1897, but annual meetings of the Association became the primary forum for telling the story of

Texas. The first annual meeting, a one-day event, met after commencement on June 17, 1897, at the University. The several papers read that day comprised the first issue of the *Quarterly*; in later years Garrison continued to publish many of the annual meeting papers. Following the advice of Dudley Wooten and others, mid-winter meetings were held in other cities "in order to acquaint the public with the Society and its aims, and to enlist universal interest."[22] This experiment did not endure, nor did an attempt to establish San Jacinto Day in April as the date for the annual meeting. The latter practice began in 1902 as a joint assembly with the Daughters of the Republic of Texas and the Texas Veterans Association, and ended after the 1904 meeting.

The Executive Council in 1904 decreed that the annual meeting would henceforth convene on March 2, Texas Independence Day. This decision proved successful. By 1907 an observer reported that attendance at the annual meeting "was the largest in its history."[23] Customarily three papers were presented consecutively, in addition to a speech or two to accompany lunch or dinner, but Garrison was not averse to making a last-minute change to take advantage of a public relations opportunity. In 1909 the legislature on short notice asked the Association to take part in a joint session. A key feature was to be a speech by Alexander W. Terrell, a member of the Texas House and the president of the Association that year. Realizing the value of such publicity, the Association canceled two of its three scheduled papers. Terrell spoke to a large audience while Eugene Barker, whose paper survived the cut, shared his limelight.

The constitution of the Association committed it not only to teaching, but also to developing an archive on the history of Texas. Precious papers and books were being lost every day. Many members could recall the destruction of much of the state library when the Capitol burned in 1881, and private collections were also being lost to fire. Within the Association ranks, Wooten lost everything when his Dallas home burned in March 1901. At the first annual meeting, in 1897, the acquisition of a library had been discussed, and a call had gone out for historical materials. University of Texas president and Association member George T. Winston gave the Association a corner of the library in the administration building, known as Old Main. Garrison supervised the area as librarian for the Association. Among the first to donate their collections was Oran Roberts, who had given first his library and then, in 1898, his papers to the University. By that time there were 216 books and pamphlets in Garrison's alcove, including books given by Swante Palm, a businessman who came to Texas from Sweden during the Republic period, and others purchased with money donated by George W. Brackenridge, a prominent businessman and University regent. The donation of Ashbel Smith's library in 1899 pushed the total number of books to 275, and this number would double in only a few years.

TSHA QUARTERS:
THE ARCHIVES CORNER

The Texas State Historical Association was crucial to the beginnings of the archival collections at the University of Texas. George P. Garrison was an adherent of the scientific school of history, which viewed the use of primary sources as indispensable in the study and writing of history. The Department of History at the University became a separate entity in 1888, with Garrison as its chairman. He brought three men to the department in its early formative years: Lester G. Bugbee in 1895, Eugene C. Barker in 1899, and Herbert E. Bolton in 1901. All four men recognized the importance of primary materials in their work as historians, and "in 1897 the history department provided the leadership in organizing what would prove to be one of the most important influences on the development of the University of Texas history collections: the Texas State Historical Association," with the objective of "collection, preservation, and publication of historical material, especially as relates to Texas." University of Texas president George T. Winston gave the Association a corner in the Old Main Library for the storage of its collections, and for its first few years the TSHA kept its collections there in a separate archive. But by 1902 most of the items donated to the Association were regularly housed in the University Library in two Texas collections—the Archives collection of documents and the Texas Collection Library of books. In 1911 the Association membership voted to formally transfer ownership of its collections to the University Library. The first recorded location of the Library was a room on the fourth floor of the University's main building (Old Main), and it was here that the TSHA had its first corner. This photograph is from 1924.

Don E. Carleton and Katherine J. Adams, "A Work Peculiarly Our Own": Origins of the Barker Texas History Center, 1883–1950," *SHQ*, 86 (Oct. 1982), 197–208 (quotation, p. 200). *Photograph courtesy of Prints and Photographs Collection, DI 01832, CAH.*

Gifts of books and archives remained the rule rather than the exception. A lack of funds dictated that little could be spent on acquisitions, though at times copies of the *Quarterly* were swapped for other organizations' publications. Garrison's most impressive archival acquisitions, in addition to the Roberts donation, were the papers of Stephen F. Austin and the Bexar Archives. The Austin papers had attracted the attention of Bugbee, who was allowed to use the material by Guy M. Bryan, who had inherited the collection. Impressed with Bugbee and with the idea of the papers being kept safe but accessible to the public, Bryan directed in his will that the material be placed in a state institution. His daughter, Hally Bryan Perry, and her brother, Beauregard Bryan, decided to give Austin's papers to the University of Texas after Garrison assured them that the collection would be put in a fireproof vault.

Walter F. McCaleb, a young graduate student in history, told Garrison in 1897 about the archives of the Bexar District, and Garrison in turn led Bugbee to them. Garrison wanted the papers placed in his University vault, but complained in 1898, "it would be rather too enlightened unselfishness on the part of the local authorities to give them up." Bugbee refused to quit and in the fall of 1899, after "much patient work and scheming" and the intervention of his friend Frank R. Newton of San Antonio, boxes containing more than 81,000 documents arrived in Austin.[24]

At Bugbee's request, money was set aside by University regents to store and index the Bexar Archives. Ernest W. Winkler, a former student of Bugbee's who had taken graduate courses from Frederick Jackson Turner at the University of Wisconsin, was hired to do the work. It proved overwhelming. Preliminary cataloging of the collection was not completed until 1932, and translation, a condition of the original transfer, did not begin until 1934, when federal funds made it possible to hire a full-time translator. Subject guides appeared in the 1960s as the papers were being microfilmed, but translation was still incomplete as the Association celebrated its centennial in 1997. Meanwhile, George Garrison, then Eugene Bolton, added greatly to the pile by going to Mexico to transcribe documents on Texas's colonial era. Garrison began the transcription program, with money from the Carnegie Institute; the program was continued by Bolton and then by others after Bolton left for California. A new University library building, designed by Cass Gilbert and completed in 1910, provided more space for the Texas Collection of books and the Association's archives.

Julia L. Sinks was effusive in her praise for "our little Bugbee. What a diver into the hidden and unknown he is!"[25] The arrival of the Bexar Archives at the University allowed Bolton to accelerate his research on both the Spanish period and the Indians in Texas, bringing him much attention and a job offer in California. And Garrison's hard work was recognized as well. When a decade of effort finally resulted in the establishment of the Texas Library and Historical Commission in 1909, he became an ex officio member in recognition of his position as the senior history professor at the University of Texas. His own accomplishments were recognized, however, when he became the first person to chair the Historical Commission. Several others on the commission were members of the Association, and they well knew Garrison's role in saving the vital historical records of Texas.

Garrison and his associates realized that it was not enough simply to preserve the records. They had to be interpreted and published for public use. Both Bugbee and Garrison planned to translate and publish not only the Bexar Archives, in accordance with their agreement with Bexar County, but also the Austin papers, which were a treasure trove of information on Texas as a province of Mexico. Unfortunately, the straitened circumstances of the Association prevented the realization of such big plans. Publication of any book, in fact, was beyond their means, a situation acknowledged by Roberts in his presidential address of 1897. He asserted that the Association's role was not to "induce the writing of a connected and complete history," but instead was "to furnish the facts for that object in the future." Sounding as Progressive as Garrison, Roberts declared that these "facts" would not be just "literary and scientific," but must "embrace material developments and everything else that tends to form the habits, character, and actions of the people of every class and condition." Roberts read a list of topics, then said, "Without further enumeration, it may be said that any and everything that the people do or think, that tends to form habits of life, or to build up prevailing institutions affecting society, constitutes material for history, and may be properly presented to this Association as such."[26]

With such a broad publishing mandate, and little money, a decision was made to focus on producing a quarterly journal. The first such publication in the United States, the *Pennsylvania Magazine of History and Biography*, had appeared just twenty years before Garrison edited his first issue of the *Quarterly* in 1897. Only two other states, Virginia and Ohio, had historical societies that printed journals in 1897. The American Historical Association published its proceedings but had not begun subsidizing the publication of a journal. Garrison's other model, the Wisconsin Historical Society, would not begin printing a quarterly until 1917. With little guidance, Garrison organized a publishing committee as provided by the constitution of his Association. He and Oran M. Roberts served ex officio, with three others chosen by the Fellows from within their own ranks: Zachary T. Fulmore, Bride N. Taylor, and Dudley G. Wooten.

Named for George P. Garrison, Garrison Hall was built in 1926, one of the group of buildings designed by Herbert M. Greene, who was chosen in 1922 by the Board of Regents to succeed Cass Gilbert as university architect. Over the course of the next decade he designed a number of campus buildings in addition to Garrison Hall in the prevailing Mediterranean-influenced Beaux-Arts style, among them Littlefield Dormitory, the Biology Building, Gregory Gymnasium, the Chemistry Building, and Waggener Hall. Situated across the West Mall from Gilbert's Battle Hall (Old Library Building), Garrison Hall is also lavishly decorated; the decorative motifs are steer heads, cacti, bluebonnets, cattle brands, and the names of the statesmen of the Republic of Texas. TSHA directors since Eugene C. Barker have had offices in Garrison Hall, and until moving to the Old Library Building in 1950, the Association offices were also in Garrison Hall. For many years the Association's annual meetings were held in the building. Christopher Long, "Herbert Miller Greene," in Tyler, et al. (eds.), *New Handbook of Texas*, III, 319. *Photograph courtesy of Prints and Photographs Collection, DI 02608, CAH.*

It soon became apparent that Garrison guided the election of publication committee members, and that he had one criterion: they should be people who would leave him alone to publish the *Quarterly of the Texas State Historical Association* as he saw fit. Taylor recalled that she discovered the content of each issue only when she got her copy in the mail. When she asked Garrison about this, he assured her that she served a useful purpose because, if she quit, someone who actually wanted to interfere with him might join the committee. Roberts certainly never complained, perhaps because his was the lead article in all four issues in the first year. Almost every prominent Association member had an article in the *Quarterly*, and many had several. Most agreed with Guy M. Bryan that "The first number is certainly worthy of the subject & the society," and they apparently thought later issues were just as good.[27] After

DEATH OF GARRISON

"...the October, 1910, number [of THE QUARTERLY] marks the end of our first epoch: the place [on the cover] occupied from the beginning by the name of Dr. Garrison as editor-in-chief is blank. He died in July, cut down, as I have always believed, by overwork, the last straw of which was the editing of the Texas Diplomatic Correspondence. In a talk I had with him a few weeks before his death, and the last time I ever saw him, he spoke of his extreme weariness and said that he was hoping that as soon as the last touch had been put to this work he might find a chance to rest and recuperate, for, he went on to say, the labor of it, added to his other duties, had become a load almost insupportable. Shortly afterward, we heard of his illness. On his death-bed, he read the proofs of the final installment of that fatal Diplomatic Correspondence, for the July QUAR-TERLY, superintended, as usual, the final preparations for the issuance of that number, and then, a few days later, was gone, cut down in his prime, and literally dying in harness—what we might call the harness of the cause of the history of Texas. The July QUARTERLY was the last number to carry his name on its cover. Three succeeding numbers came out with that sad blank, after which it was filled by the name of one of the associate editors, Dr. Barker."

Bride Neill Taylor, "The Beginnings of the State Historical Association,"
SHQ, 33 (July 1929), 14–15.

Barker and Bolton became the associate editors for the *Quarterly*, the publication committee ceased to meet at all, which seemed to suit Garrison.

Development of the *Quarterly* became a process of trial and error. Some complained when they learned they would not be paid for contributions. Rip Ford was among those who claimed that he could not afford to give away his writing. Garrison appreciated the generosity of people like William P. Zuber. A tireless advocate of veterans' rights who fought for Texas independence and for the Confederacy before becoming a founding member of the Texas Veterans Association, Zuber wrote prolifically and sent several articles to the *Quarterly*. He wrote to Garrison that he had been "amply paid by the consciousness that I have presented truthful statements to Texas history and biography."[28] Garrison himself usually penned the "Notes," which reported on historical activities and was reprinted in the *Alcalde*, the publication for former students of the University of Texas. He printed primary material in all issues, reviving an initiative begun by the *Texas Almanac* in 1857 but abandoned in 1874. His

July 1898 issue contained the first book review, a laudatory report by Robert L. Batts on Garrison's Texas government textbook. This piece was joined by an equally effusive review of Batt's annotated edition of Texas civil statutes and a third review praising Wooten's two-volume history of Texas. In 1899 Garrison began running advertisements in an attempt to help pay printing costs.

Somehow Garrison's experiment in publication succeeded. Many subsequent works that dealt with pre-1900 Texas history included references to Garrison's early issues of the *Quarterly*. Bolton's work in Mexico, for example, yielded a total of eighteen articles on Texas under Spanish rule. The first of these appeared in the *Quarterly* in 1902, and the stream continued after Bolton moved to California. He also produced more than a hundred articles for Frederick Hodge's book on North American Indians, and some of this material found its way into the *Quarterly*. Bolton's article on the French-Spanish conflict in Texas was complemented by other articles by Bugbee and Isaac J. Cox. Walter F. McCaleb, who left Austin to study under Von Holst at the University of Chicago, produced an excellent article on American filibusters into colonial Texas. Barker's early work on the slave trade in Mexican Texas, land speculation, and the San Jacinto campaign laid the groundwork for his later publications on Stephen F. Austin. There was certainly a bias in Garrison's *Quarterly* toward the colonial period and early statehood, but that was the history that was being lost as he began the Association. If nothing else, his issues of the *Quarterly* are invaluable for the primary material contributed by those who had lived through the state's formative years.

Garrison was editing the copy for yet another issue of the *Quarterly* when he died on July 3, 1910. Though confined to his bed with congestive heart disease, he had continued to work. His dedication earned him many accolades, including an honorary Doctor of Law degree from Baylor University earlier in 1910, but he always seemed to be frustrated. His plans to publish volumes of primary documents, specifically the Bexar Archives and the Austin papers, had yet to be fulfilled. A modest budget did not allow enlargement of the *Quarterly*, and persistent efforts to woo members and acquire more archival materials had yielded only small gains. He could certainly agree with David F. Houston, who in his 1908 address as president of the Association declared that they were "only at the beginning."[29] The Association had survived the conflicts of its founding, increased membership, collected books and archives, and even established a journal, but more was needed. Garrison laid strong foundations, but he knew as well as anyone that greater challenges lay ahead if the Association were to continue to grow. Fortunately for him and his organization, he had trained a dedicated successor, Eugene C. Barker, who shared his vision.

THREE

The Chief

Eugene C. Barker, 1910–1937

THE FIRST PERSON ASKED TO SUCCEED George P. Garrison was Herbert E. Bolton, but it was Eugene C. Barker who ultimately took the job. He proved to be perhaps the best choice for a difficult stage in the growth of the Texas State Historical Association. A Texan who overcame poverty to secure a doctorate, Barker was tenacious and uncompromising. In a note to Herbert P. Gambrell several years after Barker's death, H. Bailey Carroll repeated a popular description of Barker as being "about half saber tooth tiger and about half St. Francis of Assisi."[1] Others were less kind in their remarks about Barker, but they probably had never known the young man with big plans who took charge of the Association in 1910. Conflict during the Progressive Era, along with economic hardship then and during the ensuing Depression, convinced Barker that strict control over a small but loyal membership would best ensure the survival of his organization. The result was

Eugene C. Barker (1874–1956), director of the Association 1910–1937.

"My work for the Texas State Historical Association, which seems to be the starting point of this celebration, is too much emphasized. Twenty-seven years is a long period, but, given the time, twenty-seven volumes of the *Quarterly* were inevitable so long as I held the job of editor. I restricted the volumes to a very modest size. Again, my excuse is that I gave the job just about what I thought I could spare from other duties and pleasures. I am glad that you approve the result, but your generosity does not convince me that I merit such commendation. I plead guilty to longevity and concentration, no more. In effect it all comes back to the reflection that I have been allowed to do what I wanted to do in about the way that I wanted to do it. Admitting the performance of some hard and persevering labor, the program has included a good deal of plain loafing and a maximum of freedom and independence." Eugene C. Barker, "The Eugene C. Barker Portrait: Presentation, Acceptance, and Acknowledgment Addresses," *SHQ*, 46 (Jan. 1943), 315. *Photograph courtesy Eugene C. Barker Papers, DI 02310, CAH.*

The Quarterly: CHANGE OF NAME

"On recommendation of the Executive Council [at the March 2, 1912, annual meeting], the name of THE QUARTERLY was changed to THE SOUTHWESTERN HISTORICAL QUARTERLY. Though as much Texas matter will hereafter be published as was formerly, the change of name will enable the Association to enlarge the scope of THE QUARTERLY by publishing material on other portions of the Southwest. This, it is hoped, will lead to betterment of the Association's finances, and to a considerable enlargement of THE QUARTERLY."

"Affairs of the Association," *QTSHA*, 15 (Apr. 1912), 360.

the forging of an enduring image of Barker as the "Chief," a revered but grim conservator of Texas history.

Bolton declined the offer of Garrison's vacant post as chair of the history department when the University would not pay him what he wanted. The chairmanship along with the responsibility for directing the Association then went to Barker. Bolton and Barker remained close friends and worked together on several Association projects. When the presidency of the University became available in 1923, Barker campaigned hard for Bolton, but Bolton disappointed him and refused yet another offer from the Texas regents. Bolton in turn tried several times to lure both Barker and Charles W. Ramsdell to California, but both refused to leave Texas.

Barker's default appointment to direct the Association did not spark a great outpouring of enthusiasm from members. He had entered the University of Texas in 1895 by examination, having left school at the age of fourteen to work as a blacksmith after his father died. It actually took him two attempts to pass the University entrance test. He completed his bachelor's and master's degrees in 1899 and 1900 respectively, and then became an instructor in 1901 when Lester G. Bugbee departed for El Paso. His tenure as Bugbee's successor as corresponding secretary for the TSHA ended when Bolton arrived in the fall of 1901 to take that job. Barker and Bolton soon became allies, though, and served together as associate editors of the *Quarterly of the Texas State Historical Association*. Meanwhile, Barker completed a doctorate at the University of Pennsylvania and in 1908 became an adjunct professor at the University of Texas. His next promotion, to associate professor, came in 1911, after he took charge of the Department of History. He blossomed after becoming a full professor in 1913, emerging as a faculty leader, acquiring support for the University library, and writing prolifically. The perseverance that shaped his early education served him well throughout his career, and the Association clearly benefited from it.

Barker followed closely in the footsteps of Garrison as a Progressive historian. His background, if it had any influence on his career, made him perhaps more open to diversity than Garrison but just as committed to contributing to a better understanding of national development through the use of state and local sources. While American historians during the late nineteenth and early twentieth centuries focused mostly on politics, Barker's doctoral mentor at the University of Pennsylvania, John Bach McMaster, led the way in exploring social and economic topics. In his work for the Association and as a member of the national historical community, Barker maintained McMaster's interest in historical complexity, and published works that used Texas material to illustrate national patterns. He joined the Executive Council of the American Historical Association, which published his three volumes of Stephen F. Austin's papers, became president of the Mississippi Valley Historical Association, which he helped to found, and coauthored textbooks on American history. Revered by Texans for his meticulous biography of Austin, Barker, like Garrison before him, was a Progressive historian who emphasized Texas's role within the context of national development.

Barker also inherited from Garrison an able partner: Charles W. Ramsdell. Ramsdell followed in the footsteps of Lester Bugbee by studying at Columbia University, where he became a student of William A. Dunning, one of the most influential Progressive Era historians on Reconstruction. Ramsdell never quite absorbed all of the strongly pro-Southern biases of Dunning, but his dissertation on Texas Reconstruction, published in 1910, was very clearly an indictment of the Radical Republicans and their push for black empowerment. Texans "never embraced the cult of the Confederacy with quite the enthusiasm of the rest of the ex-Confederate states," but Ramsdell became well known in scholarly circles for his work on that period.[2] Like Barker, Ramsdell sat on the Executive Council of the American Historical Association and was president of the Mississippi Valley Historical Association, and in addition he served as president of the Southern Historical Association. While most Texan historians during the Progressive Era, professional and amateur, preferred to focus on the Western frontier heritage of the state, Ramsdell spoke for the Southern perspective.

Barker's editorship of the *Quarterly* reflected the interests of his professional and lay colleagues, but he clearly had the last word in all decisions. After Garrison died, Barker inherited not only his history department and his course on Southwest history, but also his research interests and his Association, which included the *Quarterly*. Ernest W. Winkler, Barker's friend and classmate who was a charter member of the Association, worked on the *Quarterly* with Barker for years, but the most interesting influence on Barker came from Herbert Eugene Bolton. As early as 1909 Bolton, from his new job in California, had pressed Garrison to expand the *Quarterly* focus to include all of the Spanish colonial borderlands. Bolton asked presidents of other universities to support his proposals, and in March 1910, three months before he died, Garrison agreed to a change in the scope of the *Quarterly*.

Barker was scarcely settled in Garrison's office before Bolton renewed his push to expand the focus and the title of the *Quarterly*. Barker agreed, but unlike Garrison he anticipated some resistance from the Executive Council and the membership of the Association. Mindful of the still-fresh image of Garrison as the conservator of Texas history, Barker wrote to Bolton that they would have to delay any changes, lest Barker appear to be an "upstart" without the proper respect for his predecessor.[3] As final preparations for the changes were being made, Barker accepted a proposal from Bolton and appointed him a coeditor of the *Quarterly*, though he rejected the notion that some issues might be published in California, where Bolton taught.

Bolton's interest in expanding the content apparently originated in his

BARKER IN THE CLASSROOM

"We, his students, have heard his patient defense of the work of the founders of Texas, as well as his impatient explosions over a very unhappy discovery of chewing gum. At times it seemed an amusing contradiction of character—amusing if you were not guilty of the chewing—and we were awed into admiration that a man so patient in the pursuit of evidence supporting the good intentions of men, and so tolerant of human frailties, excesses and failures, could become so violent over the vacuous, sophomoric chewer of gum.... But those of us who observed his dejected retreat from class knew that he was humiliated and contrite, and that his choicest castigation was silently reserved for himself. As Miss Ruby Mixon has pointed out, he would be back next time with a sheepish look on his face. After roll call his glance might sweep the seats for the offender, and, with a twinkle in his eye, he might deliver himself of a double-barrelled apology: 'If a student has no self-respect,' he once regretted, 'then he ought to be ashamed to make a fool out of his professor.'"

J. Evetts Haley, "The Eugene C. Barker Portrait," *SHQ*, 46 (Jan. 1943), 304–305.

> " I came to the settled conclusion a long time ago that people, particularly in our profession, spend too much time and effort preparing to live, while life itself is slipping away. Perhaps a sense of proportion helped to strengthen the conviction. No thoughtful person, least of all a historian, can hold much confidence in a doctrine of indispensability and perfectability. Much misery in the world is traceable to diseased egos clothed in the terrible illusion of a divine mission. In matters of small importance, the consequences are merely ludicrous; in larger spheres they may be indescribably tragic."
>
> Eugene C. Barker, "The Eugene C. Barker Portrait," *SHQ*, 46 (Jan. 1943), 314.

desire to continue using the Texas journal as a forum for publishing his research and that of his students. This became clear in the fall of 1910 when he proposed changing the title to the "Southwestern Historical Quarterly." Barker did not strongly support the idea of changing the title, but he did believe the expansion in scope might bring more articles. As he had earlier confessed to Bolton, when he "took hold" as editor in late 1910, the "bins were empty."[4] Others believed the new name would attract subscribers and thus increase revenue. Barker submitted the new title to the Executive Council for approval in March 1912, and the change was endorsed. The first number with the new title appeared in July 1912. Bolton wrote the lead article, which was about the Spanish in Texas.

The new partnership quickly unraveled. Bolton, despite his protests to the contrary, became increasingly absorbed with topics outside Texas. He insisted to Adele B. Looscan, president of the Association, in 1918, "My interest and efforts in Texas history are unabated, and I keep track of all that you and your associates are doing."[5] Barker knew better, and many years later quietly noted that Bolton responded to editorial inquiries only if he wanted something, such as having his student's paper included in the next issue. Barker had been told by Bolton to expect many California subscriptions to enhance his budget; instead he got, as H. Bailey Carroll later recalled, only six paid memberships and a small pile of manuscripts to be edited for publication. Bolton remained on the title page as coeditor until 1937, when Barker resigned, but the Chief exercised sole discretion over content and style.

Barker's solitary editorship of the *Quarterly* of course meant that the focus remained almost exclusively on Texas, his homeland and that of his loyal readers. He initially remained skeptical of the new name, but almost everyone else seemed to like it. When Looscan wrote that she hated the name, he replied, "Personally I was mildly opposed to the change myself—at least I was never very enthusiastic about it." But when "Bolton urged it," and Zachary Fulmore (then president of the Association), Charles Ramsdell, and Ernest Winkler all endorsed it, he agreed. Barker pointed out that he "managed to postpone the change for a year . . . but could not hold out longer without being thought selfish and interested for personal reasons." He assured Looscan that he printed "every thing on Texas that I have been able to get." He had to admit, though, that the "expansion of field" made it easier "to feed the Q. more easily and regularly, without crunching out a single article on Texas."[6]

In the end, the predictions of diehards that the title change would drive away Texas readers proved untrue, primarily because Barker produced a solid journal devoted principally to the history of their state. Abandoned by Bolton, Barker took charge of the material he received and forged his own journal. In the process he became by his own admission a reluctant editorial "autocrat." He had little time or inclination for close scrutiny; Bailey Carroll remembered that his predecessor "simply accepted or rejected" articles. Stung by criticism from cantankerous Samuel E. Asbury of Texas A&M University in 1938, one year after he retired as editor, Barker responded, "I did it my way, and on the whole I know it is good." He admitted that while he had printed articles that he knew were far from perfect, he published what he got. As another successor, Joe B. Frantz, remarked later, Barker inherited a "bare-bones operation" and made it work, even if when copy was a bit short he printed "another section from the almost interminable and doggedly dull diary of Adolphus Sterne."[7]

Others may have had less than complimentary remarks about him as editor, but Barker never apologized or tried to second-guess himself. In 1946 Executive Council member C. C. Jeffries proposed that the title revert to its original. Jeffries, Barker, and Louis W. Kemp, a former president of the Association and noted for his tremendous efforts at historical preservation, were appointed as a committee to discuss the idea. Barker had made it clear that he was a man loath to reconsider decisions, especially those that had proven to be correct or at least harmless, and Kemp represented the majority in the Association who agreed with him. The matter was dropped.

Barker and the Association had good reason to be proud of his work because much of it has stood the test of time. Of course, he included much on Spanish Texas. Charles W. Hackett was, with Bolton, an early contributor on this period. He earned his undergraduate degree in history at the University of Texas, and then followed Bolton to California, where he got his doctorate. After returning to teach in Austin, he became a "surrogate Bolton" for the University of Texas, earning distinction in the field of Latin American history.[8] While still a graduate student, Hackett published articles in the *Quarterly* on the Pueblo revolt of 1680, and other articles appeared after he joined the University faculty. His work on the Spanish reaction to French intrusion in colonial Texas relied in part on the groundwork laid in articles by Charmion C. Shelby and Richard Senberg. Another Bolton student, William E. Dunn, who got his doctoral degree at Columbia University, wrote solid articles on Spanish-Indian relations and the Spanish counterattack against the French in colonial Texas. And Barker certainly did not overlook the importance of primary sources for this period. One of the most useful was Fritz L. Hoffman's translation of a diary kept during Martín de Alarcón's Texas *entrada* of 1718, but there were many more.

Barker published some of his own and his students' work on Mexican Texas and the arrival of Anglo-Americans. Garrison had strictly limited Barker's Texas research to the pre-1821 period, but, after Garrison's death, Barker inherited his post-1821 research interests, along with projects such as the Austin papers and biography. Among the most notable of Barker's own scholarly contributions to the *Quarterly* were an article on slavery in the colonization of Texas and an article defending the role played by Tejanos in the war for Texan independence. In the latter article, Barker clearly revealed his break with the older interpretations of Texas history written by Anglos, who tended to emphasize the corruption and ineptness of Spanish and Mexican settlers in Texas. Garrison set the stage with his research on early Texas, Bolton

BARKER AS FISHERMAN

"[W]hile many people fish without attracting notice, Dr. Barker fishes in his own highly individualistic way. No reckless abandon marks his sport; no relaxation of the quiet dignity and reserve that distinguish him in public. He fishes with grim determination, even with deadly concentration, as if he were tracking down a slanderer of Stephen F. Austin. And after everyone else in the party has done up his line in disgust, he has been known to settle himself wearily but philosophically to the fruitless job at hand with the observation: 'When a man makes up his mind to go fishing, I don't suppose he has any choice but to fish.' Then when he does catch a big one, his companions sometimes hear a throaty chuckle as if at last he gloats a little in triumph."

J. Evetts Haley, "The Eugene C. Barker Portrait," *SHQ*, 46 (Jan. 1943), 309.

expanded the focus with his work, and then Barker, with his students, added more to a fuller, less biased understanding of colonial Texans. Mattie A. Hatcher produced an interesting study on American filibusters in colonial Texas, and Amelia Williams contributed a groundbreaking work on the Alamo. For the early Republic, Barker printed a five-part study by J. E. Winston on American popular reactions to the Texas Revolution; an influential article by Rupert N. Richardson on the constitution of 1836; and several installments by Ralph W. Steen on government in the early Republic. Richardson and Steen both became noted Texas historians, as did Carlos E. Castañeda, who contributed two useful translations of reports on Mexican Texas to Barker's *Quarterly*.

Some of the best work published by Barker in the *Quarterly* focused on the early statehood period. On politics, Frederic L. Paxson, a noted frontier historian, and Annie Middleton produced articles on the Constitution of 1845. William C. Binkley wrote on Texas claims to land ceded to New Mexico after annexation, and S. H. German contributed a good study of Governor George T. Wood. While working on her dissertation for Barker, Abigail Curlee wrote a pioneering study of Texas slave plantations. Harold Schoen later contributed a notable article on free blacks in antebellum Texas. Frontier defense received much attention from established national historians and Texas scholars alike. J. Fred Rippy in 1919 sent a timely article on Rio Grande border troubles prior to the Civil War, and Averill B. Bender wrote on United States Army operations. Both later published very influential books on their topics. Among the Texas contributors, Frank B. Lammons wrote on the Army's experiment with camels, Lena F. Koch wrote on federal Indian policy in the antebellum era, and Kenneth F. Neighbours wrote on Robert S. Neighbors's expedition to El Paso in 1849.

Barker's selection of articles on Texas history after 1860 clearly reflects an emerging bias among his contributors. There were far fewer good contributions on the Civil War period than on the post-Reconstruction era. Many who wrote about the war avoided military topics; among the best articles were one by Alma D. King on William S. Oldham, the Confederate congressman, and one by William R. Russ Jr. on Radical disfranchisement in postwar Texas. Those who wrote about Texas farming and ranching after the Civil War included William C. Holden and Roscoe C. Martin, both of whom later became popular writers whose books were published by the Association. Of note also was early research on the Grange and Farmers' Alliance by Ralph A. Smith, who had three articles printed in the *Quarterly*. Texans as they approached the centennial of their independence from Mexico preferred to focus on the positive aspects of their heritage, such as the ennobling frontier

Zachary T. Fulmore
(1912–1915)

Adele B. Looscan
(1915–1925)

T. F. Harwood
(1925–1929)

Alex Dienst (1929–1932)

W. R. Wrather (1932–1939)

Five presidents served under Barker's directorship. Adele Looscan is the longest-serving president in the Association's history. Alex Dienst is the only president ever to be ousted. *Photographs from TSHA Files.*

and romantic cowboys, and not the heartache of the Lost Cause. This became obvious in the official celebrations of 1936, when western culture obliterated almost every reference to the Southern aspects of Texas's past. As Walter L. Buenger has noted, Texans replaced Robert E. Lee—the chivalrous ideal—with John Chisum—the "innovative westerner."[9]

Barker published three volumes of Stephen F. Austin's papers and a landmark biography of Austin (inherited from Garrison and Bugbee), but the Association did not undertake a substantial book publication effort during his tenure. Barker's books, and those written by other members, for the most part had to be published elsewhere. Two works, both reprinted from the *Quarterly*, appeared with the Association's imprint: Ephraim D. Adams's edited volume of British diplomatic correspondence about Texas prior to statehood was published in 1918, and an edition of George B. Erath's memoirs followed five years later. Barker planned to publish an index to the *Quarterly*, but several efforts failed. Elizabeth H. West began one in 1911, but her abrupt resignation from the Texas State Library in 1915 slowed her work. Lack of money created another obstacle. A sales campaign in 1917, which was intended to raise money to publish West's index, brought only forty orders. In 1922 West quit the project altogether. A printed index did not appear until 1950, when the Association had more staff and money.

West's resignation from the state library, with its subsequent effect on the *Quarterly* index, was just one aspect of the Progressive Era political troubles that plagued Barker. The Progressive Era was a period of growth for some historical organizations, such as the Wisconsin Historical Society, but in Texas it was a time of bitter conflict for the University of Texas. Barker had been in charge of the Association for only a few years when he became enmeshed in the clash between Governor James E. Ferguson and the University. Barker succeeded Garrison as chairman of the Texas Library and Historical Commission. In 1915 Ferguson removed Ernest Winkler as state librarian in spite of heated protests from Barker and others. Winkler's removal led Barker to quit as chair of the Historical Commission; West, TSHA charter member and the state archivist, also left her job. Ferguson next targeted the University of Texas with his version of reform. During the summer of 1917, he vetoed the University's budget while his appointees to the Board of Regents mustered a majority vote for the dismissal of seven faculty members. Barker played a prominent role in the subsequent outpouring of public and academic protest, battling openly against what Charles Ramsdell ridiculed as Ferguson's "folly and wickedness."[10] University allies revived charges of corruption against Ferguson, who was impeached and convicted. He resigned in August 1917.

The conflict with Ferguson thrust Barker into a leadership role among the

Members

"Mr. C. M. Caldwell of Abilene has given $100 to be distributed in prizes by the History Department of the University of Texas for the best essays in local history written by high school students of Texas. The *Dallas News* will print the prize-winning essays and in addition will give $5 to each of the winners of prizes offered by Mr. Caldwell."

"News Items," *SHQ*, 27 (Apr. 1924), 335.

"Benjamin Dudley Tarlton, professor of law in the University of Texas, died at Beeville, September 23, 1919, as a result of exposure during the storm that devastated the coast."

"News Items," *SHQ*, 23 (Oct. 1919), 152.

faculty, but it also convinced him that he had to be careful with the Association. Texas politics, especially that which involved the University of Texas, appeared to be a dark and bloody ground full of those who would destroy academic integrity, which Barker valued above all else. Here he often reacted with the maternal instinct of a saber-toothed tiger rather than the self-sacrifice of a St. Francis. In 1918 he wrote to Alexander Dienst, a Temple dentist and Texana collector who later became president of the TSHA, that "if your friend [Ferguson] is not dead, he ought to be, and I wish he were." After reflecting on this notion, he confessed to Dienst that he was not entirely serious, "but I'm not going to let that person's memory worry me very much." Barker added, "If the decent people of Texas can't prevent that sort of vermin from feeding on the state I shall get out; but I'm making no preparations yet."[11] He did not step down as leader of the Association for another twenty years, but incidents like this taught him to be conservative, and perhaps overly defensive, in his management style.

Membership was a great concern for Barker when he took charge of the Association in 1910. He worried about increasing the number of members, but at the same time kept tight control over leadership. He freely admitted to Looscan as early as 1915 that the Association was "autocratically managed by a handful of people in Austin."[12] But, as he insisted later, he believed that if he did not choose the officers, no one else would and the Association would languish. At times it did appear as if there might be no more than a half-dozen people active in keeping it alive. Those who served as president during the sec-

History Department faculty, ca. 1930. *(Left to right) Top row:* Leslie Waggener Sr., 1883–1896; George P. Garrison, 1884–1910; Lester Gladstone Bugbee, 1895–1902. *Middle row:* Charles W. Ramsdell, 1906–1942; Charles W. Hackett, 1918–1951; Milton R. Gutsch, 1912–1951; Walter Prescott Webb, 1918–1963; Frank B. Marsh, 1910–1940. *Bottom row:* Rudolph L. Biesele, 1925–1956; Thad W. Riker, 1910–1951; Eugene C. Barker, 1899–1951; Frederic Duncalf, 1909–1951. At the time of this photograph Webb was chairman of the department, having taken over from Barker in 1925. *Photograph from TSHA Files.*

ond and third decades of the Association, men such as Zachary T. Fulmore and Thomas W. Harwood, agreed that Barker did right in directing the organization with a heavy hand. After all, Garrison himself had insisted that a University of Texas professor always be in charge to ensure close ties to that institution, which was always a vital source of support.

One TSHA president was chosen by Barker primarily to recruit women. The enlistment of women had declined when the Daughters of the Republic of Texas angrily divided over the fight for control of the Alamo between Adina De Zavala, a charter member of the Association, and Clara Driscoll. Governor Oscar B. Colquitt tried to negotiate a settlement between De Zavala and Driscoll in 1911 but failed. De Zavala remained in the Association, which, as a result, became estranged from the Daughters and suffered a loss of membership. This problem was compounded in 1912 when Barker, Charles Ramsdell, and Charles S. Potts produced a public school textbook on Texas history that supplanted an earlier, popular work by Anna J. H. Pennybacker. Pennybacker quit the Association and became its vocal opponent, which proved unfortunate since Pennybacker was greatly influential in women's organizations throughout Texas. Barker sourly noted in July 1912, "We have a pretty hard fight on hand . . . because most of the club women have gone wild over Mrs. Pennybacker and apparently think the supremacy of the sex depends on the defense of her book."[13]

So, in 1915, after several years of struggling to recoup the loss of women members, Barker appointed the first female president of the Association. He had appealed to Bride N. Taylor and Hally B. Perry, prominent members of the TSHA and of women's groups in Texas, for support in 1912 while appointing yet another man, Zachary T. Fulmore, to replace the late Alexander W. Terrell as president. Fulmore worked hard with Taylor and Perry, but the results were disappointing, and it was on Fulmore's advice that Barker finally selected Adele B. Looscan to be president. Apparently no one protested, either through disinterest or in continued trust that Barker knew what he was doing.

The fact that Looscan learned of her election when she read it in the *San Antonio Express* suggests the control that Barker exercised over Association matters. She told Barker that she was "inexpressibly surprised" and curious about "how this strange thing came about." Furthermore, she asked, "Who pulls the wires behind the screen of this erudite society?"[14] The answer to the second question was obvious: Eugene Barker. He selected Looscan because

"Mrs. Adele B. Looscan died at her home in Houston, Texas, November 23, 1935. She was the daughter of Andrew Briscoe, a captain in the battle of San Jacinto, and Mary Jane Harris, a pioneer resident of Harrisburg, Texas. She was President of the Texas State Historical Association from 1915 to 1925, and contributed liberally both labor and money to its maintenance. She was an able and singularly candid and detached student of Texas history. Many of her articles were published in the *Quarterly of the Texas State Historical Association*—the most notable being her history of Harris County, 1822–1845. She contributed studies also to *A Comprehensive History of Texas* (edited by Dudley G. Wooten) and to local Houston papers. During the last six or eight years of her life she was a helpless invalid."

Memorial page, *SHQ*, 39 (Jan. 1936), 252.

she was a founding member and historian general of the Daughters, remained active in the United Daughters of the Confederacy and the Daughters of the American Revolution, and was a charter member of the Texas Woman's Press Association. During the fall of 1915 she began writing to the leaders of the Texas Federation of Women's Clubs on behalf of the Association. Barker expected her efforts would have more impact if she were president. He had no way of knowing that she would serve longer as Association president than any other person.

Looscan tried to recruit men as well as women, but with both she was restricted by Barker's unofficial rule for members: quality before quantity. As he had quipped to I. J. Cox, an Association member and contributor to the *Quarterly*, "There is no desire to build up a large organization by pandering to the cheap and sensational."[15] *Dallas Times Herald* editorial writer J. P. Worley's lighthearted suggestion that jokes be printed in the *Quarterly* probably did not amuse Barker. Ramsdell had a more interesting proposal for Barker and Looscan: employ a "bright, hustling, prepossessing young man" to sell memberships in Texas cities. This plan was implemented in 1916 but "absolutely failed." After a few weeks, the man hired to peddle memberships "gave it up in disgust."[16] The reason for his failure became clear when Ramsdell tried to sell memberships and enrolled twenty-three recruits in just two days in Dallas. The younger man appeared to be what he was, a salesman, while Ramsdell was in fact a university academic, which reassured people. Unfortunately neither Ramsdell nor Barker had the time to sell memberships.

Looscan had to admit by 1922 that her efforts to increase enrollment had failed. She had proven no more able than Garrison or Barker to recruit women, and overall membership remained at about eight hundred. Looscan proposed yet another idea: sponsoring the establishment of county history societies to be affiliated with the TSHA and boost its support. A committee was organized at the annual meeting in 1923 for this purpose. Chaired by Alexander Dienst, its members included Ramsdell, retired attorney and legislator George W. Tyler, and Elizabeth H. West, who had been appointed state librarian after the impeachment of Jim Ferguson as governor. Ramsdell became the contact person for providing any assistance to the committee, excluding money. Local organizations initially responded warmly to the new program, but again it failed to generate either memberships or funds for the Association, which soon abandoned the effort.

Barker did what he could to boost interest in the TSHA by giving honorary memberships to a handful of key people in other organizations, but he continued to be restricted by his lofty ideal of a proper member. What he also realized, and what Ramsdell would not readily admit, was that the Association did not have the staff to capitalize on the increase in the number of local history groups. Barker and Ramsdell at that time were the entire staff, with a few graduate students who worked part-time. They were caught in a troubling cycle: they did not have the money to hire people, and without a staff there was little chance to forge useful alliances. The Depression, with its crushing impact on the nation and Texas, quashed whatever strong desire Barker had for recruitment. When he relinquished control of the Association in 1937, membership reportedly stood at less than five hundred.

Faltering membership, and the fact that about half of the enrolled members could not or would not pay their dues, severely reduced the Association's budget. Barker revived the idea of an endowment soon after he took control. His target was $10,000. Members gave what they could—Looscan donated $250—but the drive derailed as the outbreak of war in Europe and continued revolution in Mexico pushed Texas into a recession. Barker told Beauregard Bryan in 1914, "I discovered some weeks ago that my campaign for an endowment was ill-timed." Ramsdell, TSHA treasurer, reported to Barker, "It looks as if the Association will have to drag along until the financial stringency is over." Borrowing a phrase that Barker often used, Ramsdell added, "Someday, I hope, this hand-to-mouth struggle for existence will have passed."[17] The Texas economy recovered briefly, but timber and oil revenues could not offset a devastating drop in cotton prices after 1920, when the Executive Council voted for the first time to increase the dues of members —from two dollars to three dollars.

While the Association gained little, the University of Texas greatly benefited from Barker's futile effort to establish an endowment. In 1912 Barker convinced George W. Littlefield, a University regent and one of the wealthiest men in Texas, to buy a life membership in the TSHA. Barker continued to correspond with Littlefield on the subject of improving the library collections of the University, specifically in southern history. Littlefield, a former Confederate officer, often feuded with another prominent benefactor of the University, Regent George W. Brackenridge, a Unionist during the Civil War. Littlefield responded to Barker's prodding in 1914 by giving a check for $25,000 to establish the Littlefield Fund for Southern History. This amount, suggested to Barker by Reuben G. Thwaites of the Wisconsin Historical Society, grew as Littlefield continued to give, climaxing with a bequest of $100,000 in 1920. Barker's triumph for the University of Texas was bittersweet. Littlefield pledged $1,000 for an Association endowment if Barker could raise $9,000, but the efforts of Barker, Looscan, Ramsdell, and others fell far short. Looscan at one point suggested to Ramsdell that Littlefield be made president of the Association in her place to secure his support, but this was never done.

GEORGE WASHINGTON LITTLEFIELD
(1842–1920)

"Now What Ever you do. let it be done well and Satisfactory—It makes but little difference what a man starts in so he saves up what he makes. Unless He does that, then it will make no difference what he engages in He will do no good—So it is in life. The best men of our land Started on nothing. but they saved and built up. When you show you can be successful then the world endorses you. but if you show you are a failure then the world is afraid of you—Truth and honesty must prevail. Your word must be good in all things, or Confidence will not exist. and without Confidence no business is Safe—"

George Littlefield was born in Mississippi and moved to Texas in 1850. He grew up on the family plantation in Gonzales County, and in 1861 enlisted with Terry's Texas Rangers. He fought at Shiloh, Perryville, Chickamauga, and Mossy Creek, where he was wounded by an exploding cannon shell. He was promoted to major at Mossy Creek, and after the mid 1880s he was addressed by that title. When he came back to Texas from Tennessee he took charge of his and his brother's plantation. He married Alice Tillar in 1863 and had two children, both of whom died in infancy. Littlefield had a strong sense of family and for the rest of his life used nephews and the husbands of nieces in his business ventures.

In 1871 Littlefield put together a herd of cattle and drove it to Kansas. With his profits he paid off his debts and opened a dry goods store. He continued to buy and trail cattle, bought ranches in Texas and New Mexico, and developed his plantations.

Littlefield moved to Austin in 1883, and in 1890 he organized the American National Bank, for which he built (1910–1911) the nine-story Littlefield Building, now an office building in downtown Austin. The doors are bronze, cast by the Tiffany Company of New York, and have depictions of ranch scenes on them. Through his loans to political figures he gained political influence, and he gained interest in a number of businesses, including the Driskill Hotel (which for many years was the site of TSHA annual meetings).

In 1911 Littlefield was appointed to the University of Texas Board of Regents and in his University work came to know Eugene Barker. When Littlefield complained to Barker about the Northern bias he saw in the American history textbooks, Barker responded by emphasizing the need for archival sources from which to write better history. This ongoing discussion between Littlefield and Barker was the seed for what became the Littlefield Southern History Collection, which began in 1914 with the establishment of the Littlefield Fund for Southern History. Littlefield also gave money to the University for the Littlefield Fountain and the six statues on the South Mall, the Alice P. Littlefield Dormitory, the purchase of the John Henry Wrenn Library, and $500,000 toward the construction of the Main Building. Littlefield died on November 10, 1920, and is buried in Oakwood Cemetery.

The Littlefield Southern History Collection is one of the nation's principal resources for research on the history of the eleven southern states that seceded in 1860 and 1861. It is housed at the Center for American History on the University campus and includes five collections: the Natchez Trace Collection, the Southern History Archival Collection, the Littlefield Rare Book and Pamphlet Collection, the Southern Newspaper Collection, and the Charles Ramsdell Microfilm Collection.

When it was built in 1893, the Littlefield House was one of many Victorian houses in the neighborhood at the edge of the original Forty Acres of the University campus. When Alice Littlefield died in 1935 the house was given to the University and since then has housed, at various times, the Texas Centennial Office, the Music Department, and the Navy R.O.T.C. (which used the attic as a firing range). It is now the only surviving Victorian, surrounded by University buildings. It houses, on the second floor, the offices for Resource Development. The first floor, decorated in Victorian style, is used for special functions. The ghost of Alice is said to live in the attic.

Littlefield to Maurice Dowell, Dec. 29, 1904 (Dowell Papers, TSL), quoted in H. Bailey Carroll, "Texas Collection," *SHQ*, 68 (Oct. 1964), 243 (quotation; punctuated as in original); David Gracy II, "George Washington Littlefield," in Tyler, et al. (eds.), *New Handbook of Texas*, IV, 230–231; Kay Randall, "Littlefield Spirit Lives On: House is a Victorian Ghost of the Past," http://www.utexas.edu/features/archive/2002/littlefield.html (accessed May 24, 2006). *Photographs courtesy of Prints and Photographs Collection, DI 02305 (George Littlefield), DI 02607 (Littlefield House), CAH.*

Without an endowment, Barker struggled to pay the Association's bills and fund its activities. Receipts slowly declined in spite of efforts to increase subscriptions, solicit donations, and even loan Association funds at interest. Barker tried to get money from Brackenridge, but he, like Littlefield, gave to the University, not the Association. The war interrupted Barker's fund-raising, but he dismissed a proposal in 1919 to ask for money from the legislature. He strongly believed that accepting state funds "would in all probability introduce politics, which would be ruinous."[18] This was perhaps a strange attitude for a Progressive, since Progressives were noted for their belief in government as the source of cures for many of society's ills, but not so strange for someone like Barker who had weathered the storm of Texas politics during the Ferguson era. Barker instead put aside his own earlier reservations and asked the Executive Council to increase the annual dues in 1920, a suggestion that was strongly supported by the members. He also borrowed money to invest with the powerful business enterprise of Brown Brothers, a national firm later known as Brown Brothers Harriman. Careful management permitted the purchase of other investments, mostly bonds, but these were modest in amount and produced less revenue than the loans the Association continued to provide each year, mostly to academic members.

A new member of the University's Department of History brought an ambitious idea for raising money. Thomas P. Martin, who earned bachelor's and master's degrees under Herbert Eugene Bolton at the University of California in Berkeley and his doctorate under Frederick Jackson Turner at Harvard University, became, with Barker's endorsement, an associate professor. Martin chaired the Association's Committee on Patrons, established in 1923 to recruit members who would donate $100 or more to an endowment. The first four Patrons enrolled quickly: longtime members Adele B. Looscan, Thomas F. Harwood, and Robert L. Batts, as well as Mrs. J. A. Walker. Encouraged, Martin outlined Association plans to University of Texas president Walter M. W. Splawn. Patrons, Martin declared, would support a $500,000 endowment for hiring staff, enlarging the journal, publishing monographs and both weekly and monthly newsletters, offering scholarships and fellowships, and acquiring archives. A "memorial building," completed for the centennial of Texas independence in 1936, would house the expanded Association.[19]

Martin's logic was a bit faulty, but his enthusiasm was contagious. Looscan endorsed Martin by being the first to give. Even Barker proved supportive; as Martin wrote to Looscan, the somber Chief was "becoming almost enthusiastic." Martin, however, based his projections on the success of a committee that had been organized to raise money for building a football stadium at the University of Texas. When it became clear that Texans were much more willing to spend money on a football stadium than a history organization, Martin's interest flagged. He began applying for a big research grant for himself, writing defensively to Looscan, "I think you will agree with me when I say that the raising of endowment funds is not properly the work of a University professor, but rather that of the publicist and promoter."[20] He spent the 1925–1926 academic year in England on a fellowship from the Social Science Research Council, then demanded another year on leave, with a pay raise, from an annoyed Barker. Instead, Martin became the first faculty member asked to resign from the Department of History, and did so with Barker's emphatic approval.

Receipts for the Association in 1924–1925, the year that Martin laid his unrealistic plans for an endowment, totaled just $2,015.84. Cotton prices bottomed out at half of the World War I peak, indicating the weakness of commodities markets for Texans, and incomes fell further as the Great Depression began in the fall of 1929. Hard times made it difficult to collect the loans made by the Association or for it to sell its bonds for much-needed cash. Barker during 1934 declared that he, Charles Ramsdell, and J. Evetts Haley, a colorful former student of Barker's then working as a field agent for the University archives, would serve as a special committee to review the Association's reduced finances. They managed to sell some bonds, most notably those for German companies, but had to write off a third of the loans the Association had made. Somehow they acquired a rental house in Coleman, but expenses negated any profit. Sadly for Barker, during his last year in charge of the Association, revenue was not more than a few dollars over what it had been a decade earlier, nor had his organization increased its assets during that decade.

Lack of money may have been the reason that the annual meeting continued almost unchanged in location and attendance during Barker's tenure. Barker worried that attendance was poor, but rejected all suggestions to convene in any place but Austin. When Zachary Fulmore pushed hard for Brenham in 1914, Barker appointed him as a "committee of one to see to it." "Indifference" from around the state, as well as from Barker, forced Fulmore to give up. Adele Looscan next took up the cause, arguing for Houston, her hometown. Plans were discussed for the twentieth anniversary meeting to be held at Houston in 1917, but Barker feared attendance would be sparse with so little advance notice. Looscan had purchased advertisements in the Houston newspapers and was understandably upset when Barker decided to hold the meeting at Austin. He reluctantly endorsed a Houston meeting again in 1918, as long as Looscan agreed not to be greatly "chagrined or humiliated by small attendance and lack of interest."[21] The wartime flood of soldiers and material into the city forced another cancellation. Looscan, like Fulmore, finally abandoned the quest. In 1922, when her failing health had made it difficult for her to travel to Austin, Barker gallantly offered to hold the annual meeting in Houston, but Looscan declined.

Barker did occasionally make slight changes in the format of the annual meeting. The lack of attendance led him initially to reduce the number of presentations, but during his second decade in charge of the TSHA he made some adjustments with an eye toward expansion. He changed the meeting date to April 21, San Jacinto Day, in 1921 and 1922 because March 2 was "such a busy day around the University."[22] The revived Sons of the Republic of Texas protested that this date conflicted with their own program at the San Jacinto battlefield. Barker obligingly moved his meeting to May, then returned to April and subsequently met in either month each year, more often than not avoiding San Jacinto Day. In 1928 he expanded the program to two days to allow more presentations. In April 1922, two papers were read; in 1935 there were a dozen presentations and a dinner speaker. Barker's Texas Centennial meeting in 1936 was a triumph. Held jointly with the Mississippi Valley Historical Association in Austin, it attracted more than 150 people to hear two dozen presentations in the Driskill Hotel and Garrison Hall, completed on campus in 1926 and named in honor of the founder of the Association.

The addition of a second day permitted the initiation of a new idea to increase attendance. Incoming TSHA president Alexander Dienst wrote in 1929, "It has always seemed to me that we are just a wee bit selfish about our annual gatherings and keep our charmed circle too small. In fact, I am in close touch with rival Institutions who do not say so but who believe the U of T wants to keep this Society of ours a Baptist institution to the extent of us being 'close communicants'." Dienst added that it would encourage speakers "if the class room was chuck full of folks and not just a gathering of a few choice 'spirits' as we are." He ended, "I know it is not the object of the Association to hold the meetings in an 'aloof' way but that is the impression created." As a solution, he proposed that invitations be sent to prominent persons and organizations in Texas, asking them to come to "our two days love feast."[23] From this proposal developed the practice of having representatives speak about their local history organizations during a dinner session. Dienst presided over the first such presentation in 1930.

Barker planned to have a library devoted to Texas history on the University of Texas campus, but this did not happen until more than a decade after he stepped down as TSHA secretary. Soon after he took charge in 1910, Nathaniel L. Goodrich, University librarian, told Barker that unless he transferred control of the Texas Collection from the TSHA to the University, funds could not be made available for binding and cataloging the books. Barker

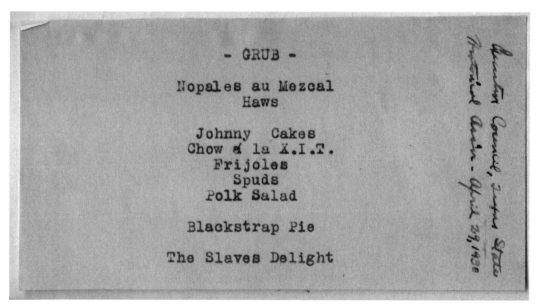

- GRUB -

Nopales au Mezcal
Haws

Johnny Cakes
Chow à la X.I.T.
Frijoles
Spuds
Polk Salad

Blackstrap Pie

The Slaves Delight

Executive Council dinner menu, from Annual Meeting, April 29, 1930. *Courtesy Subject Vertical Files, TSHA, DI 02588, a, b, CAH.*

organized a committee to review the issue, and an arrangement was made for the transfer of the Texas Collection and Association archives to the University in 1911. Barker did exact a price for this transfer. Since its opening, the University of Texas had allowed students who graduated from its affiliated high schools to enroll as freshmen without examination. While they were in high school, students in affiliated schools got copies of the *Quarterly*, purchased by the regents at half the usual rate. The Texas Department of Education's

ERNEST W. WINKLER

"With no lack of appreciation of many others, a second generation of builders must be acknowledged. Subordinate to Garrison and Bugbee in point of time, but to none in constancy of service or wisdom and volume of acquisition, I am sure that a referendum to qualified voters would put my friend and classmate, E. W. Winkler, at the head of this list. Oliver Goldsmith might have been describing him two hundred years ago when he wrote of the village school master, "... and still the wonder grew that one small head could carry all he knew." We think of him as a veritable encyclopedia of Texas history and bibliography. His knowledge is phenomenal. Whether he carries it all in his head or has mastered a perfect filing system of facts to which he always has the key, I do not know. He is our first resort, and usually our last, when we want information without working for it. We impose on him without conscience. His position, his marvelous knowledge, and his eager interest have made him the purchaser of more books and manuscripts about Texas than any other member of the University staff. No great collection of material on Texas, on the South, or on Spanish America has been bought by or for the University in the past thirty years without his previous inspection and evaluation."

Eugene C. Barker, "To Whom Credit is Due," *SHQ*, 54 (July 1950), 8.

accrediting of secondary programs ended the affiliation program and cast doubt on the future of the regents' subvention. In return for Barker's transfer of the Texas Collection and archives, the regents agreed to give $300 each year to the Association, which would provide copies of the *Quarterly* for the University's journal exchange program. This arrangement continued for more than sixty years, ending in the early 1970s.

Barker tried to secure a library for the Association after its collections were transferred, but again his initiative resulted in a gain for his University, not his organization. At the 1917 annual meeting, a committee was organized to ask for space in the Land Office building, on the Capitol grounds, for a library and museum. This scheme grew into a proposal that the state's historical archives be given to the Association and housed in the Land Office, under the supervision of Ernest W. Winkler. Barker never got his museum, but his initiative revived an idea for an on-campus museum that had originally been proposed by University president George T. Winston in 1897. Alexander Dienst read a paper on the topic before the Association at the annual meeting in 1920, and another committee formed. Composed of Dienst, Adele Looscan, Charles Ramsdell, Elizabeth H. West, University faculty members Henry Y. Benedict and James E. Pearce, Presbyterian minister and historian William S. Red, and O. M. Ball, this group initiated the establishment of the Texas Museum Association. Pearce served as president of this organization and Barker was on the Executive Council. Funds came through private donations, federal and state appropriations, and sales of commemorative coins by the American Legion. The Texas Memorial Museum opened in January 1939, with Elias H. Sellards as director in place of Pearce, who had died.

Barker remained active in acquiring library materials for the University of Texas. As George W. Littlefield gave money, Barker and Ernest Winkler, who after being fired by Ferguson became the reference librarian and curator for Texas books at the University, bought many books on Southern history for the Littlefield Collection. Charles Ramsdell served as the official director of the Littlefield Fund. The three men also purchased documents, making sure that Texas got strong attention within a program intended to enhance the University's collections on Southern history. Barker constantly wrote letters and met with potential donors. Among the most important papers he helped to acquire were those of Ashbel Smith, whose books had come to the University while Garrison was director of the Association; those of Henry Raguet, a prominent Nacogdoches merchant during the period of the Republic of Texas; and those of Joseph D. Sayers, Texas Confederate officer, congressman, governor, and regent who opposed Ferguson's efforts to reshape the University. At the same time, Barker and Winkler expanded further on Garrison's legacy by acquiring more materials for the growing Latin American Collection.

Barker acquired another useful partner to aid in the search for Texas archives when his student, West Texas rancher J. Evetts Haley, completed a master's degree and returned to work as field secretary for the Panhandle-Plains Historical Society and editor of the *Panhandle-Plains Historical Review*. In 1929 the University got a large grant from the Laura Spellman Rockefeller Memorial Fund, and Barker convinced the regents to put aside some money for acquiring Texas history materials. He hired Haley to do the legwork. Haley combed nineteen Texas counties in the first year, bringing thousands of pages of manuscripts and hundreds of books, maps, and other items back to Austin in the back of his Model A Ford. Among the best finds in Haley's five years of work for the University were the papers of rancher Charles Goodnight, eccentric naturalist Gideon Lincecum, and South Texas political boss James B. Wells Jr. In 1932 the papers of noted Texas physician, land agent, and politician James H. Starr arrived at the University, where,

J. Evetts Haley (1901–1995)

J. Evetts Haley, historian, rancher, and political activist, did his graduate work under Eugene Barker, who later hired him to find and acquire Texas history materials. Haley had been working for awhile as a collector of history materials for the Panhandle-Plains Historical Society, traveling the Panhandle in his Model-A Ford, when at a TSHA annual meeting Barker and Charles Ramsdell asked him to come to Austin and do for the University what he had been doing for the Society.

Hiring Haley was made possible by a grant in 1929 from the Laura Spellman Rockefeller Memorial Fund. Barker asked for $6,500 of the $250,000 grant in order to pay a collector and cover expenses. Barker gave Haley the discretion to pursue any collecting direction he desired. Haley later said about Barker "if you were worth hiring, he thought you ought to have some idea of what ought to be done."

Haley visited nineteen Texas counties in his first year, saving many courthouse records from destruction by loading them into his Model A and bringing them back to the University. He brought back manuscripts, newspapers, broadsides, maps, and photographs. Traveling the state with his bedroll, he followed every lead and discovered unique collections documenting the cattle industry, West Texas land speculators, doctors, buffalo hunters, the Texas Rangers, and much more. Among the important collections he secured for the University were the Charles Goodnight papers, the papers of naturalist Gideon Lincecum, the James B. Wells papers documenting South Texas politics, and the James Harper Starr papers (which included the diary of William B. Travis).

With the huge quantity of material Haley was bringing to the University, a new library was an urgent necessity, and in 1931 one was authorized. The Mirabeau B. Lamar Library was begun in 1933 and completed in 1937. By 1934 it could provide housing for all the Texas materials.

Haley in 1933 was appointed head of the Texas Historical Records Survey, with funding provided by the Civil Works Administration under the New Deal as a part of a nationwide survey of historical records. Over two hundred employees under Haley's direction collected, catalogued, and preserved materials, which were then sent to the University Archives. With the approach of the 1936 presidential election, however, Haley became head of the conservative Jeffersonian Democrats, organized in opposition to Franklin Roosevelt. In August of 1936 Haley took a leave of absence from his collecting work in order to expose "the fallacies and dangers of the so-called New Deal." The University terminated his position, citing insufficient funds. Haley charged that he had been fired for political reasons.

In the 1940s Haley again became embroiled in University politics over issues of academic freedom and University governance in the Homer Rainey affair. Haley, like Eugene Barker, sided with the Board of Regents against President Rainey, a New Deal man, and wrote a series of essays for the *San Antonio Express* (later published as *The University and the Issue*). In 1956 Haley ran unsuccessfully for governor on a platform of segregation and states' rights.

Haley was the author of many journal articles and books. Among his books are: *The XIT Ranch of Texas and the Early Days of the Llano Estacado* (1929); *Charles*

"After hunting on the Diamond A Ranch in Sierra County, N.M. Oct. 1931" (note on back of photograph). *Courtesy Prints and Photographs Collection, DI 02307, CAH.*

Goodnight: Cowman and Plainsman (1936); *George W. Littlefield, Texan* (1943); *Charles Schreiner, General Merchandise*, published by the TSHA (1944); and *A Texan Looks at Lyndon* (1964).

Haley was a Fellow of the Association, which published, in addition to his book *Charles Schreiner*, a number of his articles in the *Southwestern Historical Quarterly*. He was a central figure in the movement to have the University assign space in the Old Library Building for the Texas collections and the TSHA offices, and drafted the resolution for this that was passed by the Board of Regents in September 1946. Haley remained a member of the TSHA until his death, in Midland, on October 9, 1995, at the age of 94.

Don E. Carleton and Katherine J. Adams, " 'A Work Peculiarly Our Own': Origins of the Barker Texas History Center, 1883–1950," *SHQ*, 86 (Oct. 1982), 214, 215 (1st quotation), 216, 219, 220 (2nd quotation), 224–227; B. Byron Price, "James Evetts Haley, Sr.," in Tyler, et al. (eds.), *New Handbook of Texas*, III, 410–411.

"She is our conscience and our continuity." Coral Horton Tullis (1882–1967), ca. 1940s. Mrs. Tullis was corresponding secretary of the TSHA from 1927 to 1942. In 1942, with the death of Charles Ramsdell, who had held the position of treasurer since 1907, the Association added the office of treasurer to Tullis's responsibilities, and from 1942 until her retirement in 1967, she was re-elected annually as corresponding secretary and treasurer. Coral Tullis earned her B.A. degree from the University of Texas in 1924 and her M.A. degree in 1927. She taught in the history department from 1924 to 1959. In 1937, when the Association was forty years old, she compiled a list of all the articles printed in the *SHQ* up to that time. She had a keen interest in the Junior Historians, looking after their finances and serving as chairman of the judges for their annual writing contest. Coral Tullis retired in April of 1967 and died just weeks later, on June 22. Dorman Winfrey wrote of her: "Mrs. Tullis' ability and performance in her work always brought a flood of praise at Association meetings. Her reputation was described not only as capable, efficient, and honest, but also with such warm words as kind, generous, and lovable" (*SHQ*, vol. 71, p. 281). In 1967 the Coral Horton Tullis Memorial Prize was established for the Association by her children, John L. Tullis and Mrs. W. D. (Jean Tullis) White Sr., and continues to be awarded each year for the best book on Texas published during the calendar year. First quotation from Joe B. Frantz, *SHQ*, 70 (Jan. 1967), 359. *Photograph from TSHA Files.*

according to the agreement with the family, portions were always on display in a special case donated by his descendants.

Funding from the federal Civil Works Administration for a nationwide historic records survey, which began in 1933, enhanced Haley's work for Barker and the University. Haley became director of the Texas effort, and soon had more than two hundred people working for him at fifteen regional centers in the state. At the University, Federal Emergency Relief Administration workers labored to file, catalog, and index the flood as hundreds of thousands of pages of material poured into the archives. Barker pressed hard to have Haley appointed to the faculty, but Haley's rough manner and conservative, anti–New Deal political beliefs worked against him. When Haley joined a coalition devoted to defeating Franklin D. Roosevelt in 1936, the University of Texas discontinued his position, and the archival acquisition program ground to a halt. The Mirabeau B. Lamar Library, which opened on the University campus in 1937, gave more space for archives, but the quarters remained cramped because the Texas material had to share the shelves with the still-growing Latin American Collection.

Barker made a few changes in 1927 with an eye to reviving the Association as the Texas Centennial loomed. After an embarrassing incident, in which a part-time secretary stole Association funds, Barker, at the request of Ramsdell, hired Coral H. Tullis as full-time corresponding secretary of the organization. Ramsdell had held the title of treasurer and corresponding secretary for almost two decades, and it was with a sense of relief that he surrendered one of his tasks. Fifteen years later, when Ramsdell died, Tullis took his place as treasurer as well. A native of Quanah, Tullis had graduated from North Texas Normal College (now the University of North Texas) in 1901 and taught for five years before settling in Austin as a housewife. In 1921 she entered the University, where she earned bachelor's and master's degrees in history and undertook a teaching career that spanned thirty years. She became a vital part of the Association, which she served for forty years.

Hiring Tullis was not the only change Barker made in 1927. He stepped down as chair of the Department of History, only a year after he and his colleagues moved into new quarters in Garrison Hall; the history department gave its first doctoral degrees that year; and Barker was unsuccessfully nominated to be the president of the University. The Association became the main focus for his energy, but his efforts were nearly derailed in 1932 with the dismissal of Alexander Dienst as Association president. Dienst had become difficult to cope with, in part because of his increasing deafness, and Barker's protégé Evetts Haley led the charge in removing him. Most agreed with Barker, but some supported the ousted—and outraged—Dienst, and the conflict persisted for some time.

In 1937 Barker became one of the first at the University to be appointed a distinguished professor. That was also the year he resigned as leader of the Association. As Walter P. Webb later recalled, removing Dienst placed on Barker's shoulders a "burden" that could not be carried "indefinitely."[24] In a January 1937 note accepting a nomination to membership in the revived Philosophical Society of Texas, Barker had revealed that he was "fed to the chin with strenuous, purposeful people." He added a request, "Let's have no scheduled purpose but that of association with men and women who stand for solid accomplishments in their respective fields. Let's relax and be our natural lazy selves and follow adventure where it leads." There were big plans being made in the Association, however, and realizing that many wanted another big push for more members and revenue, Barker submitted his resignation in April 1937. He later explained to Asbury that the "proper and sensible thing seemed to be to get out from under and give others a chance to apply new (and I honestly believe) better methods—or methods that promise better development."[25]

The Executive Council appointed Barker to serve on a steering committee with two other members of the Philosophical Society who were prominent in the Association, oil executive George A. Hill Jr. of Houston and geologist William E. Wrather of Dallas. Barker seemed to be reinvigorated by his work with Hill and Wrather. In the fall of 1937 he wrote to University archivist Winnie Allen that if he "had a million dollars or so for the permanent promotion and development of the history of Texas," he would fund an endowment, increase the number of articles and develop the news section in the *Quarterly*, and inaugurate an expanded publishing program that would include a biographical dictionary of Texas and a comprehensive history of the state.[26]

The steering committee's plans brought some immediate action. The Texas State Historical Association was incorporated on January 28, 1938, almost four decades after the Executive Council first discussed such an idea. In accordance with the Association's constitution, two-thirds of the members approved this change from an unchartered organization to a chartered, non-profit educational organization. Barker, Hill, and Wrather then recruited Buckner A. McKinney, president of the Federal Reserve Bank in Dallas and active member of the Executive Council, to chair a $50,000 fund drive. They outlined their vision for the future: reshape the council to include an equal number of academics and businessmen, expand membership, and double the size of the *Quarterly* as part of a more substantial publication program that would include the production of books.

Barker and his fellow committee members had grand plans, but McKinney had few resources to pursue them. Receipts for the fiscal year that ended in April 1938 totaled just $2,538.50, and Barker admitted the Association had only "five or six thousand dollars . . . invested in rather dubious securities."[27] Efforts in the spring of 1938 focused on enlisting more Patrons, or persons who would give a hundred dollars. Webb led the charge by sending Coral Tullis a check for that amount in May. Mindful of the fiasco in recruiting Patrons ten years earlier, Barker suggested to Hill in June that they be allowed to donate the amount over a period of five years and be given the title of Sustaining Member. This was done, but progress was still slow.

RUDOLPH L. BIESELE

"Dr. Biesele was known as possibly the most meticulous professor the Department has had within the memory of any student living. Orderly in his own habits, he insisted on his students' observing the same sense of order and painstaking care that he practiced. This held true even on hurried hour examinations. An examination taken under Dr. Biesele was not read hurriedly and graded. Even in his large classes he did not return the papers until he had edited them carefully. When an examination paper was returned, Dr. Biesele had written in better ways of phrasing thoughts, had substituted more nearly precise words for the ones the author had submitted, and in the words of successive hundreds of his students, had crossed all the t's and dotted all the i's. . . . To his students Dr. Biesele was an exceptionally warmhearted and outgoing person. His own personal research was never as important to him as assisting his student. . . . Students who wanted a supervisor but who did not know any professor particularly well, would usually go to Dr. Biesele first, because of his innate kindness and gentleness. The result was that he did far more than his share of thesis supervising. In one summer, for instance, he supervised the completion of sixteen master's theses, and served as second reader on about twenty-five more. This almost incredible total, when coupled with the fact that he never slighted or hurried his supervisory chores, gives an idea of how fully his life belonged to his students."

Biesele was editor of the *Quarterly,* with Walter Prescott Webb and Charles W. Hackett, from 1937 to 1940, when Webb became managing editor and Biesele (along with Hackett and H. Bailey Carroll) became an associate editor, a position he held until his retirement in 1957.

H. Bailey Carroll, Joe B. Frantz, Robert A. Law, In Memoriam, "Texas Collection," *SHQ*, 64 (Oct. 1960), 254.

Actual direction of the TSHA and editorship of the *Quarterly* passed to three men after Barker stepped down. Charles W. Hackett, who in 1937 became like Barker a distinguished professor at the University, served as managing editor. Hackett was a native of Falls County. Working closely with him was Rudolph L. Biesele, a native of Guadalupe County who earned three university degrees while teaching school for many years. He had originally been an instructor in German, but the virulent anti-German sentiment of the World War I period had pushed him to begin teaching history at the Waco high school where he worked in that period. He completed his doctorate under Barker in 1928, then endured several one-year appointments before being hired at the University of Texas in 1931.

Hackett may have been the senior member of the trio that succeeded Barker, but he would not become the next man to take charge of the Association. That honor fell to Walter Prescott Webb, a native of Panola County who, like Biesele, taught high school before joining the University of Texas faculty in 1918, the same year as Hackett. This was just three years after Webb earned a bachelor's degree at the age of twenty-seven. He wrote a thesis on the Texas Rangers in 1920, under Barker's tutelage, and got a master's degree from the University of Texas, but an unhappy year at the University of Chicago in pursuit of a doctoral degree proved fruitless. He returned to the University of Texas and produced *The Great Plains*, a prize-winning epic that Webb, at Barker's insistence, submitted as an unorthodox dissertation for a doctorate. By 1937, when he joined Hackett and Biesele on the masthead of the *Quarterly*, Webb had written two more books: *The Texas Rangers*, an expansion of his thesis that became a popular movie in 1936, and *Divided We Stand*, an angry analysis of corporatism and regional bias in the United States.

Hackett was more interested in Latin American than Texas topics, and Webb clearly had both desire and credentials in Texas history. The latter's acceptance as director of the Association, though, was delayed when he spent the spring semester of 1938 at the University of London as a Harkness Lecturer. During his absence from Texas, Webb peppered Barker with notes that strongly indicated his great interest in taking charge of the Association. In March 1938 Webb asked what was to be done about a staff "in case Wrather and his associates succeed in raising an endowment and launching a program."[28] Webb reminded Barker, who needed no prodding, that the Association had reached a crucial point in its development. The choice of a new director was critical; if he got all the benefits of the new support network and produced nothing, it would be a shame. By June 1938 Webb had begun outlining his vision for the TSHA in letters to Barker that echoed the plans already being laid—to recruit members and raise funds.

"We do not expect the artist's work even to suggest that vast *range of expression* . . . that lies in the memory of his students and associates . . . I have sometimes thought of his face as a landscape—valleys, plains and promontories—across which sun and shadow, rain, mist and darkness sweep, changing its aspect in sensitive response to the emotional weather. Indeed, he has a most expressive face; and I think the reason why it reflects so accurately just what is going on within him is that he has never attempted any concealment. He seldom draws the curtain. . . . I have never in forty-three years seen him pose for one fleeting instant. He is positively the worst actor I ever saw. What a sorry poker player he would make, even after he had learned to tell one card from another." J. Evetts Haley (quoting Roy Bedichek), "The Eugene C. Barker Portrait," *SHQ*, 46 (Jan. 1943), 311. *Photograph from TSHA Files.*

Barker agreed with Webb that he should take direction of the *Quarterly* and the Association. Webb in the fall of 1938 reported to the Executive Council that Hackett had asked him to assume the title of managing editor of the *Quarterly*, which he was willing to do but for not more than five years. In the spring of 1939, Webb began a term of what would prove to be more than seven years in charge of the Association and its journal. Hackett remained on the title page as an associate editor until his death in 1951, and Biesele worked as an associate editor and book review editor until his retirement in 1957. Long-time supporters of the Association, including the irascible Samuel E. Asbury, wrote to express regret that Barker had quit for good, but the transfer of power had finally been made after more than a year of transition.

Barker remained on the Executive Council, and served the University as a professor or professor emeritus, until his death in 1956. Friends noted that during the first few years after he relinquished control of the Association, Barker seemed to be very tired or depressed. As a tribute, and perhaps to cheer him up, supporters presented an oil portrait of the Chief, as Barker had become known, at the annual meeting in April 1942. Evetts Haley made the principal speech, and many others spoke or sent letters praising Barker's contributions to Texas history. Barker himself, however, set the tone for years to come for what others would say about his direction of the Association. He obviously was pleased with the tributes, and the portrait to be hung in the Association offices, but he insisted, "I gave the job just about what I thought I could spare from other duties and pleasures." Months later, he wrote, "During most of its life, the Association made very little effort to do more than issue the *Quarterly*. Annual meetings were hardly more than formal business sessions to elect officers." Barker concluded sharply, "I suppose the explanation of this unambitious procedure is to be found in my own personal disposition. Nobody wanted to do anything without my active cooperation, and I did not want to take on additional responsibilities."[29]

That attitude became the common memory of Barker, and he did little to quash it. Webb later insisted to an interviewer that Barker had never been "enthusiastic" about the Association, and "cared little whether or not anyone belonged or not."[30] This may well express the feelings of Barker in retirement, but it does not do justice to the Chief who edited a fine journal, wrote books and articles of enduring value, tried different schemes to increase membership and funding, worked tirelessly to acquire archives, and sustained his Association through three troublesome decades. Barker never relaxed his rigid standards for himself or for the Association, striving always to keep the focus on Texas's role in the development of the United States. Stories about him might be as grim as the face in the painting, though it must be said that the painting was done by an artist (Robert Joy of Houston) who, by his own admission, did not like the dour Barker from the moment they met. Those who knew Barker better, however, realized they owed the Chief a tremendous debt for his leadership. No one understood this more than Walter Prescott Webb, in whose hands Barker left the direction of the Association.

FOUR

A Broader Scope and a Bigger Job

Walter P. Webb, 1939–1946

T HE SELECTION OF WALTER PRESCOTT WEBB to direct the Texas
State Historical Association placed the staid organization squarely in
the hands of an unapologetic popularizer. Webb wrote books that were
critically acclaimed by scholars, but he more often penned articles for
magazines and newspapers than for academic journals. He was a serious student of Texas history, but wrote in a much more accessible manner than his
predecessors, George P. Garrison and Eugene C. Barker. They appreciated the
efforts of Texas's amateur historians, but Webb wanted nonprofessionals to
play a greater role within the Association. He focused on creating programs to
involve everyone from school children to Texana collectors and every variety
of historian, professional and amateur, in between. In the process, Webb began
the first substantial book publication program of the Association, initiated the

Walter Prescott Webb (1888–1963), director of the Association 1939–1946.

"In the Texas State Historical Association I have no position save that of editor. I am an
employee whose employer pays no salary, a retainer without fee, a hired man without wages. I
work at the job for the same reason that Dr. Barker worked at it for more than a quarter of a century, and though I can't hope to equal him in work, I make the boast that I do equal him in compensation. I am held to the job by the same force that held him, the conviction that the cause is
a worthy one and that the work must be done by someone. . . . My morale is maintained by the
worthiness of a good cause—Texas history. In the past, for more than a hundred years men have
fought to make it; we have the opportunity to work to preserve it. As I see it we need three
things, a large number of recruits, a moderate amount of industry, and a little money." Walter
Prescott Webb, "Texas Collection," *SHQ*, 43 (July 1939), 100. *Photograph, October 1935, courtesy
Walter Prescott Webb Papers, DI 02592, CAH.*

landmark *Handbook of Texas* project, increased membership, expanded the education program by organizing the Junior Historians, and initiated a fund drive that would support his schemes after he stepped down as director.

Webb's work with the TSHA placed him, and the organization, in the vanguard of American historical research and writing. By the 1930s many in the field had grown tired of the stiff language and narrow focus of much of the "scientific" history. Early Progressives believed that history was the "handmaiden of politics," and they wrote to convey lessons applicable to the problems of the period in which they lived. Their more rigorously trained successors—their students—put aside earlier notions of practicality, and frequently readability. As a later scholar remarked, these historians "unfortunately...succeeded too well in convincing their students and the general public that history was a rarified science." As a result, "they surrendered to popularizers and journalists the historian's role as an educator of the public."[1]

The time was ripe for historians who could write sweeping syntheses, scholars with national perspective who could drop the shackles of tedious extended footnotes and assert broader views that seemed relevant. Webb fit that description. As he declared in his 1958 presidential address before the American Historical Association, what he "wanted to be was a writer, and . . . to write not only for the few but for the many."[2] He also refused to think of himself as primarily a historian of the frontier and never taught an undergraduate class on Texas. Webb, like Garrison and Barker, believed in the frontier as a breeding ground for sound values, but he used the frontier to make grand assertions about the world, reflections on life itself, not just Texas. Moving beyond the insistence of Frederick Jackson Turner's doctrine that frontier developments shaped the growth of the United States, Webb posited that the discovery of three new continents by Europeans at around 1500 led to all the changes in the western world during the next four hundred years. Not all Texans, or all his colleagues, agreed with every one of Webb's big ideas, but they enjoyed reading his work, and the Association benefited from both his influence and his fame.

Webb made it clear that in order for him to accomplish his goals for the TSHA, an adjustment had to be made in his responsibilities as a member of the University of Texas faculty. Garrison and Barker had always remained full-time members of the Department of History, but Webb needed a lighter schedule in order to have more time to implement his plans for the Association. Barker agreed, and he and Charles W. Ramsdell, who still served as the Association treasurer, asked University president Homer P. Rainey on behalf of the Executive Council to allow Webb's time to be divided between the history department and the Association. The University would pay half of his

The young Walter Prescott Webb, ca. 1910. *Photograph courtesy Walter Prescott Webb Papers, DI 02571, CAH.*

salary as a member of the history faculty and the Association would pay half.

The Executive Council's rather radical proposal regarding Webb's salary fit well with Rainey's plans to expand research at the University. Rainey also liked Webb and was impressed with his writing, especially one of his lesser-known books, *Divided We Stand*. As a native Texan concerned with the lack of development in his state, Rainey found Webb's condemnation of regional biases in business and government to be persuasive. He believed Webb wanted the same thing he did, to use University resources to enhance Texas, and so he

PRESIDENTS UNDER WEBB

"Harbert Davenport (TSHA president, 1939–1942) probably renders more generous service to history students and scholars than any other layman. He is an authority on the Rio Grande Valley as well as on the Texas Revolution. He carries a store of accurate information in his mind that causes the professional historian whose memory has worn out to despair. He shares his information with all who need it; he answers letters the day he receives them; and when any historian goes to the Valley Harbert Davenport lives up to the highest tradition of hospitality. He quits a lucrative law practice and takes to the chaparral to show the newcomer where things happened, or to the local archives where the records of them are kept. He is a severe critic whose approval, silent or spoken, is anxiously awaited by anyone who writes within his fields of knowledge."

Walter Prescott Webb, "Texas Collection," *SHQ*, 42 (Apr. 1939), 388. *Photograph from TSHA Files.*

approved the council's request in August 1939 and subsequently became one of Webb's staunchest supporters.

Webb also insisted that, for help with his ambitious programs for the Association, he needed an editorial assistant, in addition to Coral Horton Tullis as secretary. The Executive Council and the University balked at hiring an editorial assistant, and when Webb began to tire under the heavy burden of his expansion efforts, Barker secured a leave of absence for him for the 1940–1941 academic year. H. Bailey Carroll returned to Austin as Webb's temporary replacement. In 1928 Carroll, after receiving the first master's degree in history given by Texas Tech University, had become Webb's first doctoral student. He taught at five Texas colleges before completing his dissertation for Webb in 1935, and then joined the faculty at North Texas Agricultural College in Arlington while he assisted Webb with Association projects.

During his year in Austin, Carroll was still a North Texas professor, though on leave. Nevertheless, the Association bestowed upon him the titles of associate editor and assistant director, titles he relinquished when he returned to

North Texas and Webb resumed his duties with the Association. Eugene C. Barksdale, who like Carroll wrote his dissertation under Webb's direction, served for a year as Webb's assistant director, then Carroll came back to Austin for good. During the fall of 1942 Webb accepted an invitation to teach at Oxford University as a Harmsworth Professor, and Carroll took charge of the Association in his absence. Carroll's appointment included a promotion to

PRESIDENTS UNDER WEBB

Lou Kemp (TSHA president, 1942–1946) listed his two favorite accomplishments as his work with the Texas Centennial celebration, which resulted in the marking of one thousand historic sites in Texas, and his efforts to get the remains of famous Texans moved from abandoned or neglected graves to places of honor in the state cemetery. "And the names on the great bronze plaque of the San Jacinto monument—the men who won the battle of San Jacinto—are there largely because Louis Kemp researched and sifted those names carefully from the crumbling and almost forgotten rosters of a century ago." "Perhaps Lou Kemp's greatest service to Texas, however, was … [that] his life, and his whole attitude toward life, was a source of inspiration engendering in others a real respect for Texas. With great experience in the affairs of government, Lou Kemp had such a simple and profound faith in the Texas democracy that everyone who knew him was impressed. His was not a naive acceptance of the homilies and platitudes of patriotic orations, but an understanding and appreciation of the processes in our  American system. Out of his experience he drew, not cynicism as many men do, but respect, and he conveyed this fundamental feeling to all who knew him. In a world too full of scoffers, muckrakers, and detractors, Lou Kemp influenced hundreds, perhaps thousands, to dignify and respect the state and its officials."

H. Bailey Carroll, "Texas Collection," *SHQ*, 60 (Apr. 1957), 549 (1st quotation); Seymour V. Connor, quoted in ibid., 61 (July 1958), 165 (2nd quotation). *Photograph courtesy Prints and Photographs Collection, DI 02576, CAH.*

Webb with Oxford group; Webb is standing second from left. *Photograph courtesy Walter Prescott Webb Papers, DI 02577, CAH.*

WEBB AT OXFORD

"It is my hope that I may be able to do something in interpreting America to the English and also, from time to time, send back reports on English life in war-time. In this way I believe that I can perhaps render a service in interpreting the two great English-speaking peoples to each other. If I can do this I shall fulfill the purpose of the Harmsworth Professorship."

Walter Prescott Webb, "Texas Collection," *SHQ*, 46 (Oct. 1942), 183.

"Walter Prescott Webb in Oxford Study, Queen's College. Note Texas Almanac, World Almanac, and copy Junior Historian on table" (handwritten note on frame of photograph). The book Webb is reading is John Buchan's autobiography, *Memory Hold-the-Door*, published in 1940, shortly after the death of Buchan, a Scottish politician and popular writer of fiction. *Memory Hold-the-Door*, a collection of reminiscences of people and places (including Oxford) Buchan had known, is said to have been JFK's favorite book; Buchan's novel *The Thirty-Nine Steps* was crucial in the film career of Alfred Hitchcock. *Photograph from TSHA Files, courtesy Dorman Winfrey.*

Quarterly editor, a title he shared with Webb while Charles W. Hackett and Rudolph L. Biesele remained associate editors.

Depressed and unhealthy, Webb actually tried to resign from the Association while he was in Oxford, but instead cut short his stay in England and resumed his duties in Austin in 1943. He said little about why he declined the opportunity to continue as Harmsworth Professor, but some insight can be gleaned from a letter he wrote in 1938 after he returned to Texas from his first experience in England. He was "glad to be at home," he said, and "head over heels in a job that I love, and . . . among people that I know." For his many friends in the Association, the feeling was mutual. Soon after Webb's second departure for England, Carroll reported to Samuel E. Asbury, "Dr. Webb's appointment is for a period of from one to five years, at his option. We're all hoping that one year in the 'tight little isle' will be about all that he will want."[3]

Webb came home in 1943 to a new title. Although his two predecessors had officially been called the "recording secretary and librarian" of the Association, they would have been more accurately described as directors. Webb had wanted a change in title when he was appointed in 1939, "but out of deference to tradition and not wishing to excite anyone, he let the matter stand."[4] Before Webb left for Oxford he asked Carroll to make the change. Carroll in turn asked Louis W. Kemp, the popular president of the Association, to present the idea to the Executive Council in the fall of 1942. With Eugene Barker's strong support, the measure passed easily and Webb returned to Austin as "director," a title held by those in charge of the other University of Texas research centers.

What Webb clearly had in mind as he took charge of the Association in the spring of 1939 was a revitalization of the organization. He had observed that Barker "kept the Association very quiet," which Webb assumed was Barker's way to "hold it where it belong[ed]," at the University. Webb had little fear of losing control, so he told the Executive Council as early as the fall of 1938 that "the time has come for us to pursue a progressive policy." In August 1939, at about the same time that his request for a half-time appointment at the University received approval, he hosted a dinner meeting of the TSHA Executive Council to unveil his plans. He presented his ideas as simply an expansion of the initiatives undertaken by Barker, George A. Hill Jr., and William E. Wrather at the request of the Council in 1937. Those in attendance could hardly have been surprised at what they heard. It was the same list presented by Webb to a "bobtailed Houston meeting" of the Executive Council in April 1939: publish works by amateurs and professionals that would include a handbook of Texas history, expand membership, and reach out to schools to involve young people in the Association.[5]

Webb was a prolific writer, and he understood the importance of publica-

"Walter Prescott Webb," by Sylvan Dunn

It is odd that for all the years I spent at the University of Texas (Austin), before and after World War II, and in spite of all the courses I took in Garrison Hall, I never had any contact with Dr. Webb. It was much later that our paths would cross, and even then it was just a brief encounter. But it was Webbian.

At that time I was developing a graduate seminar at Texas Tech. The course was misnomered "Sociological Uses of Historical Data." This was unfortunate because (a) as it turned out, history students gained more from the course than sociology students, and (b) the writings of historian Walter P. Webb contributed more to the course than the writings of any other individual. Additionally, I was pleased that the noted sociologist William F. Ogburn heralded Webb! Ogburn, a student of social change, referred extensively to what he called Webb's theory of convergence, wherein three inventions—the revolver, the windmill, and barbed wire—converged to make possible the settlement of the arid plains by humans.

Thus I was understandably excited, during a trip to Austin, to find Dr. Webb at his desk in Garrison Hall. As he had his hat on, I had no idea if he were coming or going. It made no difference! Before me sat *the man*—a legend in his own time, the mainspring of my socio-historical career, the great disciple of Lindley Miller Keasbey, who was an innovative proponent of institutional history, which I suspected had a kinship to sociology. As quickly as possible, I mentioned Ogburn's use of Webb's theory of convergence.

Dr. Webb (and the hat) turned a Buster Keaton–like deadpan face to me and said, "What in the hell is the theory of convergence?"

SHQ, 92 (July 1988), 45–46.

tions. At the same time, he believed printed material had to be useful to a broad public. This became apparent in 1937, when his "Historical Notes" first appeared in the *Southwestern Historical Quarterly*. A revival of an earlier column, it was a folksy, often long-winded presentation of anecdotes and news about the history profession in Texas. The name became "Texas Collection" in January 1939, when Webb became the editor of the *Quarterly*. He explained the change by declaring, "If the *Quarterly* paints the Southwest in its pages, it does it with great and natural partiality, putting three or four coats on Texas [and] one very thin one on the rest of the region."[6] As a native Texan, he thought this was as it should be. He also expanded the advertisements in the

Quarterly to help pay the cost of doubling its size. Some paid cash for publicity, but others provided printing or books in return for announcements. Some members grumbled about Webb's changes, but a 1949 survey of editors of state historical journals revealed that a majority considered the *Quarterly* to be second in prestige only to the *Wisconsin Magazine of History*.

With generous subsidies from a variety of donors, Webb also led the Association into the book-publishing business. The first book to be printed, in 1943, was Carroll's *Texas County Histories: A Bibliography*, followed closely by Martin W. Schwettmann's *Santa Rita: The University of Texas Oil Discovery*, a study of the West Texas oil field that provided much of the endowment money for the University of Texas. Schwettmann's work, which began as a requirement for his master's degree at the University, yielded an unexpected benefit when Webb learned that the original drilling rig still existed. He suggested that it be brought to the campus and displayed. The machinery came to the University in 1940, and finally in 1958 it was reassembled on a permanent site on campus. Money troubles delayed Webb's publication of other books, but J. Evetts Haley's *Charles Schreiner, General Merchandise, 1869–1944: The Story of a Country Store* appeared in 1944, and J. A. R. Mosely's *The Presbyterian Church in Jefferson* was published in 1946, the year Webb retired as director. One project left unfinished by Webb was an index for the *Quarterly*. By 1945 W. A. Whatley had produced a set of index cards for the first forty volumes, but again a lack of funds delayed publication of an index until 1950.

The crown jewel of Webb's publication initiative became the *Handbook of Texas*, though it also was not completed while he was director. The staff of the

JOE B. FRANTZ ON WALTER PRESCOTT WEBB

"Webb always liked a comparison I once suggested to him, that he was like the bird who flies across and around the country, scattering seeds that he has picked up somewhere else. When the seeds sprout, the bird will be still elsewhere; he never hangs around to see the flowering of his droppings. All he knows is that he has carried the seed, though he never sees the harvest."

Speech by Joe Frantz on the occasion of dedicating a Walter P. Webb marker in Gary, Texas, April 9, 1978, in L. Tuffly Ellis, "Southwestern Collection," *SHQ*, 82 (Oct. 1978), 198.

Association was constantly bombarded with pleas for information. In 1932 the Executive Council had proposed printing a "Biographical Dictionary of Texas."[7] It would have been similar to the *Dictionary of American Biography* in style, with three thousand entries in a single volume of about 1,500 pages, and would have been jointly produced by the TSHA and the Texas Centennial Commission. Eugene Barker offered to recruit a board of editors and persuade the University to provide space for an operating staff, but he made it quite clear that he had little money. The Centennial Commission never responded favorably to the proposal despite inquiries from Barker and J. Evetts Haley. In 1937 Barker was still thinking about this biographical dictionary and said to Win-

WEBB ON ROY BEAN

"And now a word about Roy Bean. Without doubt he has received more notice and acclaim than any other tertiary character in Texas. He is more of a legendary figure than a historic character. Roy Bean's adolescence was well hidden by his gray beard. He was always standing on his head or walking on his hands to excite the admiration of other adolescents. Every frontier had such characters. Alabama had one and W. L. Fleming characterized the class by describing the Rev. A. S. Lakin. This man, said Fleming, 'told several marvelous stories of hairbreadth escapes by assassination which, if true, would be enough to ruin the reputation of northern Alabama men for marksmanship.' If the stories about Roy Bean are true, it certainly may impair the reputation of Texas lawmen for knowledge of procedure, justice or equity."

Walter Prescott Webb, "Texas Collection," *SHQ*, 43 (July 1939), 93.

"The Roy Bean myth has reached Hollywood. Goldwyn studios desires architectural data on Langtry and its buildings as of 1880–1885. Apparently, Mr. Goldwyn wants the data free, postage and all. This office is surrounded by fairly able historical investigators, graduate history students who are skilled in the use of the library. They know how to find things, but unfortunately they have to eat while they work. The Association undertakes to grant every reasonable request from Texans and members, and it has responded to unreasonable requests. It is no hazard to guess that Hollywood does not want the truth about Roy Bean any more than it did about the Texas Rangers. Roy had a lot of what Hollywood wants."

Walter Prescott Webb, "Texas Collection," *SHQ*, 43 (Oct. 1939), 245.

"MY WEBBIAN CONVERSION," BY JENKINS GARRETT

Several times on the way to my room at the Tejas Club from the Law School library about eleven o'clock in the evening, I would stop by PK's for coffee, or, if hungry and flushed with extra money, partake of the egg special. Occasionally Dr. Webb was there, or came in before I left, having come for a cup of coffee and, I believe, conversation. I presume it was a stopover on the way from his campus office to his home, which was located on the west side of what was then the forty acres. There was always dialogue between Dr. Webb and the night cook, who seemed to be a friend of long standing. Sometimes a student or two sitting nearby (including myself) would take part in the conversation. I noticed that, without appearing aggressive, he always seemed to ferret out to one degree or another the personal history of the participants, as well as their thoughts and appraisals of student life and politics. This demonstrated interest in, and curiosity about, the night cook, the students, and their viewpoints undoubtedly accounted for Dr. Webb's great insight into University life and his tremendous rapport with students.

Jenkins Garrett, ca. 1934. *Courtesy Prints and Photographs Collection, DI 02611, CAH.*

SHQ, 92 (July 1988), 47.

nie Allen, his student and collaborator, that if the TSHA had a million dollars, the publication of this work would be one of the things he would pursue.

After he took charge of the Association Webb made a reference work on Texas one of his priorities, and as early as May 1939 he was writing to Pat I. Nixon, noted medical historian and longtime member of the TSHA, "The time has come for the Texas State Historical Association to undertake some worth while work." He was more explicit in a letter of the same period to Association president Harbert Davenport, a Brownsville attorney and historian, describing how he had spoken with University officers and the Rockefeller Foundation about funding the publication of a "handbook of Texas history."

THE STAFF

*O*ccasionally in the Collection we get a glimpse of the size and identities of the
  office staff:

"My historical conscience hurts me each time I get this department
together. I do not like to deceive others, especially when I can not also
deceive myself. I know that I am not the author of many things that appear
here, some of them without quotation or credit of any sort. Texas Collection
is built up by accretion. An empty file is set up, and when some member
sends in an inquiry, his letter is answered and then is placed in the "T.C." file
for possible use. If the letter is used, credit is given.

"The main injustice of which I now complain is done to the young men
and women who make up the office staff of the Association, Miss Llerena
Friend, whose primary function is to promote the *Handbook*, Miss Betty
Brooke Eakle, who 'puts the *Junior Historian* to bed,' and to both of them,
who in Dr. Bailey Carroll's temporary absence, wrestle with the publication
headaches of the *Quarterly*. These two are assisted by Miss Beth Curtis, Miss
Maxine Smith, and Miss Deena Anderson. The cheerful Dorman Winfrey is
the general factotum who does about everything any of the others asks him
to do, does it cheerfully and well. Most of the material appearing here comes
through their hands and finds its way to my desk. They ask no credit and
receive none, even though one or more of them may write the paragraph I
use. I offer [an example] below.

'The drudgery in an editorial office would be intolerable . . . if it were not
for bits of humor that boil up and break the surface of monotony. All sorts of
requests for information pour in from all quarters, some reasonable, some
not. One gem has been posted in the office along with what the office staff
considers an appropriate answer:

'Please send me information on the Spanish. Yours truly, John Doe.

'The answer, which was not mailed, read:

'Please meet the next freight train at the station. We are shipping you the
García Library. Texas State Historical Association'."

Walter Prescott Webb, "Texas Collection," *SHQ*, 51 (Jan. 1948), 259–260.

As with other projects, Webb had taken, and expanded, an initiative from
Eugene Barker, who had wanted a biographical dictionary. Webb had a model
for his project, Frederick Hodge's handbook on North American Indians. He
wanted "a combination dictionary, biography and encyclopedia" in "two or
more volumes," with "800 to 1,000 pages each." He boldly declared, "It will be

a reference to practically any topic on Texas history and will be the most useful book that has ever been published in Texas."[8]

Webb realized that a project like the *Handbook* might be an "impossible dream," but he continued to push. Some members of the Association quickly became allies. Herbert P. Gambrell was a Barker student who like Webb secured a doctorate by submitting a published book, and then became the director of the Dallas Historical Society and a distinguished member of the faculty at Southern Methodist University. He wrote in August 1939, "The idea is, like all Webb-built ideas, a natural." Others harbored grave doubts that Webb's grand effort would ever bear fruit. Louis W. Kemp later confessed to Webb, "I voted in favor of the project but did not have the slightest idea it would ever be undertaken. I thought then, and later told you, that I thought you had a 'screw loose'." By the close of 1939 Webb had secured the support of the Executive Council, whose members may have thought, like Kemp, that they were endorsing a project that would never be completed, as had been the case with the 1932 proposal for the "Biographical Dictionary of Texas." This time, however, Webb was determined to be ready to publish his *Handbook* by 1945, so that the money set aside for the anniversary of Texas's annexation by the United States would "not all be spent for marble slabs as in 1936," the centennial of the independence of Texas. Webb believed that the Association had been "caught asleep in 1936" and should atone with something more significant in 1945.[9]

In the fall of 1940 Webb accelerated his efforts to produce a handbook. He wrote to Earl Vandale, a noted collector of Texana and member of the Executive Council, "The new year has begun and it's up to me and Bailey Carroll and you and the other officers of this outfit to see if we can not do something to make possible the preparation of what I consider to be the most needed book, the Handbook of Texas."[10] During that academic year, Webb spent much of his time and energy gathering public support for his project. Newspapers became a favorite medium, especially the *Dallas Morning News*, published by George B. Dealey, a founder of the Dallas Historical Society and Webb's supporter in earlier projects. Webb's public announcement of the *Handbook* appeared in Dealey's *Morning News* on November 17, 1940. "It would be the function of the Handbook of Texas to bring the essential part of this material out of the dark places, liberate it, put it between the covers of two great volumes, and send it forth to the world," Webb declared. Not only would the *Handbook* be by far the most useful book ever on Texas, the "people of Texas" would write it. Funds would come from a Foundation in Texas History whose sole purpose would be to produce the *Handbook*.

The Executive Council approved Webb's nominations for a board of editors in April 1941: Eugene Barker, Herbert Gambrell, Evetts Haley, Louis Kemp, Pat Nixon, William Wrather, and Webb. Beginning in 1942, Association members, University of Texas faculty, and "all persons known to be interested in Texas history" were polled to produce a list of topics for *Handbook* entries.[11] Student assistants were hired to help with compiling the results, but World War II greatly slowed progress and the list was not printed until 1945, the year Webb had originally chosen for having the volumes entirely completed and ready for publication.

Webb did not handle delays well. He grumbled in a letter to his doctoral student William R. Hogan that, thanks to the war, "things have gone to hell generally." Carroll, who increasingly took charge of the *Handbook* project, was more positive. He explained patiently to Davenport in 1943 that the work was "progressing, even if a large part of our membership is, like yourself, so tied up in war work that they cannot at present make the contributions which they would make in normal times." Carroll added, "We are pushing along some but are leaving numbers of things to be done by you and others after we take Berlin and Tokyo. We can afford to take four or five years in doing the Handbook in order to achieve the ideals set up by Mr. Webb."[12]

By the time Webb stepped down as director in 1946, he had, with Carroll's assistance, laid a solid foundation for the success of the *Handbook* project. Hundreds of authors, amateur and professional, had been recruited to write articles for what Carroll coolly told Willis R. Woolrich, the dean of the College of Engineering at the University of Texas, was the "regular encyclopedic rate": a penny per word.[13] To supplement this pool of writers, graduate students were employed as assistants and undergraduate students were recruited into a *Handbook* seminar created by Webb and Carroll in 1944. This activity allowed the Association to produce a slim pamphlet by 1945 that contained not only a list of topics but also sample articles, an encouraging review of the project to that time, and a new list of names for a fifteen-member advisory council to guide the *Handbook* to completion.

While he devoted much energy to publication, Webb did not neglect the charge of the TSHA constitution to develop an archive of Texas history. Barker proved a valuable ally in this endeavor. The Texas documents collection of William A. Philpott Jr. was acquired in late 1941 at a cost of $25,000, half of which came from the University and the remainder from a donor. Just a few years later Barker learned from Haley that the widow of Frank Kell, another wealthy businessman and well-known Texana collector, might be persuaded to donate her husband's papers and other items to the University. Haley approached regent Orville Bullington, Kell's son-in-law and Haley's ally in earlier efforts to oust Franklin D. Roosevelt, about the material, while Barker

TEXAS IN THE RIGHT HAND

"Every Texan carries the map of his state on his right hand. It was not the geographer, historian or scientist who discovered this. It was the poet, Townsend Miller. Before we speak of his poem, look at your right hand as you hold it up, palm outward, in front of you. Bend down the last three fingers at the joint, and as the poet says, 'I think you have it.' The thumb represents the trans-Pecos region with El Paso at the tip. The line from thumb to wrist is the Rio Grande with the first joint suggesting the Big Bend. Brownsville lies at about the place where the doctor feels for your pulse. A line across the base of the hand represents the Gulf coast. The eastern boundary comes down the little finger and the Red River boundary runs across the three bent joints. The index finger, fully extended, is the Panhandle."

Walter Prescott Webb, "Texas Collection," *SHQ,* 43 (Apr. 1940), 511.

wrote directly to the widow, Lula. It proved to be an easy decision for the family; Kell had already donated many books to the University of Texas during his lifetime, and he had proudly served on the Executive Council of the Association. His papers arrived in 1945, and the family subsequently provided significant funds for the maintenance and expansion of the collection.

The acquisition of the Kell Collection finally induced the regents to approve an idea that had for years been promoted by the leaders of the Association. When Webb took charge of the organization in January 1939, the Texas Collection shared space with the Latin American Collection in the Main Building. Webb and Barker led a delegation requesting that the 1910 Library Building, designed by Cass Gilbert, be given to the Association to house its archives and offices. When the Board of Regents proposed other alternatives, Webb pressed his case hard. He wrote in the "Texas Collection" that the history of Texas must "always come first" at the University. He added, "To me, and I believe to some millions of others, [Texas] is the most important place in all the world." J. Frank Dobie joined with Barker and Webb to write a letter to Kenneth H. Aynesworth, University regent and member of the Association, that said, "The Texas Collection is not something to box up and stow away in a corner. In so far as the records go, it is the heart of Texas."[14]

The 1944 donation of money by Orville Bullington to be used for the purchase of archives, and the recent arrival of Kell's collection, added weight to the TSHA's argument for a space of its own. Haley and Vandale met with

Aynesworth, and a delegation from the Daughters of the Republic of Texas met with the Board of Regents. In the fall of 1945 the regents agreed that the Old Library would be the new home of the Texas Collection and the University archives. Haley drafted a second resolution, adopted by the regents one year later, that provided for a portion of the facility to be used for Association offices. On the suggestion of Webb and others, the decision was stamped by renaming the building the Eugene C. Barker Texas History Center. It was a long-overdue honor for the Chief, who of course would insist that he did not deserve such distinction. Barker wrote to his close ally Hally B. Perry, "Naturally, I am flattered by the memorial to me, even though I feel that I have stolen Esau's blessing. So many others have contributed to the up-building of the collection."[15] Maybe the Chief believed he pulled a sheepskin over the regents' eyes in receiving such an honor, but no one could deny that he seemed pleased to win the battle for new quarters for the archives and the Association.

Walter Webb devoted much attention to increasing the membership of the Association. He believed that one of the most effective ways to do this was to personally canvass the state. The results were not as spectacular as he expected, but he made some gains before the entry of the United States into World War II interrupted his efforts. He projected a membership of as many as three thousand when he took charge, and, by 1940, gleefully reported that a "new spirit" had "caught the outfit." He bragged that the number of members had "trebled," but in fact this was not true.[16] The Association had 424 members in 1938, and membership would not actually reach 1,200 until 1942, just before Webb left for Oxford. Nonetheless, he had reason to be proud, and the Executive Council praised his efforts.

Part of Webb's success in recruiting lay in his plan to establish the Association as the coordinating body for local history groups in Texas. He informed Association president Davenport in 1939 that this was "contrary" to "past policy," but "we have a crop of museums and a large number of local societies sprouting up in all sections of the country." He added, "My plan is to envelope [sic] them, help them where possible, and gain their cooperation."[17] Webb had apparently forgotten the efforts his predecessors had made to involve existing local societies in the Association and foster the establishment of new organizations. If so, he can be forgiven because such work had been largely abandoned by Barker in the 1930s, when the Depression derailed many local historical societies. Barker also disdained women's organizations that glorified war or sought to rewrite history to suit themselves, a bias he shared with Charles W. Ramsdell. Unlike Ramsdell, who was unfailingly courteous, Barker made no secret of his feelings. A few women from groups such as the Daughters of the Republic of Texas and the United Daughters of the Confed-

Patriotic Societies
and the Association

"But whereas the Texas State Historical Association has a general interest which extends to all fields of history, the patriotic societies are highly specialized. Each one devotes itself largely to one subject, and—what is more important—in a patriotic manner. Again the Texas State Historical Association has its natural place as a co-ordinator. Its function is to make available the contributions of each patriotic group for the use of other groups and for the general historian who is supposed to bury patriotism in utter impartiality.

"The patriotic groups should not expect the theoretically impartial historians to share their patriotism. A historian, however ardent a patriot he may be personally, is supposed to divest himself of all good causes and the loves and hates they engender when he writes history. He is supposed to be as impartial and impersonal as a scientist or a perfect supreme judge. He differs from some of these, however, in that he knows and readily admits that he can not always attain his high ideal. But since he holds the ideal, he considers it his duty to scan with a critical eye all material that comes to him as historical evidence, and it makes no difference to him, or should make none, whether the material emanated from the executive mansion, the legislature, the supreme court, or from the solemn conclusions of the most patriotic body in the world.

"It is this ability to collect, combine, and analyze that enables the historians to write the final decisions, the so-called edicts of history. Among their many other services, the patriotic societies of Texas can well consider the value to themselves and to every Texan of co-operating with the Texas State Historical Association.

"The Daughters of the Republic of Texas may be taken as an example. This organization, it would seem, is a natural ally of the Texas State Historical Association. It was formed at Houston in 1891, six years before the Association was set up at Austin. In its early years, the historians received much encouragement and assistance from the Daughters of the Republic, and at one time and for a long time the historian of the Daughters was the President of the historians [Adele B. Looscan].

".... The Alamo chapter of San Antonio, the Fort Houston chapter of Palestine, and the William B. Travis chapter of Austin have become members of the Texas State Historical Association on invitation.... There is no doubt that other chapters will also join and by so doing contribute to the cause of Texas history.... We believe that the Texas State Historical Association has something to offer them in return for their interest and support."

Walter Prescott Webb, "Texas Collection," *SHQ*, 42 (Apr. 1939), 393–394.

TSHA advertisement for H. G. Wells's speaking engagement, November 14, 1940. *Photograph courtesy Subject Vertical Files, DI 02586, CAH.*

eracy were active in the Association, but more were conspicuous by their absence.

Webb did not share the biases of Barker or Ramsdell, and he made a special effort to win over the Daughters of the Republic of Texas. He spoke to a meeting in San Antonio as early as the fall of 1938, feigning ignorance of the dispute with Adina De Zavala that had alienated the Daughters from the

Association decades earlier. Of course, several Daughters rushed to tell him their side of the story, which included a denunciation of former Association president Adele B. Looscan for her support of De Zavala. Looscan had died in 1935, but De Zavala was still on the Executive Council, and Webb knew all about the earlier schism. His profession of ignorance, though, distanced him from the old controversy and encouraged Daughters to join his Association.

The renewed alliance had immediate benefits. The Daughters had struggled since 1927 to fund a scholarship, named in honor of Clara Driscoll, at the University. In the fall of 1940 Webb convinced H. G. Wells, whose popularity as a history writer was then at its peak, to speak at the University of Texas. To persuade him, Webb personally guaranteed Wells's fee of $1,000. Webb drafted his wife, who had joined the Daughters, to organize her colleagues to sell tickets. Pre-show ticket sales raised only $500, however, causing Webb a few anxious moments, but with the help of the Daughters and other allies the event ultimately made money. Webb graciously gave the Daughters a percentage of the gate receipts, and they were able to complete the funding of their University scholarship. By 1943 Webb's wife was president of the Daughters, further cementing the renewed alliance. The Executive Council's 1945 decision to make De Zavala an Honorary Life Fellow did not seem to weaken this renewed bond with the Daughters.

Webb had similar success in reaching out to students in public secondary schools in Texas. His purpose was twofold: to educate, and to prepare the next generation of members for the Association. It was a natural step for him because he had taught in high schools before coming to the University, where his duties included working with education students and teachers. During his first year at the University, Webb began printing a bulletin for history teachers, and he pushed both teachers and students to conduct local research. Clifton M. Caldwell, a University of Texas regent who had prospered in law, ranching, oil, and public service, joined with George B. Dealey, publisher of the *Dallas Morning News*, to give cash prizes in 1924 for an essay contest sponsored by Webb for high school students. The University Board of Regents in 1927 began giving Webb $100 a year to conduct local history contests at high schools. The results convinced him that "children can not only learn to like history; they can help to write it." If nothing else, Webb later wrote, he realized that recruiting students into the Association would provide "some youthful underpinning of a structure showing some symptoms of becoming antiquarian."[18]

The organization of what would become known as the Junior Historians began with Webb's 1939 proposal to sell *Quarterly* subscriptions to high schools at a reduced price. When he first came to the University, copies of the *Quarterly* had been given to University-affiliated high schools at no cost. That

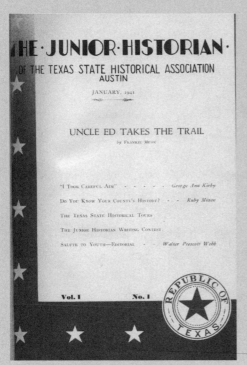

"[P]athos lies in the gulf between an old and a young generation. Youth is so immediate, so convinced that its world is the only one worth knowing. Anything that will enable youth to gain an insight into the wisdom of age is worthwhile. The Junior Historians by the nature of their work may bridge the gap between the past and the present."

Walter Prescott Webb, "Texas Collection," *SHQ*, 43 (Oct. 1939), 239.

In a survey conducted by the American Association for State and Local History in the early sixties, it was found that the earliest junior historical society was the Indiana group organized in 1938. The first magazine published was *The Junior Historian* of the Texas State Historical Association. Joe B. Frantz, "Texas Collection," SHQ, 70 (Apr. 1967), 654. *Photograph from TSHA Files.*

ended in 1911 when the Texas Department of Education replaced the University in the accrediting of high schools. Webb's plan to provide low-cost journals to high schools was approved by the Executive Council, but Wylie Parker, a member of the Association and the principal of Forest Avenue High School in Dallas, had a better idea. Conversations with Parker and others, as well as a request from the Council in August 1939 for a school outreach program, convinced Webb to expand upon his original idea. He asked an associate in early October, "What would you think of the possibility for organizing in the high schools junior historical clubs which could be affiliated with the Texas State Historical Association?"[19] The response must have been positive, because Webb soon launched the Junior Historians.

Parker's Forest Avenue High School got the first charter for a Junior Historian chapter in December 1939. Others soon followed, and in April 1940 the program held its first annual meeting, in conjunction with the Association's annual meeting in Austin. Webb carefully selected a mentor for his high school program: H. Bailey Carroll, who still worked at North Texas Agricul-

"The Junior Historian movement was an act of faith in which Webb broadcast seed in confident knowledge that God and Nature and time would take care of everything else. The Junior Historian movement was an investment in youth, not because they were talented or made high entrance scores or were class officials, but simply because they lived and needed a past to cling to."

Speech by Joe Frantz on the occasion of dedicating a Walter P. Webb marker in Gary, Texas, April 9, 1978, in L. Tuffly Ellis, "Southwestern Collection," *SHQ*, 82 (Oct. 1978), 199.

★

PROGRAM

FORTY-FOUR ANNUAL MEETING
*Texas State
Historical Association*

FIRST ANNUAL MEETING
Junior Historians

AUSTIN
April 26, 27
1940

The Junior Historians met for the first time on April 26 and 27, 1940, in conjunction with the Forty-fourth annual meeting of the TSHA. "Eleven o'clock, April 25, 1940! Every heart beat just a little faster, for at last the long awaited day had arrived. Some of us who so proudly called ourselves Junior Historians had been chosen to represent our Wichita Falls chapter of the Junior Historical Society—the sixth chapter in Texas—in the first annual meeting at Austin. We couldn't have been more excited if we had been elected to Congress. For months this trip had been the object of dreams; and now, suddenly, all those dreams had become one big beautiful reality and we were really leaving for Austin!" Marie Huper, "My Trip to the First Annual Junior Historian Meeting," *Junior Historian* (Apr. 1941), 1. *Photograph from TSHA Files.*

tural College in 1940 but happily assumed the responsibility for editing the *Junior Historian*, the official journal of the program. Carroll looked like a "colorful Texas cowboy type" and "captivated" the students with "his Stetson hat and cigar."[20] He appeared to be the incarnation of "Old Man Texas," a popular character embodying the concerns of common Texans, created years earlier by John F. Knott, acclaimed editorial cartoonist for Dealey's *Dallas Morning News* and a member of the Association. Knott greatly aided Webb by using his creation to promote the Junior Historians, and later Old Man Texas appeared on the cover of another of Webb's initiatives, the *Handbook of Texas*. By 1950 there were more than a hundred chapters of the Junior Historians, including one at the New Mexico Military Institute in Roswell, New Mexico. Cosponsored by Paul Horgan, who in 1954 would be awarded the Pulitzer Prize for his *Great River*, the New Mexico chapter was the only Junior Historian chapter ever established outside of Texas.

Despite its ultimate success, the first years of the Junior Historians were shaky. Through the late 1940s the program often operated at a loss unless it

"On the night of April 28, the Texas State Historical Association will hold its first book auction. This auction will be held at the Driskill Hotel after the annual dinner. The books, principally Texas items, will be presented by members of the Association and the proceeds will go to the Association. Governor James V. Allred made the first contribution, an old law book published in 1556. Though it does not pertain to Texas, it should be of interest to some book lover. J. Evetts Haley has presented a copy of the XIT Ranch over which collectors and dealers usually fight. . . . Some of the books will be sold 'blind,' and some of these will contain a Texas Centennial half dollar, an original document, and a five dollar bill if some one can be induced to contribute it. . . . The auctioneers will be chosen from among the members, and are sure to know far more about books than they do about auctioneering."

Walter Prescott Webb, "Texas Collection," *SHQ*, 42 (Apr. 1939), 400.

The Texas State Historical Association

Annual Dinner

MAIN BALLROOM, UNION BUILDING
FRIDAY, APRIL 26, 1940, 6:30 p.m.

Auction of Texana $1.00

Annual dinner and Auction of Texana ticket from 1940. This would have been the second auction. *Photograph courtesy Subject Vertical Files, DI 02587, CAH.*

"[*The XIT Ranch of Texas*] had been published as recently as 1929, but only 1,380 copies had been distributed before a court injunction brought sales to a halt. Dudley [Dobie] recalled that the book came up late in the day when both interest and alertness had waned. The auctioneer was a novice who knew nothing of books or Texas history. Holding up the Haley item, he called for bids, but—not comprehending the title of the book—he announced it as the "Exit Ranch." Nobody gave a hoot about the Exit Ranch. Finally a dollar bid brought down the auctioneer's gavel. Too late Dudley realized that Brother [Elijah L.] Shettles had just walked off with a mint copy of a modern rarity."

Al Lowman, *Remembering Dudley Dobie: The First Bookseller to Enrich My Life and Empty My Pockets* (San Marcos: Lagarto Press, 1993), 14.

received a subsidy from a sympathetic donor. The Executive Council realized this but agreed with Webb that the effort was "well worth continuing." The *Junior Historian* appeared with fair regularity after its first edition in January 1940 when, as Webb wrote, it made a "timid bow to the indifferent public." The journal was certainly an improvement over Webb's initial intention to cover Junior Historian news through the *Quarterly*. Having their own journal and meetings drew attention to the Junior Historians. *Time* magazine noted in 1947 that the Texas program, although not the first in the country, had, through its growth, become a model for other states, while its predecessor in Indiana stopped meeting altogether for most of the 1940s. Webb's close friend, acclaimed University of Texas folklorist J. Frank Dobie, wrote: "I don't know but when Webb gets to St. Peter, he may not have more credit there for the Junior Historians of Texas than he will have for the books he has written."[21]

Webb's efforts in recruiting adults and establishing the Junior Historians went hand-in-hand with his ideas for boosting attendance at the Association's annual meetings. The "bobtailed Houston meeting" of April 22, 1939, that served as the forum for his presentation of proposals was a one-day gathering of the TSHA in conjunction with the San Jacinto Museum of History. Four years later Webb arranged for the annual meeting to be held jointly with the Texas Folklore Society at the Driskill Hotel in Austin, after UT's Garrison Hall had been taken over by trainees from the Navy ground school. The war effort and rationing hurt attendance, but Webb noted with pride that his last meeting as director, in April 1946, attracted 219 adults, as well as a growing number of Junior Historians.

Webb believed that one successful tactic for increasing attendance at the annual meetings was his initiation of booksellers' exhibits and auctions. He first suggested an auction in the January 1938 *Quarterly*, and then implemented it and the book exhibits at the April 1939 meeting in Austin, which took place

WEBB ON HISTORICAL CONTROVERSY

"The Editor is not averse to having those who love controversy engage in it to their heart's desire, but being himself somewhat given to calm history, he reserves the right to be a little parsimonious in giving space in the *Quarterly* either to 'bunkers' or 'debunkers.' . . . Perhaps the real historian should never be able to qualify, either as debunker or a glorifier."

Walter Prescott Webb, "Texas Collection," *SHQ*, 43 (Oct. 1939), 242.

prior to the Houston gathering later that month. He expected the auction to raise money and boost attendance, and it did both. The Association made $331.55 from items given by forty-five donors, and all agreed that many more members attended than in previous years. President Davenport declared, "This was much the most interesting and enthusiastic meeting that the Historical Association has had in my time."[22] The next year proved even better when the auction earned $927.54, nearly a third of which came from the sale of a book printed at Brazoria in 1833 and signed by Stephen F. Austin. By the time Webb stepped down as director, the auction had become an eagerly awaited highlight of the annual meeting, and was often reported in newspapers around the state.

When the necessity arose, Webb revived an old practice and held periodic meetings in cities other than Austin, which continued to host all annual meetings. At about the time Webb took charge of the TSHA, the Texas State Teachers Association cut the customary history section from its yearly meeting. Webb, who believed that the teaching of Texas history was vital, found this deletion especially distressing because that section had been initiated by George P. Garrison in 1908. To sustain the spirit of Garrison's section, Webb held regional meetings jointly with the Texas State Teachers Association. He always prepared carefully by having prominent local persons host the assembly. Attendance was usually good, in excess of several hundred each time, and Webb's message proved effective. Texas history became customary in most high school curricula, although the war forced an end to the joint regional meetings after 1942. Webb further expanded on Garrison's academic legacy by recruiting Rupert N. Richardson from Abilene's Hardin-Simmons College, where he was vice-president and active in the West Texas Historical Association. Richardson, who had earned his doctorate at the University of Texas,

Quarterly TRAVELS

"Every three months twenty-five copies of the *Southwestern Historical Quarterly* travel by train and ocean liner to the far parts of the world. Copies go to Jerusalem in Asia, Montevideo in Uruguay and to other places between A and U. The *Quarterly* goes to London, Paris, Berlin, Stuttgart, Rome, Stockholm, Basel, Mexico and Canada. It is to be found in practically every university library in the United States."

Walter Prescott Webb, "Texas Collection," *SHQ,* 43 (July 1939), 87.

Webb at his desk in Garrison Hall with the *Southwestern Historical Quarterly* and the *Junior Historian*. Photograph courtesy *Walter Prescott Webb Papers*, DI 02574, CAH.

returned there in the summer of 1940 to begin an undergraduate course on Texas history.

A recurring problem for Webb in any of his efforts on behalf of the Association was a lack of money. Even before Webb became director, he was well aware of the straitened circumstances of the organization. A 1938 note accompanied his check for $100, instructing Coral H. Tullis to find a suitable purpose for his gift "looking to the time when we shall reach the end of our rainbow and find a pot of gold." In a later letter to Davenport after taking charge of the Association in 1939, Webb reported that George A. Hill Jr. was still searching for "large bequests," and confessed, "This is a field in which I am incompetent."[23] Competent or not, he had to learn, and by the fall of 1939 he was writing to prominent Texans asking for donations to fund an endowment. Despite his diligent efforts, he had raised only about $4,000 by 1940.

Webb realized that it would take at least $50,000 to publish the *Handbook*, a sobering estimate in light of his meager success at fund-raising. The total income of the Association in 1939–1940 was only $6,772.89, which represented a slight increase from the previous year. Like Barker, Webb was tired of 'nickel nursing.' He enlisted the help of men such as Regent Jubal R. Parten, who introduced him to Nelson Rockefeller. Webb talked with a representative of the Rockefeller Foundation in April 1939 and again the following month. An extended silence ensued, but in 1941 the Rockefeller Foundation began to sponsor historical studies throughout the Great Plains region and so became more interested in Webb's program. Encouraged, Webb flew to New York to meet again with Foundation officers, who expressed "guarded interest."[24] At a conference on the Great Plains hosted by the University of Nebraska in June 1942, Webb spoke on Association projects that should be funded by the Rockefeller Foundation.

The Foundation responded to Webb's lobbying by providing an initial grant of $2,500 to the Association in 1942. The purpose of their gift was to support Bailey Carroll's study of the disastrous Santa Fe expedition of 1841. The Rockefeller Foundation must have liked the result, because in 1943 they informed the Association that they would provide $5,000 annually for the next three years. Webb spent the money well, subsidizing books, the Junior Historians, and his *Handbook* project with Foundation money. The grant was renewed for three more years in 1946 and increased to a total of $18,000. Such amounts may not appear to be very much to later historians, but they are about what the Association's budget had been each year prior to Webb's becoming director.

Carroll mistakenly believed that the Rockefeller funds would enable Webb to avoid the political pitfalls of asking the Texas legislature for money. Garrison had never asked, and Barker had made it abundantly clear that he thought such a request would be a costly mistake. But Webb had big plans, and he disagreed with his predecessors and Carroll. In January 1941, not yet certain that there would be any funds from the Rockefeller Foundation, Webb reminded University president Homer P. Rainey of his earlier offer to ask for a legislative appropriation to support "research in Texas history." Webb enclosed a copy of his *Dallas Morning News* announcement of the *Handbook of Texas* project, and pointed out that financing such an effort "on a private basis" would be a "long hard task."[25]

Rainey already paid half of Webb's salary, for his position as a University faculty member, and had authorized a University contribution to the TSHA to offset its payment of the other half, but he was willing to do what he could to increase support even more. Rainey was joined in his lobbying efforts by Louis W. Kemp, who had forged links to government figures during his years

THE *Quarterly*

"[E]ven a published paper can have too many details. It will be the policy of the *Quarterly* to favor comparatively brief articles, those that tell a clear, concise story with as much economy as possible. It seems to have become a custom among students in certain institutions outside Texas to lift a chapter from a thesis and send it to the *Quarterly* for publication. Such a chapter is often not even an article. It may be, but in most cases it is a dislocation, without background, minus an introduction, sans conclusion. One suspects it is intended, like undelivered congressional speeches, 'for the record'."

Walter Prescott Webb, "Texas Collection," *SHQ*, 43 (Jan. 1940), 385.

as a leader in efforts to erect historical markers, celebrate the centennial of Texas independence, and refurbish the state cemetery in Austin. Prominent Texas businessmen such as Fred W. Frost and UT regent Clifton M. Caldwell lent their influence, and Texas historian John S. Spratt spoke privately to his friends in the Texas Senate. Webb asked only that legislative money be appropriated to the Association through the University "in order to avoid political entanglements."[26] It should never appear that the Association was attempting to be anything but an extension of Rainey's plans to expand research at the University of Texas.

The University gave the Association $2,800 in 1940–1941, when the organization first appeared as a line item in the campus budget, and Webb commenced his half-time appointment. Homer Rainey and Louis Kemp convinced the legislature to join with the University in funding the *Handbook* project, so the next year, 1941–1942, Webb received a total of $12,300 in grants from the two entities. This included $2,800 for his salary, $4,750 from the University for research in Texas history, and $4,750 from the legislature for the same purpose. The flood of money caught the Association totally unprepared, and in April 1942 a somewhat chagrined Webb had to return those first grants. The turmoil of the sudden entry of the United States into World War II had made it impossible to spend the money. Fortunately, the funding continued for four years. In 1945 the legislative grant was increased to $5,000 annually, and the University matched that amount.

The influx of state funds forced a reorganization of the Association's connection with the University of Texas. In 1943 University funding for all Association projects, including the *Handbook*, and the legislative grants to the University for the Association were merged into one budget item: the Department of Research in Texas History. Webb became the director of this department, and being thus named was another strong argument for changing his Association title to the same name (from recording secretary and librarian). Officially he became a half-time employee of the Department of Research as well as of the Department of History. This gave Webb more control over the spending of the funds from the University and the legislature, and, that same year, he was able to hire Bailey Carroll full-time, dividing the funding so that Carroll worked half-time as a faculty member and half-time for the Association.

The receipt of funds from the University and the legislature, and the creation of the Department of Research in Texas History, did not solve all of the Association's money woes. In the past these had been addressed partially through investments. In 1939 the Executive Council had decided to drop its real estate investments. The entire portfolio consisted of two houses, one in Austin and another in Coleman. The Austin house, security on an unpaid note issued by the Association, was sold immediately. The sale of the Coleman house was delayed, however, when Webb foresaw that the onset of World War II would bring development at the Army camp at nearby Brownwood. On his advice, the delayed sale of that property brought in a good profit for the Association, but this only partially offset the more than $4,000 lost when Brown Brothers, the company that handled the Association's investments, suddenly folded in 1945. Litigation dragged on for years, and an officer of the company actually committed suicide, before the Executive Council finally accepted the loss of its portfolio.

The bankruptcy of the Brown Brothers almost ruined the Association's efforts to provide more substantial funding for its publications. While he was serving as TSHA acting director in 1942 (when Webb was in England), Carroll asked the director of the New Jersey Historical Society about the best way to increase support in the business community for the Association. Carroll was told to approach bank officers, because they knew how to handle such matters. The result of his inquiries led Carroll to urge TSHA president Louis Kemp to propose creating a permanent committee of businessmen to handle the Association's "financial affairs." As for its chair, Carroll told Kemp, "There ought to be somewhere a George W. Brackenridge or a George W. Littlefield, who could be interested in the work of the Association the way these men used to be and the way they were interested in the University."[27]

The Executive Council did not agree that the management of their financial affairs should be handed over to a committee of businessmen, but they did see the practical sense of giving such a group the task of raising money. A Ways and Means Committee was approved at the April 1944 meeting, with the specific tasks of increasing the number of Patrons, Life Members, and Sustaining

Members, and selling advertisements in the *Quarterly*. Money from these efforts would be used to fund an endowment for publication. A year later the committee members were tardily announced. The chair was former regent Leslie Waggener Jr., chief executive officer of Republic National Bank in Dallas. Interestingly, he was the son and namesake of the professor who hired Garrison to teach at the University and who later became president of that institution. The other members of the committee were also businessmen who, like Waggener, shared an interest in history and in the Association.

The collapse of the Brown Brothers eliminated the small fund initially created by Eugene Barker to support the publications program, and convinced the Association to develop a more conservative investment plan. Carroll as early as 1943 had urged the TSHA to invest only in Treasury bonds. When he approached Waggener about chairing the Ways and Means Committee, he found the Dallas banker to be amenable to this strategy. Terms for the com-

WEBB ON SCIENTIFIC HISTORY

"At the last meeting of the Texas State Teachers Association there appeared on the regular program no section devoted to history. It would seem that the subject has been abolished. At least the pedagogical eraser has swept the word off the professional blackboard and written two words in its place, 'Social Science.' Now one who can make two words grow where one grew before certainly adds something—a word, but all else remains about as it was.... The adoption of the term social science is in keeping with the age. It illustrates man's inability to maintain a balance; it illustrates how much sillier adults are than children who know enough to keep equal weight on both ends of the seesaw.... [Science] is a modern obsession. It is like a fisherman's net with a two-inch mesh.... Now history, broadly interpreted, can never be caught in the scientific net. The experimental scientist can drag the waters all he likes, but he can never catch the fine spirit of history and literature. Science can contribute something, but not all, or even the most important.... It seems to me that it is far better to be a legitimate historian than a pseudo scientist, and however the social scientist regards himself, the natural scientist regards him at best as a pseudo scientist and at worst a shelter beggar under a momentarily popular roof. In any case, he is forever doomed to play second fiddle as long as he is an intruder."

Walter Prescott Webb, "Texas Collection," *SHQ*, 43 (Jan. 1940), 379–380.

mittee's investments precluded investing in any private firm, or in real estate. Carroll's target for fund-raising was also very conservative. He told Waggener that they were "not looking for miracles."[28] Here Waggener disagreed, and he set his fund-raising goal at $200,000, a miraculous amount in light of the Association's small budget. Waggener later admitted that he had little experience in asking for money, but he was so moved by Carroll's enthusiasm that he had to try. Little was gained in Webb's last year as director, but Waggener would be more successful after Carroll took charge.

Association earnings under Webb, thanks to new programs and initiatives, increased steadily. Receipts for the fiscal year ending in 1941 increased more than 100 percent from the previous year. Wartime disruptions reduced the Association's income, but in 1943 a proposal from Earl Vandale bore fruit when the Internal Revenue Service agreed that donations to the Association would be tax-free. Thus encouraged, donors gave more freely, and receipts tripled yearly—to $24,239.04 by 1946. Of course, this also included money from the Rockefeller Foundation, the legislature, and Waggener's Ways and Means Committee. With such an enhanced income, Carroll, who succeeded Webb as director, could continue investing, principally in Treasury bonds.

An increasing number of donors and new members were lured to the Association by Webb's persistent efforts at public promotion. In November 1939 he wrote to the members that memberships would make excellent Christmas gifts for "people of discrimination in lieu of red neckties and off-brand cigars." At about the same time, he began referring to the Association as "the oldest learned society in Texas." Others might predate its 1897 founding, but, he argued, it was "doubtful if any of them has had a continuous existence."[29] By 1941 the phrase was on the official stationary of the Association along with a seal. The seal had apparently been produced for the government of the Republic of Texas. Long thought to be lost, it had turned up when Benjamin Neel, a student from Menard, submitted it as an entry in a statewide contest to find exhibits for the Centennial celebration. Webb dispatched master engraver Charles Simmang of San Antonio to Menard to make a facsimile of the seal, and first used it in 1940 on cards that accompanied Christmas-gift memberships. Together with the claim to be the oldest learned society in Texas, the seal provided a look of unchallenged distinction.

Much of Webb's effort to claim the historical high ground in Texas may have been prompted by the 1936 revival of the Philosophical Society of Texas as part of the Texas Centennial excitement. The Society's establishment during the Republic predated that of the Association, but the older group, as Webb noted, had become inactive before statehood. Webb need not have worried about the Philosophical Society undercutting his support. Among the ten who

LAST LOVE

"[Webb] met Terrell Maverick, widow of former congressman and mayor Maury Maverick, flipped like a rerun of Mickey Rooney in the Andy Hardy series, and gave UT its most enjoyable romance in my fifty years on the campus. He met her at secret places with all the stealth of a CIA agent; he would give Colleen T. Kain, then administrative assistant for the Department of History, coded messages to give Mrs. Maverick; and he chased back and forth to San Antonio with all the energy of a lovesick sophomore. Once when we were going to the student union for coffee, I said to him that a rumor was going around the campus that he and Mrs. Maverick were going to have to get married. He looked at me with a grin that could have floodlit the State Capitol and said with absolute pleasure: 'You son of a bitch!'

"And then one day he was killed between Austin and San Marcos on an absolutely clear day in early March. I made some decisions about his funeral and then went to Brackenridge Hospital to see his widow. She was in intensive care, buried in bandages from toe to chin and groggy from the wreck and from the medicines she had been given. She was alert enough to recognize me and take my hand.

'He's dead, isn't he?' she asked.

After I said yes, she looked sad for a moment and then brightened.

'But God,' she said, 'didn't I give him fourteen months on the mountain top!'

He would have liked that farewell."

Joe B. Frantz, "Remembering Walter Prescott Webb," *SHQ*, 92 (July 1988), 22–23.

Note on back of photo: "Walter and Terrell (Maverick) Webb – Christmas 1962 at Prof Bill Hagan's house New Orleans (Tulane) enroute to Chicago for American Historical Meet (New sexy glasses on)."

Photograph courtesy Walter Prescott Webb Papers, DI 02593, CAH.

restored the Society were the current Association president, William E. Wrather, and Herbert P. Gambrell, a future president. Eugene C. Barker, Webb, Charles W. Hackett, and Charles W. Ramsdell were among the first invited to membership, as well as J. Evetts Haley. The Philosophical Society of Texas quickly settled into operating as a "sort of non-collegiate honor society," and members of the Association remained active in its leadership and its rank and file.[30] Of the Association directors who followed Webb, three—H. Bailey Carroll, Joe B. Frantz, and Ron Tyler—were also members of the society.

Whether or not Webb had to worry about competition, he was always trying new ways to promote the Association. He produced advance copies of his "Texas Collection" column, giving them to newspaper editors for exclusive use within their regions in return for their purchase of *Quarterly* subscriptions. He asked railroad companies to buy copies of the *Quarterly* to display in lounge cars along with the other magazines they provided. Apparently the Texas and Pacific Railroad accepted his request, the only company to do so, and by 1941 the journal could be read in their "parlor cars." Webb also asked the Texas Highway Department to provide free copies of the *Quarterly* in the "courtesy stations on the highway entrances to Texas." By the spring of 1944, with sponsors secured in part by Louis Kemp, Webb and Carroll were making broadcasts from Radio House on the University of Texas campus. Topics often changed but the theme was always the same: "Your Texas Heritage as revealed by old man Texas himself and as seen through the eyes of members of the Texas State Historical Association."[31] It was a great way for Webb to appeal directly to the public.

Webb made it clear from the beginning that he would not stay very long as director of the Association. He told the Executive Council in the fall of 1938 that he would direct the organization for no more than five years. During his first few years, making preparations to step down was a constant theme of his letters to supporters such as Harbert Davenport. Some later remembered that Webb resigned in 1943 in favor of Carroll, but that was not strictly true. That year, while in Oxford, a tired and disgruntled Webb did tender his resignation, but was persuaded to withdraw it. When he returned to Austin later in the year, he did transfer most of his responsibilities to Carroll while keeping, as he described it, only "titular direction."[32] Webb, however, did remain active on behalf of the Association, making radio broadcasts and delivering speeches about England, the proceeds of which he donated to the organization.

Although Webb continued to serve as director of the Association until 1946, by early 1944, as he confessed to Samuel E. Asbury, he spent much time "in seclusion." As Webb explained to the Rockefeller Foundation, he had "got in the mood" to "do some writing" during his "long holiday in England." His

Homer Price Rainey stands above the West Mall, with the Old Library Building in the near background below. Rainey became president of the University of Texas in December 1939. Politically, Rainey was a New Deal man, while the Board of Regents was very conservative. Almost immediately problems arose between the new president and the board, a controversy having to do primarily with tenure, book censorship, and the board's control over the daily affairs of the University. When the board ultimately fired Rainey in November 1944, a wave of protest was set off in a significant portion of the faculty and student body. Eugene Barker supported the board's decision, and "motivated by a sincere belief that a continuation of the controversy would gravely damage the University," he called for an end to the protest. It was the Rainey affair and Barker's role in it that led to the placement of the Texas history collection in the Old Library Building and the naming of the new center after Barker. J. Evetts Haley, who had also opposed Rainey and had written several newspaper articles supporting the Board of Regents, was able to put the regents' appreciation to good use in lobbying them for the building. Don E. Carleton and Katherine J. Adams, " 'A Work Peculiarly Our Own': Origins of the Barker Texas History Center, 1883–1950," *SHQ*, 86 (Oct. 1982), 224 (quotation), 225. *Photograph courtesy Prints and Photographs Collection, DI 02565, CAH.*

Friday Mountain Ranch

"Yes, I like the name of Las Cuevas. Friday Mountain Ranch is a quiet place, and it gives me a lot of time to think. I sit in the hall or out on the cistern and have all sorts of things happen here just for company. There's Bear Creek which I can turn into the Rio Grande. It runs in the same direction and has a lot of the same habits. Over here on the north I'm in Texas, and the other side is Mexico. Sometimes I'm McNelly, riding around through the brush, protecting other people's cattle. I make a sort of hero of myself. And over there behind Friday Mountain lives Juan Flores, and he's always trying to steal my cattle; we play a right good game. I gave the caves the Spanish name so that General Juan Flores will feel at home."

Friday Mountain, a peak 17 miles southwest of Austin on Bear Creek in Hays County, was named for the day the early surveyors first arrived at the location. In 1852 Thomas Jefferson Johnson founded a coeducational school on the site and named it the Johnson Institute. The school's original log buildings were built with the aid of the first students and used until 1868 when they were replaced by a two-story, ten-room limestone building with seven fireplaces.

After Johnson died in 1868, the school continued in operation by his family for another four years, then closed in 1872. The land changed hands several times over the course of the next three decades, and in 1908 was purchased by Louis Kemp (a future president of the TSHA), who sold it in 1921 to his son Thomas Jefferson Kemp. It was the younger Kemp who sold it to Walter Prescott Webb in 1942.

Webb loved the place and gradually brought the land back to grace, cutting

last book, *Divided We Stand*, had been published in 1937, and he was eager to put some new thoughts on paper. The result would be *The Great Frontier*, published in 1952. As this project grew to require more time, Webb began to consider handing over all of his TSHA responsibilities to Carroll, who by hard work "had proved that he was the one to carry on." Furthermore, as Webb explained to Wylie Parker of Dallas, "Unlike myself, he likes editing (though why I cannot understand) and now has active charge of both publications," the *Southwestern Historical Quarterly* and the *Junior Historian*.[33]

Webb may also have been depressed by the abrupt removal of his ally, Homer P. Rainey, as president of the University of Texas after an ugly fight in which Eugene Barker was among those who opposed Rainey. The University

back the encroaching cedar and restoring the soil and the native grasses.

In 1947 Webb and his friend Rodney Kidd opened a summer camp for boys at the ranch. Kidd ran the ranch and Webb continued in his management of the grasslands. From 1949 to 1956 the Austin public schools ran a program whereby sixth-grade boys and girls spent five-day turns at the ranch during the school year, in a program that stressed nature study and self-reliance.

The ranch with its old limestone building was also the setting for retreats for Webb and his friends. Roy Bedichek, on sabbatical from his University of Texas duties, spent a year at the ranch in 1947 to write his *Adventures of a Texas Naturalist*.

In 1963, shortly before his death, Webb sold the ranch to Kidd, and the Friday Mountain camp continued in operation by Kidd and his family until 1984, when the ranch was sold to the International Society for Divine Love for religious purposes. The society made so many changes to the old limestone building that the Texas Historical Commission voted in 1992 to revoke its 1964 Historic Landmark designation.

After his death in 1963, Webb's friends continued to meet at the ranch occasionally to honor his memory. On March 8, 1969, the sixth anniversary of Webb's death, friends and admirers gathered to inaugurate a perpetual memorial: the Walter Prescott Webb Great Frontier Foundation.

Thomas Jefferson Johnson, his wife, and various family members and slaves are buried in the cemetery on the ranch grounds.

Webb to J. Frank Dobie, Feb. 11, 1943 (quotation), Dobie Collection (Humanities Research Center, University of Texas at Austin), quoted in Llerena B. Friend, "W. P. Webb's Texas Rangers," *SHQ*, 74 (Jan. 1971), 322–323; Eldon S. Branda, "Friday Mountain Ranch," *Handbook of Texas Online* (accessed Nov. 10, 2005); William S. Osborn, "Johnson Institute," ibid

president simply did not agree with the regents that they, and not he, should control the University. Most of the faculty sided with Rainey, but nevertheless in November 1944 the regents fired him. This action led to a legislative investigation and censure by the American Association of University Professors, as well as the University's probation from the Southern Association of Colleges and Schools. The turmoil lasted for many years, and may well have been a factor in the 1947 dismissal of Webb's friend J. Frank Dobie, who, during the conflict, had referred to the regents as "native fascists." All in all, it was a sad time for Webb, who had leaked a report that sparked the final confrontation between Rainey and the regents. As he confided to a friend, the turmoil knocked "all the stuffing" out of him.[34]

Walter Prescott Webb, 1963, just a few weeks before he died. A note written by his secretary Eileen Guarino was attached to several photographs, of which this was one: "These are the last photographs (to my knowledge) made of Dr. Webb. They were taken in Dallas on February 18, 1963, at Dallas College of Southern Methodist University. He told me his audience there had been polite and attentive but completely unresponsive. He gave the attached speech, which I thought was sensational. He said – 'Well – it was a Monday night – and you can't win them all'."
Photograph courtesy Walter Prescott Webb Papers, DI 02568, CAH.

Webb also opposed the selection of Theophilus S. Painter as Rainey's successor, and his Friday Mountain ranch became a place for those who agreed with him to gather and grumble. Barker and Haley were not among those who attended these gatherings. Barker had sharply criticized Rainey, and became an ally of the regents who removed him. Prominent among these was Orville Bullington, who rewarded Barker's support by aiding him in the acquisition of the Kell Collection and space for the Association in the Old Library. Webb may have respected Barker's desire for peace on campus, but he split openly and acrimoniously with Evetts Haley, who wrote a series of widely reprinted articles denouncing Rainey's tolerance for Communism and support of racial integration. Alienated from Barker, his former mentor, and from other prominent members of the Association, who, like Haley, harbored ill will toward Rainey, Webb withdrew from the Association limelight to focus on writing and teaching.

Webb formally resigned as director of the Association at the April 1946 meeting of the Executive Council, and subsequently took a year's leave of absence from the University of Texas. He strongly urged the appointment of H. Bailey Carroll in his place, and the Council readily agreed. Webb retained the title of director of the Department of Research in Texas History until 1951, when he transferred that as well to Carroll. In the meantime, Carroll received half of his pay from Webb's Research budget and half from the Department of History as a faculty member, an arrangement that seemed to suit all parties. Webb stayed on the Executive Council, despite his occasional threats to resign because of some conflict or another, until his death in an automobile accident in 1963.

Despite being director for less time than any other director before or since, Webb left his own indelible stamp on the Association. His determination to broaden the organization's appeal without surrendering its academic integrity resulted in a substantial expansion of membership, activities, and publications. Lasting memorials to Webb could be seen in the Junior Historians, the new book publications program, the ongoing *Handbook of Texas* project, the enhanced budget, the Barker Texas History Center, and even the book auctions at the annual meetings. Not all of Webb's ideas worked; in 1941 his plans to host bus tours of Texas for adults and schoolchildren had to be abandoned when funds and time ran out. He had accomplished much, however, in "undertaking to give [the Association] a broader scope and a bigger job," as he had written in 1939 that he intended to do.[35] Like Barker, Webb accepted a Distinguished Professorship from the University of Texas, one of many awards for Webb during the next two decades, which also saw the continuing development of his Association initiatives under his student, H. Bailey Carroll.

FIVE

Old Man Texas Himself

H. Bailey Carroll, 1946–1966

H Bailey Carroll became the director of the Texas State Historical Association and editor of the *Southwestern Historical Quarterly* in April 1946 on the recommendation of Walter P. Webb. In 1951 Carroll succeeded Webb as director of the Department of Research in Texas History for the University of Texas, again at Webb's request. Many thus expected Carroll to continue Webb's initiatives. After all, Webb had been his doctoral professor and brought Carroll to the Association. Too, they were friends; Webb in 1935 had hosted Carroll's marriage to Mary Joe Durning at his home. Carroll declared in the *Quarterly* that he would adopt no new policies. The Association, he wrote, was "like one of the ponderous Katy locomotives. It has power, but it runs along a well defined course."[1] Within a few years, however, Carroll and Webb clashed. The latter, who remained on the

---

H. Bailey Carroll (1903–1966), director of the Association 1946–1966.

"Perhaps some statement concerning my selection as director of the Association ought to be made; actually, however, there is little to be said. Professor Webb's resignation was against my wishes and requests made on numerous occasions. At the time I took the acting directorship, upon the occasion of his going to Oxford as Harmsworth Professor of History, I made the statement that there were no new policies to announce for the Association. A half-century has fixed in a rather definite fashion the course of the Association. As a figure of speech I should say that the Association is like one of the ponderous Katy locomotives. It has power, but it runs along a well defined course. It stays on its own track and on its own division. It renders a great service in transporting freight—our freight is Texas history. . . . One final thought carrying on the railroad simile for the Association: The jeep is a worthy little fellow in his own field, but the Association can not make the quick turns and jump the ditches in the manner of the jeep. We must keep our feet on the ground, the wheels on the rails, and be prepared for the big and heavy hauls ahead." H. Bailey Carroll, "Texas Collection," *SHQ*, 50 (July 1946), 113–114. Carroll, in his office in the Barker Texas History Center, looking at galley proofs for the *Handbook of Texas. Courtesy Prints and Photographs Collection, DI 02605, CAH.*

THE *Quarterly*

"In a very real way much that governs the editorship of the *Quarterly* is custom; editorial policy is largely governed by precedents and examples established by trial and error over a half-century.

"Most of you, I am sure, have given at least some thought to what the *Quarterly* is or ought to be. I am confident that your ideas on that score are firmly fixed and that everyone is in agreement that the *Quarterly* should publish the best and only the best material available, that articles should be sound historically, that they should be contributions in some sense to the history of Texas, and that they should be of some lasting significance. An article which meets those requirements must also be a reasonable entity within itself; it must have a starting and ending point; it can not be simply a chapter wrenched from a thesis or longer study and submitted only for 'purposes of publication.'

"Probably not so many of you, however, have looked at the picture from the other side—what the *Quarterly* is not. But these negative factors have always been at least equally important in determining the editorial policy of the *Quarterly*.

The *Quarterly* is not an organ of genealogy per se ....

The *Quarterly* is not an organ of social philosophy....

The *Quarterly* does not settle, or attempt to settle, current controversy whether political, economic, religious, or personal....

The *Quarterly* is not solely a publication for any one specialized type, region, or period of Texas history...."

H. Bailey Carroll, "Report to the Executive Council,"
SHQ, 51 (July 1947), 60.

Executive Council until his death in 1963, had a broad vision of the Association's task, while Carroll seemed content with a narrower focus. Webb thought in national terms and painted his literary images with a broad brush. Carroll produced local studies that he intended for others to use to construct great theses. Both men did their best to protect and promote the Association, but their conflict led to deep divisions during Carroll's last years as director.

Carroll's breaking away from Webb, and from the legacy of earlier TSHA directors, reflected a broader rebellion by proponents of local, amateur historians against professional historians. Webb, like George P. Garrison and Eugene C. Barker, was active in history organizations with a national focus, such as the American Historical Association (AHA) and the Mississippi Valley Historical Society (later the Organization of American Historians). Carroll did join the Mississippi Valley Historical Society, but devoted himself to the American Association for State and Local History (AASLH), which was established in 1940 by historians upset with the AHA for not supporting its own Conference of State and Local History Societies. Reuben G. Thwaites of the State Historical Society of Wisconsin had chaired the initial meeting of the Conference at the AHA annual convention in 1904, but little had come of this effort. On the fiftieth anniversary of the AHA in 1934, Julian P. Boyd reported that few people attended Conference sessions, and that it had been years since its proceedings were regularly published.

Supporters blamed apathetic professional historians within the AHA for the Conference's failure. It was as a countermeasure that the AASLH organized at the 1940 Conference meeting. Observers noted a shift in focus from infusing professionalism into the work of local agencies to a new goal of promoting the acceptance of local historians in a field dominated by professionals writing national history. Amateur historians, instead of being seen as students in need of training, would be equal partners in local education and publication efforts. Conference members, which included the Texas State Historical Association, dissolved the Conference, embraced the AASLH, and took up the task of broadening the public appeal of a field believed to have become too stuffy for its own good. The results proved spectacular. From 583 groups listed in the Conference's 1936 guide to historical societies in the United States and Canada, the AASLH grew to 9,375 agencies reported in its directory fifty years later. And *American Heritage*, originally created as the flagship publication of the AASLH, became perhaps the most popular history magazine in the country.

Webb certainly understood the value of local history, but he always thought of himself as a national historian who used Texas materials. Carroll made no such pretense as he devoted much of his time to the AASLH. He served on AASLH committees as early as 1945, and during the 1950s was on their Executive Council for eight years and became a vice-president. When the AASLH met in Houston in 1952, the Association served as one of the hosts and Carroll chaired the program committee. He worked for almost a decade as chair of an AASLH national committee to oversee celebrations of the centennial of the overland mail. He became an avid promoter of historic preservation, historical markers, and local history organizations. Such topics filled his "Texas Collection" and dominated articles in the *Quarterly*. Most of the books published by the Association under Carroll followed suit. He agreed with Herbert P. Gambrell, popular Association president and respected Texas author, when he said, "The animus of this Texas School of Historians . . . is

Collectors and the TSHA

"Eight volumes of the Davy Crockett Almanacs published between 1835 and 1842, recently purchased by Edward Clark of Austin, highlight the exhibits of eight private collectors of Texana shown at the University of Texas this spring and summer in conjunction with an exhibit of material from the University's own collection. Individual copies of the almanacs are rare, and a group such as the one Clark now owns is a rare jewel in any collection of Texana. He is certainly to be commended on his efforts to bring the group to Texas where Crockett is not only a part of the history but also of the folklore of the state.

"Palmer Bradley, J. P. Bryan, Price Daniel, Jenkins Garrett, Dorsey B. Hardeman, George P. Isbell and Cooper Ragan, all members of the Association, also are exhibiting items from their collections. The eight collectors have combined a love for Texas with a love for books, seeking diligently to preserve for posterity the heritage of their state. By allowing the University to display items from their private collections, they have doubtlessly imbued in others the desire to seek out and to preserve those books and manuscripts which will lay open the past for generations to come."

H. Bailey Carroll, "Texas Collection," *SHQ*, 66 (July 1962), 146.

that local, regional, history is important, not simply because it holds sentimental interest for people of the region, but because it *is history*."[2]

Carroll's stand in defense of local history also placed him in opposition to other major trends in American historical study. Following in the well-defined footsteps of George P. Garrison, Eugene C. Barker, and Walter P. Webb, Carroll continued to emphasize the frontier, and conflict, when most prominent historians were forging a new interpretation of United States history as an ongoing process of consensus and accommodation. The social changes of the New Deal, World War II, and the cold war era included urbanization and racial integration. By focusing on the nineteenth-century frontier, Carroll avoided confronting twentieth-century issues such as poverty, illiteracy, and racism as Texas incomes and growth lagged behind national averages. Such limited vision meant that Carroll, along with many other proponents of state and local history, got pushed aside as a national flood of history doctorates embraced new topics and ideas, such as consensus. Despite this, many in the Association remained loyal to Carroll, and he had some good graduate students.

Carroll from the start realized the need to raise money for his revamped "locomotive," but he also knew that funding for the Association was "tremendously complex." His salary was paid by the University of Texas, half of it as his faculty paycheck and half through Webb's Department of Research in Texas History. In 1947, when the legislature, as part of its policy of dropping line-item appropriations for agencies sponsored by educational institutions, discontinued its annual grant of $5,000 for the *Handbook of Texas*, the University quickly increased its funding for that project. In addition to office space provided at no charge, University support by 1951, when Carroll became director of the Department of Research, totaled $20,184 each year for the Association. Carroll drolly explained to Clement M. Silvestro, director of the AASLH, that the University helped the Association "under the same philosophy that Texas Agricultural and Mechanical College expends funds for pink boll weevil control. . . . Both enterprises are supposed to do something for Texas."[3]

Carroll sought private funds to supplement his University support. As he wrote to Silvestro, "I do know that it takes both of these horses to pull our wagon."[4] At about the time that the legislature dropped its annual grant, the Rockefeller Foundation increased its financial support for the *Handbook*. This provided money to pay authors and Association employees, as well as money for prizes to students who wrote for the *Junior Historian*. Carroll also pushed for an increase in membership fees, and the Executive Council reluctantly agreed in 1949 to a raise from $3.00—the cost since 1920—to $5.00. They did not approve another such increase, in spite of requests from Carroll, until 1962, when they rejected his plea for $10.00 and settled on $7.50.

Carroll wanted to expand the book publications program of the TSHA, but apart from the Rockefeller and University funds for the *Handbook of Texas*, little could be spared for this. He realized that he could not raise much himself. He recalled in 1953, "I started my work with the Association with the high hopes of youth and the belief that it was only necessary to establish the validity of the cause and enterprise and that financial backing would be automatically secured." He learned otherwise and later confessed to the Executive Council, "I found that I could not barge into the captains of industry and talk them out of money." While he "could sell them a $5.00 membership because they would pay $5.00 to get rid of me," that obviously was not enough.[5]

Carroll welcomed Leslie Waggener Jr. as a fund-raiser. Waggener proved to be very effective at finding donors, but more important he spearheaded Carroll's successful drive to set aside all of the proceeds of his efforts as a separate book publications fund. In recognition of his tremendous achievement, Waggener was appointed honorary president of the Association for life in 1950. Tragically, he did not long enjoy this title. He died of a heart attack

Pat Ireland Nixon (1946–1949)

Earl Vandale (1949–1951)

Herbert P. Gambrell
(1951–1953)

Claude Elliott (1953–1955)

Paul Adams (1955–1957)

Ten presidents served under Carroll. *Herbert Gambrell photograph courtesy Prints and Photographs Collection, DI 02585, CAH; all others are from TSHA Files.*

Ralph W. Steen (1957–1959)

Merle Duncan (1959–1962)

Fred R. Cotten (1962–1964)

George P. Isbell (1964–1965)

J. P. Bryan Sr. (1965–1967)

WORLD WAR II

"On the active fronts of the Southwest Pacific Texans daily emblazon the record with outstanding feats of courage on land, on the sea, and in the air. Whenever I see a Texas man in command I have a feeling of confidence."—Douglas A. MacArthur, General, United States Army.

Quoted in H. Bailey Carroll, "Texas Collection," *SHQ,* 47 (July 1943), 53.

watching the University of Texas football team play in the Cotton Bowl on New Year's Day in 1951. By that time he had raised $83,588.50 to endow Association book publications. This amount exceeded the total income of the TSHA for the twenty-six years Barker had been in charge, and almost exceeded revenues for the combined forty years of Barker and Garrison. Carroll exaggerated only slightly when he declared in the *Quarterly,* "So secure are the publication funds of the Association that for at least another century the soft footfalls of Leslie Waggener should be heard in the rustling of the leaves of the Texas books done by the Association."[6]

All of Carroll's work with Association finances led to a steady increase in its resources. Thanks to a process that he had supervised since 1943, all of the Association's investments were in United States Treasury bonds. The annual return was not substantial, but Carroll argued that the organization's money was certainly more secure. The principal exception to this policy came in 1952, when he accepted $3,000 in General Foods stock to subsidize the publication of a history of Post City by Charles Dudley Eaves and C. A. Hutchinson. With no public explanation, Carroll insisted upon always listing this stock at its original value rather than its market price, which reached $21,172 by 1966, when he retired. The total assets for the Association at that time stood at $191,161 in cash and bonds, plus the $3,000 listed for General Foods stock.

As part of his effort to increase Association funds, in 1946 Carroll asked Pat I. Nixon, a well-known medical historian and the current president of the Association, to organize a membership drive. This effort fizzled, however, when older members such as Samuel E. Asbury made it clear that they opposed the "popularization" of the TSHA. Asbury grumbled that professional scholars, if they attended the annual meetings at all, "wander[ed] around like lost dogs" in a flood of amateurs whose paper presentations were poor.[7] Carroll did not agree with Asbury's unkind evaluation of nonprofessionals, but he realized that Asbury did represent an important undercurrent

of opinion. Overt efforts at recruitment ceased, but the Association grew
in membership during Carroll's
tenure. He had noted in 1943 that there
were 1,095 members. By 1953 he had
1,863 on the rolls. Growth then slowed,
but Carroll estimated there were about
2,500 when he retired.

Carroll did not share Asbury's concern about being inundated at the
annual meetings. In fact, quite the
opposite became the problem. Attendance averaged about 10 percent of
membership, except in 1950 when
some five hundred people came to the
dedication of the Barker Texas History
Center. Without exception, the annual
meetings during Carroll's tenure convened in late April or early May, at
Austin. Carroll abandoned Webb's
practice of holding regional gatherings
in other cities, explaining to all who
asked that "tradition" and "accessibil-
ity" dictated the Austin site. Annual

Leslie Waggener Jr. outside the Barker Texas History Center,
April 27, 1950. *Courtesy Eugene C. Barker Papers, DI 02578,
CAH.*

meetings also remained restricted to two days, with about a dozen papers presented consecutively so that no one had to choose among competing topics.
Those who attended Carroll's gatherings soon learned that the focus was on a
small core of supporters, both lay and professional, who came each year.
Among the faithful were colorful personalities such as Margaret B. Bier-
schwale, the historian and librarian who reportedly hired air-conditioned
ambulances to convey her from Mason to the Driskill Hotel so she would
arrive rested and looking her best.

The auction begun by Webb remained the highlight of every meeting.
Crusty Houston book-dealer Herbert Fletcher described the event as a
"miniature stock exchange during a panic." As a prominent member of the
Association well known for his cynical views on almost everything, Fletcher
took great glee in noting how J. Evetts Haley snatched every book offered on
cowboys and cattle, while "Earl Vandale of Amarillo (who has everything any-
way) sits back benignly paying much too high prices because he likes a particular author."[8] Volunteer auctioneers, most of them scholars or collectors who

Clockwise above. Evetts Haley lends the authentic Texas touch to the occasion while Herbert Gambrell and Roy Bedichek, fresh from their luncheon confessions on "How-I-Wrote-a-Book," survey the standing-room-only crowd. Lou Kemp peers under his spectacles at the item offered opposite. Bookseller Heartmann is one among the many "in the trade" that keeps a professional eye on the prices reached. On the facing page in the same order, auctioneer Timmons pushes sales against the five-fifteen deadline while Bailey Carroll puffs on his stogie. Dr. Nixon stimulates the bidding on neglected items as Carl Hertzog suffers through a new design problem as his old products sell at a premium. Herbert Davenport stays on following his pre-auction talk to enjoy the sport.

The Auction

"Far and away the most important event of any year to a book collector is the book auction at the annual meeting of the Texas State Historical Association. Five-hundred-odd books are disposed of in two or three hours of a relay of raucous and merciless auctioneers. . . . All window shopping is done before the auction starts, but once the decks are cleared, coats are discarded, sleeves rolled up and no holds are barred.

". . . . Half of the bidders are standing, waving their arms, mopping their domes; the auctioneer's runners pursue the successful voice to its origin as fast as bids are closed. Husbands bid against their wives and dealers against their own stooges. A prominent clergyman bid against a voice on the other side of the room only to find that it was his own book seller trying to buy the item for the clergyman himself. (All this time an eightsome of dealers sits around with a sort of stymied look.)

"Long before and after the carnage the collectors huddle together to gloat over their acquisitions and to compare notes on the technique of outsmarting the book dealer. Whoever said the worm had turned certainly referred to the bookworm. No bookseller could have a chance in the collectors' chosen fields of activities. . . . nor could a collection acquired for commercial purposes ever rival their personal libraries. Theirs has been the joy of a magnificent pastime and the fabulous increment in their purchases will be the least of their rewards.

"Caveat emptor, fiddlesticks! Dealers have been unhorsed so many times that most of them walk and like it."

Herbert Fletcher, "Texas Book Buyers Go Auction Mad," *SHQ*, 51 (Jan. 1948), 259–260. *Sketch by Gerry Doyle; from TSHA Files.* (For caption, see endsheets.)

were themselves interested in choice items, stalked the room, pushing prices up as best they could. Proceeds never became substantial, but the auction was popular and may well have been one of the Association's most effective recruiting tools, at least among Texana collectors.

The Junior Historians continued to be one of Carroll's primary concerns as director. Prize money provided by the Rockefeller Foundation almost tripled the number of papers submitted to the *Junior Historian*, and Carroll had to ask the University to subsidize its publication. The appearance in *Time* of a short laudatory article about the Junior Historians increased interest inside and outside the state, and by 1951 an award fund, established to honor Leslie Waggener Jr., had replaced the Rockefeller money. Ten years later, there were 1,603 subscribers in more than 150 Texas chapters. More than twice as many students as adults attended the TSHA annual meetings. Carroll's Junior Historians remained a model for similar organizations in other states, and he was asked to deliver a triumphant address about them at the annual AASLH meeting in the late summer of 1961.

A landmark survey of local and state history societies, written by Walter M. Whitehill and printed in 1962, emphasized the success of the TSHA with the Junior Historians organization. The author praised Carroll for not providing "popular history watered down for the young," but offering instead a "vehicle for printing small pieces of serious investigation carried out by students acting like adults." He added, "Professor Carroll requires high standards, is more interested in quality than quantity, and has no sympathy with the practice later developed in other states of lowering the age level to a point where fun rather than work is emphasized." Carroll continued to maintain high standards for the Junior Historians throughout his tenure as director. He wrote in 1964, "I have no direct criticism of the popular activity program, but there must be a time when one must choose between standards and numbers. Our program has gone emphatically for the almost lost art of good and factual writing."[9]

Facts also remained the focus of Carroll's work as editor of the *Quarterly*. Contributors recalled that he tolerated lapses in style but had no patience with incorrect information. Carroll exercised almost complete control over the journal's content. He retained Rudolph L. Biesele and Charles W. Hackett as associate editors, but Biesele served primarily as book review editor and Hackett rarely got very involved. When Hackett took his own life in 1951, Carroll employed Harry H. Ransom as an associate editor, and in 1957, when Biesele retired, Otis A. Singletary took his place. Ransom became the dean of the College of Arts and Sciences in 1954, and when in 1957 he became a vice-president for the University of Texas, Chester V. Kielman became the last associate editor to work with Carroll; after 1960 the title was no longer listed in the

CARROLL AND THE JUNIOR HISTORIANS

"**P**erhaps the objects of his greatest pride were the Junior Historians. Having been charged by Dr. Webb in 1940 to organize Junior Historian chapters in the public schools, he presided at the metamorphosis of an idea, saw it take root, grow, then flower into a purposeful organization of young students that soon became a living part of the Association. He edited the *Junior Historian*, a pioneering historical magazine published by and for young students. Always when possible he attended the Saturday luncheon of the Junior Historians' annual meeting . . ., his reward for the encounter being a 'fresh stimulating injection of hope for the assured future of Texas history'."

George P. Isbell, "Dr. H. Bailey Carroll, 1903–1966," *SHQ*, 70 (July 1966), 3.

FORMER JUNIOR HISTORIAN WRITES TO LLERENA FRIEND, SPONSOR AT WICHITA FALLS:

September 6, 1945

Dear Miss Friend,

I was a student of yours in the fall of '39 and spring of '40. I recall your interest in Texas history. How is the local chapter of the Texas State Historical Association progressing? I thought perhaps you would like to know that the Lone Star Flag was hoisted in Tokyo.

Our detachment of marines, from the USS San Jacinto, were in the first wave ashore in the Tokyo area. Coming from the "San Jac," they naturally had a Texas flag with them. In fact, "Zeke," one of the marine sergeants, had been carrying the flag for a long time with the avowed purpose of planting it in Tokyo. No, sorry to disappoint you, "Zeke" is not a Texan. He is from Tennessee.

As soon as the "San Jac" marines were atop the seawall at the Yokosuka Naval Base, which was in their assigned area, "Zeke" looked about for something suitable for a flag pole. Spying a Jap flag pole not far away in a gun emplacement, he sent for it and had it secured in a hole on top of the cement wall.

The bottom of the Jap flag pole fitted into the hole in the cement. An instant after he had hoisted the Lone Star flag, others of our landing forces, with honors and color guard, hoisted our national ensign.

So—as far as I know, the first flag ever to be hoisted by an invading force in the Japanese homeland was the Texas flag.

The national ensign was hoisted in front of the administration building of the Yokosuka Naval Base.

Yours truly,

(Signed) Tony R. Royster

Lt. (jg) USNR

Pilot VF No. 47

"Affairs of the Association," *SHQ*, 49 (July 1945), 175.

Quarterly. This made clear what everyone already knew: the *Quarterly* belonged to Carroll, who continued to maintain an exclusive focus on Texas, with an emphasis on the nineteenth century and local history. He expanded the use of primary material in the "Notes and Documents" section, and increased the news and bibliographic notices in the "Texas Collection."

Within his strict parameters, Carroll published articles that had lasting value. Material on Spanish Texas focused on the post-1810 era, for example, an article on Bishop Marin de Porras by Nettie Lee Benson, longtime matriarch of the Latin American Collection at the University, and another, on Napoleonic exiles at Champ d'Asile, by Jack A. Dabbs. Articles on American filibusters in colonial Texas came from J. Villasana Haggard, Harry M. Henderson, Anne A. Brindley (a future TSHA president), and Henry P. "Pick" Walker. Odie B. Faulk, a prolific writer on the Southwest, found a home in the *Quarterly* for his article on early Texas. Texas scholar Andrew F. Muir, whose article on free blacks in Texas had been published by Webb, revisited the issue of land speculation in an essay printed by Carroll. Muir also produced a study of the divided sentiment in Harrisburg during the Texas Revolution. Claude Elliott (also a future TSHA president) and noted abolitionist scholar Merton L. Dillon expanded upon earlier studies of American reactions to the Texas Revolution. For the period of the Republic, Henry W. Barton wrote about military command and control, Dorman H. Winfrey discussed Mirabeau B. Lamar and Texas nationalism, and Seymour V. Connor (another future president of the TSHA, which would also publish his book on the Peters Colony), looked at county government prior to statehood.

Carroll had an abiding interest in the early statehood period of Texas history and published good articles on a variety of topics. Ralph A. Wooster wrote on the legislature and about foreigners in antebellum Texas towns. Raymond White focused on cotton ginning before the Civil War. Thomas L. Connelly, better known as a Civil War scholar, wrote about the U.S. Army's antebellum experiment with camels in Texas. Carroll chaired a committee for a national commemoration of the Butterfield Overland Mail, and he published two articles on the overland mail, one written by J. W. Williams, Council member and author of *Big Ranch Country*, and another by Chester V. Kielman and Emmie G. Mahon.

The approach of the centennial of the Civil War brought a surge in the number of articles on that era. Interestingly, the best were not on military topics. Slave insurrections, or the pervasive fear of them, served as the subject for studies by both William W. White and Wesley Norton. Earl W. Fornell discussed arguments for reopening the slave trade in Texas. Llerena B. Friend discussed the typical Texan of 1860, while Larry Jay Gage narrowed his analysis to Austin on the eve of the war. Wooster analyzed the Texas secession convention, and Stephen B. Oates discussed efforts outside the legal arena to promote disunion. Claude Elliott wrote a groundbreaking discussion of Texas Unionists, Frank H. Smyrl also wrote about Unionism and Texans in the Federal army, and Madeline B. Stern looked at abolitionist Stephen P. Andrews (and later wrote a book about him). For Reconstruction, Elliott focused on the Freedmen's Bureau, and Otis Singletary wrote about the militia. J. E. Ericson analyzed the 1875 constitutional convention, after having another piece on the Texas bill of rights published.

Carroll did not publish much on the post-Reconstruction era, but he did include some good work on post–Civil War Texas in the *Quarterly*. J. Fred Rippy wrote on British investment in Texas ranches, and Wayne T. Alford discussed the Texas Populists and Thomas L. Nugent. Wayne Gard focused on cattle trails. John Edward Weems, author of *Weekend in September*, submitted a moving account of the 1900 hurricane that devastated Galveston. Karl E. Ashburn focused on efforts to restrict cotton production during the Depression, and Charles A. Warner analyzed the oil industry during the middle decades of the twentieth century. Leila C. Wynn, whose father Edward A. Clark served as a United States ambassador and became an important figure in the Association, sent an article on the state civil courts. Of course, Carroll did not neglect railroads. Robert L. Peterson wrote about Jay Gould, Muir discussed the impact of rail development on Houston, John C. Rayburn told the story of the New York, Texas, and Mexican Railway Company, and Texas Supreme Court judge J. R. Norvell wrote an article on the Railroad Commission.

Ethnicity became a popular topic for historians after World War II, and Carroll included a few articles on that subject. The Indians of East Texas came under the scrutiny of Marvin C. Burch, and Kenneth W. Porter wrote about the Seminole scouts. Raymond Estep discussed the role played by Lorenzo de Zavala in the Texas Revolution. Ernest C. Shearer revisited clashes between Mexicans and Anglos in the so-called Merchants War of the 1850s, a topic briefly included in a few earlier studies of border disturbances. The plight of blacks in post–Civil War Comanche County was the focus of an article by Billy Bob Lightfoot, and black Republican Norris Wright Cuney became a topic for Paul Casdorph.

With the exception of the early reprints, the first book published by the TSHA—*Texas County Histories, A Bibliography* (1943)—had been compiled by Carroll. As director, Carroll maintained an interest in book publication, but unfortunately for the broad vision intended by Webb, the topic of Carroll's initial work foreshadowed the focus of his publication efforts as director. Of the twenty-one works printed by the Association from 1946 to 1966, half were local

WALL STREET AND THE *Quarterly*

"Generally speaking one might hazard the guess that there has been little connection between Wall Street, Texas history, and the *Quarterly*. Surprisingly enough though, the *Quarterly*, while recording Texas history, acted to change the Wall Street market and Texas finance. The story should justify the *Quarterly* even in banking circles.

"For many years after the War between the States Texas municipal bonds were not eligible for purchase by the savings banks of New York. These bonds were under ban because Texas was classed as a state which had repudiated debt incurred since January 1, 1861. About 1912 C. W. Whitis, formerly of Austin but then connected with a New York bond house, became interested in making the Texas bonds eligible for purchase. Whitis knew of E. T. Miller's work on the financial history of Texas. Miller had published in the *Quarterly* a short while before: 'The State Finances of Texas during the Civil War,' *Quarterly*, XIV, and 'The State Finances of Texas during Reconstruction,' *ibid*. Whitis asked for the facts (the history) of Texas' record. The Attorney-General of New York had to be convinced. The result was Dr. Miller's 'Repudiation of State Debt in Texas since 1861,' published in the *Quarterly*, XVI (October 1912). Attorney-General Carmody was convinced that Texas was not guilty of repudiation, other than that made mandatory by the Fourteenth Amendment. The ban was lifted on Texas municipal bonds. Thus did Dr. Miller and sound historical research serve the banking and financial circles of both Texas and New York."

H. Bailey Carroll, "Texas Collection," *SHQ*, 49 (Oct. 1945), 299–300.

histories, bibliographic guides, or *Quarterly* indexes. The guides included four books in a county history series begun in 1949 (Collin, Coryell, Falls, and Young Counties). Of the remainder, few of the books discussed their subjects in a national context. One that did so was Barker's biography of Stephen F. Austin (which won the inaugural Summerfield G. Roberts Award from the Sons of the Republic of Texas), but it was a reprint.

Part of the reason for Carroll's restricted focus lay in his insistence that books be subsidized. Printing costs had to be at least partially paid by family members of the subjects or by others who had an interest. If no one provided a subsidy, then a book was not printed. Texans with money were often interested primarily in the history of Texas places and Texas people—so that was what Carroll published with their donations. Good examples were the history of Post City, by Charles Dudley Eaves and C. A. Hutchinson, and a biography of Robert A. Williamson written by Duncan W. Robinson. Carroll's search for subsidies was supplemented by Leslie Waggener's efforts to raise publication funds. This allowed the production of significant works on Manuel de Mier y Teran by Ohland Morton (after Morton's 1929 dissertation on Mier y Teran, directed by Barker, had appeared in eight *Quarterly* installments); migration into East Texas by Barnes Lathrop (a Charles W. Ramsdell student who joined the University of Texas faculty); and the Peters Colony by Seymour Connor (a Webb student who taught at Texas Tech).

The largest subsidies naturally went to the *Handbook of Texas*. Llerena B. Friend, who left the project near its end to serve as librarian for the Barker Texas History Center, and Mary Joe Carroll, who was simultaneously working on her law degree at the University of Texas, oversaw the dedicated work of graduate students, TSHA staff, and outside writers. By 1951 it was clear that the *Handbook* would actually be completed, sparking a flurry of last-minute worries. A committee created to assist in the distribution of the volumes suggested a name change, to "Treasury of Texas." The Executive Council quashed that idea, but approved a motion to bind only one-third of the three thousand printed copies. After all, they thought, the hefty two-volume set, which contained 15,986 articles in 1,930 double-columned pages, might not sell.

The Council need not have worried. The volumes appeared in December 1952, and within four months the initial run was almost completely sold out, necessitating the printing of another three thousand. Carroll was delighted to have the work finished and wrote to his old friend, Hally B. Perry, "We join with you in saying, 'Glory be, it is out'." Perry, founder of the Daughters of the Republic of Texas and charter member of the Association, joined with many others in an almost universal chorus of high praise. Her comment was sweet in its simplicity: "It charms me in many ways." The AASLH chose the *Handbook* as the outstanding publication in its field for 1953. Sales continued, generating a significant income for the TSHA for many years. Asked in 1964 whether discounts could be given, Carroll grumbled, "The Association ought not to operate like a community grocery store putting on sales items, cutting prices, and doing other things not in harmony with its dignified character." He would certainly not kill a goose that laid golden eggs. Six years later, Walter M. Whitehill wrote that the *Handbook* remained the "best systematic work of reference on any of the fifty United States," echoing the praise conveyed by those who conducted a symposium on local history at Yale University.[10]

The *Handbook of Texas* became the top money-maker for Carroll, but by 1964 a true dark horse, *The Great Hanging at Gainesville*, ranked second in book sales. The small book was the result of two traditions that had begun in 1947, the fiftieth anniversary of the Association. First, printed annual meeting

Webb and Carroll look at the *Handbook of Texas*, launched during Webb's directorship and published, in 1952, during Carroll's.

programs henceforth would have an image of two lanterns, symbolic of the pair provided by a janitor during the 1897 meeting, when the lights in the Capitol went off. Second, it became traditional that printed programs would contain a primary document, an idea initially tried by Webb in 1941 but suspended after World War II squeezed his budget. These reproductions were usually only a page or two in length, but in 1961 the Association printed the entire pamphlet on the October 1862 hanging at Gainesville. Written by Thomas Barrett, a participant, there were only three known copies of the original. Cooper K. Ragan, a lawyer and avid historian of the Civil War in Texas who later served as president of the Association, brought the tract to Carroll's attention. It proved popular and the Association quickly provided reprints of the thin booklet, which became a best seller.

Just as the *Handbook* was truly a joint legacy of Bailey Carroll and Walter Webb, they rightfully shared credit for the completion of another project: the

Handbook of Texas

If the *Southwestern Historical Quarterly* is the heart of the Texas State Historical Association, the *Handbook of Texas*, in both its incarnations, old and new, can be said to be its soul, embodying as it does the capacity to dream and plan and organize a massive research, writing, and publication endeavor that spans years and even decades in its execution, bringing together hundreds of scholars, writers, editors, administrative staff, and financial sponsors in the undertaking. That the Association has accomplished not one, not two, but three such feats is a remarkable testament to the central role it has played in the Texas history community.

The first mention of what would become the *Handbook of Texas* came in 1932 in a proposal by the Association to the Centennial Executive Committee, suggesting the preparation and publication of a biographical dictionary of Texas. Seven years later, in the "Texas Collection" of the July 1939 *SHQ*, Walter Prescott Webb first used the name "Handbook of Texas." A year after that, the first published announcement of the *Handbook* project was made in an editorial by Webb in the *Dallas Morning News* of November 10, 1940: "As yet the Handbook of Texas is but an idea, known only to me and to a few members of the Texas State Historical Association.... if it does materialize, it will be in my opinion one of the most important books that has ever come out of Texas." It took another five years before the first step toward a comprehensive encyclopedia of Texas was accomplished in the compilation and publication of *A Tentative List of Subjects for the Handbook of Texas*. Then followed seven years of concentrated effort on the part of scholars to contribute articles in their special fields. C. W. Hackett and C. E. Castañeda wrote or checked most of the articles on the Spanish period; Eugene Barker wrote the articles on colonization and furnished the material for much of the Mexican period; Claude Elliott and Ralph Steen prepared topics relating to the Civil War and statehood; Fred Cotten covered much of the material relating to Weatherford and North Central Texas; Pat I. Nixon wrote the article on med-

Eugene C. Barker Texas History Center. Refurbishing the beautiful Old Library Building, designed by Cass Gilbert and built in 1910, resolved several problems. Texas manuscripts and books were spilling from the vault and shelves in the Main Building, while Carroll maintained offices in both Garrison Hall, home of the Department of History, and B Hall, a former dormitory that had been converted into administrative quarters. The Barker Center officially opened with a gala dedication during the annual meeting of the Association in April 1950. Barker and his family graciously endured a large crowd of

ical history. The University of Texas developed student and staff writers through a course in historical writing and editing. Professional and fraternal organizations and local historical groups made contributions of writers and archives. And, in the end, as Webb had prophesied so many years before, the completed *Handbook*, published in 1952 during Carroll's directorship, was truly "the product of the combined literary genius and scholarly ability of the people of Texas.... written by the people of Texas [as the] most adequate representation of the state yet made in book form."

The *Handbook* endeavor also represents the spirit in which the TSHA and the University have worked together over the course of a century. The University, in addition to providing supplies and housing, also made funds available for paying authors for their work in writing articles and for paying the salaries of those doing part-time or full-time editorial work on the project.

The first two volumes required twelve years of work; a third, supplemental volume (published in 1976) required another dozen years, under the editorship of Eldon Branda and while Joe Frantz was director. Later, the *New Handbook of Texas* would take thirteen years in preparation, started under the direction of Tuffly Ellis and finished during Ron Tyler's tenure as director.

H. Bailey Carroll, "Texas Collection," *SHQ*, 56 (July 1952), 121–125 (quotations); Joe B. Frantz, "Introduction," in Eldon Stephen Branda (ed.), *Handbook of Texas*, III (1976), vii–viii.

The original *Handbook of Texas*, published in 1952, came in two volumes. The jacket illustration was the same on both; the volume one jacket was blue, volume two was orange. The book cloth itself was a soft slate blue with gold lettering and a Republic of Texas seal stamped in gold on the front. Volume three matched in cloth cover and design; its jacket, still with the same illustration, was aqua. *From TSHA Files.*

visitors and a long program of speeches. The highlight came when Herbert P. Gambrell, who had earned his doctorate degree under Barker, spoke. Noting how Garrison Hall and the Barker Center flanked the southern approach to the Main Building, Gambrell declared, "Garrison and Barker henceforth stand guard over the approaches to the heart and center of this University of Texas."[11]

The Barker Center provided fine quarters for the existing Texana collections of the University and room for growth as well. When it opened, the cen-

B Hall (1890–1952)

Colonel George W. Brackenridge donated money for the building that was to become legend, after hearing it said that the University of Texas was a school for rich men's sons. Brackenridge, on the Board of Regents at the time, decided to provide low-cost housing for University boys. In keeping with his desire for anonymity, the dormitory was officially named University Hall. The secret was never kept, the official name didn't last, and B Hall, for Brackenridge Hall, became the name for history.

The building, the first dormitory on the Forty Acres, was a three-story rectangular structure when it was built; two wings and a fourth story were added in 1899–1900. It ran north and south on what is now the East Mall stairs; rent was $2.50 a month, board was ten dollars a month.

What makes B Hall live on in legend are the B Hallers, the boys who in those days practically ran the University, effecting most changes in student life and activities. One of the B Hallers was the Association's own Lester Bugbee, the same who, with Garrison, made a "well-matched team pulling ahead with a single mind." Bugbee, secretary-treasurer of the TSHA in its early years under Garrison, lived in B Hall while he lectured in the history department. John A. Lomax wrote of this time: "Bugbee proposed that he and I move back (we had both lived there) to B Hall and try to work out a solution [to debt and riotous conduct]. . . . Bugbee's plan was simple: the B-Hallites in mass meeting elected at his suggestion a president and two men from each floor as an Executive Committee. . . . When a student threw a biscuit across the table, out of the hall he went. . . . Bugbee and I volunteered to pay all the business side of the proposition. . . . We hired and fired the servants, bought the groceries, and made regular financial reports to the B Hall Committee. 'The rest is up to you,' Bugbee said. 'It's your home and you are absolute bosses.' . . . Bugbee's plan worked from the start. . . . We paid our bills promptly and soon began to whittle down the deficit. On our first Thanksgiving we served as the piéce de résistance steaks from a huge deer weighing nearly two

ter held over twenty-five hundred manuscript files and about forty-five thousand books and pamphlets, along with thousands of pages of transcriptions of primary materials. The walls of the north end of the James S. Hogg Reading Room displayed the University's collection of Southwestern paintings by Dallas artist Frank Reaugh. Opening the Barker Center also provided the TSHA with a proper showcase for the Texana collection of Earl Vandale, which had been purchased at the request of University of Texas librarian Donald Coney. Vandale served as president of the Association from 1949 to 1951, and Carroll and Barker had been instrumental in persuading him to sell his collection to

This photograph of B Hall was taken in the 1930s and looks as it did during the time H. Bailey Carroll had an office there. *Courtesy Prints and Photographs Collection, DI 02606, CAH.*

hundred pounds. . . . In looking back I know now that over and over again Bugbee's sound judgment, his knowledge of human nature, his patient and persistent insistence that young men may be led but not driven, saved the B Hall experiment from disaster."

During the 1925/1926 schoolyear, B Hall closed as a dormitory and was converted to offices. In 1952 the building was razed.

"History of the Residence Halls," http://www.utexas.edu/student/housing/index; accessed Sept. 5, 2006 (1st quotation); Bride Neill Taylor, "The Beginnings of the State Historical Association," *SHQ,* 33 (July 1929), 13 (2nd quotation); John A. Lomax, "Lester Gladstone Bugbee," *SHQ,* 49 (July 1945), 33–35 (3rd quotation).

the University. The collection was the largest in the state, with more than eight thousand items, many of them rare, in four languages. Vandale had finally agreed to a sale, and the University paid him $100,000. This was an unprecedented amount of money, but Herbert Fletcher expressed the opinion of many when he said, "The acquisition by the Texas History Center of a collection like Earl Vandale's increased the value of every book already there and every book in every collection in the state. And I think it was worth about twice the amount Earl got for it."[12]

Vandale and his wife, Vada, continued to collect after the sale, and their son

Cass Gilbert and
the Old Library Building

"In this building there was a complete break with the past. During the first twenty-five years the University had been a small college, easily accommodated in a few buildings, each of which had been located without reference to plans for other buildings in the future. Between 1906 and 1910, the Board of Regents, with advice and counsel from the Faculty, attacked the problem of a future program for the location and the architecture of new buildings....There emerged in the Library Building, the cornerstone of which was laid in 1910, a structure which should stand centuries instead of years and which is a model for simplicity, convenience, and attractiveness."

Cass Gilbert's Library Building was the first separate library building on the University of Texas campus. The first library was in a room on the top floor of the Old Main Building. It was moved twice, in 1885 and 1897, and by 1903 had a regional reputation as the largest library in Texas. It was in that year, 1903, that Phineas L. Windsor became librarian. Windsor and the University administration were in accord in their devotion to the library's collection of both books and archives, and by the time Windsor's tenure came to an end in 1909, the size of the collection was such that the need for a separate building to house it was compelling.

In conceiving the new Library Building, the Board of Regents visualized it as the cornerstone and first building in a master plan for the expansion of the campus. The expansion was "to be on the grand scale, and this jewel—the Library

The library under construction, October 15, 1910. *Courtesy Prints and Photographs Collection, DI 02572, CAH.*

Barker Texas History Center, 1969 (foreground). The TSHA offices were in this building from 1950 to 1971. *From TSHA Files.*

Building, which was to be the first unit constructed of the plan—was to set the pattern of its quality." The regents wanted as architect "some recognized master in the cosmopolitan sphere, upon whom there could be no cavil, and in consequence no possible cavil upon themselves."

Cass Gilbert was selected as the University Architect in January 1910, and his preliminary design for the Library Building was accepted. Gilbert was fifty years old, a product of the School of Architecture at MIT; his major buildings would include the state capitols of Minnesota, West Virginia, and Arkansas; the St. Louis Art Museum; the New York Customs House; the United States Supreme Court Building; and the Woolworth Building in New York.

The Old Library Building and Cass Gilbert's master plan established the Spanish Mediterranean character of the University campus. In 1973 the building was renamed for William James Battle, professor of classical languages and president ad interim of the University, 1914–1916.

August Watkins Harris, "Cass Gilbert's Old Library Building: The Eugene C. Barker Texas History Center, 1910–1960," *SHQ*, 64 (July 1960), 5 (2nd–3rd quotations), 11 (1st quotation, quoting Dr. W. M. W. Splawn); "History of the University of Texas Libraries," http://.lib. utexas.edu/vprovost/history.html, (accessed Sept. 17, 2006); Jean Villeau, "Cass Gilbert," Cass Gilbert Society Web site, http://www.cassgilbertsociety.org/bio.htm (accessed Sept. 17, 2006).

John gave their later acquisitions, which totaled yet another five thousand items, to the Barker Center after their deaths, adding greatly to the immense value of the accession. In gratitude, the Executive Council, at the request of Carroll, appointed John Vandale as an Honorary Life Member of the Association, and Governor Price Daniel honored him with a commission as an admiral in the Texas Navy. The Vandale materials were certainly not the only vital additions to the Barker Center during Carroll's tenure. Items ranged from the papers of University supporters such as Leslie Waggener Jr. to the personal effects and correspondence of Texas political leaders like Andrew J. Hamilton. Dora D. Bonham funded the production of a guide to the archives, which was completed by Chester V. Kielman in 1967. Keilman, the director of the Barker Center, had been Carroll's associate editor for the *Quarterly*.

Bailey Carroll, when he had first learned of plans to renovate the Old Library rather than build a new home for the Association, had grumbled to Pat I. Nixon, "I suppose we ought to feel that a half loaf is better than no loaf at all."[13] After moving in, however, he became fiercely proud of his quarters and very protective. In 1959 he sounded the alarm that his "corner forever Texas," as J. Frank Dobie had poetically requested twenty years earlier, was in danger of invasion. Portions of the building intended for use by the Association had never been finished, and other portions were to be relegated to faculty offices for the English Department. Carroll joined with others in writing to University of Texas president Harry Huntt Ransom. Edward A. Clark, then a prominent attorney for whom Mary Joe Carroll worked, chaired an ad hoc committee for the cause, and Ransom's sympathy lay with the historians. Unfortunately for them, however, the University desperately needed space. The issue of who should be housed in the Barker Center was never resolved while Carroll was director.[14]

Carroll enjoyed more success, two years later, in what many Texans referred to as the "Second Archive War." The Texas state archives in 1956 had been unceremoniously dumped into a metal building on the outskirts of Austin. There the precious records had neither modern fire protection nor climate controls. The outcry against this move quickly swelled, and Carroll joined in. With strong support from Governor Price Daniel, a new archive building, with all the modern conveniences, opened in the summer of 1961 near the Capitol. To further enhance this victory for the Association and Carroll, the formal dedication in April 1962 was presided over by Dorman Winfrey, the new director for the Texas State Library. Winfrey had been a Junior Historian during Webb's term as director, had worked for Carroll while completing several degrees at the University, and had served as an archivist for both the State Library and the Barker Center.

TSHA Quarters, 1950–1971:
The Old Library Building

"Whereas, the Texas State Historical Association—to which Dr. Barker gave twenty-seven years of great and gratuitous editorship and leadership—stands as the officially recognized, active, and loyal liaison between this institution and the people of Texas ..., therefore, Be it Resolved by the Board of Regents of the University of Texas That Offices 101–105 inclusive, the document vault in connection with Room 102, and Room 107, of the Old Library Building, be immediately provided for The Texas State Historical Association, and its manifold activities—The Southwestern Historical Quarterly, The Texas Handbook, The Junior Historian, and its related research—and that said Association, with Professor H. B. Carroll, its director, be moved at once from its congested quarters in Garrison Hall and B Hall into these rooms ..."

Understanding that the regents appreciated the stand Eugene Barker had taken during the Rainey controversy, J. Evetts Haley lobbied the board to move the Texas history collections to the Old Library Building and to name it in honor of Barker. The above resolution was introduced in a motion by Judge D. F. Strickland and seconded by Orville Bullington.

Resolution of the Board of Regents, the University of Texas, September 20–21 (quotation), 1946, typescript, enclosed with Betty Ann Thedford to H. B. Carroll, n.d., TSHA Records, CAH; Don E. Carleton and Katherine J. Adams, "'A Work Peculiarly Our Own,' ..." SHQ, 86 (Oct. 1982), 198, 222–230.

The Executive Council of
The Texas State Historical Association
requests the pleasure of your company
at the formal opening of the
Eugene C. Barker Texas History Center
The University of Texas
at a tea and open house
on Thursday afternoon, the twenty-seventh of April
at 3 o'clock
and at a dinner at 7:30 o'clock
at the Stephen F. Austin Hotel
Austin, Texas

R.s.v.p.
Box 2131 University Station
Austin, Texas

Invitation to the opening of the Barker Texas History Center. *Courtesy of Subject Vertical Files DI 02590, CAH.*

Examining arriving documents at the new Barker Texas History Center, 1949. Left to right, University librarian Alexander Moffit, Robert B. Wilkes, Association director H. Bailey Carroll, and O. S. Franks. *From TSHA Files.*

There followed in the *Quarterly* a build-up of pride in the new quarters and anticipation for the move:

"The new home of Texas history, the Eugene C. Barker Texas History Center, on the campus of the University of Texas, is moving toward completion. Recent renovation has produced a new marble staircase in the Old Library Building. New partitioning has been carried out and the heating and lighting system has been redone. Beautiful new flooring is being laid." *SHQ,* 52 (Apr. 1949), 354.

"As this copy of the *Quarterly* goes to the printers early in October, the furniture is being uncrated for the Association's new offices in the reconditioned Old Library Building . . ." Ibid., 53 (Jan. 1950), 320.

"On January 19, 1950, the Association offices were moved from Garrison Hall to new quarters in the Eugene C. Barker Texas History Center. . . . .[T]he Association has been allotted an excellent suite of offices on the main floor. A few days later Dr. Barker moved into his new quarters also on the main floor of the building." Ibid., 53 (Apr. 1950), 474.

The building was officially opened on April 27, 1950. Eugene Barker was guest of honor at the ceremonies and gave a speech in which, as was his wont, he denigrated his own contributions and lavished praise on others: "I am gratified by these ceremonies, and grateful beyond expression to the many friends who have wished to honor me. In a sense, you have invested my name with immortality. You have linked it with an institution and a subject which we still expect to be perpetual.... Contrary to what you have heard or may infer, I can claim no unique agency in building the Texas history collections; I can hardly claim any distinction but that of having seen them grow from almost nothing to their present importance and value."

Barker spoke at length, thanking everyone from George Garrison and Lester Bugbee, who brought the Bexar Archives and the Austin Papers to the University; to Guy M. Bryan, owner of the Austin Papers; Hally Bryan Perry, Guy's daughter, who was instrumental in giving the papers to the University; E. W. Winkler, whose tenure as University librarian (1923–1924) saw an enormous increase in archival holdings; Mattie Austin Hatcher, Winnie Allen, and Marcelle Hamer, who as University archivists successively managed the Texas collections; George Brackenridge and George Littlefield, who gave so generously in the cause of collecting Texas materials; J. Frank Dobie, whose pamphlet *A Corner Forever Texas* was an early and eloquent plea for a building to house the Texas materials; members of the Board of Regents that passed the resolution creating the Barker Texas History Center; and the faculty committee that worked for five and a half years planning and preparing the building and its opening ceremonies.

Barker's list of those to be thanked gives a telescoped view of the development of a modern history department at the University, from its beginnings in the professionalization of historical research and the concern for the preservation of the primary documents of history, to the emphasis on collection, the money sought for this purpose, and the archiving of historical materials. Inherent in all is the development and growing importance of the University's natural ally in preservation and research, the Texas State Historical Association.

Eugene C. Barker, "To Whom Credit is Due," *SHQ*, 54 (July 1950), 6 (quotation), 7–12.

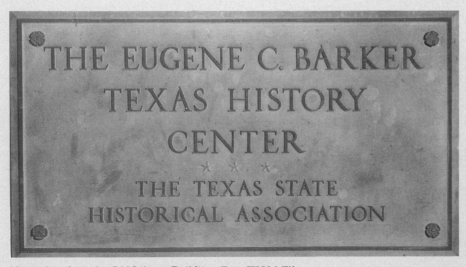

Nameplate from the Old Library Building. *From TSHA Files.*

ON AMATEUR HISTORIANS

"[M]any of our finest and most worth-while members are, both by their seriousness of purpose and native ability, amateur historians in the finest sense of the term. There are amateur historians by the score who can, and do, instruct the professionals. The strength of the Association is in its core of amateur historians who, since 1897, have always been at the very heart of the Association."

H. Bailey Carroll, "Texas Collection," *SHQ*, 48 (Jan. 1945), 407.

Carroll could also claim credit for winning the lengthy fight to place markers at important historical sites in Texas. In 1944 he began pressing for an effective historical marker program, suggesting that it be undertaken jointly by the Association and the Texas Highway Department. The Texas State Library and Historical Commission, founded in 1909 with Garrison as its first chair, had originally been responsible for markers, but in 1923 this responsibility had passed to the Texas Historical Board. The board and the Highway Department did place signs during the state centennial in 1936, prodded by activists such as erstwhile Association president Louis W. Kemp, but Carroll's demands for more brought little response, and the board disbanded in 1951. Its successor, the Texas State Historical Survey Committee, became Carroll's next target, and he peppered both newspaper editors and TSHA members with pleas for action. Finally, in 1962 the Survey Committee initiated a systematic effort to place markers at historically significant sites throughout Texas, a program that expanded even further after the committee became the Texas Historical Commission in 1973.

Carroll was successful as director of the Association, but not everyone agreed with him, especially Walter F. McCaleb. The second person ever to earn a master's degree in history at the University of Texas, McCaleb had guided George P. Garrison to the Bexar Archives, the source on which McCaleb had based his thesis, written for Lester G. Bugbee. McCaleb left Texas to work in banking, but he corresponded with Garrison, Bugbee, and Barker. When he retired, he returned to Texas and the TSHA. Walter Webb welcomed him and successfully urged that he be appointed an Honorary Life Member. Tempers soured when McCaleb began giving unwanted advice to Carroll on Association funds, telling him to diversify the organization's investments. McCaleb also had strong opinions on the *Handbook of Texas*. Finally, when McCaleb submitted a book manuscript to the Association for publication and it was rejected, the schism between him and Bailey Carroll became obvious.

Carroll in 1952 appealed to Herbert Gambrell for advice on what to do with McCaleb. Gambrell replied, "If you've got a wart-some member, give him something to keep him busy—outside your office, not in it." Carroll decided, unwisely as it turned out, to "confer" upon "Brother McCaleb" the "high office of chief investigator of accounts." In effect, McCaleb became a one-man committee to investigate the "possibility" of getting interest from the Association's checking accounts. McCaleb instead renewed his insistence that Carroll sell his beloved Treasury bonds. The breaking point came at the 1953 business meeting, where Carroll and Gambrell publicly ignored McCaleb's recommendations. Other members of the Executive Council laughed at McCaleb. For the former banker and proud protégé of Garrison, this meant war.[15]

Carroll should have read an interview with McCaleb that appeared in the May 1920 issue of *Alcalde*, the University of Texas magazine for former students. McCaleb had bragged, "There's nothing I like better than to get into a meeting and raise cain with [parliamentary procedure]." His wife had commented, "You like anything you can raise a row with." After the fateful business meeting, McCaleb sent a flurry of letters, demanding to see all Association records and accusing Carroll of ignoring the organization's constitution and by-laws. When McCaleb told UT president Logan R. Wilson that Carroll was secretive and incompetent, Wilson arranged a meeting between McCaleb and a delegation from the Association: Bailey Carroll, Coral Tullis, Walter Webb, Eugene Barker, Claude Elliott, Pat Nixon, and James Taylor. The gathering was hardly cordial, but Carroll agreed to surrender all records to McCaleb and to revise the Association's constitution. McCaleb wouldn't quit. He told the Executive Council that the records were "confused." He then accused Carroll of filling the *Quarterly* "with a reportorial melange of trivia," committing nepotism by hiring Mary Joe Carroll with Rockefeller Foundation funds, and excluding the Executive Council from important decisions.[16]

Some members of the Association sided with McCaleb, but more joined

"**M**embers of the Association . . . are hereby notified and reminded of a current widespread practice and recent innovation in the state of Texas: namely, the sales tax. . . . Full cooperation will be much appreciated, especially by Mrs. Tullis who has had the multiple problems of the sales tax dropped upon her careful accounting customs and procedures."

H. Bailey Carroll, "Texas Collection," *SHQ*, 66 (July 1962), 173.

MEMBERS

Dorman H. Winfrey, a Fellow and past president (1971–1972) of the Association, was first active in the TSHA as a Junior Historian member from Henderson, Texas. After high school he joined the army and fought in WWII. In 1946 he came to the University of Texas and worked for the TSHA until 1958, while he earned his bachelor's and master's degrees. He was the Texas State Archivist (1958–1960) and University Archivist (1960–1961). In 1962 he earned his Ph.D. and began his long tenure as director of the Texas State Library, from which he retired in 1986. It was Winfrey's idea to do a special issue of the *Quarterly* on the 100th anniversaries of the births of J. Frank Dobie and Walter Prescott Webb. He also suggested the facsimile reprint of John Cassin's 1856 *Illustrations of the Birds of California, Texas, Oregon, British and Russian America*, which the TSHA published in 1987.

In its long history the Association has profited greatly from members who are active in the organization's programs over the course of many decades. Dorman Winfrey stands as a prime example of one such member. Like links in a chain, Dorman's long tenure with the Association can be traced in the Collection sections of past issues of the *Southwestern Historical Quarterly*.

We first hear of Dorman Winfrey in 1943 when he won the Junior Historian Writing Contest for his article "General Webster Flanagan." Then, in 1944, Bailey Carroll writes in the Collection, "At present he is serving in the armed forces, but in July a check for fifty dollars arrived at his Henderson home. This was from Colonel Jim Flanagan, nephew of General Flanagan, and was in appreciation of *The Junior Historian* article."

We next hear from Winfrey in January 1945, from "Somewhere in France": "I am just wondering what the Junior Historians have on program for 1945 and whether the annual Texas State Historical Association and Junior Historian Meeting will be held. I am often reminded of the grand time our chapter had at the annual meetings, and we still consider ourselves Junior Historians at heart. Of all the pleasant high school memories, the time spent with the Junior Historian activities tops the list. My friends and I have agreed on this time and time again. Most of our group still plan to carry on the study of our county and state after the war. It is one of the things we have to look forward to when the war is won. I should be glad to receive any information on the work of the Junior Historians and the Historical Association. Also, what plans have been made for the publication of the Texas *Handbook*?"

Winfrey and Carroll corresponded throughout the war, with Carroll encouraging Winfrey to become a historian: "The way is open right here on to a Ph.D." On Labor Day weekend, 1946, Winfrey, home from the war, began working for the TSHA, in the basement of Garrison Hall where he wrapped books for sixty cents an hour. In 1948 Walter Webb writes in the Collection, "The cheerful Dorman

Winfrey is the general factotum who does about everything any of the others [on the TSHA staff] asks him to do, does it cheerfully and well." Winfrey continued working for the TSHA until 1958, and in the words of Joe Frantz "*was* the Association," where he divided his time equally between the *Quarterly*, the *Handbook*, and the Junior Historian Program, while at the same time studying for his B.A. and M.A. in history.

In 1961 Carroll writes that Winfrey has been appointed by President Harry Ransom to be university archivist; the next year we hear from Carroll that Winfrey has accepted the position of director-librarian of the Texas State Library, a position Winfrey held for the next twenty-five years.

Over the decades Winfrey and his wife Ruth Carolyn have remained involved in the Associa-

"I think you are the most promising youngster for the historical field I have encountered," Bailey Carroll wrote Winfrey during the war, "Write me when you get out of the Army." *Photograph from TSHA Files.*

tion's Junior Historian Program, anonymously giving awards in the names of some of their good friends. In 1990 the Association established the Dorman H. and Ruth Carolyn Winfrey Junior Historian Award, given annually since that time to a Junior Historian chapter sponsor for his or her work in teaching and inspiring students in the research and writing of Texas history. In announcing the award Ron Tyler wrote: "Few people can look back on fifty years with the TSHA, but in 1990 a man well known to us began his sixth decade as an active and valued member of the Association. When Dorman H. Winfrey joined the Henderson chapter of the Association's Junior Historian program in 1940—the year after it was founded by Walter Prescott Webb—little did he suspect that he was beginning a fifty-year relationship."

H. Bailey Carroll "Texas Collection," *SHQ*, 48 (Oct. 1944), 280–281; ibid., 48 (Apr. 1945), 572–573; Walter Prescott Webb, "Texas Collection," *SHQ*, 51 (Jan. 1948), 259; Carroll, "Texas Collection," *SHQ*, 64 (Jan. 1961), 400–401; ibid., 65 (Apr. 1962), 575–576; Ron Tyler, "South-western Collection," *SHQ*, 94 (Oct. 1990), 315–316.

MEMBERS

"George [Isbell] was a fixture at annual meetings of the Texas State Historical Association, where he directed the book auction for a quarter century. I assumed that responsibility for a decade beginning in the late 1960s. When he was nearly eighty, George was elected Association president, a reward that he richly deserved. He was as fine a man as I ever knew—warm, gracious, caring, the personification of decency. I remember being surprised by him once. It was in the early seventies, and I was driving to the TSHA annual meeting in Austin. Somewhere between Kyle and Buda I saw, in my rearview mirror, a green Chevy (I think) gaining on me with ease. I could make out an older driver wearing a suit, glasses, and dress hat. I was going the limit, which then was seventy. The car swung left to pass me, and when it did I cast a quick glance at the driver. It was George, by jove! He had never seemed quite the type to hold a heavy foot on the accelerator. But why shouldn't an octogenarian do eighty?"

Al Lowman, "Life and Death of a Bookstore," *SHQ*, 91 (Oct. 1987), 176–177. George Isbell was president of the Association for the year 1964–1965.

with Carroll. Evetts Haley, who had already had sharp disagreements with both Carroll and Webb, agreed that Carroll had made the organization a "one man affair" by filling the Council with "close friends" who were of "doubtful historical standing and scholarship." Herbert Fletcher had already made well known his belief that there were too many publishers of books on Texas, and so he joined the attack on Carroll's publication efforts. Many more members supported Carroll and Gambrell, who wrote to the Executive Council: "I have reluctantly come to the conclusion that Dr. McCaleb is enjoying rumpus for rumpus' sake."[17]

Carroll received strong support from an unlikely source: Walter P. Webb. They disagreed on the purpose of the Association, but neither would let McCaleb define it. Webb's letter to McCaleb struck a nerve. McCaleb, writing back, complained that though Barker approved of his accusations Webb refused to look at them. He added, "Now you come riding out on your charger—valiant and shining lance aimed at me—in defense of one you told me two or three times you were at outs with, with whom indeed you were hardly on speaking terms. Did we not discuss a possible successor in the office of director and editor?"[18] Be that as it may, Webb continued his campaign in a response to an inquiry from the Rockefeller Foundation, telling them that there had been no discrepancy in the spending of their money. He also wrote to Logan Wilson that proper changes were being made in programs. No more inquiries came from the Rockefeller Foundation, and Wilson sharply dismissed McCaleb and his controversy in a letter on May 7, 1954, the day after Webb wrote to him.

Despite Wilson's final dismissal of him, McCaleb did disrupt the close relationship between the Association and the University of Texas. The clash brought ugly charges against Carroll from others. One told Wilson that the Department of Research in Texas History had "set itself up in considerable style in the Barker Center and is reported to stand well aloof from the Department of History." The writer claimed, "Some objection has been voiced to the inaccessibility of Dr. Carroll, the Director, behind a maze of fancy offices and retarding secretaries."[19] In response, Wilson moved control of University funding for Texas research from his office to the History Department. The history faculty welcomed such a windfall, and conflict ensued as Carroll fought to retain funds for the TSHA. Relief came in 1960, when Harry Ransom, as president of the University, took charge of support for Texas research. That year Carroll received more than he had in several years, and funding continued to increase annually until he retired as director.

Carroll also had to face the challenge of integrating the Association. Since its inception, women had been welcome, and the roll contained a few Hispanic names such as charter member Adina De Zavala and University professor Carlos E. Castañeda, a prolific and respected author. Both of them became Fellows, but no one addressed the issue of admitting African Americans. The challenge became Carroll's in March 1953, when R. O'Hara Lanier, the president of Texas Southern University, wrote to ask about joining. Carroll responded truthfully, "I believe your letter raises a question in my mind which had not come up before, and I am confident there is no official rule." He claimed that his organization had accepted African Americans as members "for a number of years," but state segregation laws had kept them from attending annual meetings, which of course met at segregated hotels. He informed Lanier that he would "be quite happy" to have black members, but he could not be certain that the Executive Council would officially welcome them to annual meetings, or that white members would accept them at all.[20]

Carroll assured Lanier that he would submit the questions of African American membership and attendance at annual meetings to the Executive Council in April 1953. Lanier did not challenge his claim that the issue had not been raised earlier, or his assertion that the Association was undergoing a "period of transition" on racial issues. Instead, he politely replied, "I understand the problem mentioned in your letter of April 1, and I have no further questions to raise on this."[21] He asked to be informed of the Council's decision, but no further letter from Carroll appears in TSHA files, nor are more communications from Lanier found there. This may be because Lanier, who had many problems as the embattled first president of Texas Southern University, accomplished his purpose, which was to push the Association to address the question that was perplexing the nation. Carroll had watched from a distance as Heman M. Sweatt integrated the University of Texas Law School. He would have the first black University undergraduate, John W. Hargis, in his own class by the fall of 1955, and he would also have to confront the issue within his Association.

Carroll's suggestion to Lanier that there would probably be a "division of opinion" in the Executive Council proved to be an understatement. He wrote to the Council about Lanier's inquiry, reporting that other black schools had inquired about the same issue and explaining that hotel managers had said they would do as any organization desired. Carroll focused on the issue of attending annual meetings rather than enrollment, insisting that "For many years there have been some negro members of the Association." He concluded that while "state segregation laws or known hotel regulations kept the question [of integration] from arising" previously, "Now we have a straightforward question, and we should make a straightforward answer, difficult as it may be."[22] Rather than respond instantly, the Council created a committee. Angry members pressed Carroll to bar the door. Evetts Haley demanded a list of African American members, noting that he did not remember voting to admit any, as the Association's constitution required. Harbert Davenport, longtime member of the Executive Council and former president of the TSHA, and Merle Duncan, future president, joined with Haley, pointing out that a strict adherence to the requirement that all admissions be approved by a vote of the members would prevent African Americans from joining.

Carroll's response was practical but hardly valiant. He wrote to Duncan, "I regret that the Negro question had to arise. . . . You know that I stood for segregation as long as possible. But the Supreme Court put Negroes in the Pullmans with me, put Negroes in my classes, in the Chuck Wagon [the University cafeteria], and the like." He added that the American Historical Association had admitted black members, adding, "Whether I like it or not, the major questions of segregation have been fought and lost." Many hotels no longer refused service to African Americans, which thus eliminated a "practical solution to our problem." Carroll insisted that to preserve the close relationship with the University of Texas, the Association had to follow its example and admit African Americans. He appealed to her loyalty by adding, "Honestly two or three Negro members are not enough to warrant our dealing a lingering death blow to one of the most civilized institutions in the state."[23]

In his responses, Carroll continued to insist that the Association already had black members. His staff combed the rolls and found three: Artemisia Bowden, the indomitable dean of St. Philip's junior college for blacks in San Antonio, Clarence W. Norris of the same city, and John A. Jackson of Wichita Falls. Black institutions also had subscriptions to the *Southwestern Historical Quarterly*: St. Philips, Prairie View A&M College, and Texas Southern, the last probably hastily added as a response to Lanier's inquiry. Bowden was the most senior African American member, having joined in 1940, but she by no means could claim to be the first to apply for membership. That honor lay with S. H. Burford, an African American physician from Columbus who was invited to join in 1900. Burford had responded with a note to Lester G. Bugbee that explained that he was a "native born negro of Texas" but had "concluded to submit my name should I not be laboring under too great a disability." He would be pleased to be a member unless "my color debars me," adding poignantly, "it is very improbable that I should ever attend one of its (Ass.) sessions." There is no indication that Burford received a response from Bugbee, though others apparently did join under these terms.[24]

Integration remained among the principal issues within the Association in April 1954, when the Executive Council organized a committee, chaired by Fellow Joseph W. Schmitz of St. Mary's University, to produce a revised version of the organization's constitution. Issues raised by McCaleb, such as defining the position of director, were easily addressed. About black members, Article III of the amended constitution reserved to the Council the right to exclude any "undesirable" members. The requirement that members vote on admissions was deleted.[25] The nation was changing, and the Association changed with it. The increase in the number of minority members, especially African Americans, during the remainder of Carroll's term as director was slow, but the Council never officially opposed the admission of anyone.

The revised by-laws adopted with the amended constitution authorized the Executive Council to create as many committees as it saw fit. By the early 1960s this issue had become critical, with members pushing for more active committees. In a 1961 note to William C. Pool about Association matters, including Pool's biography of Barker, Carroll snapped, "We must be careful not to have an organization operated in the manner of the Garden Club of Texas." He pointedly reminded Pool that, without his endorsement, important topics—such as a Fellow nomination pressed by Pool—would not be approved by the Council. Cooper K. Ragan got an equally sharp response when he wrote, "I honestly believe the Association can be benefited by active committees." Carroll charged that members who wanted more committees simply wanted to wrest control of the budget from him. He and Leslie Waggener Jr. had written the financial rules, and he would not allow anyone to undo what they had done. He seemed to be especially testy about the General Foods stock to which he had clung for almost a decade. He quipped, "Believe me, there is no law that the Texas State Historical Association cannot be given stocks, shetland ponies, or anything we might want to accept."[26]

Much of Carroll's unhappiness with committees lay in their potential for creating a dominant leader, especially one who might later serve as president of the Association. As early as 1949 Carroll pushed successfully for an official two-year term limit for TSHA presidents. He had earlier opposed appointing faculty from other Texas schools to that office, as had his predecessors, but the imposition of a term limit led him to drop that restriction. In 1959 Merle Duncan of Baylor University became president, and was the first since 1949 to serve more than two years. It was hardly an honor. Joe B. Frantz, who succeeded Carroll as director in 1966, remembered that Duncan's presidency was a "blood bath period" that "threatened" the "very existence" of the Association. He added that this was not Duncan's fault. In fact, she "showed more courage than any person has a right to expect, she rapped some knuckles rather hard, she flashed fire on a few occasions (I can see her eyes snapping right now), and through it all she ever remained the composed, gracious lady."[27]

Duncan remained in office because Carroll did not want the senior vice-president, Fred R. Cotten, to succeed her. Cotten had a law degree from the University of Texas, but spent more than fifty years of his life tending the family's undertaking business and furniture store in Weatherford. He and Bailey Carroll fought over many issues. Cotten advocated ceding the Association's publication effort to the University of Texas Press; Carroll of course would not do this. More important, Cotten supported Walter Webb's criticism of Carroll's focus on local history. This was ironic because those who visited Weatherford, including John Graves as he was writing *Goodbye to a River*, found Cotten's historical interest to be "focused tightly on his own county."[28] Cotten would talk for hours about Parker County but often dismissed topics that involved adjacent counties. Perhaps he, like others, believed the Association should play a broader role than he assumed for himself.

Carroll complained to Cotten in 1961, "It would really be unthinkable for the two of us to try to lead the program." The Executive Council acceded to Carroll's wishes and kept Duncan as president for a third year. Webb angrily dissented, declaring that a tombstone should be placed on the grave of Cotten's association with the TSHA stating that "He was stung by pismires and grasshoppers."[29] Perhaps the comparison to noxious small insects stung the

Council, or perhaps it was the sad sight of the colorful Cotten, always an enthusiastic booster of the organization, sidelined with no official duties. In 1962, despite Carroll's best efforts to impose a one-year limit, Cotten began serving the first of his two years as president.

Carroll, in a makeshift apology to Cotten, did make clear his objections to those who opposed him. He resented anyone's assertion that "Texas history is 'thin' history." He added, "I do believe in local and state history and believe that these are the cornerstones of all history." He would never, though, allow differences of opinion to endanger the close relationship between the University of Texas and the Association. The bond of over sixty years was "worth saving," and was "bigger and more significant than individual personality conflicts."[30] During Cotten's tenure, he and Carroll squabbled over publication of the Bexar Archives (a long-considered project that would be partly addressed by the microfilming of the collection beginning in 1966), but otherwise Cotten's presidency was quiet. A positive end to the feud came when the Council, responding to suggestions from many parties, adopted a one-term tenure with an alternation between academics and nonacademics, defined a clear line of succession among the vice-presidents, and organized a nominating committee for TSHA officers.

Much of Carroll's difficulty during his last few years as director can be attributed to declining health. Admittedly, Carroll may never have been as healthy as he appeared. During his first year as director, he wrote to Pat I. Nixon that the pace made him feel "like the superintendent of a three-ring circus." Months later, Carroll reported to Nixon that he had suffered a "fatigue collapse." Carroll's doctor ordered a reduction of duties, and Webb, whose health had also collapsed during his first years as director, taught Carroll's classes and wrote the "Texas Collection" until Carroll recovered in the late summer of 1947. During the Executive Council meeting of April 1961, as conflict mounted over committees and Cotten, Carroll suffered "an all American stroke" and was taken to the hospital. Ten days after returning home, he suffered "fairly hurtful burns" when his house burned.[31] He lost everything and was once again hospitalized, but he was deeply touched by the great outpouring of sympathy and gifts from Association members and across the state. He continued to suffer vision loss, and in the fall of 1965 endured a series of heart attacks. He could not attend the April 1966 meeting due to illness, and less than a month later, on May 12, 1966, H. Bailey Carroll died. His resignation as director of the Association had been given to the Executive Council just two weeks before.

Nineteen years earlier, in April 1947, the *Dallas News* had praised the Association on its fiftieth birthday, declaring, "Never a stuffed-shirt organization

Dr. H. Bailey Carroll

Whereas, Dr. H. Bailey Carroll has resigned as Director of the Texas State Historical Association for reasons of poor health; and

Whereas, He has devoted his life to the cause of Texas history; and

Whereas, He has stimulated interest in and generated enthusiasm for Texas historical scholarship among thousands of Texans; and

Whereas, He has cherished the lamp of Texas history received by him from George Garrison and Eugene C. Barker and passed it to scores of dedicated scholars; and

Whereas, He has served this Association faithfully for nearly a quarter of a century; and

Whereas, His ceaseless efforts have contributed to the growth of this Association into one of the largest state historical associations in the nation and made the *Southwestern Historical Quarterly* an editorial model for all such journals; and

Whereas, He has successfully promoted the financial development of the Association; and

Whereas, He pioneered the Junior Historian Movement in Texas and has worked tirelessly for more than a quarter of a century to build it into one of the most effective organizations of its kind in the country; and

Whereas, This Association and the officers and members of the Executive Council thereof will sorely miss his guidance and wish to pay homage to these services he has rendered; now, therefore, be it

Resolved, That the Texas State Historical Association at its annual meeting of April 29-30, 1966, does hereby express its profound gratitude and sincerest best wishes to Dr. H. Bailey Carroll and does direct that copies of this Resolution be printed in the *Southwestern Historical Quarterly* and distributed among appropriate personnel, and educational and historical agencies.

April 29, 1966

This resolution honoring H. Bailey Carroll was passed by the Executive Council at the annual meeting of the Association on April 29–30, 1966. *SHQ*, 70 (July 1966), f. 109.

or one devoted to mere reminiscence and back-scratching, the Association has set its aims high and has maintained admirable standards of historical research and writing." Carroll greatly enhanced this image in the eyes of Texans. As historian James D. Carter wrote to Robert C. Cotner, who worked with Carroll in the Department of History and served as book review editor of the *Quarterly*: "Bailey was not always right, nor was he as diplomatic as he should have been at times, however, he probably did more to put the Association on a sound financial base than any other person in it and did more to encourage and develop new historical writers than any other editor of the *Quarterly*."[32]

As director, Carroll put his all into the Association and knew there were many who appreciated what he did. About those who criticized him, Carroll had a simple answer. He wrote to an associate in 1962, shortly after deciding not to resign amid yet another controversy over the TSHA's presidency, "I do not have to tell you that from beginning to end there have been some persons who have not liked what I have done. Anyhow, my procedure has maintained

"In my early days I was familiar with a long established frontier custom of 'pounding the preacher.' ...A few days ago I received one of the most pleasant surprises of my life. I refer to being 'pounded' with Texas books by my colleagues, associates, and friends. The burns on my body had healed without scar, but the loss of my books was still a raw and open wound to my spirit. Books have always been much more than mere possessions to me; they have been a part of my life—a part of my very being." [There follows a list of the seventeen "finest selections of Texana available" given to Carroll by members of the history department, the Executive Council of the TSHA, and personal friends.]

H. Bailey Carroll, "Texas Collection," *SHQ*, 65 (Oct. 1961), 258–259.

the highest of standards both financially and editorially." Perhaps recalling the scholarly tradition of his predecessors as director of the Association, Carroll concluded, "The enterprise has stood for the validity of the past as revealed in Texas experiences." He was intensely proud of his home state, and had been compared in his appearance to "Old Man Texas" cartoonist John Knott's quintessential Texan. He probably would have been pleased to hear a student say that some watched him from the classroom windows as he arrived each day, certain that "anyone so Texan as Dr. Carroll had to come to class on a horse."[33]

Six

In the Shadow of Webb

Joe B. Frantz, 1966–1977, and L. Tuffly Ellis, 1977–1985

Joe B. Frantz took charge of the Texas State Historical Association in 1966 with a determination to make some changes. Raised mostly in Weatherford, he was amiable and unpretentious and had good credentials. He had attended Weatherford College, earned a degree in journalism from the University of Texas, completed a master's thesis under the direction of Eugene C. Barker, worked as an archivist, and served in the U.S. Navy during World War II before deciding to pursue a doctorate in history. Walter P. Webb became his mentor and friend, and Frantz joined the University of Texas faculty in 1949. Ten years later, he was a professor, an author with several books that combined sound research with a lively style, and chair of the Department of History. In the 1960s he became active in the Association and served on the Executive Council. Elected unanimously by the Council to succeed H. Bailey Carroll, Frantz injected new vitality into the organization. His

Joe B. Frantz (1917–1993), director of the Association 1966–1977.

"Limits for the future of the Association don't exist. True, we will always be hedged in by interior linemen known as Time, Money, and Personnel, but each of these opponents can be blocked out of the play through perseverance and shrewd promotion. Thus, we members of the Association can dream our dreams, knowing that the real test will come when, to change the figure, we try to saddle and ride those dreams. . . . The problem is not so much to dream, as to translate dreams into realities. Here is where the membership has to be enlisted, here is where co-operation has to be complete and inspired. We would like to make the Texas State Historical Association of the future fully worthy of all the people who have gone before. We would like to make it worthy of you. Most of all, we would like to see it live up to the promise of the generations now in the schoolrooms and those generations unborn whose proper future should be carved out of a profound and intelligent respect for the past that has nurtured them." Joe B. Frantz, "History Looking Ahead," *SHQ*, 70 (Jan. 1967), 371. *Photograph from TSHA Files.*

initiatives were expanded upon by L. Tuffly Ellis, his student and meticulous second-in-command who succeeded him as director.

Frantz represented a return to the academic vision of Webb. Like his predecessor Carroll, he had studied under Barker and Webb, but unlike Carroll, Frantz adopted the broad national perspective of his two mentors. He became active in the Organization of American Historians (OAH), which began as the Mississippi Valley Historical Association, as well as the American Historical Association (AHA). Barker was a founder and later became president of the OAH, and Webb served as president of both the OAH and the AHA. Frantz's interest in Carroll's favorite group, the American Association for State and Local History (AASLH), on the other hand, actually declined as time passed. Although Frantz wrote a history of Texas as part of an AASLH project for the national Bicentennial, relations between the Association and the AASLH lapsed under him, and by 1986 the AASLH guide to historical societies did not list the TSHA, which apparently did not return the customary questionnaire. This may have been an oversight due to Ellis's resignation as director that year, but also may well have been due to changes that had accrued in both organizations. While the AASLH focused its efforts mostly on museums and amateur historians, and declined in size and prestige, Frantz and Ellis brought professionals and nonprofessionals together in a successful expansion of the TSHA.

Frantz and Ellis shared Webb's view that history should have a broad focus and should be accessible to a wide public. This was fortuitous at a time when Texas, like the nation, was changing. In the 1960s and 1970s, newcomers to the political and corporate arena, especially women and ethnic minorities, wanted their stories told more fully. During the same time period, the Texas economy was shifting, and agriculture was losing ground to industry and service jobs. New problems of urbanization and immigration became acute. Frantz shared

---

L. Tuffly Ellis (1927–), director of the Association 1977–1985.

"During my eight-year tenure as director I have sought to chart a new and more scholarly course for the Association by broadening its base, raising its visibility, and strengthening it financially. . . . Whatever success my efforts have achieved are due to the many friends, in and out of the academic world, who time after time said yes when I asked them to do something for the Association. . . . I leave the directorship with a sense that all is in good shape. There is much to do. It will be difficult, costly, and will require strong and full support of the new director by the entire Council; but almost everything in life worth doing has its price. I leave with the confidence that the history department and the Barker Texas History Center will remain the intellectual home of the Association and that the Council will choose a new director who is both an excellent scholar and a fine administrator, and that the Association will enter a truly intellectual golden era." Ellis's last Director's Report, May 15, 1985 (TSHA Files), *Photograph courtesy Tuffly Ellis.*

THE STAFF: 1967

"Visitors who have not dropped in for several years will find an almost complete change of personnel, if not of positions. Alwyn Barr has moved on to Purdue, David Gracy is at Texas Technological College, and Sam Suhler is with the field service of the Texas State Library in Corpus Christi. The past several senior secretaries have all responded to the call of incipient motherhood, so that we are faced with a new office manager every nine months or so or else replacing the secretary's chair, which evidently is jinxed. However, Miss Suann Waight, one of the more recent mothers, is due to return to her post before this essay appears. Her imminent return is reassuring, since it is nice to have someone who knows where the files are and the combination to the vault.

"An attempt is being made to give everyone a definite assignment, though a small staff like ours must invariably be prepared to help with everyone else's chores. Thus, Frances Parker runs the Junior Historian program; Barbara Cummings, preparation of the supplemental volume of the *Handbook of Texas*, abetted by James C. Martin and Karen Collins, each of whom is responsible for specific

the interest of his predecessors in traditional topics and sources, but, prompted by changing audiences and perspectives, he made use of new resources to bring heretofore untold history to light. In adjusting to new demands Frantz and Ellis demonstrated the academic flexibility of their Progressive heritage. George P. Garrison, Eugene C. Barker, Walter P. Webb, and H. Bailey Carroll had embraced new ideas and perspectives in explaining the Texas frontier. Joe Frantz and Tuffly Ellis would expand the academic horizons even further, and record a new phase in the state's history.

It helped the Association that Frantz enjoyed a national reputation. Throughout his career, he busied himself with projects that had popular appeal, such as directing Lyndon B. Johnson's program for an oral history of his presidency. This project occupied much of Frantz's time from 1968 until 1974 and brought him much favorable exposure that proved useful as professional interest in state and local history declined. The University of Texas, in an attempt to guide history students into national and international topics, had eliminated Texas history as a field for the doctorate degree, but Frantz was able to use his renown in maintaining the University's support for the TSHA. Frantz also made good use of his popularity with the general public. As he had written upon taking office as director, the Association badly needed a "strong resurrectional and promotional hand." His speeches focused on "expansion

types of articles; Wayne Cutler, the *Quarterly*; Kenneth Ragsdale, a former professional musician, assists on the *Quarterly* and doubles on another instrument, "Riding Line," the newsletter; L. Tuffly Ellis, assistant editor and assistant director of Research in Texas History (one-third time), just about anything that comes up; Dianne Prescott, probably fled to New Mexico by this time, secretarial and budgeting duties; and various bevies of pretty clerical assistants, sturdy mail clerks, and one general factotum, Randall Paul of Brownwood, who looks after everything that the remainder of us don't get done.

"I have purposely left one other employee out of this picture. She is Mrs. Coral H. Tullis, who has been minding our money and paying our bills since 1927, which is the year Babe Ruth hit sixty homers and the Yankees beat the Pittsburgh Pirates four straight in the World Series. As funsters used to say of Secretary of the Treasury Andrew Mellon, seven editors have been privileged to serve under Mrs. Tullis— Herbert E. Bolton, R. L. Biesele, Charles W. Hackett, Eugene Barker, Walter P. Webb, H. Bailey Carroll, and Joe B. Frantz. She is our conscience and our continuity."

Joe B. Frantz, SHQ, 70 (Jan. 1967), 359.

and renewed aggressiveness." Tuffly Ellis carried out that game plan back at the office, where, during Frantz's absences, he took care of daily affairs.[1]

Joe Frantz, like Eugene Barker, was not everyone's first choice for the job of director, and, like Walter Webb, when Frantz accepted the position he did not intend to stay long. Some had wanted William H. Goetzmann for director, but by 1966 he had established the American Studies program at the University, and continued to be engaged in its development. So, despite Frantz's assertion that he would serve for only three years, Chancellor Harry H. Ransom chose him to take over as TSHA director. Frantz outlined his vision for revitalizing the Association at a Lubbock luncheon on September 24, 1966. It was a remarkable speech, and appeared in the *Southwestern Historical Quarterly* the following January. It touched on almost every aspect of his plans, with a focus on decentralization. Frantz noted that Carroll had, in his last years as director, begun delegating authority by creating a program committee for annual meetings. Frantz would expand on this initiative, throughout his eleven, not three, years as director.

Decentralization for Frantz began soon after he took over as director, with the hiring of L. Tuffly Ellis as assistant director. Ellis would ultimately be responsible for the day-to-day duties that had for many years been the job of Coral H. Tullis. In April 1967 the eighty-four-year-old Tullis, who had served

Seymour V. Connor
(1967–1968)

Wayne Gard
(1968–1969)

Rupert N. Richardson
(1969–1970)

Cooper K. Ragan (1970–1971)

Dorman H. Winfrey (1971–1972)

Ten presidents served under Joe B. Frantz. *Photographs from TSHA Files.*

Roger N. Conger
(1972–1973)

Anne A. Brindley
(1973–1974)

Ralph A. Wooster
(1974–1975)

Billy Mac Jones (1975–1976)

Dan E. Kilgore (1976–1977)

Ernest Wallace (1977–1978)

F. Lee Lawrence (1978–1979)

Ben H. Procter (1979–1980)

Ben E. Pingenot (1980–1981)

Eight presidents served under L. Tuffly Ellis. *Photographs from TSHA Files.*

Marilyn M. Sibley (1981–1982)

J. P. Bryan Jr. (1982–1983)

Edward A. Clark (1983–1984)

Clifton Caldwell (1984–1985)

as secretary, treasurer, and indispensable assistant to Barker, Webb, Carroll, and briefly Frantz, retired. Frantz accepted her retirement with regret, but he had prepared for her departure by having Ellis in place. As Frantz had explained to the Executive Council: "I'm involved in too many things, and I am also mortal." Asserting, "We should always have a possible successor in training," he with their approval had appointed his former student as his understudy. Coral Tullis, who had taught history at the University from 1927 until 1959, died just two months after her retirement from the TSHA. Dorman H. Winfrey, who had known her for more than two decades, declared in the *Southwestern Historical Quarterly* that she had earned "a permanent place as a grand lady among Texas women," and with funds from her family, the Association initiated an annual award in her memory for the best book on Texas history. [2]

Tuffly Ellis joined the history faculty at the University of Texas in 1966, two years after completing his dissertation under Frantz. A fourth-generation Texan from Houston, Ellis later described himself as a "direct lineal descendant, figuratively speaking, of George P. Garrison."[3] He had taken classes under Webb, who had studied under Barker, Garrison's student. Frantz, his mentor, had also studied under Barker and Webb, reinforcing Ellis's connection to their perspectives on Texas history and to the Association. Ellis had earned undergraduate and graduate degrees in business, at the University of Texas and the University of Houston respectively, and then attended Catholic seminary and taught before returning to Austin to study under Frantz for his doctoral degree. After graduating, Ellis taught at Del Mar College and Lamar University before accepting Frantz's invitation to work for the TSHA. Ellis played a dual role as a member of the University of Texas faculty and a leading figure in the revitalization of the Association, and his pay was divided between the Department of History and the Department for Research in Texas History, the Association's University identity.

Ellis's arrival freed Frantz to serve on federal advisory councils, direct Lyndon Johnson's oral history project, organize an "International Symposium in Honor of Walter Prescott Webb," and produce a long list of publications and speeches. Frantz developed the habit of announcing ideas and leaving Ellis to implement them, which Ellis did in exemplary style. Frantz told the Executive Council in 1970, "sometimes my role is little more than titular. . . . More and more I just bask in his limelight." He added that Ellis's "driving personality" was the source of most of the advances made by the Association since his arrival.[4] In 1975 Ellis became associate director, and in September 1977 he succeeded Frantz as director of the Association and the Center for Studies in Texas History (the new name for the old Department of Research in Texas History). Ellis also took over as editor of the *Quarterly*.

THE EXECUTIVE COUNCIL:
FRANTZ ON COMPOSITION OF

"Undoubtedly the membership of the Executive Council will continue to be what the Association is, a mixture of professional historians, talented amateur or avocational historians, and people who just like to be around where history is being studied or discussed, or who love to buy and read books. Actually, experience shows that the continuity and drive for an Association such as this one come from the nonprofessionals, who are generally more generous with their energies to the cause of regional history than are the professionals, who are most intimately concerned with professional advancement."

Joe B. Frantz, *History Looking Ahead: The Present and Future of the Texas State Historical Association*; reprinted from *SHQ*, 70 (Jan. 1967), 366.

The Executive Council (and others), taken at the 75th annual meeting in March 1971, at the Stephen F. Austin Hotel in Austin. *Standing (left to right):* Edward Hake Phillips, F. Lee Lawrence, L. Tuffly Ellis, Rupert N. Richardson, Wayne Gard, T. R. Havins, Leavitt Corning Jr., Al Lowman, Joe B. Frantz, William C. Pool, [?], Escal Duke. *Seated (left to right):* Dan Kilgore, Ralph A. Wooster, Cooper K. Ragan, Anne Brindley, Dorman H. Winfrey, Roger N. Conger. *Photograph from TSHA Files.*

Frantz, with Ellis's assistance, made the Association's publications program one of the first targets of attention. Frantz said in 1966 that he would expand the size of the *Quarterly* and broaden its scope. The first step was a facelift. For this, he hired designer Carl J. Hertzog, the founder of the Texas Western Press and a longtime member of the TSHA who had, under Carroll, designed several limited editions of Association publications. At Ellis's request, Hertzog and his partner, El Paso artist José Cisneros, replaced the stodgy green cover of the *Quarterly* with a design that featured the use of a painting or a photograph for each issue. Cisneros added a calligraphic logo, and the terrazzo medallion from the rotunda floor of the Texas Capitol was added to the title page—a suggestion from Wayne Cutler, a doctoral student and editorial assistant who later edited the James K. Polk Papers at the University of Tennessee. Inside, illustrations were added, in a trend that culminated in a series of illustrated articles on Texas cities. An enlarged "Southwestern Collection" supplanted the old "Texas Collection."

The reaction to the new design, which made its debut with the July 1967 issue, was generally favorable, but there were a few grumbles. Frantz may well have remembered Webb talking about the reaction he'd received when he changed the cover from brown to green in 1940. Harbert Davenport, then president of the Association, had told Webb, "Losing the old brown bound *Quarterly* is like losing an old friend."[5] For some, losing the green *Quarterly* was just as difficult, but most enjoyed the changes and later welcomed the addition of photographs to the annual meeting programs.

Frantz initially continued the reportorial style of Carroll in the "Texas Collection," but after he renamed it, there was a sharp swing back to the folksy approach of Webb. There was one significant departure from both of his predecessors: Frantz stressed bibliography more than they, including long comments on books, articles, and archival accessions. To make room for this, reports on history events were removed to a newsletter, *Riding Line*, which appeared in the fall of 1966. Edited by Kenneth B. Ragsdale, who handled many other tasks for the Association, the quarterly publication was intended "to bring the membership into closer communication."[6] Most important, it created space in the "Southwestern Collection" for Frantz to expound on items with broader appeal, which most members appreciated. Ellis discontinued the *Riding Line* in 1975, incorporating much of its content into a longer "Southwestern Collection," which included bibliographic material as well as membership news.

Tuffly Ellis became the protaganist in Frantz's determination to improve the content of the *Southwestern Historical Quarterly*. David G. McComb, Frantz's student and biographer, has written that by 1966 the *Quarterly* was "known for sloppy documentation with a touch of cronyism in its publication."[7] McComb's words are perhaps a bit strong, but they reveal a perception, pervasive at the time, that needed to be addressed. Carroll had an editorial board but rarely consulted it. Frantz appointed a new board to assist Ellis in reviewing all potential articles. The list of reviewers grew as the process matured, but Ellis made all final decisions, issuing a style manual and having all footnotes checked by a staff that included A. C. Greene, formerly of the *Dallas Times Herald*. Frantz also suggested choosing a new book review editor every three years. Robert C. Cotner of the University of Texas served first, then Jim B. Pearson, a Webb student who followed in his mentor's footsteps by joining the University faculty as a liaison between his colleagues and Texas secondary school teachers. Pearson later became a dean at the University of North Texas. Robert A. Calvert of the University of North Texas, who later chaired the History Department at Texas A&M University, served as book review editor until 1980, when Norman D. Brown of the University of Texas succeeded him.

Peer review and close editing caused grumbling from some, but Ellis stood his ground. He explained to Calvert that "on occasion even the big guns may need to be reworked. But you know how sensitive academic people are. We don't like to offend them, but we do want to help them avoid making fools of themselves. That is part of an editor's job." The improvement became very evident, and Ellis pointed that out to anyone who asked. He declared proudly in 1968, "I think in the last two years that the quality of manuscripts submitted has improved and the standards of our journal have been raised considerably—although there is still room for improvement."[8] Most readers agreed, and Frantz never challenged Ellis's strict style and high standards. When Ellis became director, his dedication to the *Quarterly* remained strong and was still a primary concern as he contemplated retirement. Turning the direction of the *Quarterly* over to managing editor George B. Ward in 1985, Ellis admonished him never to compromise the academic integrity of the journal.

Frantz also instituted the idea of having thematic issues of the *Quarterly*. Cattle ranching became the focus of the first such number in 1967, then Spanish colonization, Reconstruction, cotton, and labor. Of particular interest was a 1973 issue on African Americans in Texas. Alwyn Barr initially suggested the topic in 1968, but it took five years for enough articles to squeeze through the editorial process. Meanwhile, a session on the history of African Americans in Texas was included in the annual meeting for 1971 and was well received, as was the ultimate issue of the *Quarterly*. Also in 1973, an issue of the *Quarterly* was devoted to an article by Ron Tyler on Mexican War lithographs. Since many of these were reproduced in color, the J. M. West Texas Corporation paid much of the cost of production. The Tyler article was reprinted separately and became one of two Tyler books published by the TSHA during Frantz's term as director. Ellis did not produce many thematic issues as director, but in 1982 he did publish an issue on the University's centennial.

Ellis as editor, both under Frantz and during his own tenure as director, published outstanding articles on almost every era of Texas history. For the Spanish period, Robert S. Weddle became the heir of a rich tradition that began with Herbert E. Bolton, extracting an excellent article on San Juan Bautista from his book on the same subject, and Benedict Leutenegger translated a 1792 report on the San Antonio missions. Nettie Lee Benson and Wilbert H. (Bill) Timmons submitted articles on the 1810 revolution in Mexico and its influence on Texas. Jesús F. de la Teja and John R. Wheat together wrote a piece on San Antonio from 1820 to 1832. Paul D. Lack took another look at slavery's influence in the Texas Revolution, and Margaret S. Henson discussed pro-Mexican sentiment in Texas prior to 1836. James W. Pohl and Stephen L. Hardin coauthored a study of the military aspects of the Texas Revolution, and Michael P. Costeloe and John H. Schroeder, respectively, explored Mexican and American press and popular opinion on that conflict. C. Alan Hutchinson, coauthor of the TSHA's earlier book on Post City, wrote a thought-provoking piece on how Texans missed an opportunity to curry the support of Federalists in Mexico; and Josefina Zoraida Vásquez analyzed the Texas issue within the context of Mexican politics in the decade after independence was won.

The period of early statehood also received much attention. Randolph B. Campbell and Richard Lowe analyzed agriculture and the relationship between wealth and power in antebellum Texas, and Cecil Harper produced a case study of slavery in Hunt County. Campbell also wrote articles on the Nashville Convention of 1850 and on the Whig Party. Ralph A. Wooster wrote an analysis of the American Party, and James A. Baggett focused on the Constitutional Union Party and the Republicans. Roy Sylvan Dunn wrote in 1967 about the Knights of the Golden Circle, a topic originally covered by C. A. Bridges in 1941. Also in 1967, Ron Tyler wrote an installment in a long-running dispute over the Callahan expedition, which Ernest C. Shearer initially discussed in 1951. Mark Nackman wrote a piece on Texas citizen-soldiers that later became a part of his book on Texas nationalism. The beginnings of Texas urbanization received the attention of Earl F. Woodward and Susan Jackson, and Wilbert Timmons wrote on antebellum El Paso. Previously neglected topics, such as religious newspapers and the ill-fated La Réunion colony, were discussed by Wesley Norton and Randel V. Davidson, respectively.

As in previous years, articles on Texas in the Civil War focused on many subjects. Walter L. Buenger expanded greatly upon earlier studies of Union-

The Association and the University

"The Association, lacking an endowment, would never have gotten beyond the *Quarterly* and the annual meeting functions without the financial aid of the University and the moral support of the history department. Thus the Association and the cause of Texas history owe the University a great debt of gratitude and all of us should recognize that fact.

"At the same time, however, the Association has served the University well. It has played an important role in bringing historical materials to the institution. The *Quarterly* and annual meeting have served as outlets for the work of UT scholars. The *Handbook of Texas* provided a training ground for many graduate students to learn the methods of historical research and editing. The Junior Historian program brings hundreds of the state's brightest youngsters to the campus every year or so, many of whom eventually become UT students.

"But the Association serves another vital function for the University. It provides an outlet through which the University can serve its constituency, the people of Texas, with a viable organ committed to continually holding the long, varied, and diverse history of this state before its citizens. For the University to do otherwise would be a failure in its public trust.

"….The University and the Association must work closely together for the benefit of both institutions. They both have an obligation to those whom they serve: the people of Texas and the historical and intellectual community at large."

L. Tuffly Ellis, "Southwestern Collection," *SHQ*, 82 (Apr. 1979), 428–429.

ists while working on a landmark book on the topic. Good biographies of military and political leaders, Union and Confederate, were produced by Robert L. and Pauline Jones, Claude H. Hall, Dale A. Somers, Alwyn Barr, Billy D. Ledbetter, Matthew Ellenberger, and Randy J. Sparks. Tyler wrote an article on the wartime trade in cotton that complemented two others in the same issue on antebellum cotton-marketing by Abigail C. Holbrook and postwar cotton-trading by Tuffly Ellis. For the Reconstruction period, Alton Hornsby's article on the Freedmen's Bureau was followed by several from Barry Crouch, and Ann P. Baenziger focused on the state police. Political topics provided the content of articles by Robert W. Shook and Philip J. Avilo. A. C. Greene wrote about Austin immediately after the war ended, and Wooster discussed who had wealth in postwar Texas.

The Gilded Age and its aftermath in Texas received much attention as topics diversified in the *Quarterly*. Robert A. Calvert wrote about farmers in the late nineteenth century, and James R. Green submitted an article on tenant farmers during the first decades of the twentieth century. There were also good articles on labor unions by James V. Reese. Lewis L. Gould's research for a book on Texas Progressives yielded an article for the *Quarterly*, and Adrian Anderson focused on one noted Texas Progressive, Albert S. Burleson. Progressive reform in Galveston and Beaumont became the focus for pieces by Bradley K. Rice and Paul E. Isaac. H. Roger Grant's study of electric railways complemented an article by Everett L. DeGolyer Jr. on the decline of Texas railroads.

In the 1970s and 1980s many *Quarterly* contributors emphasized ethnicity. Lawrence A. Cardoso wrote about Mexican migration to Texas during the Mexican Revolution. Solid articles on racial conflict between blacks and whites came from Robert V. Haynes, Garna L. Christian, and James M. SoRelle. The University centennial issue contained an article by Michael L. Gillette about Heman M. Sweatt and the integration of the UT Law School; in an earlier issue Gillette wrote a piece about the growth of the National Association for the Advancement of Colored People. Darlene C. Hine wrote on the Texas experience with black disfranchisement. Perhaps one of the most striking inclusions was Ada de Blanc Simond's memoir of growing up as an African American in Texas.

New topics appeared frequently in the *Quarterly*. Fane Downs wrote about Texas pioneer women, and Mary Ann Lamanna discussed the Women's Commonwealth of Belton. David C. Humphrey tackled a very different aspect of women's history in an article on prostitution in Austin. Randy Roberts and James W. Pohl focused on sports history; Roberts analyzed the career of black boxer Jack Johnson, and Pohl discussed Dana X. Bible, the popular University of Texas football coach. Ellis also had an interest in historiography and printed some of the first such articles, including pieces from Ralph A. Wooster on the early statehood period, Edgar P. Sneed on Reconstruction, and Walter Rundell on oil production. Ellis did not avoid controversy, printing pieces on hotly debated subjects such as Baptist minister J. Frank Norris, written by C. Allyn Russell, and McCarthyism in Houston, by Don E. Carleton. Environmental history emerged with articles from Robert S. Maxwell on W. Goodrich Jones, the "Father of Texas Forestry," and Dan L. Flores on the ecological impact of the Spanish entry into Texas. Both Willard B. Robinson and Keith L. Bryant analyzed historic architecture, and Emily F. Cutrer discussed art work in the Texas Capitol. Art also provided some new perspectives on the Alamo, as presented by Don Graham and others.

Frantz's expansion of the publications program included a popular revamping of the *Junior Historian*. Under Kenneth B. Ragsdale's direction, the size increased (although students still wrote every article) and, in September 1970, the title changed to *Texas Historian*. Dorman H. Winfrey, a Webb student who in 1971 became the first former Junior Historian to serve as Association president, wrote a history of the organization for its seventy-fifth anniversary. In it, he explained that "Dr. Frantz observed that with the 18 year olds voting and having to serve in the Army, teenagers did not want to be called junior any more."[9] Perhaps not, but sentiment ensured that only the journal, not the program, got a new name. The publication also got a new format, designed by William R. Holman, professor of the History and Art of the Book at the University of Texas. A prize-winning designer, and like Carl Hertzog a favorite of Texas collectors, Holman used color and refined the use of photographs. At the same time, in a move that mirrored changes in the *Quarterly*, a newsletter appeared for Junior Historians, the *Roadrunner*.

Frantz's determination to reach a broad popular audience influenced his decisions in book publications. He agreed to cosponsor, with the University of Texas Press, a paperback reprint series. Before Frantz left, this joint effort produced new editions of fifteen Texas history classics. Fittingly, the first were by Association stalwarts: Barker's biography of Stephen F. Austin and Llerena B. Friend's work on Sam Houston. The success of this undertaking prompted Tuffly Ellis to initiate a hardcover reprint series that belonged solely to the TSHA. Fred H. Moore provided the funds, and the series was named for him and his wife, Ella Mae Moore. The first title was William C. Binkley's classic, *The Texas Revolution*, which received additional funding from organizations that wanted a copy put in every junior and senior high school library in the state. New editions of Mary A. Holley's *Texas*, a memoir by Stephen F. Austin's cousin; Fred W. Hodge and Theodore H. Lewis's *Spanish Explorers in the Southern United States*, a 1907 rarity; and William B. Parker's *Through Unexplored Texas* also appeared before Ellis departed in 1985. Parker's work, which was a chronicle of an 1854 U.S. Army exploration along the Red River, was reproduced from a copy provided by J. Clifton Caldwell, longtime sponsor of the Junior Historians and past president of the Association.

In addition to the reprint series, the TSHA under Frantz also published six new books, several of which won awards. The topics were diverse: Nancy Barker had two volumes on the French legation in the Texas Republic, William C. Holden wrote on the Espuela Ranch, Ron Tyler wrote two books on Mexico (its war with the United States and its role in the American Civil War; both books designed by William R. Holman), and William G. Kerr wrote about Scottish finance in frontier America. Nancy Barker's contribu-

Nancy Barker, holding *The French Legation*, with longtime TSHA editor Barbara Stockley, at the annual meeting in 1971. *Photograph from TSHA Files.*

"William R. Holman, more reverently known as Bill Holman to just about everybody interested in fine printing, ... turned out his first 'book' when he was in the seventh grade. The teacher asked for one of those over-long notebooks of printed articles about the government, and Holman went a step beyond his teenage colleagues. From that time forward he was hooked on bookmaking. . . . For the Association Holman designed Nancy N. Barker's *The French Legation in Texas*. The transparent jacket which has aroused so much comment among collectors of fine books is his idea. He also designed *The Texas Historian*, successor to *The Junior Historian*; the two most recent programs for the annual meeting [1970 and 1971]; and a new letterhead for the Association stationery." Joe B. Frantz, "Southwestern Collection," *SHQ*, 75 (Oct. 1971), 235–236.

tions represented a continuing link with the TSHA. Both she and Llerena B. Friend belonged to the American History Club of Austin, several of whose members had been active in founding the Association more than seventy years earlier.

Tuffly Ellis also printed popular books in paperback. In 1980, for the Fred H. and Ella Mae Moore Texas History Reprint Series, Ellis published *Texas Vistas*, a useful compilation of *Quarterly* articles, edited by Ralph A. Wooster and Robert A. Calvert. With additional funds from Moore, Ellis acted on a suggestion from TSHA president F. Lee Lawrence, a prominent East Texas attorney and Moore's cousin, and began printing paperbacks to be sold at Texas historic sites. James M. Cotten later provided an endowment for this series, the Fred Rider Cotten Popular History Series as it was eventually called, named in honor of his father, a former president of the Association. The first in this series was a study of the Old Stone Fort in Nacogdoches, written by Archie McDonald and published in 1981. The second, *The Battle of the Alamo* by Ben H. Procter, came five years later, when McDonald was president of the Association. By 1997 the series had grown to eleven titles.

A unique and ultimately very successful publication for the Association was *Contours of Discovery*, a portfolio of maps and a companion booklet, compiled by James C. Martin and Robert S. Martin and published in 1982. J. Conrad Dunagan, a popular businessman from Monahans and a member of the Executive Council, provided the initial funds for the project. To the delight of Ellis, when he told Dunagan that the maps would be more effective if printed in color, Dunagan simply wrote a substantial check to cover the cost. The portfolio had great appeal—a popular Mexican restaurant chain even laminated the maps into their tabletops—and it has been reprinted many times. Two years after the publication of the map portfolio, Martin and Martin published their book *Maps of Texas and the Southwest, 1513–1900*, with the University of New Mexico Press. The book quickly went out of print and the negatives were destroyed. Popular demand for the book continued, however, and in 1999 TSHA editors painstakingly recreated the entire book from scratch and reprinted it in the Moore Texas History Reprint Series with a new introduction and many new color plates. Like the map portfolio, this book has proved to be one of the Association's best selling publications.

Dunagan and Moore were not the only providers of subsidies to Ellis, who proved adept at finding money for books. The Texas Education Association funded Ralph Wooster and Robert Calvert's compilation, *Texas Vistas*. The King Foundation sponsored a similar anthology of articles from the *Junior Historian*, under the catchy title, *Tracks on the Land: Stories of Immigrants, Outlaws, Artists, and Other Texans Who Left Their Mark on the Lone Star State* (1985). The Pate Foundation subsidized the publication of *Samuel H. Walker's Account of the Mier Expedition* (1978), edited by Marilyn M. Sibley, a fifth-generation Texan and chair of the History Department at Houston Baptist University, who gave her proceeds to the Association. The Kempner Foundation paid for *Black Leaders: Texans for Their Times* (1985), by Alwyn Barr and Robert Calvert, and also paid for indexes to twenty volumes of the *Quarterly*. Private donors contributed to the publication of a handsomely illustrated, two-volume edition of Jean Louis Berlandier's *Journey to Mexico during the Years 1826–1834* (1981). Private funds were also found for *Sangers': Pioneer Texas Merchants* (1978), Leon J. Rosenberg's study of the Sanger brothers and their department store, and for *Southern Community in Crisis: Harrison County, Texas, 1850–1880* (1983), Randolph B. Campbell's analysis of Harrison County during the Civil War. The Tarrant County Historical Society paid for *Log Cabin Village, A History and Guide* (1980), Terry G. Jordan's study of the log cabin village in Fort Worth.

To encourage authors, Frantz and Ellis began giving prizes. Under Bailey Carroll, the Association had given an award for the best article in each year's volume of the *Quarterly*, the W. Scott Schreiner Award, named for a supportive University of Texas regent whose family established the Schreiner Institute in Kerrville. Despite Carroll's strong support, funds for this award ran out and Frantz asked the Executive Council to create a new award for articles. Named for H. Bailey Carroll, it was first given in April 1967, to Sylvan Dunn for his article "The KGC in Texas, 1860–1861." Two months later, Coral H. Tullis died, and her children funded another award to be given for "any . . . enduring work" on Texas.[10] The first recipients of the award, in May 1968 at the annual meeting in San Antonio, were the University of Texas staff who microfilmed the Bexar Archives. The Ernest Wallace Award, with funding from the Red River Valley Historical Association, was given each year to the best *Quarterly* article on West Texas. The first of this award went to William R. Johnson in 1976 for his "Rural Rehabilitation in the New Deal: The Ropesville Project." That same year, the Daughters of the Republic of Texas began the Kate Broocks Bates Award, giving it to Eldon S. Branda for his work on the third volume of the *Handbook of Texas*.

The Executive Council in 1976 decreed that the Tullis Award would go only to book authors. The Bates Award also usually went to book authors, but all manner of creative people were honored by being elected as Fellows, whose number was increased to seventy-five through a 1984 change in the by-laws. Another distinction was given by the Association in honor of lifetime achievement. Beginning in 1975, with funding from the Texas Education Association, an award was presented every year for "outstanding leadership in promoting understanding of the American way of life."[11] Rupert N. Richardson of Hardin-Simmons University was the first recipient, followed by Robert H. Thonhoff, county judge and historian; former governor Price Daniel; Ralph W. Steen of Stephen F. Austin University; Julia K. Garrett, Fort Worth high school teacher (who earned a doctoral degree under the direction of Herbert E. Bolton); and Ernest Wallace of Texas Tech University. All were authors as well as educators, and Richardson, Thonhoff, Steen, and Wallace also served

COTTEN POPULAR HISTORY SERIES

"James M. Cotten of Weatherford has given the Association $50,000 to endow the Popular History Series in the name of his father, Fred Rider Cotten, who was a longtime member and former president of the Association. The series, which is dedicated to providing readable, accurate, and brief histories of historical sites, will be named the Fred Rider Cotten Popular History Series."

Ron Tyler, "Southwestern Collection," *SHQ*, 96 (July, 1992), 113.
Photograph from TSHA Files.

as presidents of the TSHA. By the early 1980s, in accordance with the wishes of the donor, the focus shifted to those who helped with Junior Historians. The award thus went to secondary and middle school teachers such as Willie Lee Gay, Lee Bennett, and David Robertson.

Most of the books published under Frantz and Ellis were scholarly, but no potential audience was neglected. The Association reprinted *Texas History Movies*, a cartoon compilation that told the story of Texas through 1885. Mobil Oil Corporation through the mediation of Fred H. Moore donated the copyright in 1961, after distributing more than three million copies to schools over many years. The Association organized a review board, removed material deemed ethnically offensive, and re-titled the revised work, *Texas History Illustrated*, to indicate that it had been updated. The *Houston Chronicle* paid for printing fifty thousand copies, which sold quickly. In subsequent printings, the original title of this much loved classic was restored.

The Association pushed into new territory in 1969 when it began producing audiovisual materials. With funding from the Moody Foundation, Jim Seymour, later a popular columnist for *PC Magazine*, made a movie about the Big Thicket. It proved quite popular in spite of Seymour's concerns that his creation was imperfect. Frantz chided him in his annual report, "The [film] director has some misgivings about the film, which proves that he is not infallible where public taste is concerned."[12] The Association also sponsored photographer James E. Alvis's short film, *Timepiece: A Recollection of Rural Faces*. Funded by the National Endowment for the Humanities, it was a record of changes as Texas became more urban. A three-roll filmstrip about Texas architecture, entitled *History is My Home* and made by Willard B. Robinson with financial support from the Texas Historical Foundation, became available in 1980. Kenneth B. Ragsdale and David C. DeBoe produced guidebooks for the set.

The crown jewel of Frantz's publication program, as it had been for Webb's and Carroll's, was the *Handbook of Texas*, but it proved to be a troublesome treasure. When he took office, the *Handbook* was the best selling book published by the Association. For more than five years, the Executive Council had been discussing a revision, and focused on the need for a third volume. Barbara Cummings initially directed this project, and in July 1967 Frantz announced that more than five hundred authors had completed 90 percent of the 3,622 articles for the third-volume supplement. Early in 1968 both Frantz and Ellis predicted the imminent publication of the volume, and in May the Council authorized the production of five thousand copies. No books appeared, however.

Production of the third volume of the *Handbook* had become the job of Eldon S. Branda, who came to the Association in January 1967 as a research assistant. Branda had studied at the University of Texas, Trinity College in Dublin, and the University of Iowa. He was a perfectionist. Months of delay stretched into years as his "meticulous demand for accuracy and fine editing" meant that every line had to be edited and all sources had to be checked. The work slowed even more when Branda became involved in the production of the film *Timepiece*. Ellis was pleased with Branda but not with the "many errors" Branda was wont to uncover in *Handbook* contributions. Ellis wrote to a friend in 1970, "I am leaving it to Jean Dixon to make the prediction on the publication date. If you see her on the cocktail circuit in Washington, ask her to look into her crystal ball." Frantz was more optimistic: "We are so convinced

Jim Seymour filming *The Big Thicket: A Vanishing Wilderness. Photograph from TSHA Files.*

of the value of this third volume of the handbook that we are going to get it out regardless of cost, if I have to hock Darrell Royal to make it."[13]

Time eroded even Frantz's optimism. In 1974 he told the Executive Council, "Some men dream of stumbling into buckets of gold, while other men dream of scoring winning touchdowns and leading victorious armies. The director's Walter Mitty dream consists of an annual report that won't mention the Handbook of Texas." Three more years passed before he was able to tell the Council, in April 1977, that the third volume had been printed a few months earlier. About Branda he remarked, "I learned never to hold a perfectionist to a deadline, but to take pride when the nearly perfect product finally appears."[14] Originally expected to be about three hundred pages long, the work ended up being over eleven hundred pages, and included about 3,600 articles. Branda's volume had more on cultural and social topics than the original, and included many revisions of older articles. The Council in 1953 had authorized the binding of two thousand copies of the first two volumes. In 1977 they bound ten thousand copies of Branda's supplement, reflecting the *Handbook*'s strong sales record.

Branda received both the Tullis Award and the Bates Award for his work, and then, in 1978, left the Association. The TSHA had scarcely recovered from the protracted birth of his *Handbook* supplement when Ellis offered a more ambitious idea. He asked the Executive Council in May 1980 if the Association should produce yet another supplemental volume or a "new revised edition" of the *Handbook of Texas*. He later told the Council that members voted "overwhelmingly" in favor of a new set.[15] His plan for the project was bold. Branda spent about $60,000 on his project. Ellis, despite sagging membership and shaky finances, declared that he would need $2.4 million—more than the Association had ever before raised—to hire a managing editor and print a set of six volumes by 1997, the Association's centennial. To take advantage of the swelling flood of Texas scholarship, every article of the projected twenty-five thousand entries would be new, and, as with Branda's supplement, the approach would be interdisciplinary. Like the first *Handbook*, there would be topical entries, but there would be thematic entries as well. The Council accepted Ellis's proposal during the annual meeting at El Paso in 1981—with one change. They approved F. Lee Lawrence's suggestion that the new *Handbook* appear in 1995, the sesquicentennial of the annexation of Texas, rather than in 1997. Ellis had been calling for a proper recognition of the anniversary of the annexation, so he agreed.

Ellis's ambitious plans to expand the Association's staff to produce a new *Handbook* built upon efforts that had begun under Frantz. After arriving at the Association, Ellis often found himself thrust into the role of ringmaster as the staff grew to meet the challenge of expanding programs. Frantz cheerfully admitted that his assistant director had to be responsible for "just about anything that comes up," explaining that his own tasks appeared to be to "Stay out of everyone's way, dream, talk on the 'phone, and write letters to the Executive Council."[16] Just as Frantz found a partner in Ellis, Ellis acquired an indispensable associate and friend in Colleen T. Kain when she joined the staff in 1974 as administrative assistant. Before that time, she had been Frantz's secretary when he chaired the History Department, and had worked with Frantz on the LBJ oral history project. She became a mainstay of the Association, continuing with the organization for another eleven years after Ellis retired in 1985.

One of the first full-time staff members added after Ellis arrived fulfilled the role for which he was hired many times over. Frantz told his audience at Lubbock in 1966 that he wanted a "full-time field representative."[17] Others had spent much time and energy publicly promoting the Association in the past, but no one had been paid to do only that. Frantz found the right man already working on his staff. Kenneth B. Ragsdale, a music teacher and local bandleader, had returned to the University of Texas in 1966 to get his doctorate in history. Frantz wanted a 'historymobile' to tour the state and promote historical awareness. As the vice-chair of the Texas Chisholm Trail Centennial Commission, he committed the TSHA to a similar project. Together with state organizations in Kansas and Oklahoma, the Association had a lounge car refitted by the Atcheson, Topeka, and Santa Fe Railway as a traveling museum

Colleen T. Kain with composer Aaron Copland at the Walter Prescott Webb International Symposium, 1972. The event was sponsored by the University of Texas and financed by Association member C. B. Smith Sr., a former Webb student and automobile dealer in Austin, and Maj. Jubal R. Parten, Houston oilman and University regent. Joe B. Frantz, then director of the TSHA, was chair of the organizing committee. In addition to Copland, the core group of 33 luminaries —an architect, a physicist, an anthropologist, a diplomat, a literary critic, a philosopher, a sociologist—also included a group of bright young people from a variety of disciplines ("to challenge the statements of the giants") and over a hundred observers. The symposium took place on the top floor of the LBJ Library. Kain and Copland are at a barbecue for the group, held at Webb's Friday Mountain Ranch. For a delightful description of the symposium, see David G. McComb, *Travels with Joe, 1917–1993: The Life Story of a Historian from Texas* (TSHA, 2001), 31–33. *Photograph courtesy Colleen T. Kain.*

for the 1967 centennial of the Chisholm Trail. Ragsdale oversaw the installation of exhibits, and the project was a resounding success. Among those in attendance was John W. Crain, who later directed the Dallas Historical Society, became a vice-president of the Summerlee Foundation, and would one day serve a term as TSHA president. In 1968 the traveling exhibit went to Japan, where it again proved very popular.

The AASLH gave the rail car an Award of Merit, and Frantz bragged to University of Texas president Norman Hackerman, "We think we have done the University, the State, the Region, and the Nation a real service." More important, he had found his field representative in Ragsdale, whose degree would be delayed until 1974 while he worked for Frantz. Ragsdale's first task

Kenneth B. Ragsdale, director of educational services, 1966–1977. *From TSHA Files.*

was the Junior Historian program, which despite the cheerings of Frantz and Ellis had declined to only sixty-nine chapters. Ragsdale worked with Frances V. Parker, who had edited the *Junior Historian* since 1959. When she departed in 1969, Frantz wrote that her colleagues would miss her "unfailing good humor, strict sense of order, and pleasantly barbed wit." Ragsdale became the director of education services and Larry Perry was hired as associate editor of the journal. Perry resigned in 1972, and Lucretia Graham took his place, helping Ragsdale until budget cuts eliminated her position in 1975. With Frantz's support, Ragsdale led the Junior Historians down the "long road back." He traveled thousands of miles every year, as did Perry and Graham. As Ellis noted, Ragsdale had "a wonderful ability for winning people over." By 1977 the number of chapters stood at 139 with about 4,500 members, of whom 1,200 attended the state meeting that year.[18]

Ragsdale's success with students came in part because of his History Awareness Workshops, which he developed as an expansion of the sponsors' breakfasts that took place at the annual meetings of the Junior Historians. The first workshop was held in November 1969, and five more followed within a few months. The programs were open to the public but were chiefly intended to provide history materials for primary and secondary school teachers. Results came quickly; Ragsdale credited the workshops with the founding of eleven new chapters of Junior Historians, the first new chapters in ten years. New growth allowed the Junior Historians to meet separately from the Association for the first time in March 1970, when the students met at the Institute of Texan Cultures in San Antonio.

When Ragsdale retired in late 1977, four months after Frantz left, Ellis endorsed the establishment of a fund named in honor of Ragsdale to support awards for Junior Historians. This was in addition to the prizes funded by the Leslie Waggener memorial account and another award initiated in 1977 in memory of Kate Harding Bates Parker, great-granddaughter of Oran Milo Roberts and one of six family members who were patrons of the Association. Other donors, such as J. F. Wood III of Nixon, sponsored Junior Historian chapters in their hometowns. At the TSHA, Ragsdale's successor was David C. DeBoe, who earned a doctorate at Tulane University and had taught at the University of Texas at Arlington. Ellis viewed the Junior Historian program as a "very effective recruiting vehicle for the University," and DeBoe worked to make it even more so.[19] During his first year, with the help of Executive Council member Robert A. Nesbitt of Galveston, DeBoe received $50,000 from the Moody Foundation, the largest contribution ever made to the Association up to that time. With additional funding from the Texas Educational Association, students conducted their first regional meetings, and by 1981 there were seven regional meetings each year and separate annual meetings for both junior high and senior high students.

Ragsdale's legacy to the Association included more than his work with younger students. College undergraduates had been involved in the Association for years. For example, Brownie Ponton, a University of Texas junior, coauthored a paper that was read in December 1897 at the winter meeting of the TSHA and published in the *Quarterly*. Frantz encouraged undergraduate participation in the TSHA by offering a reduced membership rate, and he endorsed Ragsdale's proposal for a collegiate program named in honor of his mentor, Walter P. Webb. The first chapters of the Walter P. Webb Historical

Junior Historians, April 21, 1978, with then Austin mayor Carol Keeton McClellan [Strayhorn]. *From TSHA Files.*

Society were founded at Lubbock Christian College and Wayland Baptist College in October 1973. Any student interested in Texas history could join, and the number of chapters reached twenty-one before DeBoe took over as education director. The Webb chapters were involved in many projects, including sponsoring the Junior Historians, and had their own state convention during the Association's annual meetings. J. Clifton Caldwell endowed awards for outstanding students and chapters in memory of his grandparents, Clifton M. and Cora Caldwell, who in 1924 had given money to Webb to fund student prizes. C. Gwin Morris, the academic dean for East Texas Baptist College, sponsored an annual publication for the Webb Society for a trial period of two years. The first edition of *Touchstone*, which publishes student papers, appeared in 1982.

Kenneth Ragsdale also served as the secretary for the Collectors' Institute, which had formed in August 1968, in the J. Frank Dobie Room of the Undergraduate Library at the University. Jenkins Garrett, a University of Texas regent, Fort Worth attorney, and well-known *aficianado* of Texana, chaired the initial meeting of collectors. The Association, along with the Harry H. Ransom Humanities Research Center, cosponsored the Collectors' Institute. Over 150 people enrolled at the official organizational meeting in November 1968, and the membership eventually reached about 200. Garrett served as the president for the duration of the institute, presiding over both the annual fall meetings and the spring clinics on collecting, repairing, and preserving printed and archival material. Frantz admitted in his annual report for 1973 that "the success of the Institute has far exceeded my expectations."[20] The Association continued as a sponsor until 1980, when the institute disbanded.

Ragsdale's History Awareness Workshops became so popular that in 1973 an advisory committee of the Association produced a guide for teaching Texas history. Ellis then proposed that the TSHA sponsor an Institute of Texas Studies at the University each summer for middle-school and secondary-school history teachers. The notion was not entirely original; as director, Webb had the Association host summer sessions for teachers that focused on Texas history. Ellis's programs were more elaborate. Each session lasted two weeks and provided an interdisciplinary look at Texas that included politics, culture, economics, and geography. Each attendee received graduate credit, which helped meet state requirements for in-service education.

Ellis's first institute, in June 1974, enrolled forty-seven teachers. The next summer the institute attracted a full slate of fifty teachers; its highlight was a lecture by J. Evetts Haley, who thus ended a lengthy self-imposed exile from the TSHA and the University that had begun when he and Webb clashed. Frantz reported that while Haley "wove his stories of the cattle kingdom, the

Third annual gathering of the Collector's Institute, San Antonio, November 21, 1970. Jenkins Garrett is presiding. Designer Carl Hertzog and artist José Cisneros are seated to his left. *From TSHA Files.*

students responded to his mood like musicians to a master conductor."[21] In subsequent years, attendance remained strong, and the summer institute became a model for programs at other colleges and universities. In the summer of 1983 the institute expanded to include a special program on research in Texas history. Meanwhile, the number of annual teacher workshops climbed to about a dozen, enrolling hundreds of people; in addition the Association sponsored lectures all over the state, often in partnership with other schools and agencies.

David C. DeBoe in 1981 added another branch to the Association's education outreach program. The year before, the National Endowment for the Humanities provided $750,000 to Case Western Reserve University for student history programs under the direction of David D. Van Tassell, a former member of the history faculty at the University of Texas. Part of Van Tassell's task was to support regional history fairs in conjunction with a "National History Day," to be held annually. He did not forget Texas, whose Junior Historians provided the model for his program, and gave the Association a grant in 1981 to implement a Texas History Day. The key became a competition for students to make history exhibits. Those who did well at Texas History Day, the state fair, went on to National History Day in Washington, D.C., with the generous support of Texas businessmen. At the national competition Texans excelled, winning a disproportionate share of the awards. By 1985, the fifth

Texas History Day under DeBoe's direction, more than seven hundred students participated.

Tuffly Ellis added even more staff to support the production of his *New Handbook of Texas*. Thomas W. Cutrer, who had a doctorate in American Civilization from the University of Texas, arrived in 1982 from the Institute of Texan Cultures in San Antonio to be associate director of the Association. Anders Saustrup became the first managing editor of the *New Handbook*, but he departed in 1983 and Cutrer took charge. Roy R. Barkley, who had a doctoral degree in English and had worked on both Branda's *Handbook* supplement and the *Dictionary of Middle English* at the University of Michigan, joined as an editor for the *New Handbook*. George B. Ward, with a University of Texas doctorate earned under Joe Frantz and William Goetzmann, was hired as an assistant to Ellis and soon became managing editor of the *Quarterly* and director of publications. In all, Ellis had more than two dozen staff at the TSHA offices by 1985, and many more worked at eight other universities and colleges around the state. In addition, he had advisory editors, including faculty from other schools and prominent authors such as James Michener, who admired the original *Handbook* and found the Association to be a wonderful source of information for his epic novel, *Texas*.

In an effort to increase Executive Council participation and share responsibility, Frantz and Ellis increasingly included the Council in Association affairs. In Frantz's first report, he urged that the Council, not the director, should nominate Executive Council officers and members. On a motion by Roger N. Conger, a future TSHA president, the Council declared in May 1968 that the outgoing president would chair a Committee on Nominations, along with four other committee members that he or she would appoint. The four would include two members from the Council and two outside members; one member had to be a Fellow. At that time the Association had four vice-presidents, and each year, with the senior vice-president becoming president, the Committee had to fill a vacancy in the line of succession. The vice-presidents were reduced to two after 1973 on a motion by Wayne Gard, himself a former president. Frantz also asked for term limits for Council members. On another motion by Conger in 1968, the Council resolved that members could not serve more than six years. All changes were incorporated into a revised constitution in 1975. Five years later, to combat perceptions of the Council as a "closed corporation," another amendment supported by Ellis added three members to the Executive Council (for a total of seventeen, counting the officers), and reduced the term of each member to four years.[22]

Frantz made recruitment of new TSHA members a primary mission for the reorganized Executive Council. He was not certain exactly how many

The Interim Director takes time out from his busy day so that he might practice his skills at balancing the academic and lay interests of the Association.

AMATEURS AND PROFESSIONALS

"But the Bible says that no man can serve two masters, and sometimes the Bible makes a firm believer out of me. We have walked that two-master tightrope between the talented amateurs and the professionals. And though we have slipped now and then, we have never fallen flat on our faces. We have remained reasonably upright."

Joe B. Frantz, "Eleven Years—A Summing Up," *SHQ*, 81 (July 1977), 43.

members there were when he became director, but his canvass of the Association mailing list revealed about two thousand names. This became the starting point for a membership drive led by chairman A. Ray Stephens, one of Webb's last doctoral students and a member of the history faculty at the University of North Texas. Stephens announced a goal of five thousand members, but this proved impossible despite his best efforts and those of Anne Brindley and Billy Mac Jones, presidents of the Association in 1973 and 1975, respectively, and his successors as chair of the membership drive. Membership peaked at about 3,700 in 1974, when Frantz gleefully crowed, "If we had two-score Joneses and Brindleys, we would have to move our offices to a gymnasium just to handle the traffic."[23] Unfortunately, because many newcomers did not renew memberships, the number of members had tumbled to 3,052 when Frantz stepped down in 1977, though he noted in his last report that overall membership during his term had grown 50 percent. Under Ellis, the numbers increased slightly through the hard work of Council members such as Stephens and Ben H. Procter, a Texas Christian University professor and a president of the TSHA.

Under Joe Frantz much of the true value of recruiting lay not in numbers, but in subtle shifts in the kinds of people who joined the Association. A principal focus of Stephens's push was teachers and other history professionals in Texas, and the number of academics at the annual meetings increased markedly. At the same time, a conscious effort was made to contact people from groups that had been noticeably absent from the Association. As late as 1968 a Texas professor had asked Frantz and Ellis if it would be all right for an African American girl to serve as a page during the annual book auction. Ellis assured him that she would be welcome, and he and Frantz worked hard to make sure that such a question would not be thought necessary again. George Woolfolk of Prairie View A&M University wrote to Frantz, "Thanks again to the best friend a man has ever had. Without such outside encouragement, I would have to throw in the towel and quit."[24] Sadly, change did not occur quickly enough at all levels. Woolfolk resigned as a vice-president of the Association as his turn to serve as president approached, claiming poor health. Some suspected that in fact he understood that not everyone would welcome an African American president. On the other hand, by 1971 Félix D. Almaráz Jr. had recruited 182 members, most of them students and Hispanic. The Council at Frantz's request made Almaráz an Honorary Life Member, and he later became president of the TSHA.

A key component of Frantz's effort to increase membership was his decision to hold some of the annual meetings in places other than Austin and to expand the annual meeting program. In 1966 the annual meeting attracted two hundred people to Austin, where they could hear eight speakers in three consecutive sessions. Ten years later, seven hundred could choose from fifty-one papers read in seventeen sessions, held concurrently over three days in Galveston. The first annual meeting to be held outside Austin in several decades was held in San Antonio in 1968, the 250th anniversary of that city and the year it hosted Hemisfair. Austin remained the site for most of the annual meetings under Frantz due to resistance from older members and the Executive Council, but the Association also met in Fort Worth, Waco, and Dallas. As director, Tuffly Ellis continued to alternate locations and expand programs, meeting in Houston and San Antonio as well as in Austin. In 1981 the TSHA met in El Paso, for the first annual meeting west of the Pecos River and the first held jointly with the Historical Society of New Mexico.

To further expand the Association's influence, Frantz revived semiannual

Welcome to El Paso. Annual meeting, 1981. *From TSHA Files.*

Texana Auction, 1981

"The George P. Isbell, Robert C. Cotner, and Franz Scholes Memorial Auction of Southwestern Americana, conducted by Charles G. Downing and Brad H. Smith, netted $5,132. The special edition of Tom Lea's *King Ranch*, procured by Association president Ben E. Pingenot from the King Ranch and enhanced by a preliminary original sketch by artist-author Tom Lea, sold for $2,200, the highest amount ever paid for an item at a TSHA annual meeting. Association vice-president J. P. Bryan, Jr., was the purchaser.

"J. P. made his trip to El Paso worthwhile for the Association, as his total purchases at the auction amounted to $3,050. F. Lee Lawrence, Clifton Caldwell, S. L. Abbott, Brad Smith, Fred White, Sr., Ron C. Tyler, and Bill Stallings all made purchases in excess of $100."

L. Tuffly Ellis, "Southwestern Collection," *SHQ*, 85 (July 1981), 68.

regional meetings, convening in Abilene, Brownsville, El Paso, Fredericksburg, Galveston, Jefferson, Lubbock, Marshall, Nacogdoches, and Victoria. After 1974 the regional meetings were discontinued due to lack of money. The Association also began charging a registration fee for annual meetings. For years there had been a charge for luncheons and dinners at the meetings, but the sessions had been free. The institution of registration fees did not dampen attendance. Over eight hundred people registered for twenty-seven concur-

Texana Auction, annual meeting 1968, at the Lone Star Brewery in San Antonio. Auctioneers that year were Eldon Branda, Wayne Cutler, J. C. Martin, and Ken Ragsdale. Dan Kilgore and J. P. Bryan Sr. can be seen on front row, right; Jenkins Garrett is midway back on the aisle (with hand raised); Nettie Lee Benson (in white-collared blouse) is farther back on the aisle. Joe B. Frantz is standing in the far back corner, right. *From TSHA Files.*

rent sessions at the meeting in 1985, Ellis's last meeting as director.

Much of Ellis's success with annual meetings came from having other groups meet jointly with the Association. Ellis himself participated in the revival of the Texas Catholic Historical Society at the Association's meeting in 1976. That group continued to meet in conjunction with the Association and to sponsor sessions on Catholic history. By 1980 there were half a dozen others that met either regularly or occasionally with the Association, including the venerable Texas Folklore Society, whose efforts had intertwined with those of Texas historians so often in the past. In 1985 eleven outside societies hosted thirteen sessions. Strong participation was reflected not only in attendance but also in an increase in profit from the popular annual auction of books, documents, and Texas ephemera. Those who wanted a less frenzied manner of adding to libraries browsed the exhibits of publishers and booksellers, who returned to the annual meetings at Frantz's invitation in 1967.

The Association, while tending to various other projects, always remained mindful of its original mandate to assist in collecting Texas archives. Joe Frantz

The Association and the Barker Texas History Center/Center for American History

Since its inception the Barker Texas History Center has been intricately bound with the Association in the endeavor to promote the study of Texas history through the collection, preservation, and publishing of primary source materials. The opening ceremonies for the Center took place as a part of the Association's annual meeting in 1950 and the Center was named for Eugene C. Barker, a past director of the Association. Barker Center directors—Llerena B. Friend, Chester

(continued on page 201)

Llerena B. Friend was synonymous with the Barker Texas History Center from its opening in 1950 to her retirement in 1970. She was the supreme bibliographer of the Texas Collection and built it into a world-class research library. Friend's connection with the TSHA began when she was the Junior Historian sponsor from Wichita Falls. She later came to Austin and worked for many years as an editorial and research assistant for the *Handbook of Texas*. During her years with the TSHA she took one course a semester at the University and in that way ultimately earned her Ph.D. in history. Her dissertation, *Sam Houston: The Great Designer*, was published as a book and was awarded the Summerfield G. Roberts Award for 1954. She remained active in the Association throughout her life, winning the H. Bailey Carroll Award for her article "W. P. Webb's Texas Rangers," which appeared in the January 1971 *SHQ*. At the time of her death in 1995 Llerena Friend was a Fellow and Honorary Life Member of the Association. *SHQ*, 58 (Apr. 1955), 554–555; Ron Tyler, et al. (eds.), *New Handbook of Texas*, III, 2–3. *Photograph from TSHA Files.*

Chester V. Kielman came to the University in 1941 at the age of 16; by the time he was 18 he was in the U.S. Army, not returning to his academic career until after the war. He received his B.A. in 1948 and his M.A. in 1952. From 1953 to 1960 he worked at the Association as an associate editor for the *Quarterly* and assistant editor for the *Junior Historian.* In 1962 he was named university archivist and in 1970, when Llerena Friend retired, he became librarian and director of the Barker Center. He compiled a massive *Guide* to the University of Texas Archives (published in 1968), oversaw the microfilming of the Bexar Archives, and played a leading role in organizing the Society of Southwest Archivists. In 1968 the TSHA recognized Kielman's work by electing him a Fellow. *SHQ*, vol. 84 (July 1980), 89–90. *Photograph from TSHA Files.*

Don E. Carleton, director of the Barker Center from 1979 and later director of the Center for American History from its beginning in 1991, came to the University of Texas in 1979 after receiving his B.S., M.A., and Ph.D. from the University of Houston and serving as director of the Houston Metropolitan Research Center from 1975–1979. Throughout his tenure at the University of Texas, Carleton has been closely involved with the work of the Association, serving on the *Southwestern Historical Quarterly*'s Editorial Advisory Board (1980–1990), as advisory editor for the *New Handbook of Texas* project (1983–1996), as senior editor for the Barker Texas History Center series in the TSHA publications program, and on the Association's Executive Council/Board of Directors (1998–2002). His book *Red Scare! Right-Wing Hysteria, Fifties Fanaticism, and Their Legacy in Texas* won the TSHA's Coral Horton Tullis Award for the best book on Texas in 1985, and in 1998 the Association published his *A Breed So Rare: The Life of J. R. Parten.* Carleton was elected a Fellow of the Association in 1991. *Photograph from TSHA Files.*

V. Kielman, and Don E. Carleton—have all been active members of the Association, serving on its board and its various committees, and all have been elected Fellows of the Association.

From its beginnings in 1897, the Association "felt the duty of immediate action in order that the sources of Texas history may be preserved," and to this end they collected books, manuscripts, periodicals, archives, and newspapers. By 1902 everything was being deposited in the University Library on the fourth floor of the Old Main Building. When in 1911 TSHA members voted to formally transfer ownership of its collections to the University, the items donated included: 293 books, 431 state reports (bound), 1,072 state and society reports (unbound), 836 magazines and quarterlies, 73 miscellaneous publications, 434 foreign publications, and 165 pamphlets. The TSHA materials were catalogued and put into the University's general library system as additions to the Texas Collection Library (books), the Newspaper Collection, and the Archives Collection.

By 1937 a new library had been completed for the growing collections. Named the Mirabeau B. Lamar Library, it included space for all the Texas materials: the Newspaper Collection was on the ground floor; the Archives Collection was on the first floor; and the Texas Collection Library of books was on the third floor, sharing space with the Latin American Collection and under its librarian, Carlos Castañeda.

With the continued growth of the Texas Collection, a cry was taken up for it to have its own separate quarters, and this was finally realized in the Eugene C. Barker Texas History Center. The Association, keeping its status as an independent organization, also moved into the new quarters, and for the first time the Association offices and all the Texas collections—newspapers, archives, books— were together in one place. In 1971, when the Barker Center moved to the new Sid Richardson Hall, the Association offices also moved, demonstrating again the close connection between the two organizations and their common goals in the work of Texas history.

In 1991 the Barker Center became a division of the newly organized Center for American History, which until 1994 was a unit of the General Libraries; in August 1994 it became an independent operating unit on campus.

Don E. Carleton and Katherine J. Adams, " 'A Work Peculiarly Our Own,' ..." *SHQ*, 86 (Oct. 1982), 206, 222–230; *The Texas State Historical Association, Report of Organization, Constitution, List of Members* (pamphlet; n.p. in TSHA Files), 1 (quotation); *Bulletin of the University of Texas, Fifteenth Biennial Report of the Board of Regents* ... (University of Texas, 1912), 61; Katherine J. Adams, "The Barker Texas History Center," *Handbook of Texas Online* (accessed Oct. 19, 2006).

as director was a cheerful accomplice for Harry Ransom, who was a voracious procurer of books and manuscripts for the University. Together they acquired so many new Texana materials that the Barker Texas History Center soon became crowded. Frantz also noted as early as 1966 that University administrators were always visiting "to see if a cubic foot somewhere in our lair is not being used." When plans for an LBJ presidential library on the eastern edge of campus were expanded to include other new buildings, a solution presented itself. In 1971 the Barker Center, and the offices of the Association, moved to the new Sid Richardson Hall, adjacent to the new Johnson Library. The edifice was officially dedicated on January 21, 1971. It was a welcome change of venue, but Frantz admitted later, "The move . . . alleviates the crowding of people and materials, but we will miss the graciousness and character of the old Texas History Center."[25]

More space allowed yet more acquisitions, and the TSHA often played an active role in bringing in new archival treasure. In 1972 the Barker Center received the papers of Jesse H. Jones, the powerful Houston businessman who chaired the Reconstruction Finance Corporation during the Depression. Association member John H. Jenkins, a Texana collector and publisher, purchased the Edward Eberstadt collection of books and manuscripts in 1975 and sold the Texas portion to the Barker Center. One of the largest collections in private hands at that time, the Eberstadt accession pushed the number of volumes in the center to about 110,000, with eighteen million items in archival collections and more than two thousand titles in the newspaper section. More came after Tuffly Ellis became director, including the papers of Lt. Gov. Martin M. Crane. Don E. Carleton, a Dallas native with three degrees, including a doctorate, from the University of Houston and experience as director of the Houston Metropolitan Research Center, took charge of the Barker Center in 1979 when Chester V. Kielman retired after seventeen years. Kielman, who had worked for the Association as a graduate student, not only left behind a great archive as a legacy but also wrote a guide to the collections.

The growth achieved under Frantz and Ellis cost a lot of money. When Frantz took office, he praised Bailey Carroll for closely managing Association funds, but declared that he would diversify investments. The Executive Council at his request eliminated by-laws that restricted investment, and they created a finance committee, which sold Carroll's government securities and invested in corporate stocks. As Frantz approached his tenth anniversary as director, the energy crisis and concerns about economic unrest prompted the Council to demand a return to a conservative policy of purchasing only federal securities or certificates of deposit. Frantz called instead for a drive to increase the endowment, the first such campaign since the 1940s. The target was

Four Dedicated Gentlemen

Among the host of devoted members, lay and academic, who have come forth to add their time and expertise to what Tuffly Ellis envisioned as "the true flowering of the Association," four can be singled out—for their contributions to the *New Handbook* project and to the organization in general—as representative of Ellis's ideal lay member, having "political and economic clout that will assist the Association in raising its visibility among the general public and strengthen the institution's financial status, as well as having a deep interest in the history of our state."

All four men were born in the ten-year period between 1906 and 1915. All had risen to the tops of their professions—an oil executive; two lawyers, one also a U.S. ambassador; a businessman; all were committed to higher education; all were Texans by birth. Gentlemen of the first water in probity and decorum, all were philanthropists who throughout their lives gave generously to their communities, serving on boards of universities, hospitals, and historical foundations. All had been widely recognized, with long résumés of honors conferred, and professorships, buildings, libraries, and ships named for them.

Edward A. Clark (1906–1992), a native of San Augustine in East Texas, was senior partner in the Austin law firm Clark, Thomas, Winters, and Shapiro. Mr. Clark was committed to encouraging scholarship in Texas studies and while president of the Association (1983–1984) and chairman of the Development Committee made the funding of the *New Handbook* project his number one priority. While ambassador to Australia under Lyndon B. Johnson, he was so active in promoting the interests of his native state that he was known as the ambassador from Texas rather than from the United States. He planted yellow rosebushes in the embassy garden and wore on his watch chain a miniature map of the Lone Star state. "For the last four years I got to know and to visit Edward A. Clark frequently. My only regret here is that I didn't know him earlier in my career. From the very beginning he grasped fully the potential and the significance of the *Handbook* project and he never lost faith in the Association's ability to produce the work." (Tuffly Ellis, last director's report, May 1985.)

Fred H. Moore (1909–1985), a native of Comanche in North Texas, began his career in 1935 as a field geologist for Magnolia Petroleum. When Magnolia merged with Mobil Oil Mr. Moore moved to New York and took charge of oil exploration and production for North America; in 1961 he became president of the North American company and director and vice president of the worldwide company. Mr. Moore retired in 1967 and moved to Austin, where he soon began to work his magic for the University of Texas and the Texas State Historical Association. He served on the Executive Council on two different occasions, and, like Mr. Clark, was chairman of the Development Committee, directing his efforts toward the funding of the *New Handbook* project. In 1983 he was named hon-

Edward A. Clark

orary life president of the Association. In his last director's report Ellis wrote, "Over the past eight years no one has been closer or more helpful to me than Fred H. Moore. Every thought I had about the Association I bounced off of him. He has ridden every mile of the fence with me for this period. Every director or head of an organization should have such wise counsel. On almost every idea we were in complete agreement, but when we were not, he was able in the kindest way to express his disagreement."

J. Conrad Dunagan (1914–1995), a native of Midland, Texas, attended the University of Texas and began his long career with the bottling business as the manager of the Coca-Cola Bottling Company in Monahans. By 1983 he had risen to the position of president and chairman of the board of the company. He became a member of the Association in 1958, served a term on the Executive Council and was president for 1986–1987. Like Clark and Moore, Mr. Dunagan played a central role in the raising of funds for the *New Handbook*, and, through the Dunagan Foundation, contributed significant support to many Association projects. He also established through his foundation a fellowship for the research and writing of *New Handbook* articles. "Perhaps the most important thing that Mr. Dunagan has done for the Association is to lend us his knowledge and advice. He is the rare and selfless advisor whose every word carries thought and meaning." (Ron Tyler, "Southwestern Collection," *SHQ*, 90 [July 1986], 85–87.)

A. Frank Smith Jr. (1915– 1994) was born in in Detroit, Texas, and grew up in Houston, where he received his B.A. from Rice University

Fred H. Moore

in 1937. Three years later he received his law degree from the University of Texas and joined the law firm of Vinson and Elkins. Mr. Smith worked on behalf of educational and medical causes and was on the board of trustees of hospitals and medical schools as well as of law schools, museums, and various foundations. Mr. Smith's dedication to the research, writing, and teaching of Texas history led him to the TSHA, where he served as president (1990–1991) and as a member of the Executive Council. During his term as chairman of the Development Committee he helped raise many hundreds of thousands of dollars for the *New Handbook* project and other Association programs. (Ron Tyler, "Southwestern Collection," *SHQ*, 94 [July 1990], 107–109.)

Although the primary contribution of each of these four men was toward the funding of the *New Handbook*, each also took an active interest in all things pertaining to the Association and, especially, its staff, providing advice and critical direction in such matters as salaries and quality health insurance benefits. These four men were known and appreciated at all levels of the staff, from director to part-time mail clerk.

Photographs from TSHA Files.

J. Conrad Dunagan and A. Frank Smith

$500,000. While only a fraction of that amount was raised, Frantz was still able to report to the Council in the fall of 1976 that assets and receipts had increased greatly since he had become director. While deficits had become commonplace, money was always found to cover expenses. The Executive Council dropped its demand for a more conservative fiscal policy.

The turmoil in the Association's budget during the 1970s reflected in part the fluctuating funds at the University of Texas. Frantz once described the relationship between the University and the Association as "a sort of common law marriage replete with intricacies and mutual consent . . . as irrevocable as if it were contractual," which of course it had never been. "Indeed it may be more intimate because of the absence of any hard-and-fast boundaries. . . . You almost need a scorecard to know the ground rules, but they are real and fast. And usually they have a logical reason, or if not, a sound historical reason. Or else they just 'growed'."[26] When Frantz became director, two-thirds of the Association's budget came from the University. His salary, and Ellis's, was paid through the Department of History and the Department of Research in Texas History. Such financial support from the University, which also included the quarters provided for the Association, allowed more funds from other sources to be spent on projects.

University support for the Association more than doubled while Frantz was director, but trouble did surface. In August 1970 a concerned Ellis wrote to Association president Cooper K. Ragan, "It seems that about every 25 years the University goes through a trauma of academic upheaval." Ellis was more explicit in a letter to another associate, "The University is obviously in a great mess and is likely to explode this fall."[27] His fears focused on the conflict between Dean John Silber and Frank Erwin, the chair of the University Board of Regents. Their clash generated a real threat that the legislature might cut research funds, but the crisis passed when Silber left the University. Five years later, in 1975, embattled University president Lorene L. Rogers confronted budget shortfalls. One solution was to cut support for Texas research. Ellis, on the advice of Frantz, organized a letter-writing campaign, but Rogers held firm. Ellis had to reduce staff and programs. Just two years later, the legislature slashed University research funds, and Association funding once more declined. Ellis cut his staff again, and then increased membership dues to cover other losses.

At the request of President Rogers, the Association agreed to a reorganization of their University funding. The Department of Research in Texas History became the Center for Studies in Texas History in the fall of 1978, and the next year the center became a line item in the University's budget. The legislature would not accept this, however, and again Ellis resorted to a letter-writing campaign to secure University support. The arrival of Peter T. Flawn as University president finally brought stability. Dean Robert D. King of the College of Liberal Arts became an ally as well, giving more funds and administrative support to the Association through the Center for Studies in Texas History. By 1985, when Ellis departed, the University provided not only the salary of the director but also that of seven staff members.

Ellis believed that the solution to the Association's money woes lay in creating an endowment, an idea he had advocated since 1971, when he wrote, "Our problems are not so serious that they cannot be corrected by a half-million dollars." Frantz tried, but as Ellis acknowledged when he became director, his "most pressing task" remained the endowment.[28] J. P. Bryan Jr. stepped forward to chair a development committee. Bryan's roots lay deep in Texas; he was a descendant of Stephen F. Austin's sister, Emily Austin Bryan, and his father was the president of the TSHA when Frantz succeeded Bailey Carroll. As a student, the younger Bryan graded papers for Carroll, and he later earned a law degree from the University of Texas. Prosperity in the oil business allowed him to follow in his father's footsteps as a Texana collector and to establish Pemberton Press, with Austin book dealer John H. Jenkins III. Bryan announced he would get $500,000 in five years. In short order, membership categories were reorganized and all proceeds, apart from a small amount for operating expenses, were put into the endowment.

Edward A. Clark and Fred H. Moore joined Bryan as leaders in boosting the endowment. Clark, a former United States ambassador to Australia and a regent for the University of Texas, was a longtime member of the Association from East Texas, and Moore, a friend of Ellis's, had retired as president of Mobil Oil Corporation and used his many connections to promote education. Ellis later quipped that Clark knew "virtually everyone in Texas who counted," and those he didn't know, "Moore did." As a fund drive began in 1980, Ellis made his ambition clear. As a model for his aspirations he pointed to the Wisconsin Historical Society, which received almost $500,000 each year from its members and enjoyed an annual budget "in excess of $6,000,000."[29] Clark, Moore, and Bryan all worked hard, and by 1982 they approached their goal.

The "Texana Auction of the Decade" in 1982 provided a successful, and dramatic, close to the initial fund-raising phase. Planned by Bryan and others for four years, the black-tie affair in Houston generated over $300,000 in ticket sales, auction proceeds, and related transactions. Buyers took home an impressive array of merchandise, ranging from the usual trove of books, documents, maps, and pictures to furniture, guns, collectibles, militaria, quilts, boots, wine, vacation packages, two miniature horses, and a genuine Long-

TUFFLY ELLIS AND THE STAFF

"A puzzling aspect of contemporary Texas is the state's failure to realize that as its natural resources decline, it will become increasingly important to rely on the most important resource of all, the human mind.... I urge the Council to take a more enlightened view and to insure that the Association compensate its staff in a way that is commensurate with their responsibilities and abilities. It has been with the thought of building human resources as it relates to the Association that I have sought to develop the staff as it now exists."

"I urge the Council to be solicitous of the staff. My affection for them has grown as I have seen them ably handle successfully the enormous demands made on them. Every day is full.... It is not unusual for many staff members to work ten hours per day and not to take all the compensation time due them. I never ask them to work overtime. They do it on their own."

L. Tuffly Ellis's last Director's Report, May 15, 1985 (TSHA Files).

horn bull. And when all the pledges were paid, Ellis reported that the total raised from the fund drive was $601,455. At Fred Moore's suggestion, Ellis had bronze plaques made to honor generous donors and placed them in the lobby of Sid Richardson Hall, home to the Association's offices since 1971.

Ellis celebrated the successful conclusion of his first fund drive, and immediately began planning another one, to raise an additional $1,000,000. His plans for the *New Handbook of Texas* required at least that much, and ultimately much more. Ed Clark took charge of the Development Committee, and Ellis, Moore, and TSHA president Marilyn M. Sibley met with state officials to ask for funds. More profitably, at the request of the Executive Council, Moore and Clark visited University vice-president William S. Livingston in the fall of 1981 to ask for a new position in the Center for Studies in Texas History. Their message was compelling; as Ellis explained, "The Association can maintain the status quo or it can become a truly influential factor in the educational and intellectual life of the state." Livingston had already asked University president Peter T. Flawn not to approve the proposal. After meeting Moore, whom he discovered to be a "charming and elegant man," Livingston changed his mind, and in February 1982 Flawn approved the new funds.[30] Perhaps Flawn, a geologist, was influenced as well by Mobil's earlier

Some of the Tuffly Ellis "hires"—members of the core staff as it was at the time Ellis retired in 1985. From left: Debbie Brothers (administration), Paul Cecil (*Handbook* editor), Mary Standifer (publications senior editor), Colleen T. Kain (executive assistant), Janice M. Pinney (publications editor), George B. Ward (publications director, managing editor of the *Quarterly*, and assistant director), Ann Russell (bookkeeper), David C. DeBoe (education director), Joe Coltharp (photographic archives volunteer), Douglas E. Barnett (*Handbook* editor, would succeed Tom Cutrer as *Handbook* managing editor and associate director), Tim Cavanee (mail clerk), Evelyn Stehling (administration, would succeed Colleen as executive assistant), Tom Cutrer (*Handbook* managing editor and associate director), Maryanne Brain (receptionist), Roy Barkley (*Handbook* senior editor). Some of the staff and the *Handbook* research assistants are not shown here.

The management staff—Colleen Kain and Evelyn Stehling (administration), George Ward (publications), David DeBoe (education), and Doug Barnett (*Handbook*)—hired by Tuffly Ellis in the early 1980s, didn't begin to disintegrate until the late 1990s. Colleen retired in 1996, David died of cancer in 1997, George retired and Evelyn left in 2003, and Doug left in 2005 (leaving the *Handbook* in the hands of Mark Odintz who has been with the project since the mid 1980s). Longevity of the staff has been a hallmark of the Association, if not the secret ingredient to its success. Roy Barkley was with the TSHA until 2003, when he took early retirement as a result of University budget problems that affected the funding for his position; Mary Standifer moved from publications to the *Handbook* and stayed until that project was completed in 1996; volunteers Joe Coltharp and Bill Carssow (not shown) worked with our photographic archives until the fall of 2004; Janice Pinney is still working with publications in 2007. This team continuity has engendered a standard of productivity and efficiency that would not be possible for such a small group, were it to be ever changing in composition.

Photograph from TSHA Files.

gift to the University of a valuable seismic exploration ship, named the *Fred H. Moore*, in honor of Moore.

Securing more support from the University of Texas was just the first step for Clark and Moore, who succeeded Clark as the chair of the Development Committee. They recruited business leaders such as A. Frank Smith Jr., a prominent attorney active in education and community development in Houston. Smith had been a board member for the Cullen Foundation, and in 1984 that foundation donated $200,000 to the Association, eclipsing all earlier gifts. Clark and Moore also convinced others to sponsor students and faculty to work for the *New Handbook* at the University in Austin and at other campuses and institutions. J. Conrad Dunagan, for example, funded the Association's first permanent research fellowship, at the University of Texas-Permian Basin, and Price Daniel Sr. established a research position at the regional archive near his home in Liberty. During his last year as director, Ellis wrote that Clark and Moore "forever changed the Association. Their commitment and efforts on behalf of the Texas State Historical Association has enabled us to aspire toward goals that we didn't even dream of ten years ago. Their brand is indelibly stamped on this outfit."[31] The Executive Council warmly agreed; Fred Moore became an honorary life president of the Association, and Ed Clark was later elected president.

Joe Frantz had achieved almost all of his objectives by 1977. His election in 1966 had been hailed as the end of a hard era for the Association and had proven to be so. As President Seymour V. Connor wrote then, "a long period of friction and dissension . . . should be over." Frantz kept the Executive Council informed of plans and tried to keep their meetings, which he referred to as the "annual April blood letting," as pleasant as possible. His final report was typical: "I want to tell you how very much I appreciate all your courtesies, cooperation, and patience during the past eleven years. I realize that you undoubtedly had plans and ideas for improving the Association, some of which have not been accomplished. On the other hand, I am a great believer that we should always seek more than we achieve, which may be a way of salving my conscience for what does not get done."[32] He remained at the University as the first recipient of the Walter Prescott Webb Chair of History and Ideas. He was president of the Western Historical Society and the Southern Historical Society, published a lively history of the University of Texas (a project Webb had often talked about undertaking), and ended his career as an endowed professor at Texas A&M University-Corpus Christi.

Tuffly Ellis was not as fortunate as Frantz. Some resented the changes that he had initiated under Frantz's direction; Frantz's tendency to act without the approval of the Executive Council added to the tension. For example, Frantz

> " After all, life comes always from within, never from without. And
> inside me is nearly sixty years of watching and thinking and keeping
> quiet and turning over in my mind, and I want to share this while I have
> time. If no one cares for what I have to say, I will still have had the pleasure
> of getting it said. And after all, any artist writes or paints or composes
> mainly for himself. Otherwise, he's a hack, no matter how talented or com-
> mercial. And I've been a hack long enough—whether a high-class hack or a
> low-class hack is beside the point. I want to choose my own topics and set
> my own deadlines, except for that one deadline over which I have no con-
> trol. And if hard work will accomplish it, I'll set that one uncontrollable
> deadline as far in the future as possible."
>
> Joe B. Frantz, "Eleven Years—A Summing Up," *SHQ*, 81 (July 1977),
> 43–44.

in 1968 heard about W. D. Smithers's fine collection of Trans-Pecos photographs and sent Ken Ragsdale to investigate. Ragsdale reported that Smithers
had thousands of pictures on topics ranging from bootleggers and cowboys to
the U.S. Army expedition into Mexico in 1916. Smithers wanted $15,000 for
the lot, but Harry Ransom did not have that much in his Humanities Research
Center budget. In his book on the University (*The Forty-Acre Follies: An Opin-
ionated History of the University of Texas*), Frantz claimed that he loaned the
money to Ransom from Association funds, and that Ransom had repaid the
loan quickly. Frantz was "titillated" that his Association, "hirpling along on
$100,000 a year," could loan money to the University of Texas with its "billion-
dollar endowment." The Council protested that he gave the money without
asking them, but Frantz did not apologize. He recalled, "I would rather get the
job done than quail before the timidities of bureaucracy."[33] Be that as it may,
his independent action prompted the Council to form a committee to review
finances, and resentments would not entirely fade.

Frantz anticipated that Ellis might have problems as his successor. He confessed in his final report, "We have . . . been accused of making some people
uncomfortable in the Association." He added, "We recognize that we are not
gifted at petting some difficult people and making them feel as if the Association is their private club, but we hope that if we disappointed some, we have
made many more happy." There were definitely some unhappy members when
Frantz broke an Executive Council tie by casting his vote in favor of Ellis as
director. And when Frantz polled the Council by letter on the topic of raising
membership fees in May 1977, the responses included a few growls from members who preferred actual meetings, where issues could be discussed. The clear

The Executive Council:
Ellis on Composition Of

"Traditionally, the Council consists of half academicians and half non-academicians. Both groups have very definite functions to perform, and, of course, both parties should be deeply committed to the furtherance of the Association's welfare. Generally, the presidency alternates between a non-academician and an academician.

"I view membership on the Council in a different light than do some members, including people on the present Council and some of the general membership. Given the Association's present needs, a love of Texas history and attendance at meetings, etc. should not be the only criteria for a Council position. Before a person is considered for placement on the Council, the Nominations Committee should ask of itself, 'What can this individual do for the Association, not what can the Association do for the individual,' to paraphrase the words of the late President John F. Kennedy. The Association's mission today is too costly, and its commitment for intellectual development is too strong for members to be nominated to this important body solely because they have had a longtime love affair with Texas history....

"Academicians should be chosen on the basis of their determination and willingness to perform for the Association scholarly tasks: write and critique articles for the *Quarterly*, prepare numerous excellent entries for the *Handbook*, give lectures at our summer institute and lecture series, write book reviews, solicit their professional colleagues to do likewise, and so on. The academicians are professionally trained to do these functions, and if they carry out these responsibilities effectively, they render the Association a great service that is the equivalent of a monetary contribution.... For the most part the academicians cannot be expected to raise large sums of money for the Association. They do not perform such tasks for their universities, and in most instances they do not have the contacts to do such work effectively.

"Along with their interest in Texas history and the Association, non-academicians should bring another type of expertise in whatever is their field. They should have political and economic clout that will assist the Association in raising its visibility among the general public and strengthen the institution's financial status, as well as having a deep interest in the history of our state.

"A combination of the Council members from the two areas that possess the characteristics I have enumerated would witness the true flowering of the Association. The foundation is set, now it is time to erect the edifice that will be truly an intellectual force in the state. One only need be aware of the advancement of the University of Texas during the past six years when a very able but low profile Board of Regents and a highly capable scholar/administrator [Peter T. Flawn] worked closely and effectively to bring the University to the edge of greatness and excellence."

From L. Tuffly Ellis's last Director's Report, May 15, 1985 (TSHA Files).

signs of unrest led Frantz to write that he had "mixed feelings" about his directorship, but "the party had to end sometime, and the guest has to leave."[34]

Much of the concern about Tuffly Ellis focused on assumptions about his
attitude toward amateurs in the Association. Ellis was a trained professional
historian with high standards. As assistant director he noted with pleasure the
increase in the number of both professional and nonprofessional members,
and he included both in all programs. Commenting on the annual meeting in
1971, however, he had candidly written, "I do think by and large . . . that the
professional historian is a better bet than the amateur historian." Joe Frantz
agreed and thought one of his greatest accomplishments was bringing profes-

Sid Richardson Hall, a far cry—architecturally as well as geographically—from the beautiful
Old Library Building at the center of campus. This photograph looks on the middle portion of
the long, tri-sectioned building. The TSHA moved into the western side of the third (top) floor
of this middle portion in 1971; the Barker Texas History Center (now the Center for American
History) occupies the first and second floors and the eastern half of the third floor. A corner of
the Latin American Collection can be seen to the right (south); to the left is the LBJ School of
Public Affairs. The LBJ Library and Museum is to the left of the fountain. The complex is on
the easternmost stretch of campus, with Interstate 35 just a stone's throw behind it. The solace
in the new TSHA quarters is its view, the large office windows looking out over the campus,
with its red-tiled roofs and clock tower. *Photograph courtesy Prints and Photographs Collection, DI
02598, CAH.*

sionals into the TSHA at a time when academic interest in local history was waning elsewhere. Time and experience softened Ellis's attitude toward amateur historians. By 1977, when he became director, it could honestly be said that Ellis was "uniquely qualified" to maintain the "delicate balance of professional historians holding university positions and 'non-professionals'."[35]

Ellis had expected the "tough" fight over his appointment, and he worked hard to push beyond it. At the end of his first year, the Council congratulated him for a smooth transition. He urged teamwork between professional and nonprofessional as projects such as the new *New Handbook* got underway. He explained, "The TSHA has always been interested in both the academic and non-academic historian. I suppose during various periods of its history one group or another has exerted more influence than some would want. But a problem of that nature is to be expected from its dual character. Both groups have much to offer and both are wanted and needed."[36] Exccutive Council meetings, though, became longer and more contentious. Ellis was often challenged to defend his proposals, especially those that involved spending or investing funds.

Ellis's *New Handbook* proved to be both a successful device for unity and the source of much stress. The project provided a clear goal that both the professional and the nonprofessional historian could embrace. At the same time, it provided fund-raisers with a tangible product they could use in recruiting more donors. Many believed the project gave the Association a new lease on life. The *Handbook* required constant effort, though, and the Council wanted Ellis to be present at every step along the way. In the fall of 1980, his relationship with the Council began to deteriorate when he asked for a leave of absence to work on his book about the Civil War cotton trade in Texas. The Council, which had only recently approved the *New Handbook* and initiated a fund drive for it, refused the leave but gave Ellis a substantial pay increase. Ellis renewed the request several times and was denied each time. Finally, in 1985, on a motion introduced by A. Frank Smith, seconded by Fred Moore and unanimously adopted, Ellis was given permission to go on leave. But in May 1985, on the eve of his departure, he resigned as director of the Association. Three months later, frustrated with the controversy and saddened by the death of Fred Moore in July, Ellis resigned as director of the Center for Studies in Texas History.

Ellis in his final report discussed the creation of an Executive Council that would keep a balance between scholars and nonacademics with political and business ties that could be used to advance the Association. He declared, "The foundation is set; now is the time to erect the edifice that will be truly an intellectual force in the state."[37] He and Joe Frantz together had greatly expanded on the foundation laid by their predecessors. In their zeal to enhance the legacy of Walter Prescott Webb, they had left few programs untouched. At every level of the Association, many more people were involved. Funding had increased, and research had been made available to a public that appeared to be more eager to learn than ever before. Tuffly Ellis and Joe Frantz dominated Texas history for almost two decades. During that time, they set high standards and would be a hard act to follow. They could hardly have anticipated the accomplishments of the last decade of the Association's first century, when the organization fell into the capable hands of Ron Tyler, a longtime friend of both Frantz and Ellis.

SEVEN

Completing the First Century

James W. Pohl and Ron Tyler

A
s it approached its one-hundredth birthday in 1997, the Texas State Historical Association had more publications, educational programs, and members than ever before. When Tuffly Ellis went on leave in the summer of 1985, James W. Pohl was appointed acting director, on Ellis's recommendation. That fall, when Ellis suddenly resigned, Pohl became the interim director. A year later, in September 1986, the Association welcomed Ron Tyler, the first permanent director of the Association since George P. Garrison who had not earned his doctoral degree at the University of Texas. Tyler, however, was a friend of Ellis's and shared his vision of what the Asso-

---

Ron Tyler (1941–), director of the Association 1986–2004.

"The Texas State Historical Association represents a once-in-a-lifetime opportunity that I simply cannot pass up. The rich history of this state gives every Texan a special sense of identity; I look forward to helping in the process of researching, documenting, and sharing that special identity." Tyler, a Fellow of the Association since 1978, came to the Association from the Amon Carter Museum in Fort Worth, where he had been director of publications since 1974 and acting director from 1979 to 1980. At the time he was selected to be director, Tyler was serving as president of the TSHA. During his nineteen years as director, Tyler brought the Association to the forefront as a publisher of high-quality illustrated books devoted to Texas history. "Tyler's greatest legacy to the TSHA might be in what he has brought not only to our publications but also to our graphic sensibilities. . . . As a result of what we learned working with him, we are far better educated and discerning when it comes to the visual. . . . the influence of his 'eye' will continue to be seen for a long time to come in our published works." Tyler, a member of the UT history department, left the Association in January 2005, but continued to teach at the University until June 2006, when he returned to the Amon Carter Museum as its director. In a tribute to Tyler's contributions to the connections between art and history, the TSHA has established the Ron Tyler Award for Best Illustrated Book on Texas History and Culture. Ron Tyler, "Southwestern Collection," *SHQ*, 90 (July 1986), 84 (1st quotation); Janice Pinney, ibid., 109 (Apr. 2006), 556 and 562 (2nd quotation). *Photograph courtesy Ron Tyler.*

James W. Pohl (1931–), director of the Association 1985–1986.

"The Association is very pleased that Dr. James W. Pohl is serving as interim director for 1985–1986 while the Association begins the search for a new director. Jim's steady hand and his long experience as a scholar and administrator make him an ideal person to oversee the Association during this critical transitional period." For his interim year with the TSHA, Pohl took a leave from his position in the history department at Southwest Texas State University, where he had long taught and had served as chairman of the department, chairman of the faculty senate, and as a member of the president's council. Pohl had earned his Ph.D. from the University of Texas and was a longtime member of the Association. At the time of his selection as interim director he was serving as the advisory editor on sports for the *New Handbook*, a role in which he continued through publication of the *Handbook*. After stepping down as interim director, Pohl served the next year as president of the Association. His scholarly contributions and publications in military history and sports history were recognized by the Association in 1994 when he was elected a Fellow. George Ward, "Southwestern Collection," SHQ, 89 (July 1985), 76. *Photograph from TSHA Files.*

ciation should be. This vision was firmly rooted in the traditions and policies of their predecessors, but also stressed inclusiveness as American historians explored new fields in social and cultural history. Fortunately Tyler inherited not only a blueprint but also a great staff that facilitated new efforts in publications—including the *New Handbook of Texas*—continuing education for students and working adults, and recruitment of members. As a result, the Association enjoyed more prestige and impact at the end of its first century than its founders had ever envisioned.

Jim Pohl proved to be a good choice for acting and interim director. His calm demeanor and popularity combined with his solid reputation as a scholar served both him and the Association well during his fifteen months in Austin. A Fellow of the Association who taught at Southwest Texas State University (now Texas State University), Pohl was the author of many books, especially in military history; he was also well known for the humorous caricatures he drew of his associates (and himself). Pohl had studied for his doctorate at the University of Texas alongside Ellis, and shared his zeal for a new *Handbook of Texas*. When he stepped down as interim director, Governor Mark White made him an admiral in the Texas Navy for his work, and Tyler wrote of him in the *Quarterly*: "The Association has many good friends, but Jim Pohl is among the best." As TSHA president for 1987–1988, Pohl continued to work closely with Tyler.[1]

Ron Tyler, assistant director for collections and programs at the Amon Carter Museum, stepped down as president of the Association—J. Conrad Dunagan graciously took his place—and became the director on September 1, 1986. A Temple native with a doctorate from Texas Christian University, Tyler was a Fellow of the TSHA and well known to the Executive Council and the membership. He received the H. Bailey Carroll Award in 1973 for his article in the *Quarterly* on Mexican War lithographs, and the Coral H. Tullis Award in 1976 for his book, *The Big Bend: A History of the Last Texas Frontier*. The TSHA had published two of his earlier works, both in 1973: *Santiago Vidaurri and the Southern Confederacy*, and *The Mexican War: A Lithographic Record*. Tyler brought to the Association not only solid credentials but also strong ties to other state organizations, such as the Philosophical Society of Texas, for which he began serving as secretary in 1988.

Pohl and Tyler both benefited from the support of key staff members. As it had under Ellis, the Association continued to expand its programs under Pohl and during Tyler's years as director. The core of the staff hired by Ellis provided crucial leadership through this period and for years afterward. George B. Ward, who came in 1984 as managing editor of the *Southwestern Historical Quarterly*, also served as the director of the book publications pro-

Presidents under Tyler

Archie P. McDonald (1985–1986)   J. Conrad Dunagan (1986–1987)

Jenkins Garrett (1988–1989)   Robert A. Calvert (1989–1990)   A. Frank Smith (1990–1991)

Archie P. McDonald served as president under James Pohl. Ron Tyler served briefly in 1986, then when he became director, J. Conrad Dunagan took his place as president, serving out the remainder of the 1986–1987 term. James W. Pohl (1987–1988) is not pictured here (see p. 218). *Photographs from TSHA Files.*

Max S. Lale (1991–1992)

Alwyn Barr (1992–1993)

Randolph B. Campbell (1993–1994)

Robert H. Thonhoff (1994–1995)

Félix D. Almaráz Jr. (1995–1996)

Cissy Stewart Lale (1996–1997)

Margaret Swett Henson (1997–1998)

Paul G. Bell (1998–1999)

Norman D. Brown (1999–2000)

Al Lowman (2000–2001)

Presidents continuing with Tyler into the first few years of the Association's second century. *Photographs from TSHA Files.*

Jerry D. Thompson (2001–2002)

Shirley Caldwell (2002–2003)

George N. Green (2003–2004)

"One of the best TSHA friends that any of us has had is Colleen Kain, administrative assistant at the Association since 1974. . . . Colleen brought to everything the Association did a touch of class and a spirited style that she always credited to her Irish heritage. Of course we'll always just remember it as 'the way Colleen did it'—and that was always the best." Colleen T. Kain's connections to Texas history began in 1957 when, as a freshman at the University of Texas at Austin, she began working part-time as secretary to the history department's graduate advisor. Within a few years Colleen was serving as administrative assistant to the department's chairmen—including Robert Divine, William H. Goetzmann, and future TSHA director Joe B. Frantz—a position she held until 1968. Her connections to Texas history were strengthened during those years by working with some of the department's Texas history stalwarts, including Walter Prescott Webb and H. Bailey Carroll, both former directors of the Association. As secretary to the graduate advisor, Colleen worked with and befriended a generation of UT history graduate students, including David G. McComb, Robert A. Calvert, and James W. Pohl, all of whom went on to become accomplished Texas historians and important members and officers of the TSHA. In her time at the Association Colleen played a significant role in all of the organization's programs—education, publications, and administration—in addition to meticulously coordinating the annual meeting each year. George Ward, "Southwestern Collection," *SHQ*, 99 (Apr. 1996), 547–548 (quotation). *Photograph courtesy Colleen T. Kain.*

gram and worked on a variety of other projects. Douglas E. Barnett joined the Association staff in 1982 as a graduate research assistant for the *New Handbook*, and in 1988 Tyler made him the managing editor of that program, which came to include an innovative online component and several other related research projects. David C. DeBoe served as the director of educational programs, as he had under Ellis, until his untimely death from esophageal cancer in the fall of 1997. Last but certainly not least, Colleen T. Kain, who had worked for Ellis and Joe B. Frantz, continued under Pohl and Tyler, handling daily administrative affairs and coordinating annual meetings until her retirement in 1996. Evelyn Stehling, who began working with Kain in 1983, succeeded her when she left.

The demands on the TSHA staff, and their increasing responsibilities, meant that this small group, which originally worked together in a somewhat collective fashion, began to break into four distinct but interlocking divisions, formalized under Jim Pohl: publications, *Handbook*, education, and administration. Under Tyler's leadership, it became apparent that the four divisions needed to be independent units with their own budgets. This was done, creating greater opportunities for each division director to pursue unique but mutually supportive objectives. With this capable team of division directors, Tyler provided an overarching vision, pushing forward and expanding activities in all four areas.

As published authors, Jim Pohl and Ron Tyler placed great emphasis on publications. Under Tyler, the Association continued to print special editions of the *Southwestern Historical Quarterly.* These editions included issues devoted to: J. Frank Dobie and Walter P. Webb, the Texas Capitol, the sesquicentennial of Texas independence, the Alamo, Reconstruction, and the Mexican borderlands. In keeping with popular tradition, Tyler retained the "Southwestern Collection" section as a potpourri of historical news and com-

"David DeBoe was a true Renaissance man of his profession: he was a teacher, an editor, a writer, a student of pedagogy. He was devoted to the continued improvement of the teaching of history in this state. He was determined to give all the tools and support he could possibly provide to those who were charged with the responsibility of passing on our common heritage to the next generation."

David C. DeBoe (1942–1997) earned his graduate degrees at Tulane University and taught history at the University of Texas at Arlington, then, after a brief stint as director of educational services for the Texas Bureau of Economic Understanding, in 1978 he joined the staff at the TSHA as director of educational services, a position in which he found his true calling and one he held until his death, building upon the already strong programs bequeathed him by his predecessor Kenneth Ragsdale. Among David's proudest accomplishments was the development of the history fair competition in Texas. Under his leadership, Texas students won more National History Day awards than any other state. "The fact that so many students return to the contest as judges after graduation illustrates beyond words the impact David had on them." DeBoe initiated the Summer Institute historical tours, which took place at the beginning of each summer and ultimately developed into the Heritage Travel Program. He also edited both the *Texas Historian*, the magazine of the Junior Historians, and *Touchstone*, the publication of the Walter Prescott Webb Historical Society. John Britt, "Southwestern Collection," *SHQ*, 101 (Jan. 1998), 367–372 (quotations). *Photograph from TSHA Files.*

For two decades, George B. Ward filled many roles: assistant director of the TSHA, managing editor of the *Southwestern Historical Quarterly*, and director of publications. The publication program he headed has "a continuity that stretches back to George Garrison and our first *Quarterly* published in 1897." The many books and *Quarterlies* published over the past century "are confirmations of our momentum, set going more than one hundred years ago. They are like well-worn shoes nailed firmly to the deck, holding one publications director after the next on course through the vicissitudes of publishing. They are big shoes to fill and have a proud lineage: Garrison, Eugene Barker, Walter Prescott Webb, Bailey Carroll, Joe Frantz, Tuffly Ellis, Jim Pohl, Ron Tyler, and George Ward. George was the first to head a separate publications department and the one to bring our books program to maturity." At the time of his retirement, George commented about his years at the TSHA: "For the last twenty years some of my fondest memories have to do with colleagues and friends I have met through the TSHA. I simply can't imagine a job in the world of Texas history that would have allowed me to get to know such a vast array of wonderful people—scholars, ranchers, governors, slackers, novelists, oilmen, cowboys, lawyers, liars, and all the rest. . . . When I sit in my office and look west, I see the University campus and the Texas Hill Country in the distance—both of which have been great sources of inspiration. Looking the other way, across the piles of manuscripts and author correspondence that fill my office, I see several shelves full of twenty years of *Quarterlies* and TSHA books—a fair number of them award-winners—and I feel a real sense of accomplishment and pride." George Ward, "Southwestern Collection," *SHQ*, 106 (Apr. 2003), 603–605; first quotations from Janice Pinney, ibid., 110 (July 2006), 113–114. *Photograph from TSHA Files.*

ments on items of interest about Texas history, broadly interpreted. This section regularly provided notices of museum exhibits, events and meetings of various historical organizations, publications, and archival acquisitions.

Every issue of the *Quarterly* benefited from the editorship of George Ward, who in 1989 became the assistant director of the Association in addition to being managing editor of the journal and director of publications. Ward supervised every aspect of producing the *Quarterly* and proved particularly adept at working with authors to bring out the best in their manuscripts. For example, he worked closely with F. Todd Smith on his manuscript, "The Kadahadacho Indians and the Louisiana-Texas Frontier, 1803–1815," which appeared in the

July 1991 *Quarterly* and won the Western History Association's Ray Allen Billington Award for the outstanding article published that year on the history of the American West. After he won the award, Smith, a highly regarded scholar from the University of North Texas, kidded Ward about putting him through an editorial wringer. Others may well have recalled how Tuffly Ellis, when he passed control of the journal to Ward, had instructed him to maintain the high editorial standards of the journal at all costs.

Ward in turn received great support from a group of talented and dedicated associate editors, including Mary M. Standifer, Janice M. Pinney, Mary Jo Powell, Martin D. Kohout, Victoria Moreland, William V. Bishel, and Holly Z. Taylor. Standifer began working for the *Quarterly* as an assistant editor under Joe Frantz in 1974, and, in yet another example of the benefits to the Association of staff longevity and continuity, she did much to set the editorial standards for the *Quarterly*, standards that continue to be transmitted, editor to editor, to this day. Pinney, who trained under Standifer, originally joined the staff in 1981 as a fact checker and later advanced to research assistant, then

"Doug Barnett was always there. At first he was a graduate student working part-time but eventually he assumed larger and more important roles until he became one of the real solid rocks of the organization. As managing editor of the *Handbook* project, a leader in our online programs, and in many other ways, Doug made major contributions to the TSHA and the University. He was a dogged worker and a good colleague." Douglas E. Barnett was with the Association from 1982 to 2005. He came as a graduate student in geography to work as a research assistant on the *New Handbook* project. He left as assistant director of the Association. In the intervening 23 years Doug served as managing editor of the *New Handbook* and the *Handbook of Texas Online*, and coordinated development of the *Portable Handbook of Texas* and the *Handbook of Texas Music*. During his last five years he also served as assistant director for Research and Information Services, in which capacity he coordinated development of the Association's Web site and served as project director for the Association's Digital Gateway to Texas History, leading project development efforts for digital projects such as the *Southwestern Historical Quarterly Online*, Texas Day by Day, and My Texas. George Ward, "Southwestern Collection," *SHQ*, 109 (Oct. 2005), 261 (quotation). *Photograph courtesy Doug Barnett.*

Evelyn Stehling came to the Association in 1983, after graduating from Angelo State University with a B.A. in history. Her strong work ethic was immediately apparent and she quickly climbed up through the ranks from receptionist to membership secretary to educational services assistant to, in the end, executive assistant to the director, a position she held for her last eight years at the Association. Evelyn's capacity for work and her organizational skills are truly phenomenal. While she was working with David DeBoe she organized the mechanics of National History Day competitions involving close to a thousand competitors over a period of a day and a half—coordinating judges, meeting spaces, staff, volunteers, speakers, and meal functions. As executive assistant she did the same for annual meetings and the meetings of the Philosophical Society of Texas. Like Colleen Kain before her, she also supervised the Association's administrative support staff in all its myriad daily tasks. Everything Evelyn did was done meticulously and with unfailing reliability. *Photograph from TSHA Files.*

assistant editor, and in 1994 to associate editor. Taylor came as a Phi Alpha Theta fellow while she was a graduate student at the University of Texas, and assumed Bishel's position as associate editor when he left in 1997 after a year's tenure. Pinney and Taylor also edit Association books, and Ward left the *Quarterly* in their hands when he retired in 2003, declaring that Pinney and Taylor were among the best editors in the field of Texas history. Norman D. Brown, the Barbara White Stuart Professor of History at the University of Texas and an Association Fellow, served as book review editor for fifteen years. When he left in 1995, Paula M. Marks of St. Edward's University and then Jesús F. (Frank) de la Teja took his place. For his loyalty, or endurance, Brown was made an Honorary Life Member of the Association, and he became its president in 1999.

The special issues of the *Quarterly* took extra time and effort, but those on the Alamo and the Texas Capitol proved to be especially popular, winning commendations from the American Association for State and Local History (AASLH). The additional attention paid to the topical issues, however, occasionally threw the *Quarterly's* timetable behind schedule. The October 1982 special issue on the University of Texas put the *Quarterly* in a position of desperately playing catch-up for a period of several years, and it was finally with the efforts of Jim Pohl, who made the journal's schedule his mission during his year as interim director, that the *Quarterly* became firmly settled into its erstwhile timely schedule. Moving some of the Association news items to a revived *Riding Line*, resurrected in 1987 with the assistance of Kenneth B. Ragsdale, who had helped establish the original one in 1967, put the finishing touches on this process. Martin Kohout, associate editor at the time of the newsletter's revival, created a new look for it, and subsequent associate editors added its writing and production to their responsibilities. To encourage more submissions to the *Quarterly*, George Ward in 1989 began to hold *SHQ* workshops at the annual meetings to answer questions and provide submission instructions.

Special issue or not, the *Southwestern Historical Quarterly* continued to present significant work on every period of Texas history. Donald E. Chipman, author of a landmark work on colonial Texas, produced a study of Cabeza de Vaca, and Nettie Lee Benson submitted an article on the Texas question in Mexican politics prior to 1834. Joseph W. McKnight and Howard Miller each reexamined Stephen F. Austin, and James E. Crisp discussed the image of Sam Houston in published versions of his speeches and the veracity of reports on how Davy Crockett died at the Alamo. Todd Smith expanded the focus with his award-winning article on the Kadohadacho Indians, and H. Allen Anderson produced a similarly fine study of the Delaware and Shawnee in Texas

Getting the *Southwestern Historical Quarterly* back on schedule was a priority with Interim Director Jim Pohl. "The not-what-one-exactly-would-call-brilliant Interim Director but the dogged-to-a-fault interim editor issues his last orders." *Cartoon by James W. Pohl, 1986; from TSHA Files.*

THE *Quarterly*: APRIL 1993

"This issue of the *Quarterly* represents something of a milestone for the Association, since it is the first issue produced entirely on disk, using the latest desktop publishing technology....This process provides greater control over and flexibility in the editorial and production processes, as well as a significant savings in the production costs of each issue, since we now bypass the typesetting step entirely."

Ron Tyler, "Southwestern Collection," *SHQ*, 96 (Apr., 1993), 577.

from 1820 to 1845. Primary sources for the colonial period included Sam D. Ratcliffe's presentation on the destruction of the San Saba mission and a translation, submitted by Elizabeth A. H. John and Adán Benavides Jr., of a 1785 diary kept by Pedro Vial and Francisco Xavier Chaves.

Texas during the first half century after statehood became the focus of many excellent writers, but the period of the Civil War and Reconstruction drew perhaps the most attention. Richard B. McCaslin and James A. Marten provided perspectives on Unionism in Texas drawn from their books on the topic. Carl H. Moneyhon and Barry A. Crouch, both of whom produced influential books on Reconstruction in Texas, submitted articles on that turbulent and controversial period, focusing on education and historiography respectively. Gregg Cantrell published an article about black politician John B. Rayner and an article about racial violence during Reconstruction. Randolph B. Campbell, the author of acclaimed works on slavery in Texas, provided a glimpse of material from his work on the local impact of Reconstruction in Texas with an article on district judges of the period.

There were many good articles on twentieth-century topics as well. Ronald E. Marcello extracted material from his extensive oral history project to produce an award-winning study of Texas prisoners of war and construction of the Burma-Thailand railroad in 1942–1944. Other notable articles were those by Christie L. Bourgeois on Lyndon B. Johnson's enlistment of blacks into the Democratic Party, Christopher S. Davies on urbanization in Texas, and McCaslin on the integration of the University of Texas (which built on a landmark study by Michael B. Gillette that appeared in the special UT centennial edition of the *Quarterly* in 1982). Terry G. Jordan, an influential writer who taught geography at the University of Texas and held the Walter P. Webb Chair after Joe B. Frantz, tackled a daunting subject when he analyzed migration into Texas from 1836 to 1986, an article which followed earlier pieces on immigration by him and Homer Lee Kerr.

Economic and social topics remained a great concern of those who wrote for the *Quarterly*. Charles W. Macune Jr. discussed his famous ancestor, C. W. Macune of the Farmers' Alliance, in both a book and a *Quarterly* article. Association staff member Douglas E. Barnett contributed from his research on raising Angora goats on the Edwards Plateau. Harold L. Platt focused on a very different enterprise: oil and the growth of Houston. Articles on Tejanos increased in number in the *Quarterly* during the late 1980s. One of note was Carole E. Christian's analysis of the experience of Mexican Americans from Texas in World War I. Another was an award-winning study, by Emilio Zamora, of Mexicans who worked in the Texas oil industry during World War II.

Familiar subjects in Texas history were also revisited, from new perspectives. For example, in the special edition on the Alamo, authors paid more attention than before to the symbolic impact of prominent persons and events, including pictorial materials. Susan P. Schoelwer's extensive analysis of artists' perspectives on the Alamo won a Carroll Award. This emphasis on illustrations was not unique to the Alamo issue—Tyler brought his interest in such material to the Association from the Amon Carter Museum and greatly increased the sophisticated use of pictures in every volume of the *Quarterly*. The new perspectives on the Alamo provided a fitting scholarly capstone to more than a century and a half of Alamo discussions at a time when Texas was celebrating the sesquicentennial of its independence.

The *Southwestern Historical Quarterly* served as a fine forum for disseminating new research on Texas, but it certainly was not the only bully pulpit for the Association. Tyler, as his fifth year as director came to an end, drolly noted in the *Quarterly*, "you have probably noticed that our book publication program has expanded."[2] Beginning in 1989, cash grants were given from the surplus funds in the Tullis Award account for those who presented the best papers at the annual meeting. This grant money was later made available to those who submitted research proposals for books or articles. In 1994 another fellowship, named in memory of publisher John H. Jenkins III, promoted the production of an article, book, or exhibit. Along with generous grants from many foundations and individual sponsors, such support complemented the aid provided through older awards such as the Carroll, Tullis, and Kate Broocks Bates Awards. The Association under Tyler thus continued to actively promote research and publication not only of articles in the *Quarterly*, but also of good books.

Tyler had considerable experience at the Amon Carter Museum in producing beautiful publications, so his increased emphasis on books, along with his enhanced subsidy programs, brought a flood of new titles on a wide vari-

VOLUNTEERS

Throughout its history the TSHA has depended on and benefited greatly from volunteers. Six can be singled out for their steady commitment and long service, stretching over decades.

Mike Heaston, Tom Munnerlyn, and Dorothy Sloan, all experts in the field of rare books, have helped us with our annual auctions each year, going over the donated books with a connoisseur's eye, writing detailed descriptions, and compiling our auction catalogues. Dorothy has also served as auctioneer for many of our live auctions. It is through the influence of book dealers like Heaston, Munnerlyn, and Sloan that other book collectors give to the Association auctions and that the auctions attract the interest of astute collectors. Tom, Mike, and Dorothy have all been made Honorary Life Members of the Association for their work.

Joe Coltharp and William (Bill) Carssow came to our offices every Tuesday, from Labor Day to Memorial Day, for the better part of two decades, cataloguing and filing all the hundreds of photographs that had accumulated over the course of the century. Mr. Coltharp retired from the University's Harry Ransom Humanities Research Center, where he was the curator of photography, caring for the Helmut Gernsheim collection and the W. D. Smithers collection, among others. Mr. Carssow came to us after retiring from his Austin law practice. They retired again in 2004, at the age of 91, leaving us with an organized file of photographs and many fond memories.

Arthur (Art) K. Leatherwood worked on the *New Handbook* project for 20 years, coming once a week to work with various aspects of the *Handbook* program. Mr. Leatherwood's first extensive project was "Art's List," a comprehensive list of physical features to be covered in the *Handbook*. Among his last projects were the "Texas Connection" lists which highlight *Online Handbook* articles that relate to other cities around the country. In between, he wrote hundreds of articles for the *Handbook* on a wide range of topics, including: the Medal of Honor

ety of Texas topics. In 1989 the TSHA published *The Methodist Hospital of Houston: Serving the World*, by Marilyn M. Sibley, a former president of the Association and a Fellow (five years previously Sibley had won the Tullis and Bates Awards for *Lone Stars and State Gazettes: Texas Newspapers before the Civil War*, Texas A&M University Press, 1983). In 1992 Kenneth Hafertepe's *Abner Cook: Master Builder on the Texas Frontier*, one of the first extensive biographies of the man who designed the Governor's Mansion and other landmark buildings, was published; and in 1993 Margaret S. Henson and Deolece Par-

recipients, the Shelby Expedition, Santa Gertrudis Cattle, the Horned Lizard, and the Seventh Bombardment Wing. When Art left the TSHA in 2003 it was his third "retirement," the first being from the U.S. Air Force, the second from his career as a high school social studies teacher.

Photographs from TSHA Files.

Mike Heaston

Tom Munnerlyn

Dorothy Sloan

Art Leatherwood

Bill Carssow (left) and Joe Coltharp at their 80th Birthday Party, TSHA kitchen, 1993.

malee's *The Cartwrights of San Augustine*, about one of the first families to settle in East Texas, went to press. The centennial year of the TSHA, 1997, saw the publication of Susanne Starling's *Land is the Cry! Warren Angus Ferris, Pioneer Texas Surveyor and Founder of Dallas County*, and John Miller Morris's *El Llano Estacado: Exploration and Immigration on the High Plains of Texas and New Mexico, 1536–1860*, which won seven awards from various organizations. Tyler also increased the number of reprints among the Association's publications. One of the most significant was *Basic Texas Books* by John H. Jenkins III.

Jenkins, who had published hundreds of books at Pemberton Press and through his own Jenkins Company, had been hailed by J. P. Bryan Jr. as the "Alcalde of Texana."[3] His list of 224 titles representing four hundred years of Texas history was first published in 1983, then revised and reprinted by the TSHA in 1988.

Tyler and Ward continued to expand upon Ellis's original initiative with the Fred R. Cotten Popular History Series, which was endowed by his son, James M. Cotten, himself a once-powerful Texas legislator. By 1997 there were nine more paperbacks on historical sites in Texas to join the two printed under Ellis. The nine new titles included Jessica Foy and Judith Linsley on the McFaddin-Ward House in Beaumont, two by Kenneth Hafertepe on the French Legation in Texas and the Ashton Villa in Galveston, Michael V. Hazel on Dallas, Margaret S. Henson on the Samuel May Williams house in Galveston, David C. Humphrey on Austin, Jim Pohl on San Jacinto, Craig Roell on Goliad, and Robert Wooster on Fort Davis. All of these titles sold well, and this, along with the Cotten endowment, allowed the series to grow.

Publication of new editions of classic works also continued within the Fred H. and Ella Mae Moore Texas History Reprint Series. Ellis had originally begun this series with an endowment from Moore. Ward, as publications director, worked closely with Moore and an advisory group to select titles and find appropriate scholars to write introductions for these reprints of books that were no longer in print and available only in expensive rare editions or in a few research collections. Titles produced under Tyler's direction included D. W. C. Baker's *A Texas Scrapbook* . . . (an 1875 classic with more than six thousand entries), Evelyn M. Carrington's *Women in Early Texas* (first printed in 1975 by John H. Jenkins III), David B. Edward's *The History of Texas* (an antebellum classic with an introduction by Margaret S. Henson), Lewis L. Gould's *Progressives and Prohibitionists: Texas Democrats in the Wilson Era* (with a new introduction by the author, who was the Eugene C. Barker Centennial Professor of American History at the University of Texas), and Frank S. Hastings's *A Ranchman's Recollections.* . . . Too, the Moore Series included compilations from the *Southwestern Historical Quarterly*, including sixteen articles on the Texas State Capitol and another fourteen on Texans in the Civil War, *Shades of Blue and Gray*, edited by Ralph A. Wooster.

In addition to the single-volume works listed, Tyler and Ward included many multivolume works in the Moore Series. The first was Dudley G. Wooten's *A Comprehensive History of Texas, 1685 to 1897*. Originally published in 1898, it contained the complete text of Henderson K. Yoakum's 1855 history of Texas as well as chapters written by many founding members of the Association, including Wooten. The other sets were Dorman H. Winfrey and

MEMBERS

"On a recent trip I made to El Paso I visited Bill and his gracious wife, Laura. Everywhere we went former students spoke to him. They remember him as being a tough but interesting teacher. Perhaps that accounts for his receiving the Amoco Foundation Teaching Excellence Award in 1975.

"Bill graduated from high school in Fort Worth and then went to Park College in Missouri for his bachelor's degree. He took his M.A. at the University of Chicago, graduating in 1940. After his tour in the service during World War II, he entered the University of Texas and received the doctorate in 1949. He then went to El Paso to teach at Texas Western College, as UTEP was then called. Timmons devoted the next thirty years to teaching, to researching, and to writing, and to serving his community. All of these things he does well. He also plays a mean piano, as many of you who attend the annual meeting know. One of my great delights at an annual meeting is to see Bill Timmons and Terrell Webb sit down at a piano and entertain the onlookers."

L. Tuffly Ellis, "Southwestern Collection," *SHQ*, 83 (Jan. 1980), 292.

"Mr. and Mrs. Texas," Bill and Laura Timmons, dance to "The Yellow Rose of Texas" at the Happy Birthday, Texas sesquicentennial party, annual meeting 1986.

James M. Day's *The Indian Papers of Texas and the Southwest, 1825–1916* (a five-volume reference), William H. Emory's *Report on the United States and Mexican Boundary Survey* (three volumes designed by Bill Holman, with thirty-seven color plates, and an introduction by William H. Goetzmann, the Jack S. Blanton Professor of History at the University of Texas), and Goetzmann's trio of books on the West: *Army Exploration in the American West, 1803–1863* (first printed in 1959), *Exploration and Empire: The Explorer and the Scientist in the Winning of the American West* (which won a Pulitzer Prize when it was first published in 1967), and *New Lands, New Men: America in the Second Great Age of Discovery* (originally published in 1986).

Tyler also established a cooperative publishing venture with Don E. Carleton, director of the Center for American History (CAH) at the University

Associate editors for the publications department, Mary Standifer and Janice Pinney, at the annual meeting in Galveston, 1987. *Photograph from TSHA Files.*

of Texas, which succeeded the Barker Texas History Center as the primary archive of University and TSHA collections. The CAH came about as the result of a 1991 reorganization that recognized the growth of the University's archives into fields not envisioned by those involved in its early years. The Eugene C. Barker Texas History Collection was subsumed under the new center, which also held many other materials acquired through the Association, as well as the Littlefield Southern History Collection, and the archives of the University itself, in addition to several other subdivisions. The first result of the TSHA/CAH publishing collaboration was Frank N. Samponaro and Paul J. Vanderwood's *War Scare on the Rio Grande: Robert Runyon's Photographs of the Border Conflict, 1913–1916*, which featured photographs taken by Runyon during the Mexican Revolution. Next came Caleb Coker's *The News from Brownsville: Helen Chapman's Letters from the Texas Military Frontier, 1848–1852*. R. C. Hickman's *Behold the People: R. C. Hickman's Photographs of Black Dallas, 1949–1961*, which presented his photographs of blacks in Dallas from 1949 to 1961, was third. The fourth book was *Imaginary Kingdom: Texas as Seen by the Rivera and Rubí Military Expeditions, 1727 and 1767*, edited by Jack Jackson and William C. Foster. Lawrence Goodwyn's *Texas Oil, American Dreams: A Study of the Texas Independent Producers and Royalty Owners Association*, and Nancy B. Young and Lewis L. Gould's *Texas, Her Texas: The Life and Times of Frances Goff*, appeared in time for the centennial of the Association.

The study of history through images fascinated Tyler, and he devoted much energy to printing works about visual resources. Some were simply guidebooks, such as David Haynes's *Catching Shadows: A Directory of Nineteenth-Century Texas Photographers*. Though produced only in paperback, this work marked the beginning of an important era in TSHA publishing in that it was the first to be typeset entirely on a desktop computer by Association staff. Tyler himself edited *Prints and Printmakers of Texas: Proceedings of the Twentieth Annual North American Print Conference*, a compilation of materials

Walter Prescott Webb described the original *Handbook* as the "product of the collective literary genius of the people of Texas." That was true of the *New Handbook* as well. More than 3,000 authors and readers researched and wrote the more than 23,000 articles in the six-volume print edition. In-house, the *New Handbook* was handled as its own separate project with its own staff for core functions such as research and writing, editing, and data entry. Between 1982 and 1996 more than 100 people served in one capacity or another on the *Handbook* staff. *Photographs from TSHA Files.*

from the conference, which was sponsored by the Association and held in Austin in the fall of 1988. Other Association publications on visual materials were more elaborate, specialized compilations, such as Robert Reid's *Picturing Texas: The FSA-OWI Photographers in the Lone Star State, 1935–1943* and Alan Govenar's *Portraits of Community: African-American Photography in Texas.* Even more complex, and costly, were works such as *Art for History's Sake: The Texas Collection of the Witte Museum*, by Witte curator Cecilia Steinfeldt. The Association later named a research fellowship in arts and material culture in Steinfeldt's honor.

Outside funding had to be secured for the largest pictorial projects. The Summerfield G. Roberts Foundation funded Tyler's edited facsimile of *The War Between the United States and Mexico, Illustrated*, by George W. Kendall, New Orleans editor and war correspondent. That work, designed by W. Thomas Taylor of Austin, and with half-tones printed by David Holman, received a design award from the Texas Institute of Letters. The Summerlee Foundation, through the San Jacinto Museum of History, paid for publishing William H. Goetzmann's lively text, *Sam Chamberlain's Mexican War: The San Jacinto Museum of History Paintings*, which included over 160 color paintings from the museum's collections. The success of that work prompted the publication of *My Confession: Recollections of a Rogue*, a more complete version of Chamberlain's memoir edited by Goetzmann and funded by the Summerfield G. Roberts and Carl B. and Florence E. King Foundations of Dallas. All together, this trio of books provided an interesting look at the Mexican War era, which has often been overshadowed in American history by the Civil War. The Summerlee Foundation also served as the copublisher of an Association edition of John Cassin's *Illustrations of the Birds of California, Texas, Oregon, British and Russian America*, designed by Bill Holman and printed by David Holman (1991). Cassin, a Smithsonian Institution ornithologist, included those species in his 1856 work that he believed had been overlooked by John J. Audubon in his more famous book. Robert McCracken Peck, fellow of the Academy of Natural Sciences in Philadelphia, provided an introduction for the new edition.

In the late twentieth century, cowboys still represented a romantic perspective on preindustrial life that appealed to many. Tyler did not neglect that small but significant slice of Texas history. Laura Wilson's photographic book, *Watt Matthews of Lambshead*, focused on a remarkable Texas character: a Princeton graduate who devoted his life to running his family's ranch in Shackelford County. Tyler was proud of the work, which received several awards. In cooperation with the DeGolyer Library at Southern Methodist University, the Association also sponsored the open-ended Cowboy and Ranch Life Series.

New Handbook of Texas

"**O**ne reason we are aware of the approaching deadline is that we have been spending quite a bit of time lately with designer David Timmons, who is the genius behind the attractive formats of many of our books. Working with a generous $10,000 grant for design, provided by Al and Darlyne Lowman, we have employed David to design the *New Handbook* and to provide production oversight throughout the process to guarantee the quality of production that we all want. Al is well into his biography of El Paso designer and printer Carl Hertzog, so the grant for the design of the *New Handbook* obviously springs from a professional as well as a personal interest on his part. We have often commented on the fact that David is also from El Paso. He is a former Association employee and his father, W. H. Timmons, is professor emeritus at the University of Texas at El Paso and a long-time Association member."

Ron Tyler, "Southwestern Collection," *SHQ*, 98 (July 1994), 112–113.

The first reprint in this series was the *History of the Cattlemen of Texas: A Brief Resume of the Live Stock Industry of the Southwest . . .*, a 1914 rarity reprinted with a new introduction by Association Fellow Harwood P. Hinton. By 1997 there was a second title in the series: Mary Kidder Rak's *A Cowman's Wife*, a 1934 classic with a new introduction by Sandra L. Myres, a prolific author and former member of the Executive Council.

With the vision and ambition of Tyler, and under the guiding hand of Ward and his editors, the TSHA's publications program grew from the foundation established by Ellis into one of the largest and most respected scholarly publishers of Texas and Southwestern history. Its titles won numerous state and national awards, and the Association was praised for its breadth of subject matter and its willingness to undertake difficult and singular projects. For example, few presses could produce the three-volume, oversized Emory report on the boundary survey with its many color plates and fold-out maps, but with Tyler's imagination and the strong support of numerous foundations the Association was able to accomplish this task. The Association also kept a focus on the broad public without sacrificing scholarly credibility in its approach to history from diverse perspectives. A common thread in all publications remained the care with which books were developed, edited, and designed.

Many critics noted that the Association's books not only contained fine scholarship but also were among the most attractive volumes being produced anywhere. Much of the credit for this goes to David Timmons, who began working with the TSHA as an editor for the *Quarterly*, and, after establishing his own design business, became the primary designer of Association books and dust jackets.

The capstone of Association publication efforts remained the *New Handbook of Texas*. When Jim Pohl became the interim director, he found that in nearly four years of work only a tiny fraction of the intended number of articles had been completed. Despite a concerted effort, less than 1 percent of entries were finished when Tyler took office. Under the guidance of a newly instituted advisory committee that included William H. Goetzmann and Terry G. Jordan of the University of Texas and Randolph B. Campbell of the University of North Texas, Tyler reorganized the Association staff to increase efficiency. Douglas E. Barnett, a doctoral candidate in geography at the University of Texas, had been serving as director of research for the project, and succeeded Thomas W. Cutrer as managing editor. Nancy Baker Jones became the new director of research, and Cecil Harper Jr. assumed Jones's vacated position as assistant director of research. Mark F. Odintz, a *Handbook* staff writer, succeeded Harper as assistant director of research in the summer of 1989 and succeeded Jones as director of research in 1992. All of these changes were duly reported in *Hotline*, a newsletter begun in 1989 to report on the progress of the *New Handbook*.

Barnett implemented a more focused production process for articles, and new staff members were hired at the University of Texas and other institutions. In all, approximately 90 percent of *New Handbook* entries were produced by Association employees. Sixty-nine scholars served as advisory editors, who not only wrote articles but also supervised the production of entries written by students and associates working within a consortium of twenty-eight Texas colleges, universities, research centers, and historical organizations. The TSHA, with financial support from the University, also selected several professors to come to Austin as scholars-in-residence. This small group included Association Fellows Randolph B. Campbell and Robert Wooster. Wooster was the author of several books published by the TSHA and later became a member of the Executive Council and president of the Association; Campbell proved indispensable as an advisory editor and later president of the Association. Yet another Fellow, Harwood P. Hinton, who edited the journal *Arizona and the West* for many years, joined the Association staff as a senior editor for the project after his retirement from the University of Arizona.

Technology greatly facilitated the production of the *New Handbook*, and it was out in time for the Association's centennial. The technical innovation that had facilitated publication of the old *Handbook* was an electric typewriter, which arrived at the TSHA offices in 1947. The device, invented by Texan James F. Smathers, allowed speedy typing of multiple carbon copies of articles for review. Tuffly Ellis, who as director of the Association had proposed the new *Handbook*, boldly embraced more modern technology during the first stages of the ambitious project. In remarks to an editorial board meeting in May 1984, Ellis declared that all information for his *New Handbook* would be entered into a computer database. By 1995, he predicted, computers would be as common in homes as televisions and telephones were in 1984. At his insistence, all of the production of the *New Handbook* was done with computers. This tremendously enhanced the ability of staff, with the aid of "resident computer shaman" Paul F. Cecil, to correct all entries quickly, keep track of contributions from over three thousand authors, and continue the regular updating of entries prior to the final publication deadline.[4]

Tremendous pressure came from all quarters to increase the number of articles in the *New Handbook* on often overlooked groups, such as minorities and women. This was a reflection of the changing nature of the history profession itself, and was a continuation of a process that had begun with Eldon Branda's third volume of the original *Handbook*. With special funds from several agencies, most notably the Texas Committee for the Humanities, the Association organized five conferences to generate topics and promote discussion. When George Ward arrived in 1984, one of the first tasks he was assigned by Ellis was to organize these conferences. The first, on religion in Texas, was followed quickly by one on women in Texas, convened in the fall of 1985 and featuring state treasurer Ann Richards, later governor of Texas, as a keynote speaker. A conference on African Americans in Texas followed a year later. Under the supervision of Nancy Baker Jones, a second conference on women met in the fall of 1990, and during the spring of 1991 a conference focused on Mexican Americans in Texas. Each conference attracted hundreds of participants. The two on women and the one on Mexican Americans won awards from the AASLH. Jones reinforced her success with the women's conferences by producing, with the assistance of Debbie M. Cottrell, an archival bibliography on women in Texas History, and by coediting, with Fane Downs, *Women and Texas History: Selected Essays*. Another conference-inspired publication, *Mexican Americans in Texas History*, was compiled by Emilio Zamora, Cynthia Orozco, and Rodolfo Rocha. Both books were published by the TSHA.

The impact of the special conferences soon became evident. The original *Handbook* contained approximately 17,000 articles, only a small fraction of which focused on women (230 entries), African Americans (94 entries), and

TRADITIONAL EVENTS OF THE ANNUAL MEETING.

Bidding for the silent auction.

Auctioneers Dorothy Sloan and J. P. Bryan.

Guests and speakers: Lady Bird, David McComb, Margaret Henson, Liz Carpenter and Laura Bush, Arnoldo De León.

Photographs from TSHA Files.

The registration table: David DeBoe (left), Colleen Kain, and (stopping by to help) Joe Frantz.

The Book Exibits room: Francis E. (Ab) Abernethy (left) and Alex Pratt browsing.

Historians in earnest conversation: Randolph B. (Mike) Campbell (left) and Walter Buenger; Margaret Swett Henson and Ellen Temple; A. Frank Smith and Al Lowman.

New Fellows: Jack Jackson (1991) and Paula Mitchell Marks (1993). William H. Goetzmann congratulates Paula.

Book-signings: William C. Foster signs his La Salle Expedition to Texas; Ty Cashion (white shirt) signs his Pigskin Pulpit while associate editor Holly Taylor helps with sales.

Mexican Americans (63 entries). The redesigned *New Handbook* provided 954 articles on women and women's topics, 525 on blacks, and 476 on Mexican Americans. The *Handbook* conferences also promoted a greater focus on women and minorities in the *Southwestern Historical Quarterly* and in the selection of books published by the Association. As a direct response to an initiative proposed by participants in the 1990 conference on women, the Association established an annual award for books on Texas women, named in honor of Austin writer Liz Carpenter, who had been Lady Bird Johnson's White House press secretary. In addition, the TSHA regularly scheduled sessions on women at its annual meetings, and jointly sponsored some of these with the Texas Foundation for Women's Resources.

A completed *New Handbook* slowly emerged from the mass of entries channeled through the editors. Tyler told the Executive Council in May 1989 that just 25 percent of the articles had been completed. One year later, the *New Handbook* was 37 percent complete, then 52 percent in 1991, 65 percent in 1992, 72 percent in 1993, 79 percent in 1994, and finally 88 percent in March 1995 as the deadline approached for sending the text to the printer. Feverish effort was devoted to the editing of the last entries, and research assistant Kendall Curlee searched far and wide for the array of illustrations Tyler had argued should be an essential component of the *New Handbook*. Delays ensued when the text was discovered to be about a thousand pages longer than expected, but Tyler stressed that quality was more important than speed. As he wrote to the Executive Council, "we decided not to rush the last-minute preparations any more than necessary, because we did not consider a two or three month delay in a fourteen-year project extraordinary."[5] As a preview of what was to come, he published, in cooperation with the Victoria County Historical Commission, the *Handbook of Victoria County*, which was primarily a compilation of Victoria County articles written by Craig H. Roell for the *New Handbook*.

Finally, in June 1996 the first sets of the *New Handbook* were shipped from the printer. It was a truly Texas-sized achievement that presented 23,640 entries accompanied by 76 color and 611 black-and-white illustrations. In all, the six bound volumes contained 6,945 pages. All of the 42 pounds of text, about 10.7 million words, had been painstakingly typed by in-house staff on computers (as were many of the organization's books and the *Quarterly* by 1996). The volumes proudly bore the title *The New Handbook of Texas*. Other titles had been seriously considered by the Executive Council, but the original label, with only the slight but obvious change of adding 'New,' had been kept because it was a "shorthand term that lovers of Texas history instantly recognize."[6]

One should never judge a book by its cover, but *The New Handbook of Texas* looked every bit as impressive as its contents were intended to be. Longtime

TSHA member Al Lowman, a well-known bibliophile and "connoisseur of well-designed books," and his wife Darlyne provided the funds to hire David Timmons to design the volumes.[7] Timmons hailed from El Paso like Carl Hertzog, another favorite book designer for the Association, and like Hertzog had designed many other works on Texas, many of which Lowman had sold as auctioneer at the annual meeting auctions. Timmons's father, W. H. Timmons of the University of Texas at El Paso, is a noted Texas historian and Association stalwart who is much in demand at gatherings not only for his scholarship but also his skill as a piano player. Timmons's design for the *New Handbook* was unveiled in September 1994 at a meeting of the Texas Association of School Boards, which was helping with the sale of sets to school libraries and other buyers.

To no one's real surprise, the *New Handbook* proved to be immensely popular. The initial print run of 5,079 sets sold in less than a year. In fact, more than 82 percent of the sets had been sold before they were printed, and a second printing was scheduled for early 1997, in time for the centennial meeting of the Association. Among the many people who worked on the *New Handbook*, perhaps Lawrence L. Graves, popular historian from Texas Tech University and an advisory editor and author for the *New Handbook*, provided the best expression of their sentiments. He wrote, "Every now and then I look back on the early days of it and am still surprised at the size of the job and that it ever got finished, and at how well it was done." Another advisory editor, noted borderlands historian David J. Weber of Southern Methodist University, wrote in a lighter vein: "Just lugged home my 6 volumes of the *Handbook*, added steel reinforcements to my shelves, unpacked them and put them atop the Texana section—they are beauties."[8]

In commemoration of both the production of the *New Handbook* and the centennial of the Association, Robert Thonhoff, a *Handbook* author, award-winning Fellow, and former president of the TSHA, successfully introduced a motion to have bronze replicas cast of the lanterns that were used when the Capitol lights were shut down during the first meeting of the Association in 1897. Not only did the replicas adorn the head table at the centennial meeting, and pictures of them once again appear on the program, but heavy bronze bookends were crafted in their image to be sold as accompaniments for sets of the *New Handbook*. The bookends were unveiled at the 1997 meeting, and proceeds from their sale contributed to a centennial fund drive.

The *New Handbook* broke new ground not only in its content and design, but also in the decision to provide the entire text online. Again the initial push for this came from Tuffly Ellis, who was greatly influenced by associates such as Anders Saustrup and Jim Seymour. While employed by Ellis to prepare lists of possible articles, Saustrup in April 1982 attended a Texas Library History Colloquium. There he met Harold Billings, director of the University of Texas libraries, who suggested that the *New Handbook* should be a "sort of data bank that would spew out info at a moment's notice."[9] Seymour suggested to Ellis that the volumes be made available on CD-ROM. By the time Tyler inherited the project, technology had again advanced, with the development of the Internet, and Tyler met with Billings to discuss making the volumes available online.

Billings played a key role in the production of the online version of the *New Handbook* and was even influential in one final tweaking of Ellis's original concept. Ellis had intended to provide the electronic text only to those who paid for a subscription, but Tyler, taking advice from Billings, decided to provide access free of charge to anyone with a computer. The online version of the *New Handbook*, a cooperative project of the Association and the University libraries, became available in February 1999. It continues to be regularly updated and has hundreds of articles not found in the published volumes. And its keyword search feature made Ellis's original plans to print a comprehensive index volume, a feature many had said would have enhanced the old *Handbook*, unnecessary.

While the *New Handbook* project was still underway, Tyler wrote, "We have always said that one of the greatest benefits of the *Handbook* is that we are training scholars for the future."[10] Hundreds of students at many Texas educational institutions had been involved in writing and editing the entries for the *New Handbook*. That mission continued after publication of the work, not only in the updating of the online version, but also in the publication of several related works. Editors Roy R. Barkley and Mark F. Odintz oversaw production of the *Portable Handbook of Texas*, published in the fall of 2000. A thick single volume containing 2,300 entries and four hundred illustrations (many of which were not in the original volumes), it was intended to be a useful distillation of the *New Handbook*. To enhance its appeal, it was prefaced with a compact history of Texas, and it had an index. In 2003 a handsome single-volume *Handbook of Texas Music* was published with an advisory board that included George Ward, Roy Barkley, Doug Barnett, Cathy Brigham of Concordia University, Gary Hartman of Southwest Texas State University (now Texas State University), Casey Monahan of the Texas Music Office, and Dave Oliphant of the University of Texas. With a total of about four hundred entries, the volume expanded greatly upon the music entries in the *New Handbook*, and added more than 125 illustrations.

The completion of the *New Handbook of Texas* was a great success for Ron Tyler and the Association, not only because of its huge impact as a historical resource, but also because it represented a triumph over financial adversity. Tyler inherited a budget in crisis in 1986. His problems became more acute with a growing list of other publications and projects in addition to the completion of the *New Handbook*. In August 1985, with Jim Pohl as interim director, Edward A. Clark had begun assembling a new Development Committee, confidently expecting that the grant denied by the National Endowment for the Humanities (NEH) the past May would soon be forthcoming through a new application. Tyler was on this committee and he well understood that the matching fund requirement of the federal grant meant that a total of over $600,000 was at stake. The second request for NEH funding also failed, and by the summer of 1986 the Association had suffered cuts in state support as well. Tyler scrambled and found funds to keep almost all of his staff, but he still faced a huge shortfall in funding for the *New Handbook* and other publication projects.

The effort to produce the *New Handbook* ultimately required the Association to raise more than three million dollars, much more money than it had ever raised previously. The value of the efforts made by Clark, "fund-raiser extraordinaire," prior to his death in 1992 cannot be exaggerated, but he did not work alone.[11] Hardworking members of the Association such as A. Frank Smith Jr., J. Conrad Dunagan, and Jon P. Newton, a Texas legislator and University of Texas regent, succeeded Clark as chair of the Development Committee. The committee's effectiveness was also enormously enhanced by the work of others such as J. P. Bryan Jr. and Jack S. Blanton, a law school graduate of the University who became the chief executive officer of a Texas oil company and chaired the University Board of Regents. Together they built upon the financial foundation Clark had laid with the assistance of his friend Fred H. Moore at the beginning of the project.

The NEH ultimately gave more than $701,000 to the *Handbook* project, but private foundations more than matched this figure. An impressive total of $1.25 million came from six organizations: the Brown Foundation (Houston), the Cullen Foundation (Houston), the Fondren Foundation (Houston), Houston Endowment, the Summerfield G. Roberts Foundation (Dallas), and the Summerlee Foundation (Dallas). In 1984 the Association established four councils to recognize various levels of financial contributions to the *Handbook* project. By 1996, when the *New Handbook* was published, the NEH and these six foundations had been joined by fifteen other foundations, the Texas Committee for the Humanities, and Mrs. Fred H. Moore in the Alamo Council, a group that contained donors of $50,000 or more. Seven organizations and individuals comprised the San Jacinto Council, whose members gave $25,000 to $50,000. Al and Darlyne Lowman joined A. Frank Smith, Harwood and

Ann B. Hinton, and J. Clifton Caldwell, as well as fourteen other donors, in the Ranger Council, a rank that signified a donation of $10,000 to $25,000. Finally, no fewer than 140 individuals and organizations joined the Republic of Texas Council by giving $1,000 to $10,000. In all, more than fifty foundations supported the project, along with hundreds of individuals. Their donations, large and small, made the *New Handbook* a reality.

Despite heroic efforts, the *Handbook* project did sometimes stumble due to a lack of funds, occasionally with distressing repercussions. A delay in NEH funding coupled with a decline in donations led to staff cuts in the summer of 1992. Decisions were made with a focus on the condition of the project; a change in focus from writing to production seemed to make it clear who needed to be retained in order to complete the *New Handbook* on time. Five writers, two editors, and three research assistants departed, sparking a controversy that centered on claims that cuts in staffing had been made in such a way that the number of articles on women and minorities would be reduced. Inquiries were launched by federal agencies, and lawsuits were filed against the Association, but the Executive Council endorsed the decisions and in the end federal authorities found no reason to pursue the matter. Because by 1992 most of the articles had already been written and the initial editing had been completed, the turmoil over staff cuts had little real effect on the project's contents or timetable. Thanks to federal and private funds, and the hard choices made to reduce the budget, the *New Handbook* project ran in the black by the summer of 1993 and continued to do so through its publication in 1996.

While Tyler struggled to keep the *New Handbook* on a sound financial footing, by 1992 he found that, as a result of the increased expenditures for staff, the annual meeting, and the *Quarterly,* his general fund accounts were strained. Strong book sales had helped to cover shortages, with well over $500,000 from the publications fund being moved into the general fund to cover debts, but after two years of declining revenues, hard decisions had to be made. Efforts were made to increase endowments, and the unpopular measure of increasing the annual meeting registration fee had to be adopted as well. In 1993 the cost of registration rose from $10.00 to $25.00. This was still reasonable when compared to the cost of attending conferences sponsored by other historical organizations. Some members grumbled, but meeting attendance did not decline. As with the *Handbook* budget, adjustments in income and a bit of belt-tightening put the general fund in the black by the summer of 1993, which was beneficial to all concerned with the future of the Association. In 1997 the Association reported cash reserves of $297,043, and more than $3.7 million in investments.

Part of the ongoing problem in raising funds for the Association lay in the fact that money had to come from a static membership. While similar organizations in other states boasted a long membership list, the Association may well have been a victim of its own success in popularizing Texas history. By the time the *New Handbook* appeared in 1996, more than eight hundred historical societies operated in Texas. Most of these had been established after 1970, when Kenneth B. Ragsdale and others were stumping the state for Texas history and the TSHA. Other states had launched similar efforts, but none enjoyed more success than the Association did in Texas. Unfortunately for the Association, as enlistments in local organizations soared, those in the state organization stagnated, despite membership drives chaired by prominent members such as J. Conrad Dunagan. Tyler reported in March 1997

Honorary Life Member José Cisneros at the annual meeting in 1992, some of his drawings on auction in the background. *Photograph from TSHA Files.*

that membership stood at 3,754. While this was much larger than the small group that had founded the Association, it reflected an annual growth of only 2 percent during the past decade, and most of this growth actually came in the three years just prior to the Association's centennial year. Of course, any membership count excluded the dozens of free copies of the *Quarterly* sent to members of the Texas legislature and to other individuals as part of the Association's mission.

The big event every year for the members continued to be the annual meeting, which Tyler in 1997 described proudly as being "somewhat different from a run-of-the-mill scholarly get-together." While other organizations strained to become more 'professional'—which often meant little more than being more exclusive—the Association's convention strove to be ever more "eclectic" and "broad-based."[12] When budget concerns led to an increase in registration fees, loyal members and their guests continued to attend in good numbers. In 1992, the last year that the fee was $10.00, about six hundred people attended the annual meeting in Austin. There they could choose from among thirty sessions and workshops (many sponsored by other organizations), two auctions, a special auction of works by José Cisneros, and several receptions. Four years later, when the fee had risen to $35.00, 742 people attended the one-hundredth annual meeting of the Association, and the program again included sessions jointly sponsored by other well-respected scholarly groups such as the Texas Catholic Historical Society, the Texas Historical Commission, and the Society of Southwestern Archivists. The centennial meeting was in Austin, but during Tyler's first ten years as director, the organization also met in Houston, Dallas, San Antonio, and, for the first time, Lubbock.

A mild crisis loomed as preparations were being made for the centennial celebration. An impressive fete was planned for March 1997, with music provided by Association stalwart Ken Ragsdale and his orchestra. Costs rose, so the registration fee increased to $50.00. This sparked genteel protests from some longtime members, perhaps the most prominent of whom was Al Lowman, who thought the increase in the registration fee should not be instituted until after the centennial meeting. Texas historian Stephen L. Hardin wrote Tyler, "damn it, Ron, we do *not* have to gouge our members just because others do." Holding forth in language that recalled the mission espoused by the founders of the Association, Hardin declared that if the fee remained so high, "Then wealthy lawyers and stuffy academics can hobnob and not be bothered by the likes of public school teachers, graduate students, and retired folks. When that occurs, however, they will have destroyed a tradition that has lasted now for more than a hundred years. I hope they won't."[13]

The Executive Council did not lower the registration fee for the centennial meeting, and attendance did not drop significantly. Texans from all walks of life with an interest in history came to Austin, and more sessions than ever before were presented. The presidential address was given by Cissy S. Lale, only the fifth woman in the Association's long history ever to serve as president and the first spouse of a former president to serve. She is a prolific writer and active in many organizations; her husband Max, a civic leader, journalist, and historian, served five years before her. Despite the high costs of the meeting, the Association made money. As usual, the popular live and silent auctions of books and Texana made a solid profit, confirming their reputation as the "premier fund-raising event" for the Association and providing a much needed supplement to the revenue from registration fees.[14] Too, more book and collectible dealers displayed their wares, and more publishers paid for advertisements in the annual program, an innovation that Tyler had introduced.

For Association insiders, the triumph of the 1997 centennial meeting was accompanied by a hint of sadness. It was the first gathering in many years that had not been orchestrated by Colleen T. Kain, who retired in August 1996 after working for the University of Texas for thirty-nine years. Kain began working for the UT History Department in 1957, when she enrolled at the University as a freshman. In 1968 she joined the Oral History Project on Lyndon B. Johnson, a team of scholars and administrative staff directed by Joe Frantz. The group spent the academic year 1968–1969 in Washington, D.C., collecting oral history interviews on Johnson. On her return to Austin at the end of that year, Kain continued to work for the project at the University of Texas until the tapes were turned over to the Lyndon B. Johnson Library in 1973–1974. In January 1974 Kain joined the administrative staff of the Texas State Historical Association, and in her twenty-two years with the Association she was executive assistant to four directors—Joe B. Frantz, L. Tuffly Ellis, James W. Pohl, and Ron Tyler.

Upon her retirement, the Executive Council thanked Kain with a resolution that declared the "working title of 'Style and Grace Under Pressure' [should] be reserved for her future biography." George Ward afterward noted in the "Southwestern Collection" that she received an Ima Hogg Historical Achievement Award from Winedale Historical Center Advisory Council for her many contributions to Texas history. He added, "Colleen brought to everything the Association did a touch of class and a spirited style that she always credited to her Irish heritage."[15] Again in the TSHA tradition of continuity born of long staff tenure, Evelyn Stehling, who had worked with Colleen since 1983, succeeded her in a seamless transition and proved to be just as indispensable in the work of the organization.

Adults were not the only people who attended Association events. When universities came under fire during the last part of the twentieth century for ignoring education in favor of research, the University of Texas did not escape unfriendly scrutiny. University administrators, searching for evidence of their impact on public education for all age levels, found that they in fact had for years been sponsoring a strong effort in the field of education. The Association's extension programs—which included the Junior Historians, the Walter P. Webb Society, Texas History Day, the Summer Institute, the History Awareness Workshop, and numerous other in-service education programs—provided educational support for both students and teachers. These efforts had a great impact on young people and served as a vital link between amateur and professional historians, as well as between public history and the academy. As such, they more than met the concerns of those who assailed the University, providing a fitting capstone for the Association's efforts in publication, research, and education.

The Junior Historians approached their fiftieth anniversary in 1989 with renewed confidence in a strong future. When Ron Tyler took office as director, the student organization suffered from reduced membership due to the Texas legislature's withdrawal of official support for extracurricular activities. Amendments in that legislation, along with the efforts of an advisory committee created by Tyler to assist David C. DeBoe, TSHA advisor for the Junior

EDUCATIONAL PROGRAMS

The educational programs of the Association began in 1939 when Walter Prescott Webb, TSHA director and world-renowned historian of the American West, founded the Junior Historian program to encourage young Texans to learn more about their state and local history. In the early 1970s the educational programs were expanded further when the Association held its first History Awareness Workshop and, a year later, the first Summer Institute of Texas Studies. The Workshop was designed to introduce Texas history teachers to content

Jo Ann Stiles, of Lamar University, and John Britt, honors coordinator at Lee College, have been the mainstay of our educational outreach efforts for many years.

as well as methods and techniques for involving young people in the study of history. The Institute brought middle school and high school history teachers to the University campus for a two-week graduate seminar with various scholars of Texas history. In 1980 the Association further expanded its educational programs when it began its Texas History Day program, the state affiliate of National History Day, and built it into one of the nation's leading secondary student research programs.

Lee College in Baytown has long been associated with the TSHA through its sponsorship of a Webb Historical Society chapter, by publishing *Touchstone*, the TSHA's journal for showcasing undergraduate historical research, by co-sponsoring the History Awareness Workshops, and by leading the Heritage Travel Program, the heir to the old Institute of Texas Studies, which ran from 1974 to 1996. The Travel Program is a one-week traveling seminar focusing on a specific subject in Texas history each summer.

Photographs from TSHA Files.

Historians, brought an increase in chapters and in attendance at the organization's annual meetings. In 1986 about eight hundred students attended the yearly convention; by 1990 the number recovered to approximately two thousand, representing 130 chapters. In addition to earlier awards for exhibits and writing, Dorman Winfrey provided an annual prize for the best essay, named in honor of Tuffly Ellis, and Ellen Temple of Lufkin sponsored the Minnie

Fisher Cunningham Memorial Award for the best article on a woman or women in the *Texas Historian*, the journal of the Junior Historians.

DeBoe also continued to supervise the growth of the Walter P. Webb Society for college-age members of the Association. In 1989 Austin College founded the twenty-eighth chapter of the Webb Society. The attendance at their annual meetings, which took place in conjunction with the TSHA

Clifton Caldwell presents the C. M. and Cora Caldwell Memorial Award for Excellence in History to a Webb Society student at the 1996 meeting of the Society. The award was established in 1974 and is named for Clifton's grandparents. Winners have their papers published in *Touchstone*, the Society's journal, and give presentations of their work each year when the Webb Society convenes at the TSHA annual meeting. Students and sponsors of the Webb Society also meet each fall at an historic location for on-site learning. *Photograph from TSHA Files.*

annual meetings, averaged about 150. East Texas Baptist University was for almost two decades the sponsor of the Webb Society journal, *Touchstone*. When it asked DeBoe to be relieved of the responsibility for the undergraduate publication, Lee College provided new quarters, and the Association paid the publication costs. DeBoe continued to edit the journal. John Britt, honors coordinator at Lee College, later recalled that DeBoe was an "exacting but forgiving editor," meticulous to a fault but quick to laugh when unseen "gremlins" slipped a typographical error into a title.[16]

DeBoe worked hard as coordinator for the Junior Historians and the Webb Society and as editor for their respective publications, but he always had time for even younger students. Hundreds turned out every year for Texas History Day under his direction. In truth, the event by 1990 had become a two-day affair and had to move from its original site at the Student Union on the University of Texas campus to a more spacious outlying hotel. Texas students from 1986 to 1993 won more National History Day awards than students from any other state, which made DeBoe very proud. Their success was also a source of great pride to the many supporters of Texas History Day, some of whom sponsored their own awards, such as the Jane Y. McCallum Memorial Award for the best entry on women, the Willie Lee Gay Award for the best entry on African American history, and the C. M. and Cora Caldwell Memorial Award for Excellence in History.

Texas History Day, part of the National History Day program, is a yearlong educational program that culminates in an annual state-level history fair for students in grades six through twelve. The TSHA coordinates the Texas competition, from which the top two winners in each category go on to compete at the national level in Washington, D.C. David DeBoe, who began the state program in 1980, "was a fervent believer in the National History Day program. And he knew more than anyone else that talent alone was not enough; it took an incredible amount of commitment to hard work and an unrelenting dedication on the part of both the students and their teachers to win." John Britt, "Southwestern Collection," *SHQ*, 101 (Jan. 1998), 369.

DeBoe was justifiably proud of his work with students, but ulitmately became frustrated with the summertime Institute of Texas Studies, hosted for teachers by the TSHA on the University of Texas campus. Attendance remained good until 1989, when state officials reduced the credit hours for the course from six to three and increased the cost by requiring three weeks of instruction rather than the traditional two. Enrollment plummeted that year, and the institute was canceled. A revised version of the program enrolled sixteen students the next year; in following years enrollment increased as the Association mailed thousands of copies of *Insight*, the newsletter of the institute, to teachers throughout Texas. This publication continued until 1997 and earned commendations from both the AASLH and the Texas Historical Commission. In 1996 the institute program was reorganized as the Summer Institute and became a popular traveling seminar dealing each summer with a different topic in Texas history.

To reach more teachers, the Association also continued to sponsor workshops at sites all over the state. Several hundred teachers attended the Summer Institute and the workshops every year. At the same time, sales of *Teaching Texas History: An All-Level Resource Guide*, developed from institute materials and printed with a grant from the Texas Committee for the Humanities, remained brisk, and demand continued for other handbooks produced by DeBoe.

In the early fall of its centennial year, 1997, the Association suffered a great loss in the death of David DeBoe, who lost a hard fight with esophageal cancer. In 1994 David had received the first-ever Governor's Award from the Texas Historical Commission for his work with the Junior Historians, the Webb Society, Texas History Day, and the Summer Institute, and in 1996 the History Channel selected him as an Outstanding History Educator for that year. Truly, as John Britt later remembered, DeBoe found in the Association "his true calling and the perfect forum for his multiple talents and his apparently inexhaustible energy."[17] DeBoe died just five days before he was to receive an award for lifetime achievement from the AASLH.

The Association's original mandate included the development of an archive as well as publication and education, and its members continued to find treasures. Perhaps one of the most intriguing discoveries came in February 1987, when Houston attorney Mark E. Steiner called director Ron Tyler. While reading the will of Peter W. Gray, who had died in 1874, Steiner noticed that Gray had bequeathed his library and papers to the Grand Lodge of Texas until a permanent state historical association could be founded. Tyler consulted with Fort Worth attorney, and future TSHA president, Jenkins Garrett, and then approached the Grand Lodge through the intercession of former president Roger N. Conger of Waco, where the Grand Lodge Library was

Willie Lee Gay presents the 2003 Willie Lee Gay Award to Michael Johnson and Ahmeed Muhammed of Houston for their project titled "40 Acres and a Mule." *From TSHA Files.*

JUNIOR HISTORIANS

Willie Lee Gay is representative of many of our Junior Historian sponsors from around the state who have worked with the Association in the Junior Historian and National History Day programs, and without whose dedication and commitment those programs could not have thrived as they have.

As a career teacher with the Houston Independent School District, Mrs. Gay taught Texas history at Carter G. Woodson Middle School and sponsored the Woodson Junior Historians, Chapter 244, for fifteen years. At her retirement, former Woodson Junior Historians established through the Association the Willie Lee Gay Permanent Endowment Fund. The fund is to be used to provide a permanent annual award for Junior Historians who write the best essay or build the best exhibit on African Americans in Texas. At the ceremony celebrating her retirement David DeBoe, director of the Association's educational services, presented Mrs. Gay with a TSHA Certificate of Commendation for her outstanding achievement in the preservation and advancement of Texas history in her work as a teacher and a Junior Historian sponsor.

Willie Lee Gay was also involved with groups such as the Harris County Historical Commission and the Houston Preservation Alliance. Her working relationship with Governor Ann Richards led to her appointment as the first African American to serve as a THC commissioner (1991–1997). In 2003 she created the Willie Lee Gay Collection of her historical archives related to African Americans in the Houston area. The collection is housed at Texas Southern University, her alma mater.

"Southwestern Collection," *SHQ*, 91 (July 1987), 79–80; Texas Historical Commission, *The Medallion* (Jan./Feb. 2006), 3.

FORMER PRESIDENTS

Former presidents of the Association were honored in a reception at the Capitol Complex Visitors Center during the 1996 annual meeting. Shown here, left to right, are: Ron Tyler (1986), Cissy S. Lale (1996–1997), Félix D. Almaráz Jr. (1995–1996), Clifton Caldwell (1984–1985), Marilyn M. Sibley (1981–1982), Ben E. Pingenot (1980–1981), Ben H. Procter (1979–1980), Ralph A. Wooster (1974–1975), Dorman H. Winfrey (1971–1972).

Jenkins Garrett (1988–1989), James W. Pohl (1987–1988), Archie P. McDonald (1985–1986), Robert H. Thonhoff (1994–1995), Randolph B. (Mike) Campbell (1993–1994), Alwyn Barr (1992–1993), Max S. Lale (1991–1992), and Robert A. Calvert (1989–1990). *Photographs from TSHA Files.*

located. In short order, Gray's collection of documents and books arrived at the offices of the Association, whence they went to be archived at the Center for American History.

The arrival of Gray's collection at the University of Texas ended a sporadic hunt that had spanned nine decades. Gray had been a member of the Congresses of the Republic of Texas and the Confederate States of America, and Henderson K. Yoakum's 1855 history of Texas was dedicated to him. He was president of the short-lived historical society founded by Ashbel Smith and others in Houston in 1870, and a member of the similarly ill-fated history organization that met with Oran M. Roberts as president in Austin in 1874. In May 1898 Adele B. Looscan had responded to an inquiry by George P. Garrison with the information that she did not know exactly what had happened to Gray's papers. She and Eugene C. Barker also wrote to each other on the same subject in 1916, and Ingham S. Roberts resurrected the topic in 1923, again with no result. The establishment of the Barker Texas History Center was approved by the regents in 1945, and in 1946 Louis W. Kemp read Gray's will to the Executive Council. The Council in turn appointed Harbert Davenport to negotiate with the Grand Lodge for the materials. Earl Vandale had acquired some of them, which apparently were among the materials he later sold to the University. The portion acquired by Tyler, which included twenty-two rare imprints, represented the completion of Gray's bequest to a permanent state historical association.

In a way, the acquisition of Gray's donation symbolized the completion of a journey for the Association. Prior to the establishment of the Association in 1897, Texans had long wished and worked for a state historical organization. The members of the Association in 1997 could look back on a century of remarkable achievement. Their organization had not only survived, but had become a model for others in publication and education. History groups in other states might have more members, or more money, but none could rightfully claim to surpass the Association in accomplishments. George P. Garrison and his associates had intended to lead the way in publishing Texas history; the *Southwestern Historical Quarterly* and the *Handbook of Texas* became models not only for Texas organizations, but for organizations in other states as well, and the long list of monographs and guides published by the Association includes many titles that have become the standard texts in their fields. At the same time, hardly a history curriculum in any school in Texas has not been influenced by the work of the TSHA. In its first century the Association has laid a foundation for the continuation of its mission far into the future. And in so doing, its members, amateur and professional, have provided a remarkable legacy to the Lone Star state.

The TSHA Centennial Birthday Cake.

Bill Moyers speaking at the banquet.

Francis (Ab) Abernethy and Jo Ann Stiles at the reception.

William H. Goetzmann signs copies of his new TSHA book, *My Confession: Recollections of a Rogue*.

Luci Baines Johnson talks with Robert Berdahl, president of the University of Texas at Austin, following his speech at the Women in Texas History Luncheon.

The Executive Council: *(first row, left to right)* Jenkins Garrett, Dora Guerra, Margaret S. Henson, Cissy S. Lale, James H. McPhail, and Robert H. Thonhoff: *(back row)* Charles Spurlin, Sharon Crutchfield, William Foster, Ron Tyler, Dudley Dobie, John Crain, Paul Gervais Bell, George N. Green, and Chester R. Burns. Paul D. Lack is not shown.

Editor's Epilogue

"It seems that about every 25 years the University goes through a trauma of academic upheaval," Tuffly Ellis wrote a few years before the 1978 budget cuts that resulted in a reorganization of the Association's funding through the creation of the Center for Studies in Texas history. In the spring and summer of 2003, as if right on cue, the balance that has existed between the Texas State Historical Association and the University of Texas for more than a century began once again to slip. In an early tremor that would set off reverberations that are still being felt four years later, the University, in an effort to tighten its budget, offered many of its employees an incentive for early retirement. One of the TSHA staff members, Roy Barkley, senior editor for

J. C. Martin, director of the Association, 2004–present

"My involvement with the Texas State Historical Association has been a work in progress for most of my adult life. In high school I was a member of the Junior Historians, and as a freshman at the University of Texas I had my first direct introduction to the Association, in the person of Dr. Bailey Carroll, sitting behind the desk I now use, at the TSHA offices in the old Barker Texas History Center. The next year I attended my first annual meeting, at the Driskill Hotel." Martin worked as editorial associate for volume three of the *Handbook of Texas* under Bailey Carroll and later Joe Frantz and Tuffly Ellis. After working at the White House and for two years in Austin with President Johnson on his memoirs and personal correspondence, he worked as assistant director for the Barker Texas History Center and as director of special collections and research libraries (including the Jenkins Garrett Library) and founding director of the Cartographic History Library at the University of Texas at Arlington. Martin was then appointed executive director of the San Jacinto Museum of History, a position he held for twenty years before returning to the University of Texas to work first in development and then, in the fall of 2004, answering the call to serve as interim director of the TSHA; since that time, he has used his long experience as "one of the finest historical administrators in the Southwest" to help guide the organization through one of its most challenging and tumultuous periods. Martin's tenure has coincided with the work on *At the Heart of Texas*, which has benefited in countless ways, but none more crucial than his unerring instinct and support for the process itself. Martin is the author of two Association publications, *Contours of Discovery* and *Maps of Texas and the Southwest*. He has served on the Executive Council (1990–1994), as chair of the annual meeting program committee and the Carroll awards committee, and as a member on many other TSHA committees. Martin is a member of the Philosophical Society of Texas, and has served as president of the Texas Association of Museums, as well as on its Executive Council. Martin chaired the Summerlee Commission on Texas History (1989–1992), working with Ron Tyler, John Crain, and dozens of Association members, as well as leaders in education and preservation from across the state. In returning to the TSHA as its interim director, Martin comes full circle to where he first began his career in the service of Texas history. "I do not doubt for a minute that the future of the Association will be as bright and exciting as its colorful, productive, and meaningful past. The history of the TSHA has always been about people—extraordinary people—and we still have them in abundance." *SHQ*, 108 (Jan. 2005), 389 (quotation).

the *Handbook* project, was affected by this, and retired before the end of that fiscal year. George Ward, director of publications since 1983, also coincidentally retired in May of that year, and Evelyn Stehling, executive assistant, who had worked with the Association since the early 1980s, left that summer for another job on campus.

Throughout the remainder of 2003 and into the next year, tension grew between the University and the Association, and, as J. P. Bryan points out in his Foreword, it became apparent that over a long stretch of seemingly balmy times the University had somehow lost its sense of the Association, its work and history. Relations between the Association and the College of Liberal Arts became contentious and in the summer of 2005 the TSHA's University component, the Center for Studies in Texas History, was moved from Liberal Arts and put under the Center for American History, with the idea that the TSHA would also keep its connection to the University through the CAH. Ron Tyler's nineteen-year term as director had come to an end the previous January, and J. C. Martin had been asked to serve as interim director until the TSHA's relationship with the University could be clarified—what promised then to be only a few months.

Another period of tension followed upon these developments, which resulted in a de facto separation of the TSHA from the Center for Studies in Texas History and, over time, the departure of additional TSHA staff. And yet, something held. The publications program has continued to publish its several books a year, as well as the *Southwestern Historical Quarterly*. The publications marketing program continues to develop its in-house endeavors along with its collaborative effort with the Texas A&M University Press Consortium. Work progresses on the *Online Handbook* and the Digital Gateway. Our educational programs continue to grow, with 850 students participating in this spring's Texas History Day competitions. The annual meeting, which this year drew over 800 attendees, is thriving, with plans for a joint meeting next year with the Hispanic History of Texas Project. A rapid turnover in staff has steadied, and there are the first intimations of a new core team forming.

Richard McCaslin researched and wrote *At the Heart of Texas* long before the tensions with the University of Texas came about. For several years the book manuscript circulated amongst longstanding members and staff of the TSHA, and, under the tutelage of George Ward, was revised many times in response to suggestions made by these insightful readers. Then for a year or two after George retired, the manuscript sat in a box in our publications office, awaiting its turn to come to a front burner again. Kent Calder, during his short tenure as publications director, got the book back on schedule, turning it over to me and—graciously sanctioned by McCaslin—giving me a long rein in

Transition Presidents under J. C. Martin

John W. Crain (2004–2005)

Robert A. Wooster (2005–2006)

Larry McNeill (2006–2007)

Jesús F. de la Teja (2007–2008)

Photographs from TSHA Files.

During his short tenure as director of publications (November 2003–July 2006) Kent Calder made the manuscript for *At the Heart of Texas* a priority in the publications schedule, and his encouragement and support for the project were decisive in giving the book its final shape. Kent is also responsible for putting the late Jack Jackson together with money from our Armstrong Fund to result in Jackson's last book, *New Texas History Movies*, published this spring by the TSHA.

working with it. For the year and a half that I have worked on the book, the tension between the University and the Association has been very much a part of the environment in which I have worked.

It has been very interesting to me to read through all the old Collection sections of past *Quarterlies*, 1897 to the present, in the light of what was happening around me. The troubled times made me especially receptive to the components that have for over one hundred years given the Association its tensile strength and resilience. Foremost among these has been the relationship with the University of Texas.

As McCaslin details in this book, five attempts were made between 1837 and 1890 to establish a historical society in Texas. After a short time all of these organizations failed for lack of dependable funding, and it was only with George Garrison's linking the Texas State Historical Association with the University of Texas that success was finally achieved in 1897. Joe Frantz called it a common law marriage, "replete with intricacies and mutual consent. . . . You almost need a scorecard to know the ground rules, but they are real and fast."

A second component to the Association's strength during its first one hundred years has been the relationship between its lay and academic members, the professor and the collector, the scholar and the oil man. Garrison gave the first shape to this when he proposed that the position of president be held by a lay member, thereby giving the Association's lay component its position of power and influence and insuring that the scholarly integrity of the organization remain always in the hands of an academic, who would hold the joint position of professor in the history department and director of the Association. This has changed through the years, with the honors and responsibilities of the lay and the academic board member becoming more convergent and more nuanced. As can be seen throughout the book, all the directors have reflected on this relationship, but it was Tuffly Ellis who in his last director's report wrote about it most thoughtfully, describing the academic's task as being the organization's scholarly work, and the nonprofessional's task being to bring economic and political clout to the raising of the organization's visibility among the general public, likening this collaborative effort to what the University achieved during the tenure of President Peter T. Flawn and his Board of Regents—a talented scholar/administrator and a powerful and able but low-profile governing board.

The third component in the mix is the rare longevity of the Association staff. To name but a few examples, Coral Horton Tullis, corresponding secretary and treasurer, had a tenure of forty years; Colleen Kain, executive assistant, twenty-two years; Evelyn Stehling, twenty years; George Ward directed the publications program for twenty years; Doug Barnett was with the *Handbook* project for twenty-three years, Mark Odintz is now in his nineteenth year with the *Handbook*; Sandra Gilstrap (administration) and Beth Bow (publications) have been with the Association for twelve years, Holly Taylor (publications) for eleven. And if you look at the list of our Executive Council members (Appendix E), you will see that many of them, especially in the early years, served ten, fifteen, twenty years.

In the summer of 2003 tension with the University began over budget cuts, but this kind of tension and transient turbulence had arisen regularly over the century: Walter McCaleb's accusations against Bailey Carroll and his handling of University funding, for example, temporarily put askew the TSHA's close relations with the University. The relationship was destabilized again when budget cuts under University president Lorene Rogers resulted in Ellis's having to cut Association staff. But in these and other instances described by McCaslin, the mutually held sense of obligation to the people of Texas provided for the successful buffeting of the storm.

As this book goes to press, the University of Texas has given the Texas State

Historical Association a draft of a letter stating that, in its view, the missions of the two organizations have diverged substantially over the years, and, given the demands for space on campus, asking the TSHA to make other arrangements for offices and staff members traditionally provided by the University. A letter has gone out to the membership informing it of this decision.

What the lasting outcome will be of this most recent development is yet to be seen. Will it turn out in retrospect to be just the latest 25-year storm, a little more intense perhaps, coming at the Association's century mark? Or is there something different this time? Is it perhaps that the days of the gentlemen's agreement are past? Has something happened in the University's attitude toward Texas history? Have there been changes over the years within the Association that have distanced us from the University?

These are questions for another time. The dust has to settle first; all the stories have to be told. But even in the midst of the sandstorm a few things can be discerned: within the TSHA, key people who had been hired by the early 1980s and had worked together as a team for the better part of two decades began to leave, some for natural reasons, some later as a result of the uncertain relationship with the University of Texas. Transitions are by nature start-and-stop, lurching. And yet, through it all, our programs have not stalled—and there is pride in the thought that a less-rooted organization could not have achieved this underlying continuity in the midst of such flux.

As for the University and the TSHA, the question is more poignant. As this book so vividly demonstrates, the Association and the University have been so closely woven in their endeavors that it is impossible to draw a distinct boundary between them. Consider, for instance, the University's Texas history collections. The impetus for these came from the Association. The initial and most pressing reason and stated mission for the Association's existence was to collect and preserve the documents of Texas history. The University gave the Association its first "corner" for its collections; then the Association, in 1911, formally donated its collections of books and archives to the University, in return for cataloguing and binding. But even more interwoven than that donation are the many collections that the University acquired as a result of the Association's drive and interest in collecting. J. Evetts Haley was hired by the University to travel the state and collect documents, but it was at the behest of Eugene Barker, who was director of the TSHA with its mission to collect and preserve. And how does one parse the contributions of the two entities in the acquisition of the Kell Collection, the Philpott Collection, the Bexar Archives, the Vandale Collection, the libraries of Swante Palm and Ashbel Smith, the papers of Stephen F. Austin? Where would the Texas collections be without the Texas State Historical Association? Where would the collections

RALPH ELDER

For over 35 years few important books dealing with Texas history were published without the expert research assistance and guidance of Ralph Elder. During his entire adult life, Ralph never worked anywhere other than the Eugene C. Barker Texas History Center (Center for American History). He was first hired in the summer before his freshman year at the University of Texas (Austin) by Texas history giant, Dr. Llerena Friend. For years Ralph, his colleague and friend Mary Beth Fleischer, and *Miss* Friend (as she preferred to be called) guided the development of the Texas Collection at the University into the last word in Texas bibliography. After the early 1970s, their combined knowledge of Texas history in general, and the contents of the Texas Collection in particular, rested with Ralph, and his genuine eagerness to be helpful to researchers was a key ingredient to many successful research projects.

Many of those researchers were TSHA employees engaged in writing and editing *Handbook* articles, book manuscripts, *Quarterly* articles, and a myriad of related projects. They all became spoiled to ignoring the card catalog when all they had to do was ask Ralph. And he never failed to come up with the right answers and in record time. Years ago he lost count of the

Ralph Elder, in a pose familiar to all of us who have approached him with questions at his desk in the reading room of the Center for American History. *Courtesy Ralph Elder.*

number of "Acknowledgments" in which he was thanked, and he was always considered to be the "go to" guy by the Board of Regents, top University of Texas administrators, a host of colleagues and friends from universities across the state, as well as the otherwise lost incoming freshman student. Ralph is imbedded in the history of TSHA, the University of Texas, and in the hearts and minds of grateful students everywhere.

Ralph formally retired from University employment on August 31, 2005, but has accepted a half-time appointment as research archivist with the Center for American History, where he currently works on special research projects, including the UT Oral History Project.

University of Texas president Larry Faulkner presents Elder with a certificate of appreciation for 35 years of service. *Courtesy Ralph Elder.*

be without the University of Texas? It has been a truly symbiotic endeavor, and to attempt to apportion these collections now would need a Solomon. For one hundred years it has been one piece of cloth. It was Walter Prescott Webb's writing, as director of the Association in the *Southwestern Historical Quarterly*, that the history of Texas must "always come first" at the University that led ultimately to the Texas Collection being given for the first time its own separate quarters, in what would be named the Eugene C. Barker Texas History Center. The first two (of three) directors of the Barker Center, now a component of the Center for American History, were trained at the TSHA, Llerena Friend as editorial and research assistant for the *Handbook*, and Chester Kielman as associate editor for the *Quarterly* and assistant editor for the *Junior Historian*; the third, Don Carleton, has been an active member of the Association, serving on its Executive Council and its committees.

Then, with no one really noticing it, the cloth must have begun to thin and wear out. As long as the weather was calm the threads held, but in the summer of 2003 a not untypical storm hit, and this time the cloth has come dangerously close to tearing. It will take the passage of time and then curious and objective research to figure out how all the forces came together to bring this about. How did we lose the scorecard, what real and fast rules did we each, over time, forget or neglect? Perhaps it began as early as 1971 when the Association moved from the Barker Texas History Center in the middle of campus, where the buildings named for Garrison and Barker "[stood] guard over the approaches to the heart and center of this University of Texas." In moving to the far eastern edge of campus, isolated, where a special effort had to be made to sustain what had once been a natural and daily contact between Association and University personnel, was the first small but irrevocable step taken toward what has culminated in 2007?

The Association leaves to the University the legacy of all its many Texas history collections. The Association takes from the University one hundred years of development and growth, its *Southwestern Historical Quarterly* continuously published without one issue missed in one hundred and ten years, its *Handbook of Texas* and *New Handbook of Texas*; its scholarly reputation further solidified in its one hundred and sixty books published between 1917 and 2007. In looking back over the lists of Executive Council/Board of Directors members, the presidents, the Fellows, one can see a line of powerful and distinguished protectors of Texas history, from 1897 to the present.

It may be that we will one day look at this book's ending as having come full circle back to its beginning—an organization looking to establish itself in the world as a free agent. In the nineteenth century every attempt at this proved to be unsuccessful. In the twenty-first—with a century of work and tradition behind us and a vital membership established—if the old venture must be pursued again, it will be with resolve and the exhilaration of spirit that comes with "something worth fighting for." We will miss the balmy days of old, but will reach for the best of what has been bequeathed us by George Garrison, Eugene Barker, Walter Prescott Webb . . . to meet whatever challenges might confront us.

And if we compare where we are now with where we were a century ago, our roots are not only much deeper, they are much more widely planted. Not only our members, but our board of directors, our committees, and our supporters come from every part of the state and beyond, and dozens of universities and colleges are represented in our academic members. In this sense the Association might be said to have grown beyond the University, at least in its ballast.

Still, there cannot help but be a profound sense of loss if these two institutions that have meant so much to the study of Texas history part ways. There will surely be feelings of regret on both sides as time passes and the emotion of the moment subsides. But, at this pivotal moment when separation seems a very real possibility, it is somehow fitting that the common endeavor is memorialized so well in this history. The Texas State Historical Association and the University of Texas have truly been at the heart of Texas studies, and this book assures that that long chapter in the history of both institutions has been done justice and will not now ever be forgotten.

When the second book is written, a hundred years hence, the current turbulent transition, which now seems so everlasting and its events and speculations so compelling, might, after only a page or two of exposition, show our future self settled quickly back to sympathy with Eugene Barker's bygone one, "fed to the chin with strenuous, purposeful people" and ready once again to "have no scheduled purpose but that of association with men and women who stand for solid accomplishments in their respective fields," to "relax and be our natural lazy selves and follow adventure where it leads."

Janice Pinney
May 2007

Appendix A

CONSTITUTION OF THE TEXAS STATE HISTORICAL ASSOCIATION
ADOPTED MARCH 2, 1897

ART. I. NAME

This Society shall be called THE TEXAS STATE HISTORICAL ASSOCIATION.

ART. II. OBJECTS.

The objects of the Association shall be, in general, the promotion of historical studies; and, in particular, the discovery, collection, preservation, and publication of historical material, especially such as relates to Texas.

ART. III. MEMBERSHIP.

The Association shall consist of Members, Fellows, Life Members, and Honorary Life Members.

(a)*Members.* Persons recommended by the Executive Council and elected by the Association may become Members.

(b)*Fellows.* Members who show, by published work, special aptitude for historical investigation may become Fellows. Thirteen Fellows shall be elected by the Association when first organized, and the body thus created may thereafter elect additional Fellows on the nomination of the Executive Council. The number of Fellows shall never exceed fifty.

(c) *Life Members.* Such benefactors of the Association as shall pay into its treasury at one time the sum of ($50) fifty dollars, or shall present to the Association an equivalent in books, MSS., or other acceptable matter, shall be classed as Life Members.

(d)*Honorary Life Members.* Persons who rendered eminent service to Texas previous to annexation may become Honorary Life Members upon being recommended by the Executive Council and elected by the Association.

ART. IV. OFFICERS.

The affairs of the Association shall be administered by a President, four Vice-Presidents, a Librarian, a Secretary and Treasurer, and an Executive Council.

The President, Vice-Presidents, and Secretary and Treasurer shall be elected annually by the Association from among the Fellows.

The Professor of History in the University of Texas shall be *ex officio* Librarian of this Association.

The Executive Council, a majority of which shall constitute a quorum, shall consist of the following:

The President.
The four Vice-Presidents.
The Librarian of the Association.
The State Librarian.
Three Fellows.
Five Members.

The Association, immediately after organizing, shall elect three Fellows to serve on the Executive Council one, two, and three years, respectively, the term of each to be decided by lot. Thereafter, one Fellow shall be elected annually by the Association for the term of three years.

The Association, immediately after organizing, shall likewise elect five members to serve on the Executive Council one, two, three, four, and five years, respectively, the term of each to be decided by lot. Thereafter, one Member shall be elected annually by the Association for the term of five years.

ART. V. DUES.

Each Member shall pay annually into the treasury of the Association the sum of two dollars.
Each Fellow shall pay annually into the treasury of the Association the sum of five dollars.
Life Members and Honorary Life Members shall be exempt.

ART. VI. PUBLICATION COMMITTEE.

A Publication Committee, consisting of five persons, shall have the sole charge of the selection and editing of matter for publication. The President and Librarian of the Association shall be ex officio members of this committee; the remaining three members shall be chosen annually by the Fellows from the Executive Council.

ART. VII. AMENDMENTS.

Amendments to this Constitution shall become operative after being recommended by the Executive Council and approved by two-thirds of the entire membership of the Association, the vote being taken by letter ballot.

PRESIDENT.
O. M. Roberts.

———

VICE-PRESIDENTS.

Dudley G. Wooten,   William Corner,
Guy M. Bryan,   Mrs. Julia Lee Sinks

———

LIBRARIAN.
Geo. P. Garrison.

———

Secretary and Treasurer.
Lester G. Bugbee

———

Executive Council

O. M. Roberts	Geo. P. Garrison,	Mrs. Dora Fowler Arthur,
Dudley G. Wooten,	Eugene Digges,	Rufus C. Burleson,
Guy M. Bryan,	Z. T. Fulmore,	M. M. Kenney,
William Corner,	C. W. Raines,	R. L. Batts,
Mrs. Julia Lee Sinks,	F. R. Lubbock,	Mrs. Bride Neill Taylor.

From: *The Texas State Historical Association. Report of Organization. Constitution. List of Members.* Pamphlet, n.d., in TSHA Files; copy in O. M. Roberts Papers, Box 2G66, folder 90-99, Center for American History, University of Texas at Austin.

The Texas State Historical Association Bylaws

Amended March 3, 2000, March 2, 2001 and March 5, 2004

Article I. Name

The name of this Society shall be THE TEXAS STATE HISTORICAL ASSOCIATION, sometimes referred to herein as "Association."

Article II. Purpose

The purpose of the Association shall be to foster the appreciation, understanding, and teaching of the rich and unique history of Texas and by example and through programs and activities encourage and promote research, preservation, and publication of historical material affecting the state of Texas.

Article III. Membership

There shall be two classes of membership in the Association:

3.1 *Member.* A Member is a person or entity interested in supporting the purpose of the Association and is current with payment of dues. In all matters governed by the vote of the membership a Member shall be entitled to one vote. A Member must be present to vote, and the right to vote cannot be delegated by proxy, except in the case of a legal entity, such entity may designate an individual present at the meeting to cast its vote.

3.2 *Honorary Life Member.* A person who has rendered eminent service to Texas or to the Association may be elected an Honorary Life Member by a vote of two-thirds (2/3) of the members of the Board of Directors present at the meeting in which the vote is taken. Such member shall be exempt from the payment of dues.

Article IV. Meeting of the Membership

4.1 *Annual Meetings.* Annual meetings of the Association shall be held at a place in the state of Texas and at such times as may be determined by the Board of Directors. At the annual meeting officers and members of the Board of Directors shall be elected and votes taken upon those matters in which the vote of the membership is provided for in these Bylaws.

4.2 *Special Meetings.* Special meetings of the membership may be called only upon an affirmative vote of eleven members of the Board of Directors. The Secretary of the Association shall notify the members in writing of the date, place, and purpose of the special meeting, all as determined by the Board of Directors. Such notices shall be effected by depositing said notice with the United States Post Office at least two weeks before the date of said meeting.

Article V. Fellow

A person of any classification of membership who has demonstrated through published works with a special aptitude for historical investigation relating to the state of Texas may be elected by the Board of Directors a "Fellow of the Texas State Historical Association." Their election shall be announced at the first annual meeting of the Association after their election. In any given year the number of Fellows elected, if any, shall be within the sole discretion of the Board of Directors; however, at no time shall there be more than three persons elected as Fellows of the Association each year.

Article VI. Officers

6.1 *Officers, Election, and Term.* The officers of the Association shall consist of a President, a First Vice President, a Second Vice President, and a Secretary. To be eligible to serve as an officer one must be a member in good standing in the Association except that of Honorary Member. Officers shall serve for a term of one year except as may be otherwise provided in Section 6.2 of the Bylaws. The President shall report to the Board of Directors, and the Vice Presidents and Secretary shall report to the President.

The First Vice President shall be the President Designate and shall succeed to the office of President upon the expiration of the President's term of office. The Second Vice President shall be First Vice President Designate and shall succeed to the office of First Vice President upon the expiration of the term of office of the First Vice President.

6.2 *Election of Officers.* At the annual business meeting of the Association the Nominating Committee shall submit a written report containing the names of its nominees for the various offices of the Association, other than Secretary, and for the Board of Directors vacancies, which are to be elected by the membership under the provisions of the Bylaws. After the report the Nominating Committee nominations may be made from the floor. A nominee receiving the highest vote of the membership present at the meeting shall be elected to the respective offices and vacancies. Should there be more than two nominees for a position there shall be a run-off if no one nominee receives a majority of the votes present. Those elected at the annual meeting shall take office at the adjournment of the meeting at which they are elected.

6.3 *Vacancies.*

(a) Should the office of President for any reason become vacant, the first Vice President shall succeed to the office of President and serve as President for the remainder of the unexpired term, and shall also serve as President for the following one-year term for which he/she would have served had the vacancy not occurred.

(b) Should the office of First Vice President become vacant for any reason, the Second Vice President shall succeed to the office of First Vice President and serve as First Vice President for the remainder of the unexpired term, and shall also serve as First Vice President for the following one-year term for which he/she would have served had the vacancy not occurred.

(c) Should the office of Second Vice President for any reason become vacant, that office shall remain vacant until the next annual meeting of the Association.

6.4 *Duties of President.*

(a) The President shall be the Executive Officer of the Association, and he shall serve as Chairman of and preside at all meetings of the Board of Directors.

(b) The President shall appoint all standing and special committees of the Association, except for the Publications Committee.

(c) The President shall be an ex-officio member of all committees.

6.5 *Duties of the First Vice President.* In the event of the absence of the President, the First Vice President shall assume the duties of the President and perform such assignments and duties that may be assigned to him by the President or the Board of Directors.

6.6 *Duties of the Second Vice President.* The Second Vice President shall perform those assignments that may be made to him by the President or the Board of Directors.

6.7 *Duties of the Secretary.* The Secretary shall be elected by the members of the Board of Directors. The Secretary shall keep the minutes of all meetings of the Board of Directors, attest all documents executed by the Association when required, and perform such other duties as may be assigned by the Board of Directors.

ARTICLE VII. BOARD OF DIRECTORS

7.1 The management of the affairs of the Association shall be vested in the Board of Directors, which shall consist of the President, the Vice Presidents, the two immediate past Presidents, and sixteen (16) elected members. The elected members of the Board of Directors shall serve for a term of three (3) years, with a maximum service of six (6) years and no members of the Board of Directors shall serve more than six (6) years continuously unless his term has been extended by the fact that he has been elected an officer of the Association. In the event an elected member of the Board of Directors is elected an officer of the Association, that person shall continue on the Board in the capacity of an officer and a vacancy shall thereby be created in the membership of the Board, which vacancy shall remain vacant until the vacancy is filled by the Nominating Committee. The President may not appoint a member of the Board of Directors to the Nominating Committee in the year in which that member will be eligible for a second three (3) year term.

7.2 The Board of Directors shall meet at least twice each year, the first during and at the site of the annual membership meeting and the second, or any additional meetings, upon the call of the President at such place and at such time as may be set by the President. A quorum for a meeting shall be a majority of those serving on the Board of Directors at the time such meeting is called. Each member present at a meeting shall have one vote, and voting shall not be by proxy.

7.3 The powers of the Board of Directors shall be:

(a) The Board of Directors shall appoint the Director of the Association.

(b) Under circumstances not otherwise provided for in the Bylaws, the Board of Directors shall be empowered to fill vacancies in all offices of the Association, and the person so appointed shall serve until the succeeding annual meeting of the membership. In the case of the death or resignation of a member of the Board of Directors, the Nominating Committee shall make recommendation to the Board of Directors as to a replacement, subject to approval by the membership at the next annual business meeting. The replacement term shall not count as part of a normal term unless the replacement takes place during the first three (3) months of the former member's term.

(c) The Board of Directors may create such additional offices or such standing and special committees as it may deem necessary and proper in carrying out the purposes and activities of the Association.

(d) The Board of Directors shall direct and be responsible for the financial matters of the Association, including the control and investment of the assets of the Association, with power to purchase or sell securities or other property held or needed by the Association.

(e) The Board of Directors shall be the final authority on all matters of personnel, including salaries, as may be recommended to the Board of Directors by the Director.

(f) The Board of Directors at any regular or called meeting shall, with two weeks prior written notice to the members of the Board, have the power to create or discontinue various levels of membership as it may deem in the best interest of the Association and establish or amend the amount of the dues applicable to each membership classification. The Board shall determine the rules and procedures by which members shall be dropped from the membership rolls.

(g) The sixteen elected members of the Board of Directors shall be elected by the members at the annual meeting of the Association on a staggered basis. The Board of Directors shall determine the order in which the staggered elections are to be administered.

(h) Eleven members present and voting shall constitute a quorum for conducting business of the Association at any regular or called meeting of the Board.

7.4 The members of the Board of Directors of the Association shall not be liable to the Association or its members for monetary damages for an act or omission in the board member's capacity as a board member, except that this amendment shall not eliminate or limit the liability of a board member for any of the matters described in Article 7.06B (1) – (5) of the Texas Miscellaneous Corporation Laws Act.

7.5 The Board of Directors by a two-thirds (2/3) vote of the Board may designate a former member of the Board as a Lifetime Honorary Member of the Board in recognition and appreciation of outstanding contribution to the Board and the Association, but such individual shall not have the right to vote on any matter before the Board.

Article VIII. Director

8.1 The Director shall be appointed by the Board of Directors and shall be the Chief Operating Executive of the Association. The Director shall be responsible for all operations of the Association, subject to the policies set by the Board of Directors. He shall be directly responsible to and report to the Board of Directors.

8.2 The Director must be an individual holding an academic or staff appointment to the Department of History of The University of Texas at Austin.

8.3 The Director shall be the Editor of the *Southwestern Historical Quarterly* and shall appoint the Associate Editor and Editorial Assistants of the *Quarterly* as needed. In this connection the Director shall be responsible for seeing that the material published in the *Quarterly*, including the Book Reviews section, shall have a bearing upon the history of Texas.

8.4 The Director shall be directly in charge of all employed personnel of the Association.

8.5 The Director shall, subject to the concurrence of the Board of Directors, annually select members of the Publications Committee and shall serve as Chairman of the committee. In this connection, in addition to the Director and President of the Association, the Publications Committee shall consist of no more than eight (8) members, not less than four (4). Not less than four (4) of the appointed committee members shall be either Fellows of the Association or members of the Board of Directors.

8.6 The Director shall serve as an ex-officio member, without voting privileges, of the Board of Directors and of all standing and special committees of the Association, except that he shall have voting privileges as a member of the Publications Committee.

Article IX. Publications

The Association shall from time to time undertake such publications as may be recommended by the Director and the Publications Committee and approved by the Board of Directors. The principal publication of the Texas State Historical Association shall be the *Southwestern Historical Quarterly*, and it shall have precedence over all other publications of the Association.

Article X. Committees

10.1 Standing committees of the Association shall be as follows:

(a) *Membership Committee.* The number serving on the Membership Committee shall be determined by the President and shall be appointed by the President. This committee shall have the responsibility of seeking and obtaining new members of the Association as well as the renewal of existing memberships, and of making recommendations to the Board of Directors with respect to the level of dues to be assessed by the Association.

(b) *Nominating Committee.* Prior to the adjournment of the annual meeting the incoming President elected to serve during the ensuing year shall name his appointees to the Nominating Committee. This committee shall be composed of a Chairman, who shall be the outgoing President of the Association, and four other members, two serving as current members of the Board of Directors and two from the general membership. This committee shall recommend to the Association membership nominees for the office of President, First Vice President, and Second Vice President, and members of the Board of Directors. The election of the officers and Board of Directors shall be voted upon at the business session of the annual meeting of the ensuing year. The announcement of the names of this committee prior to the adjournment of the annual meeting will give the members of the Association an opportunity to suggest nominees to the committee during the year prior to the annual meeting of the ensuing year. The committee's report shall be delivered to the President not later than five days before the next ensuing annual meeting, with a copy to the Board of Directors. The Chairman or a member of the committee designated by the Chairman shall present the committee's report at the annual meeting upon the call of the President.

(c) *Development Committee.* The members of the Development Committee shall be appointed by the President. This committee shall take leadership in the development work of the Association.

(d) *Finance Committee.* The members of the Finance Committee shall be appointed by the President. This committee shall review periodically the financial operations of the Association, including investments, and make such recommendations to the Board of Directors as it may deem appropriate.

(e) *Program Committee.* Each incoming President shall appoint a Program Committee for the annual meeting two years hence, which committee shall plan and be responsible for carrying out the program for the meeting of the Association to be held two years hence. The members of the committee shall be appointed by the President only after consultation with the Chairman of the committee.

(f) *Handbook Committee.* The President shall appoint a *Handbook* Committee, which shall consist of not more than eight (8) members, half of which shall be members of the Board of Directors. The purpose of this committee is to be available to the Director for consultation in all matters relating directly to the publication of the *Handbook.*

(g) *Resolutions Committee.* The Resolutions Committee shall be appointed by the President to serve for one year and to prepare and present to the membership for a vote at the ensuing annual meeting of the Association those resolutions it deems proper and timely. Such resolution may be amended on the floor at the annual meeting. Should an individual seek to present a resolution not presented by the committee, such resolution may be presented for consideration at the annual business meeting of the Association, provided such resolution is presented in writing to the

President prior to the time the business meeting is called to order. This limitation on the presentation of a resolution may be overruled by a vote of two-thirds (2/3) of the members present and voting.

(h) *Bylaws Committee.* The President shall appoint the members of the Bylaws Committee. The Committee shall word the bylaws to reflect the intent of the recommendations from the Board of Directors.

(i) *Audit Committee.* The Audit Committee shall be appointed by the President and shall audit the books and records of the Association annually, and report its finding to the Board.

(j) *Archives Committee.* The President shall appoint the members of the Archives Committee. The Archives Committee shall review matters concerning archives and archives records, and furnish reports to the Board upon request.

(k) *Education Committee.* The Education Committee shall be appointed by the President. Its purpose is to assist the director of education in planning the Association's education programs and it shall make reports to the Board.

(l) *Term of Appointment.* All appointees to committees and special committees shall serve for a term of one year; however, members of committees are eligible to be reappointed.

10.2 Special committees may be constituted as may be deemed necessary and proper by the President or by the Board of Directors.

Article XI. Balance of Officers and Board of Directors

For many years there has been an established custom that the presidency of the Association be alternated from year to year between academic and nonacademic members and that membership of the Board of Directors likewise be balanced substantially between these two groups. An academic member is described as an active or retired employee of an accredited academic institution.

This custom is hereby incorporated into the Bylaws with the recognition that limited flexibility must be exercised where unusual circumstances dictate.

Article XII. Operating Policy

The President shall make all appointments within two (2) months of the President taking office. The President and Director shall publish a calendar, within the President's first two (2) months, of anticipated scheduling of all committee meetings for the remainder of the President's term of office. The President and Director shall write and transmit letters of high expectation to new Board of Directors members, specifically emphasizing the duty of regular attendance. The Nominating Committee shall attempt to interview candidates for the Board of Directors and meet only when all members can attend. The Director shall report regularly to the Board of Directors, committee chairs, and the President.

Article XIII. Amendments

Amendments to the Bylaws shall be first approved by the Board of Directors and then be approved by a two-thirds (2/3) vote of the members of all dues-paying classifications present and voting at any annual meeting, provided that the notice of the substance of the proposed amendment shall be included or inserted in the announcement of the annual meeting of the Association.

ARTICLE XIV. ADOPTION OF BYLAWS

These Bylaws shall be effective upon the affirmative approval of two-thirds (2/3) of the Board of Directors and by a two-thirds (2/3) vote of the current membership present and voting at an annual meeting of the Association.

By the adoption of these Bylaws, the undated "The Constitution of the Texas State Historical Association" adopted in 1975, and all amendments thereto, are amended in their entirety, and these Bylaws, together with the Charter of the Association issued by the Secretary of State of the state of Texas on January 28, 1938, shall constitute the sole governing documents of this Association.

Adopted at the ninety-seventh annual meeting, Houston, March 5, 1993. (From TSHA Files.)

Appendix B

List of Charter Members

Fellows

Hon. Guy M. Bryan, Quintana.
Lester G. Bugbee, Austin.
William Corner, San Antonio.
Col. R. S. Ford, San Antonio.
Judge Z. T. Fulmore, Austin.
Judge R. R. Gaines, Austin.
Prof. George P. Garrison, Austin.
A. C. Gray, Houston.
Ex-Governor F. R. Lubbock, Austin.
Judge C. W. Raines, Austin.
Ex-Governor O. M. Roberts, Austin.
Mrs. Julia Lee Sinks, Giddings.
Hon. Dudley G. Wooten, Dallas.

Members

Mrs. Dora Fowler Arthur, Austin.
Casey Askew, Tyler.
H. G. Askew, Austin.
William Aubrey, San Antonio.
Prof. W. J. Battle, Austin.
Prof. R. L. Batts, Austin.
Gen. H. P. Bee, San Antonio.
Dr. Milton J. Bliem, San Antonio.
J. Alleine Brown, Austin.
Hon. Beauregard Bryan, Brenham.
Miss Hally Ballinger Bryan, Quintana.
President Rufus C. Burleson, Waco.
Hon. J. M. Carlisle, Austin.
Rev. Dr. Wallace Carnahan, San
    Antonio.
Miss Lilia M. Casis, Austin.
Captain James B. Clark, Austin.

Mrs. James B. Clark, Austin.
Hon. George Clark, Waco.
Hon. John H. Cochran, Sweetwater.
Charles Corner, Austin.
J. J. Cox, San Antonio.
Mrs. Ella Dancy-Hall, Austin.
Miss Mary Decherd, Austin.
Judge Leroy G. Denman, Austin.
Col. Eugene Digges, Austin.
Judge Peyton F. Edwards, El Paso.
Miss Anna Ellis, Austin.
Prof. H. F. Estill, Huntsville.
Ira J. Evans, Austin.
Wilbur L. Evans, Austin.
Prof. Thomas Fitz-Hugh, Austin.
H. P. N. Gammel, Austin.
Eugene A. Giraud, Austin.
Judge R. S. Gould, Austin.
John Granger, Austin.
John A. Green, Sr., San Antonio.
Mrs. S. F. Gulick, Corsicana.
Hon. T. S. Henderson, Cameron.
Ex-Governor J. S. Hogg, Austin.
E. M. House, Austin.
Reagan Houston, San Antonio.
William R. Houston, Dallas.
Ex-Governor R. B. Hubbard, Tyler.
Judge Sam J. Hunter, Fort Worth.
Col. John G. James, Austin.
Mrs. Jenkins, Houston.
R. M. Johnston, Houston.
R. A. Judd, Austin.
Major M. M. Kenney, San Antonio.

Gen. W. H. King, Sulphur Springs.
Mrs. M. Looscan, Houston.
B. F. Louis, Marlin.
W. F. McCaleb, Carrizo Springs.
Regent J. H. McLean, Georgetown.
Hon. J. H. McCleary, San Antonio.
Robert E. McCleary, Austin.
J. Magnenat, Austin.
Clarence H. Miller, Austin.
A. W. Orr, Omen.
Hon. T. M. Paschal, Castroville.
James E. Pearce, Austin.
Mrs. L. C. Pease, Austin.
Miss Julia M. Pease, Austin.
Judge H. Clay Pleasants, Galveston.
Hon. William L. Prather, Waco.
Prof. Sylvester Primer, Austin.
G. A. Quinlan, Houston.

Hon. John H. Reagan, Austin.
Major A. J. Rose, Austin.
Dr. William B. Seeley, San Antonio.
Morris Sheppard, Austin.
Hon. Seth Shepard, Washington, D.C.
Hon. James L. Slayden, San Antonio.
Col. Robert G. Street, Galveston.
Mrs. Bride Neill Taylor, Austin.
Mrs. Kate S. Terrell, Dallas.
Judge E. W. Townes, Austin.
Mrs. A. V. Winkler, Corsicana.
President George T. Winston, Austin.
Dr. Joe S. Wooten, Austin.
Dr. Thomas D. Wooten, Austin.
Col. R. M. Wynne, Fort Worth.
William H. Young, ———
Miss Adina de Zavala, San Antonio.
Miss Mary de Zavala, San Antonio.

From: *The Texas State Historical Association. Report of Organization. Constitution. List of Members.* Pamphlet, n.d., in TSHA Files.

Appendix C

DIRECTORS

George P. Garrison, 1897–1910
Eugene C. Barker, 1910–1937
Charles W. Hackett, 1937–1939
Walter P. Webb, 1939–1946
H. Bailey Carroll, 1946–1966
Joe B. Frantz, 1966–1977
L. Tuffly Ellis, 1977–1985
James W. Pohl, 1985–1986
Ron Tyler, 1986–2004
J. C. Martin, 2004–

Appendix D

TSHA Presidents (Chronological from present)

Jesús F. de la Teja, 2007–2008
Larry McNeill, 2006–2007
Robert A. Wooster, 2005–2006
John W. Crain, 2004–2005
George N. Green, 2003–2004
Shirley Caldwell, 2002–2003
Jerry D. Thompson, 2001–2002
Al Lowman, 2000–2001
Norman D. Brown, 1999–2000
Paul G. Bell, 1998–1999
Margaret S. Henson, 1997–1998
Cissy Stewart Lale, 1996–1997
Félix D. Almaráz Jr., 1995–1996
Robert H. Thonhoff, 1994–1995
Randolph B. Campbell, 1993–1994
Alwyn Barr, 1992–1993
Max S. Lale, 1991–1992
A. Frank Smith, 1990–1991
Robert A. Calvert, 1989–1990
Jenkins Garrett, 1988–1989
James W. Pohl, 1987–1988
J. Conrad Dunagan, 1986–1987
Ron Tyler, 1986
Archie P. McDonald, 1985–1986
Clifton Caldwell, 1984–1985
Edward A. Clark, 1983–1984
J. P. Bryan Jr., 1982–1983
Marilyn M. Sibley, 1981–1982
Ben E. Pingenot, 1980–1981
Ben H. Procter, 1979–1980
F. Lee Lawrence, 1978–1979
Ernest Wallace, 1977–1978

Dan E. Kilgore, 1976–1977
Billy Mac Jones, 1975–1976
Ralph A. Wooster, 1974–1975
Anne A. Brindley, 1973–1974
Roger N. Conger, 1972–1973
Dorman H. Winfrey, 1971–1972
Cooper K. Ragan, 1970–1971
Rupert N. Richardson, 1969–1970
Wayne Gard, 1968–1969
Seymour V. Connor, 1967–1968
J. P. Bryan Sr., 1965–1967
George P. Isbell, 1964–1965
Fred R. Cotten, 1962–1964
Merle Duncan, 1959–1962
Ralph W. Steen, 1957–1959
Paul Adams, 1955–1957
Claude Elliott, 1953–1955
Herbert P. Gambrell, 1951–1953
Earl Vandale, 1949–1951
P. I. Nixon, 1946–1949
L. W. Kemp, 1942–1946
Harbert Davenport, 1939–1942
W. R. Wrather, 1932–1939
Alex. Dienst, 1929–1932
T. F. Harwood, 1925–1929
Mrs. Adele B. Looscan, 1915–1925
Z. T. Fulmore, 1912–1915
A. W. Terrell, 1907–1912
David F. Houston, 1905–1907
John H. Reagan, 1899–1905
Dudley G. Wooten, 1898–1899
O. M. Roberts, 1897–1898

Appendix E

EXECUTIVE COUNCIL/BOARD OF DIRECTORS, 1897–2007

Names and dates as listed in the *Southwestern Historical Quarterly*, 1897–2007

(The name was changed to Board of Directors at the annual meeting, March 2004.)

Paul Adams, 1948–1963
Raye Virginia Allen, 1999–2004
Félix D. Almaráz Jr., 1983–1996
Mary Margaret McAllen Amberson,
 2003–2007
Charles H. Armstrong, 2005–
Watson Arnold, 2004–
Dora Fowler Arthur, 1897–1917
Samuel E. Asbury, 1923–1939

Richard Bailey, 1987–1992
Eugene C. Barker, 1902–1905, 1943–1948
Nancy N. Barker, 1973–1977
Alwyn Barr, 1982–1987, 1990–1993
J. W. Barton, 1919–1921
W. J. Battle, 1899–1918
R. L. Batts, 1897–1912
Paul G. Bell, 1988–1999
R. L. Biesele, 1939–1956
Milton J. Bliem, 1906–1912
Herbert E. Bolton, 1905–1910
George W. Brackenridge, 1915–1917
Anne Brindley, 1967–1975
John C. Britt, 2004–
S. P. Brooks, 1903–1915
Norman D. Brown, 1988–1993,
 1996–2001
Beauregard Bryan, 1899–1914
Guy M. Bryan, 1897–1901 (died during
 term)
J. P. Bryan Sr., 1959–1969
J. P. Bryan Jr., 1979–1984

Lewis R. Bryan, 1919–1921
Walter L. Buenger, 1987–1992, 2005–
Lester G. Bugbee, 1901 (died during
 first year)
Rufus C. Burleson, 1897–1901 (died
 during term)
Chester R. Burns, 1992–1997

Clifton Caldwell, 1975–1984
Shirley W. Caldwell, 1991–1996,
 1999–2004
Robert A. Calvert, 1977–1988
Randolph B. Campbell, 1987–1994
Gregg Cantrell, 2005–
Don E. Carleton, 1997–2002
Paul H. Carlson, 2003–2007
Lilia M. Casis, 1913–1918
Edward A. Clark (HLM)*, 1979–1991
J. L. Clark, 1925–1938
Luther W. Clark, 1907–1912
Michael Collins, 1996–2001
Roger Conger, 1966–1974
Seymour V. Connor, 1956–1969
Allyson Cook, 1996–2003
William Corner, 1897–1898
Leavitt Corning Jr., 1969–1973
Fred R. Cotten, 1949–1967
James Crain, 2004–2007
John Crain (HLM), 1993–2007
R. C. Crane, 1915–1922
Carolina Castillo Crimm, 2007–
Sharon Crutchfield, 1992–1997

*Honorary Life Member

Executive Council/Board of Directors, 1897–2007

Retta Murphy, 1939–1941
Menton J. Murray, 1985–1990
Joseph Myers, 1907–1908
Sandra L. Myres, 1984–1989

Joseph Milton Nance, 1963–1969
Robert A. Nesbitt, 1976–1983
Jon P. Newton, 1984–1989
P. I. Nixon, 1939–1965

H. J. O'Hair, 1929–1930
Roger M. Olien, 1988–1993

Jim B. Pearson, 1980–1989
Julia C. Pease, 1916–1918
Ben E. Pingenot, 1971–1982
James W. Pohl, 1980–1984, 1986–1987
William C. Pool, 1968–1972
Anna Powell, 1928–1946
B. Byron Price, 2005–
Ben Procter, 1970–1981

Gilberto Quezada, 2000–2005

Cooper K. Ragan, 1962–1972
C. W. Raines, 1897–1906
Charles W. Ramsdell, 1907–1941
Harry H. Ransom, 1957–1960
Fred Rathjen, 2000–2005
John H. Reagan, 1899–1904 (died during term)
W. S. Red, 1928–1932
Rupert N. Richardson, 1962–1971
Marilyn D. Rinehart, 1991–1996
Ingham S. Roberts, 1926–1932
O. M. Roberts, 1897–1898
Joseph Schmitz, 1951–1965
Marilyn M. Sibley, 1973–1983
Julia Lee Sinks, 1897–1904
A. Frank Smith (HLM), 1983–1993
C. B. Smith Jr., 1981–1986
Charles D. Spurlin, 1995–2000
Ralph Steen, 1946–1968
A. Ray Stephens, 1971–1974
Jo Ann Stiles, 2003–2007
Cornelia Branch Stone, 1915–1918
Rex Strickland, 1946–1956

Bride Neill Taylor, 1897–1918, 1928–1931
James Taylor, 1950–1962
Lonn Taylor, 2006–
Jesús F. de la Teja, 1998–2003, 2005–2007
A. W. Terrell, 1907–1912
B. V. Thompson Jr., 1978–1982
Jerry D. Thompson, 1994–2003
Robert H. Thonhoff, 1983–1988, 1992–1995
L. N. Throop, 1926–1927
Wilbert H. Timmons, 1970–1976
John C. Townes, 1900–1922
Coral Horton Tullis, 1955–1966
George W. Tyler, 1925–1927
Ron C. Tyler, 1976–1984

Earl Vandale, 1939–1952
Frances B. Vick, 2005–
Ethel Rather Villavosa, 1915–1918, 1933–1939

Leslie Waggener, 1949–1950
Ernest Wallace, 1962–1970, 1974–1979
David M. Warren, 1953–1959
Jim A. Watson, 1991–1996
Walter P. Webb, 1947–1962
David J. Weber, 1998–2003
Cecil "Eddie" Weller, 2007–
Fannie Wilcox, 1933–1944
Amelia Williams, 1939–1948
Clayton W. Williams, 1981
J. W. Williams, 1956–1971
James Wilson, 1996–2001
Janice Woods Windle, 2000–2005
Dorman H. Winfrey, 1962–1973
E. W. Winkler, 1907–1938
W. D. Wood, 1905–1906
George R. Woolfolk, 1972–1981
Ralph A. Wooster, 1968–1976
Robert A. Wooster, 1999–
Dudley G. Wooten, 1897–1913
J. L. Worley, 1910
W. E. Wrather, 1931–1954
William P. Wright, 1999–2004

Adina de Zavala (HLM), 1919–1954

Appendix F

The constitution of the Association provides that "members who show, by published work, special aptitude for historical investigation may become Fellows. . . . In any given year the number of Fellows elected, if any, shall be within the sole discretion of the Board of Directors; however, at no time shall there be more than three persons elected as Fellows of the Association each year."

Past Fellows (year elected)

Sam Acheson, 1943
Ephraim D. Adams, 1917
Paul Adams, 1953
S. E. Asbury, 1941
Eugene C. Barker, 1902
Nancy N. Barker, 1971
W. J. Battle, 1952
R. L. Batts, 1898
Nettie Lee Benson, 1969
R. L. Biesele, 1933
W. C. Binkley, 1965
Herbert E. Bolton, 1902
Mrs. John Henry Brown, 1897
Guy M. Bryan, 1897
Eleanor C. Buckley, 1918
Lester G. Bugbee, 1897
Robert A. Calvert, 1990
H. Bailey Carroll, 1947
James D. Carter, 1965
Lilia M. Casis, 1899
Carlos E. Castañeda, 1927
Charles E. Chapman, 1918
A. K. Christian, 1918
Robert Carlton Clark, 1904
J. L. Clark, 1933
Roger N. Conger, 1967
Seymour V. Connor, 1954
O. H. Cooper, 1903

Bethel Coopwood, 1899
William Corner, 1897
Robert Cotner, 1960
Fred R. Cotten, 1953
I. J. Cox, 1902
R. C. Crane, 1941
Barry A. Crouch, 1995
Charles H. Cunningham, 1918
Harbert Davenport, 1929
James M. Day, 1965
Adina de Zavala, 1915
Alex. Dienst, 1915
J. Frank Dobie, 1941
Merle M. Duncan, 1953
William Edward Dunn, 1911
Claude Elliott, 1941
Chris Emmett, 1941
H. F. Estill, 1897
Lawrence J. FitzSimon, 1954
Paul J. Foik, 1931
John S. Ford, 1897
Earl Fornell, 1967
Joe B. Frantz, 1952
Llerena B. Friend, 1955
Z. T. Fulmore, 1897
R. R. Gaines, 1897
Herbert P. Gambrell, 1936
Wayne Gard, 1954

Julia Kathryn Garrett, 1941

George P. Garrison, 1897

Ellen C. Garwood, 1959

S. W. Geiser, 1941

Lewis L. Gould, 1991

A. C. Gray, 1897

A. C. Greene, 1990

James K. Greer, 1947

Charles W. Hackett, 1913

J. Villasana Haggard, 1947

J. Evetts Haley, 1929

Mattie Austin Hatcher, 1908

T. R. Havins, 1959

Margaret Swett Henson, 1987

George A. Hill, 1938

William Ransom Hogan, 1948

Abigail Curlee Holbrook, 1927

W. C. Holden, 1933

W. Eugene Hollon, 1974

D. F. Houston, 1903

Hobart Huson, 1970

Fannie Chambers Gooch Iglehart, 1897

Jack Jackson, 1991

C. C. Jeffries, 1961

John H. Jenkins III, 1967

Terry G. Jordan, 1979

L. W. Kemp, 1937

M. M. Kenney, 1898

Chester V. Kielman, 1968

Dan E. Kilgore, 1991

Rudolph Kleberg Jr., 1900

Barnes F. Lathrop, 1950

Tom Lea, 1997

Leonard Lemmon, 1903

Walter E. Long, 1959

Adele B. Looscan, 1900

F. R. Lubbock, 1897

William R. Manning, 1915

Thomas Maitland Marshall, 1915

Robert S. Maxwell, 1984

W. F. McCaleb, 1899

Stuart McGregor, 1944

E. T. Miller, 1905

Andrew F. Muir, 1967

Sandra L. Myres, 1984

Joseph M. Nance, 1965

Kenneth F. Neighbours, 1982

C. T. Neu, 1910

William W. Newcomb, 1970

P. I. Nixon, 1941

William H. Oberste, 1972

William A. Owens, 1988

Anna J. H. Pennybacker, 1897

Carmen Perry, 1988

Ben E. Pingenot, 1996

William C. Pool, 1957

C. S. Potts, 1941

Anna Powell, 1928

C. W. Raines, 1897

Charles W. Ramsdell, 1908

Harry H. Ransom, 1954

Dora Neill Raymond, 1941

John H. Reagan, 1897

Rupert N. Richardson, 1929

Carl Coke Rister, 1948

O. M. Roberts, 1897

Ingham S. Roberts, 1917

Willard B. Robinson, 1985

E. M. Schiwetz, 1976

Edmond J. P. Schmitt, 1899

Joseph Schmitz, 1941

Harold Schoen, 1938

Florence Johnson Scott, 1972

L. F. Sheffy, 1947

Charmion Shelby, 1933

Seth Shepard, 1898

Marilyn McAdams Sibley, 1974

Harold B. Simpson, 1972

Julia Lee Sinks, 1897

W. Roy Smith, 1902

Harriet Smither, 1923

C. L. Sonnichsen, 1951

Lota M. Spell, 1969

J. S. Spratt, 1959

J. Lee Stambaugh, 1959

Ralph W. Steen, 1943

Thomas W. Streeter, 1947

Rex W. Strickland, 1965

Virginia H. Taylor, 1970

A. W. Terrell, 1907

Francis X. Tolbert, 1967

John C. Townes, 1899

Philip C. Tucker III, 1918
George W. Tyler, 1923
Earl Vandale, 1947
David M. Vigness, 1965
Ethel Zivley Rather Villavaso, 1905
Ernest Wallace, 1954
Frank A. Wardlaw, 1977
Walter Prescott Webb, 1923
John Edward Weems, 1993
Elizabeth H. West, 1912

Amelia W. Williams, 1933
J. W. Williams, 1961
O. W. Williams, 1900
Ruthe Winegarten, 2003
Mrs. A. V. Winkler, 1897
Ernest William Winkler, 1904
George R. Woolfolk, 1986
Dudley G. Wooten, 1897
J. L. Worley, 1909
W. E. Wrather, 1933

CURRENT FELLOWS, THROUGH 2007 (YEAR ELECTED)

Francis Edward Abernethy, 2002
Félix D. Almaráz Jr., 1986
T. Lindsay Baker, 1987
C. Alwyn Barr, 1971
Adán Benavides Jr., 1994
Norman D. Brown, 1990
Walter L. Buenger, 2000
Randolph B. Campbell, 1985
Don E. Carleton, 1991
Paul H. Carlson, 1992
Donald E. Chipman, 1994
Garna Christian, 2004
Michael L. Collins, 2005
Ana Carolina Castillo Crimm, 2005
Gilbert R. Cruz, 2000
Light T. Cummins, 1993
Arnoldo De León, 1987
Roy Sylvan Dunn, 1967
L. Tuffly Ellis, 1989
Odie B. Faulk, 1965
T. R. Fehrenbach, 1975
Dan L. Flores, 1990
William C. Foster, 2001
William H. Goetzmann, 1989
David B. Gracy II, 1992
Don Graham, 1989
George N. Green, 1989
William C. Griggs, 1996
James L. Haley, 2007
Kenneth E. Hendrickson Jr., 2002

Diana Davids Hinton, 1992
Harwood P. Hinton, 1997
Elizabeth A. H. John, 1978
Billy Mac Jones, 1967
Thomas Heard Kreneck, 2006
Paul D. Lack, 1994
Al Lowman, 1988
Richard B. McCaslin, 2006
David G. McComb, 1988
Archie P. McDonald, 1984
Joseph McKnight, 2004
Malcolm D. McLean, 1967
Paula Mitchell Marks, 1993
Carl H. Moneyhon, 2000
David J. Murrah, 1996
Stephen B. Oates, 1968
Roger M. Olien, 1989
J'Nell L. Pate, 1994
James W. Pohl, 1994
Ben H. Procter, 1968
Kenneth B. Ragsdale, 1987
Fred Rathjen, 2007
John C. Rayburn, 1967
Joyce Gibson Roach, 1997
Charles M. Robinson III, 2003
Lou Rodenberger, 2001
Stanley Siegel, 1987
Elizabeth Silverthorne, 1997
James M. Smallwood, 1995
F. Todd Smith, 2006

Thomas T. Smith, 2003

Charles Spurlin, 2004

Lonn Taylor, 2007

Jesús F. de la Teja, 2001

Jerry D. Thompson, 1992

Robert H. Thonhoff, 1980

Andrés Tijerina, 1997

W. H. Timmons, 1968

Ron Tyler, 1977

Frank E. Vandiver, 1970

David J. Weber, 1985

Robert S. Weddle, 1969

John R. Wheat, 2005

Dorman H. Winfrey, 1961

Ralph A. Wooster, 1965

Robert A. Wooster, 2002

Donald E. Worcester, 1981

Appendix G

1917

British Diplomatic Correspondence Concerning the Republic of Texas, 1838–1846. Edited by Ephraim Douglass Adams.

1943

Santa Rita: The University of Texas Oil Discovery, by Martin W. Schwettmann. Illustrated by Tom Lea. (1958 Reprint, designed by Carl Hertzog.)

Texas County Histories: A Bibliography, by H. Bailey Carroll. Foreword by Walter Prescott Webb.

1944

Charles Schreiner, General Merchandise: The Story of a Country Store, by J. Evetts Haley. Illustrations by H. D. Bugbee. Designed by Carl Hertzog.

1946

The Presbyterian Church in Jefferson, by J. A. R. Moseley. Drawings by Harold Bugbee.

1947

El Sal del Rey, by Walace Hawkins. Illustrated by José Cisneros. Designed by Carl Hertzog.

1948

Judge Robert McAlpin Williamson: Texas' Three-Legged Willie, by Duncan W. Robinson.

Terán and Texas: A Chapter in Texas-Mexican Relations, by Ohland Morton. Introduction by Eugene C. Barker.

1949

Check List of Texas Imprints, 1846–1860. Edited by Ernest W. Winkler. Foreword by Thomas W. Streeter.

The Life of Stephen F. Austin, Founder of Texas, 1793–1836: A Chapter in the Westward Movement of the Anglo-American People, by Eugene C. Barker. (Second Edition.)

Migration into East Texas, 1835–1860: A Study from the United States Census, by Barnes F. Lathrop.

1950

Cumulative Index of the Southwestern Historical Quarterly, *Vols. I–XL, July 1897–April 1937.* Introduction by H. Bailey Carroll.

1951

Western Falls County, Texas, by Lillian Schiller St. Romain.

1952

The Handbook of Texas (2 vols.). Edited by Walter Prescott Webb and H. Bailey Carroll.

Post City, Texas: C. W. Post's Colonizing Activities in West Texas, by Charles Dudley Eaves and C. A. Hutchinson. Foreword by Jesse H. Jones.

1955

Texas History Theses: A Check List of the Theses and Dissertations Relating to Texas History Accepted at the University of Texas, 1893–1951. Compiled and edited by H. Bailey Carroll and Milton R. Gutsch.

Theses on Texas History: A Check List of Theses and Dissertations in Texas History Produced in the Departments of History of Eighteen Texas Graduate Schools and Thirty-Three Graduate Schools Outside of Texas, 1907–1952. Compiled and edited by Claude Elliott.

1956

A History of Young County, Texas, by Carrie J. Crouch. Foreword by Harry Yandell Benedict.

1958

A History of Collin County, Texas, by J. Lee Stambaugh and Lillian J. Stambaugh.

1959

The Peters Colony of Texas: A History and Biographical Sketches of the Early Settlers, by Seymour V. Connor. Illustrated by Frances Pearce. (Reprint 2006.)

1960

Cumulative Index of the Southwestern Historical Quarterly, *Vols. XLI–LX, July, 1937–April, 1957.*

1961

The Great Hanging at Gainesville, Cooke County, Texas, October, A.D. 1862, by Thomas Barrett. Preface by H. Bailey Carroll.

The Junior Historian Movement in Texas: A Guidebook and History. Edited by H. Bailey Carroll and Frances V. Parker.

1963

George Washington Diamond's Account of the Great Hanging at Gainesville, 1862. Edited by Sam Acheson and Julie Ann Hudson O'Connell.

1964

Check List of Texas Imprints, 1861–1876. Edited by Ernest W. Winkler and Llerena B. Friend.

1965

A History of Coryell County, Texas, by Zelma Scott. Foreword by H. Bailey Carroll.

1968

The Republic of Texas. Edited by Stephen B. Oates. Joint publication with the American West Publishing Company.

1970

The Espuela Land and Cattle Company: A Study of a Foreign-Owned Ranch in Texas, by William Curry Holden. Foreword by Joe B. Frantz.

Talks on Texas Books: A Collection of Book Reviews by Walter Prescott Webb. Compiled and edited by Llerena Friend. Foreword by Joe B. Frantz.

1971

Eugene C. Barker: Historian, by William C. Pool.

The French Legation in Texas, Volume I: Recognition, Rupture, and Reconciliation. Translated and edited by Nancy Nichols Barker. Foreword by John Connally. Designed by William R. Holman.

1973

The French Legation in Texas, Volume II: Mission Miscarried. Translated and edited by Nancy Nichols Barker. Designed by William R. Holman.

The Mexican War: A Lithographic Record, by Ronnie C. Tyler. Introduction by Stanley R. Ross.

Santiago Vidaurri and the Southern Confederacy, by Ronnie C. Tyler.

1974

Texas History Illustrated.

1976

The Handbook of Texas: A Supplement, Volume III. Edited by Eldon Stephen Branda. Foreword by Joe B. Frantz. Dustjacket designed by Gerald Emelyn Branda.

Scottish Capital on the American Credit Frontier, by W. G. Kerr. Foreword by Charles Wilson.

1978

Samuel H. Walker's Account of the Mier Expedition. Edited by Marilyn McAdams Sibley.

Sangers': Pioneer Texas Merchants, by Leon Joseph Rosenberg.

1979

The Texas Revolution, by William C. Binkley.

1980

Cumulative Index of the Southwestern Historical Quarterly, *Vols. 61–70, July, 1957–April, 1967.*

Journey to Mexico during the Years 1826 to 1834, by Jean Louis Berlandier (2 vols.). Translated by Sheila M. Ohlendorf, Josette M. Bigelow, and Mary M. Standifer. Introduction by C. H. Muller. Botanical Notes by C. H. Muller and Katherine K. Muller.

Log Cabin Village: A History and Guide. Text by Terry G. Jordan. Catalogue by Bettie A. Regester and Selden A. Wallace. Photography by Elna Wilkinson. Preface by Nevin E. Neal. Drawings by Tony Crosby.

Texas Vistas: Selections from the Southwestern Historical Quarterly. Compiled by Ralph A. Wooster and Robert A. Calvert. (Revised 1987, 2006.)

1981

Black Leaders: Texans for Their Times. Edited by Alwyn Barr and Robert A. Calvert.

History is My Home: A Survey of Texas Architectural Styles (Filmstrip). *Teachers' Guide*, by Kenneth Ragsdale, David C. DeBoe, and Willard B. Robinson.

The Old Stone Fort, by Archie P. McDonald.

1982

Contours of Discovery: Printed Maps Delineating the Texas and Southwestern Chapters in the Cartographic History of North America, 1513–1930, A User's Guide, by Robert Sidney Martin and James C. Martin. Foreword by J. Conrad Dunagan.

1983

The People's Architecture: Texas Courthouses, Jails and Municipal Buildings, by Willard B. Robinson.

A Southern Community in Crisis: Harrison County, Texas, 1850–1880, by Randolph B. Campbell.

1984

Cumulative Index of the Southwestern Historical Quarterly, *Vols. 71–80, July, 1967–April, 1977.*

Spanish Explorers in the Southern United States, 1528–1543. Edited by Frederick W. Hodge and Theodore H. Lewis. Dustjacket designed by David Timmons. (Reprint 1990.)

Through Unexplored Texas: Notes Taken during the Expedition Commanded by Capt. R. B. Marcy, U.S.A., in the Summer and Fall of 1854, by W. B. Parker. Introduction by George B. Ward. Dustjacket designed by David Timmons. (Reprint 1990.)

1985

A Ranchman's Recollections: An Autobiography, by Frank S. Hastings. Introduction by David J. Murrah. Designed by Deborah E. Brothers and George B. Ward.

Teaching Texas History: An All-Level Resource Guide, by David C. De Boe, Barbara F. Immroth, and Jane Manaster. (Revised 1989.)

Texas, by Mrs. Mary Austin Holley. Introduction by Marilyn McAdams Sibley. Dustjacket designed by David Timmons. (Reprint 1990.)

Tracks on the Land: Stories of Immigrants, Outlaws, Artists, and Other Texans Who Left Their Mark on the Lone Star State. Edited by David C. De Boe and Kenneth B. Ragsdale. Designed by Deborah E. Brothers and George B. Ward.

1986

The Battle of the Alamo, by Ben H. Procter.

A Comprehensive History of Texas, 1685 to 1897 (2 vols.). Edited by Dudley G. Wooten. Publisher's Preface by William G. Scarff. Introduction by Seth Shepard.

Texas History Movies. Introduction by George B. Ward. Designed by Deborah E. Brothers and George B. Ward.

1987

Report on the United States and Mexican Boundary Survey: Made under the Direction of the Secretary of the Interior, by William H. Emory. (Vols. I and II, parts I and II). Introduction by William H. Goetzmann. Publisher's foreword by the Texas State Historical Association.

1988

Basic Texas Books: An Annotated Bibliography of Selected Works for a Research Library, by John H. Jenkins. Designed by William R. Holman. (Revised edition.)

1989

The Battle of San Jacinto, by James W. Pohl.

A History of the French Legation in Texas: Alphonse Dubois de Saligny and His House, by Kenneth Hafertepe.

The Methodist Hospital of Houston: Serving the World, by Marilyn McAdams Sibley. Preface by A. Frank Smith Jr. Designed by David Timmons.

Twentieth-Century Texas: A High School Texas Studies Curriculum Guide, by William C. Hardt, Jack Sheridan, and David C. De Boe.

Watt Matthews of Lambshead. Photographs and text by Laura Wilson. Introduction by David McCullough. Designed by Eleanor Caponigro.

1990

The Handbook of Victoria County. Prepared by the staff of the *Handbook of Texas.* Foreword by Charles D. Spurlin. Dustjacket designed by David Timmons.

The History of Texas; or, the Emigrant's, Farmer's, and Politician's Guide to the Character, Climate, Soil and Productions of That Country: Arranged Geographically from Personal Observation and Experience, by David B. Edward. Introduction by Margaret S. Henson. Dustjacket designed by David Timmons.

Junior Historian and Walter Prescott Webb Historical Society Sponsors' Handbook, by David C. De Boe.

Women and Texas History: An Archival Bibliography. Preface by Nancy Baker Jones.

1991

Army Exploration in the American West, 1803–1863, by William H. Goetzmann.

A History of Ashton Villa: A Family and Its House in Victorian Galveston, Texas, by Kenneth Hafertepe. Designed by David Timmons.

History of the Cattlemen of Texas: A Brief Resumé of the Live Stock Industry of the Southwest and a Biographical Sketch of Many of the Important Characters Whose Lives are Interwoven Therein. Introduction by Harwood P. Hinton.

Illustrations of the Birds of California, Texas, Oregon, British and Russian America, by John Cassin. Introduction by Robert McCracken Peck. Designed by William R. Holman.

A Shared Past: Texas and the Untied States Since Reconstruction, by William C. Hardt.

A Texas Scrap-Book: Made up of the History, Biography and Miscellany of Texas and Its People, by D. W. C. Baker. Introduction by Robert A. Calvert. Designed by David Timmons.

1992

Abner Cook: Master Builder on the Texas Frontier, by Kenneth Hafertepe. Dustjacket designed by David Timmons.

The McFaddin-Ward House, by Jessica H. Foy and Judith W. Linsley. Designed by David Timmons.

The News from Brownsville: Helen Chapman's Letters from the Texas Military Frontier, 1848–1852. Edited by Caleb Coker. Foreword by Don E. Carleton. Designed by David Timmons.

Progressives and Prohibitionists: Texas Democrats in the Wilson Era, by Lewis L. Gould.

The Samuel May Williams Home: The Life and Neighborhood of an Early Galveston Entrepreneur, by Margaret Swett Henson. Designed by David Timmons.

Teachers' Guide to the Handbook of Texas. Edited by David C. De Boe and William C. Hardt.

War Scare on the Rio Grande: Robert Runyon's Photographs of the Border Conflict, 1913–1916, by Frank N. Samponaro and Paul J. Vanderwood. Foreword by Don E. Carleton. Designed by Wind River Press.

1993

Art for History's Sake: The Texas Collection of the Witte Museum, by Cecilia Steinfeldt. Introduction by William H. Goetzmann. Designed by George Lenox.

The Cartwrights of San Augustine: Three Generations of Agrarian Entrepreneurs in Nineteenth-Century Texas, by Margaret Swett Henson and Deolece Parmelee. Dustjacket designed by David Timmons.

Catching Shadows: A Directory of Nineteenth-Century Texas Photographers, by David Haynes. Cover designed by David Timmons.

A Cowman's Wife, by Mary Kidder Rak. Introduction by Sandra L. Myres. Dustjacket designed by David Timmons.

Exploration and Empire: The Explorer and the Scientist in the Winning of the American West, by William H. Goetzmann. Dustjacket designed by David Timmons. (Reprint 2000.)

Sam Chamberlain's Mexican War: The San Jacinto Museum of History Paintings, by William H. Goetzmann.

Women and Texas History: Selected Essays. Edited by Fane Downs and Nancy Baker Jones. Keynote essay by Elizabeth Fox-Genovese. Designed by David Timmons.

1994

Behold the People: R. C. Hickman's Photographs of Black Dallas, 1949–1961, by R. C. Hickman. Preface by Barbara Jordan. Foreword by Don E. Carleton. Designed by Wind River Press.

Fort Davis: Outpost on the Texas Frontier, by Robert Wooster.

Picturing Texas: The FSA-OWI Photographers in the Lone Star State, 1935–1943, by Robert L. Reid. Designed by David Timmons.

Remember Goliad! A History of La Bahía, by Craig H. Roell.

The War Between the United States and Mexico, Illustrated, by George Wilkins Kendall. Illustrations by Carl Nebel. Introduction by Ron Tyler. Designed by W. Thomas Taylor.

Women in Early Texas. Edited by Evelyn M. Carrington. Introduction by Debbie Mauldin Cottrell. Preface by Barbara Likan.

1995

Imaginary Kingdom: Texas as Seen by the Rivera and Rubí Military Expeditions, 1727 and 1767. Edited by Jack Jackson. Annotations by William C. Foster. Foreword by Don E. Carleton. Designed by Martin Kohout. Dustjacket designed by David Timmons.

The Indian Papers of Texas and the Southwest, 1825–1916. Edited by Dorman H. Winfrey and James M. Day. Introduction by Michael L. Tate.

Lone Star Blue and Gray: Essays on Texas in the Civil War. Edited and with an introduction by Ralph A. Wooster. Designed by Martin Kohout. Cover designed by David Timmons.

New Lands, New Men: America and the Second Great Age of Discovery, by William H. Goetzmann. Dustjacket designed by David Timmons.

The Texas State Capitol: Selected Essays from the Southwestern Historical Quarterly.

1996

My Confession: Recollections of a Rogue, by Samuel Chamberlain. Edited by William H. Goetzmann. Designed by David Timmons.

The New Handbook of Texas (6 vols.). Edited by Ron Tyler, Douglas E. Barnett, Roy R. Barkley, Penelope C. Anderson, and Mark F. Odintz. Publisher's preface by Ron Tyler. Designed by David Timmons.

Portraits of Community: African American Photography in Texas, by Alan Govenar. Designed by David Timmons.

Texas Oil, American Dreams: A Study of the Texas Independent Producers and Royalty Owners Association, by Lawrence Goodwyn. Foreword by Don E. Carleton.

1997

Austin: A History of the Capital City, by David C. Humphrey.

Dallas: A History of "Big D," by Michael V. Hazel.

El Llano Estacado: Exploration and Imagination on the High Plains of Texas and New Mexico, 1536–1860, by John Miller Morris. Dustjacket designed by David Timmons.

Prints and Printmakers of Texas: Proceedings of the Twentieth Annual North American Print Conference. Edited and with an introduction by Ron Tyler. Designed by Martin D. Kohout. Dustjacket designed by David Timmons.

Texas, Her Texas: The Life and Times of Frances Goff, by Nancy Beck Young and Lewis L. Gould. Preface by Ann W. Richards. Foreword by Don E. Carleton. Designed by William V. Bishel. Dustjacket designed by David Timmons.

A Wild and Vivid Land: An Illustrated History of the South Texas Border, by Jerry Thompson. Foreword by A. R. Sanchez Jr. and Brian E. O'Brien. Designed by David Timmons.

1998

A Breed So Rare: The Life of J. R. Parten, Liberal Texas Oil Man, 1896–1992, by Don E. Carleton. Designed by David Timmons.

Fifty Miles and a Fight: Major Samuel Peter Heintzelman's Journal of Texas and the Cortina War. Edited and with an introduction by Jerry Thompson. Designed by David Timmons.

The La Salle Expedition to Texas: The Journal of Henri Joutel, 1684–1687. Edited and with an introduction by William C. Foster. Translated by Johanna S. Warren. Designed by David Timmons.

Land is the Cry! Warren Angus Ferris, Pioneer Texas Surveyor and Founder of Dallas County, by Susanne Starling. Designed by William V. Bishel. Dustjacket designed by David Timmons.

Pigskin Pulpit: A Social History of Texas High School Football Coaches, by Ty Cashion. Foreword by O. A. "Bum" Phillips. Designed by Holly Zumwalt Taylor. Dustjacket designed by David Timmons.

1999

Chronicles of the Big Bend: A Photographic Memoir of Life on the Border, by W. D. Smithers. Foreword by Kenneth B. Ragsdale. Designed by William A. Seymour. Dustjacket designed by David Timmons.

Civil War Texas: A History and a Guide, by Ralph A. Wooster.

Fort Lancaster: Texas Frontier Sentinel, by Lawrence John Francell.

Maps of Texas and the Southwest, 1513–1900, by James C. Martin and Robert Sidney Martin. Designed by Emmy Ezzel. Dustjacket designed by David Timmons.

McKinney Falls: The Ranch Home of Thomas F. McKinney, Pioneer Texas Entrepreneur, by Margaret Swett Henson.

2000

Galveston: A History and a Guide, by David G. McComb.

Mexican Americans in Texas History: Selected Essays. Edited by Emilio Zamora, Cynthia Orozco, and Rodolfo Rocha.

The Old Army in Texas: A Research Guide to the U. S. Army in Nineteenth-Century Texas, by Thomas T. Smith. Designed by David Timmons.

The Portable Handbook of Texas. Edited by Roy R. Barkley and Mark F. Odintz. Foreword by Ron Tyler. Designed by David Timmons.

William Pitt Ballinger: Texas Lawyer, Southern Statesman, 1825–1888, by John Anthony Moretta. Foreword by Don E. Carleton. Designed by Janice Pinney. Dustjacket designed by David Timmons.

2001

Forgotten Texas Census: First Annual Report of the Agricultural Bureau of the Department of Agriculture, Insurance, Statistics, and History, 1887–88, by L. L. Foster. Introduction by Barbara J. Rozek. Designed by Janice Pinney.

Mistress of Manifest Destiny: A Biography of Jane McManus Storm Cazneau, 1807–1878, by Linda S. Hudson. Designed by Holly Zumwalt Taylor. Dustjacket designed by David Timmons.

Travels with Joe: The Life Story of a Historian from Texas, 1917–1993, by David G. McComb. Designed by Janice Pinney. Dustjacket designed by David Timmons.

2002

Documents of Texas History. Edited by Ernest Wallace, David M. Vigness, and George B. Ward. Cover designed by David Timmons.

Giant under the Hill: A History of the Spindletop Oil Discovery at Beaumont, Texas, in 1901, by Judith Walker Linsley, Ellen Walker Rienstra, and Jo Ann Stiles. Preface by Michel T. Halbouty. Designed by Janice Pinney. Dustjacket designed by David Timmons.

A Revolution Remembered: The Memoirs and Selected Correspondence of Juan N. Seguín. Edited by Jesús F. de la Teja. Cover designed by David Timmons.

Valor across the Lone Star: The Congressional Medal of Honor in Frontier Texas, by Charles M. Neal Jr. Foreword by Jerry Thompson. Designed by Holly Zumwalt Taylor. Dustjacket designed by David Timmons.

2003

Almonte's Texas: Juan N. Almonte's 1834 Inspection, Secret Report & Role in the 1836 Campaign. Edited by Jack Jackson. Translated by John Wheat. Designed by Janice Pinney.

Along Forgotten River: Photographs of Buffalo Bayou and the Houston Ship Channel, 1997–2001, With Accounts of Early Travelers to Texas, 1767–1858, by Geoff Winningham. Designed by David Timmons.

The Handbook of Texas Music. Edited by Roy Barkley, Douglas E. Barnett, Cathy Brigham, Gary Hartman, Casey Monahan, Dave Oliphant, and George B. Ward. Foreword by George B. Ward. Introduction by Roy R. Barkley.

I Would Rather Sleep in Texas: A History of the Lower Rio Grande Valley and the People of the Santa Anita Land Grant, by Mary Margaret McAllen Amberson, James A. McAllen, and Margaret H. McAllen. Foreword by Jerry Thompson. Designed by David Timmons.

The La Salle Expedition on the Mississippi River: A Lost Manuscript of Nicolas de La Salle, 1682. Edited and with an introduction by William C. Foster. Translated by Johanna S. Warren. Designed by David Timmons.

Saving Lives, Training Caregivers, Making Discoveries: A Centennial History of the University of Texas Medical Branch at Galveston, by Chester R. Burns. Designed by Holly Zumwalt Taylor. Dustjacket designed by David Timmons.

2004

Civil War & Revolution on the Rio Grande Frontier: A Narrative and Photographic History, by Jerry Thompson and Lawrence T. Jones III. Designed by David Timmons.

Fort Worth: A Texas Original! by Richard F. Selcer.

Sea of Mud: The Retreat of the Mexican Army after San Jacinto, An Archeological Investigation, by Gregg J. Dimmick. Designed by David Timmons.

Texas and the Mexican War: A History and a Guide, by Charles M. Robinson III.

2005

Fort Concho: A History and a Guide, by James T. Matthews.

Road, River & Ol' Boy Politics: A Texas County's Path from Farm to Supersuburb, by Linda Scarbrough. Designed by David Timmons.

S. Seymour Thomas, 1868–1956: A Texas Genius Rediscovered, by Cecilia Steinfeldt. Foreword by John W. Crain. Designed by David Timmons.

Tejano Epic: Essays in Honor of Félix D. Almaráz, Jr. Edited by Arnoldo De León.

2006

A Brave Boy & a Good Soldier: John C. C. Hill & the Texas Expedition to Mier, by Mary Margaret McAllen Amberson. Designed by David Timmons.

A Brave Boy & a Good Soldier: John C. C. Hill & the Texas Expedition to Mier. Educator Guide, by Jana Magruder.

The Texas Republic: A Social and Economic History, by William Ransom Hogan. Foreword by Gregg Cantrell. Cover designed by David Timmons.

Texas Towns and the Art of Architecture: A Photographer's Journey, by Richard Payne. Foreword by Stephen Fox. Designed by David Timmons.

2007 *(Spring)*

At the Heart of Texas: One Hundred Years of the Texas State Historical Association, 1897–1997, by Richard B. McCaslin. Foreword by J. P. Bryan. Illustrated and with captions and sidebars by Janice Pinney. Designed by David Timmons.

New Texas History Movies, by Jack Jackson. Foreword by John Wheat. Designed by David Timmons.

New Texas History Movies, Special Educator's Edition, by Jana Magruder. Designed by David Timmons.

On the Border with Mackenzie; or, Winning West Texas from the Comanches, by Robert G. Carter. Foreword by Charles M. Robinson III. Dustjacket designed by David Timmons.

THE FRED H. AND ELLA MAE MOORE TEXAS HISTORY REPRINT SERIES

(For this and the following series lists, the primary author or editor is given; for other information as to introduction, foreword, designer, etc., see the above general list.)

The Texas Revolution, by William C. Binkley (1979).

Spanish Explorers in the Southern United States, 1528–1543, ed. by Frederick W. Hodge and Theodore H. Lewis (1984).

Through Unexplored Texas: Notes taken during the Expedition Commanded by Capt. R. B. Marcy, U.S.A., in the Summer and Fall of 1854, by W. B. Parker (1984).

Texas, by Mrs. Mary Austin Holley (1985).

A Ranchman's Recollections: An Autobiography, by Frank S. Hastings (1985).

A Comprehensive History of Texas, 1685 to 1897, ed. by Dudley G. Wooten (1986).

Report on the United States and Mexican Boundary Survey: Made Under the Direction of the Secretary of the Interior, by William H. Emory (1987).

Basic Texas Books: An Annotated Bibliography of Selected Works for a Research Library, by John H. Jenkins (1988).

The History of Texas; or, the Emigrant's, Farmer's, and Politician's Guide to the Character, Climate, Soil and Productions of That Country: Arranged Geographically from Personal Observation and Experience, by David B. Edward (1990).

Army Exploration in the American West, 1803–1863, by William H. Goetzmann (1991).

A Texas Scrap-Book: Made up of the History, Biography and Miscellany of Texas and Its People, by D. W. C. Baker (1991).

Progressives and Prohibitionists: Texas Democrats in the Wilson Era, by Lewis L. Gould (1992).

Exploration and Empire: The Explorer and the Scientist in the Winning of the American West, by William H. Goetzmann (1993).

Women in Early Texas, ed. by Evelyn M. Carrington (1994).

The Texas State Capitol: Selected Essays from the Southwestern Historical Quarterly (1995).

The Indian Papers of Texas and the Southwest, 1825–1916, ed. by Dorman H. Winfrey and James M. Day (1995).

New Lands, New Men: America and the Second Great Age of Discovery, by William H. Goetzmann (1995).

Lone Star Blue and Gray: Essays on Texas in the Civil War, ed. by Ralph A. Wooster (1995).

Maps of Texas and the Southwest, 1513–1900, by James C. Martin and Robert Sidney Martin (1999).

Forgotten Texas Census: First Annual Report of the Agricultural Bureau of the Department of Agriculture, Insurance, Statistics, and History, 1887–88, by L. L. Foster; ed. by Barbara J. Rozek (2001).

A Revolution Remembered: The Memoirs and Selected Correspondence of Juan N. Seguín, ed. by Jesús F. de la Teja (2002).

Documents of Texas History, ed. by Ernest Wallace, David M. Vigness, and George B. Ward (2002).

The Texas Republic: A Social and Economic History, by William Ransom Hogan (2006).

On the Border with Mackenzie; or, Winning West Texas from the Comanches, by Robert G. Carter (2007).

Fred Rider Cotten Popular History Series

The Old Stone Fort, by Archie P. McDonald (No. 1; 1981).

The Battle of the Alamo, by Ben H. Procter (No. 2; 1986).

The Battle of San Jacinto, by James W. Pohl (No. 3; 1989).

A History of the French Legation in Texas: Alphonse Dubois de Saligny and His House, by Kenneth Hafertepe (No. 4; 1989).

A History of Ashton Villa: A Family and Its House in Victorian Galveston, Texas, by Kenneth Hafertepe (No. 5; 1991).

The McFaddin-Ward House, by Jessica H. Foy and Judith W. Linsley (No. 6; 1992).

The Samuel May Williams Home: The Life and Neighborhood of an Early Galveston Entrepreneur, by Margaret Swett Henson (No. 7; 1992).

Fort Davis: Outpost on the Texas Frontier, by Robert Wooster (No. 8; 1994).

Remember Goliad! A History of La Bahía, by Craig H. Roell (No. 9; 1994).

Austin: A History of the Capital City, by David C. Humphrey (No. 10; 1997).

Dallas: A History of "Big D," by Michael V. Hazel (No. 11; 1997).

McKinney Falls: The Ranch Home of Thomas F. McKinney, Pioneer Texas Entrepreneur,
  by Margaret Swett Henson (No. 12; 1999).
Fort Lancaster: Texas Frontier Sentinel, by Lawrence John Francell (No. 13; 1999).
Civil War Texas: A History and a Guide, by Ralph A. Wooster (No. 14; 1999).
Galveston: A History and a Guide, by David G. McComb (No. 15; 2000).
Texas and the Mexican War: A History and a Guide, by Charles M. Robinson III (No.
  16; 2004).
Fort Worth: A Texas Original! by Richard F. Selcer (No. 17; 2004).
Fort Concho: A History and a Guide, by James T. Matthews (No. 18; 2005).

BARKER TEXAS HISTORY CENTER SERIES

*War Scare on the Rio Grande: Robert Runyon's Photographs of the Border Conflict,
  1913–1916*, by Frank N. Samponaro and Paul J. Vanderwood (No. 1; 1992).
*The News from Brownsville: Helen Chapman's Letters from the Texas Military Frontier,
  1848–1852*, ed. by Caleb Coker (No. 2; 1992).
Behold the People: R. C. Hickman's Photographs of Black Dallas, 1949–1961, by R. C.
  Hickman (No. 3; 1994).
*Imaginary Kingdom: Texas as Seen by the Rivera and Rubí Military Expeditions, 1727
  and 1767*, ed. by Jack Jackson; annotations by William C. Foster (No. 4; 1995).
*Texas Oil, American Dreams: A Study of the Texas Independent Producers and Royalty
  Owners Association*, by Lawrence Goodwyn (No. 5; 1996).
Texas, Her Texas: The Life and Times of Frances Goff, by Nancy Beck Young and Lewis
  L. Gould (No. 6; 1997).
William Pitt Ballinger: Texas Lawyer, Southern Statesman, 1825–1888, by John Anthony
  Moretta (No. 7; 2000).

DEGOLYER LIBRARY COWBOY AND RANCH LIFE SERIES

*History of the Cattlemen of Texas: A Brief Resumé of the Live Stock Industry of the
  Southwest and a Biographical Sketch of Many of the Important Characters Whose Lives
  are Interwoven Therein* (No. 1; 1991).
A Cowman's Wife, by Mary Kidder Rak (No. 2; 1993).

TEXAS COUNTY AND LOCAL HISTORY SERIES

Western Falls County, Texas, by Lillian Schiller St. Romain (No. 1; 1951).
A History of Young County, Texas, by Carrie J. Crouch (No. 2; 1956).
A History of Collin County, Texas, by J. Lee Stambaugh and Lillian J. Stambaugh (No.
  3; 1958).
A History of Coryell County, Texas, by Zelma Scott (No. 4; 1965).

A Note on Sources

This work, in seeking to be a discussion of the history of the Texas State Historical Association within the context of the evolving historiography of Texas and the United States, relies on a broad variety of sources. When the focus was expanded to include as much of the personal history of the Association as possible, the bibliography became even more complex. Certainly not every available source was used, but an honest effort was made to incorporate materials that were significant in both quantity and quality.

There are many books on the evolution of historical study in the United States. Among the most useful are two written by W. Stull Holt: *The Historical Profession in the United States* (Washington, D.C., 1963), and *Historical Scholarship in the United States* (Seattle, WA, 1967). For the emergence of professional historians, see two works by J. Franklin Jameson: *The History of Historical Writing in America* (New York, 1891; reprint, New York, 1961), and "The American Historical Association, 1884–1909," *American Historical Review*, 15 (Oct. 1909), 1–20. The early annual reports of the American Historical Association are also helpful, as well as a fine compilation of statistics and other information by William B. Hesseltine and Louis B. Kaplan, "Doctors of Philosophy in History," *American Historical Review*, 47 (July 1942), 765–800. For an interesting later regional perspective, see David D. Van Tassel, "The American Historical Association and the South," *Journal of Southern History*, 23 (Nov. 1957), 465–482.

Much less attention has been paid to the development of historical associations in the United States. The standard studies remain Walter M. Whitehill, *Independent Historical Societies* (Boston, 1962), and again David D. Van Tassel, *Recording America's Past* (Chicago, 1960). Another older work, Leslie W. Dunlap, *American Historical Societies, 1790–1860* (Madison, WI, 1944), provides background on the period preceding the Texas State Historical Association, while Clifford L. Lord (ed.), *Keepers of the Past* (Chapel Hill, NC, 1965), provides both useful information and interesting anecdotes. In addition, some information can be gleaned from Betty P. Smith, *Directory: Historical Agencies in North America*, 13th ed. (Nashville, 1986). For more about the creation of the American Association for State and Local History, see Henry E. Bourne, "Work of Historical Societies," and Frederick W. Moore, "First Report of the Conference of State and Local Historical Societies," both of which are in the *American Historical Association Annual Report, 1904* (Washington, D.C., 1905), as well as Julian P. Boyd, "State and Local History Societies in the United States," *American Historical Review,* 40 (Oct. 1934), 10–37. A more optimistic view can be found in Walter M. Whitehill's "Local History in the United States," *Times Literary Supplement*, Nov. 13, 1970. One of the best histories sponsored by local organizations is Lana Ruegamer, *A History of the Indiana Historical Society, 1830–1980* (Indianapolis, 1980).

Texas historiography has fortunately become the subject of more careful scrutiny in the past few decades or so, although a study produced outside the state may be the first on the topic. James S. Payne completed his dissertation, "Texas Historiography in the Twentieth Century: A Study of Eugene C. Barker, Charles W. Ramsdell, and Walter P. Webb," at the University of Denver in 1972. Nearly twenty years later, an authoritative summary of Texas historiography appeared: *Texas Through Time: Evolving Interpretations*, edited by Walter L. Buenger and Robert A. Calvert (College Station, TX, 1991). Laura L. McLemore analyzed the first Texas historians in her ground-breaking dissertation that was published as *Inventing Texas: Early Historians of the Lone Star State* (College Station, TX, 2004). Other useful works on the writing of Texas history include Stephen Stagner, "Epics, Science, and the Lost Frontier: Texas Historical Writing, 1836–1936," *Western Historical Quarterly,* 12 (Apr. 1981), 165–181, and Kenneth B. Ragsdale, *The Year America Discovered Texas: Centennial '36* (College Station, TX, 1987). Finally, much about the evolving image of Texas, including Texans' perspectives on their own history, can be gleaned from Maury Forman and Robert A. Calvert, *Cartooning Texas* (College Station, TX, 1993).

Those familiar with Texas historiography know that many authors have produced fine works that provide solid contextual foundations for studies such as this one. Among the most useful are Randolph B. Campbell, *Gone To Texas: A History of the Lone Star State* (Oxford, 2003), Lewis L. Gould, *Progressives and Prohibitionists: Texas Democrats in the Wilson Era* (Austin, 1973), Norman D. Brown, *Hood, Bonnet and Little Brown Jug* (College Station, TX, 1984), and Walter L. Buenger, *The Path to a Modern South: Northeast Texas between Reconstruction and the Great Depression* (Austin, 2001). These authors and many others also wrote for the monumental *New Handbook of Texas* (Austin, 1996), six thick volumes of historical treasure produced by the Association that will remain invaluable to those interested in Texas for years to come.

This book also benefited from the sporadic efforts of Texas historians to record the accomplishments of the Association and similar organizations in the state. For a discussion of early historical societies in Texas, beyond the material covered by McLemore, see three works: Dorman H. Winfrey: *A His-*

tory of the Philosophical Society of Texas, 1837–1987 (Austin, 1987), *90 Years of the Daughters: History of the Daughters of the Republic of Texas* (Waco, TX, 1981), and June Moll (comp.), *The American History Club, 1893–1993* (Austin, 1993). On the Association, the first significant efforts were Thomas F. Harwood, "Review of the Work of the Texas State Historical Association," *Southwestern Historical Quarterly,* 31 (July 1927), 3–32, and Bride Neill Taylor, "The Beginnings of the State Historical Association," *Southwestern Historical Quarterly,* 33 (July 1929), 1–17. Eugene C. Barksdale in 1942 wrote a longer manuscript entitled, "Texas Historical Association History and Accomplishments in Forty-Five Years Reviewed," but it was never published and remains among the files at the Center for American History. L. Tuffly Ellis did publish a report, "The Texas State Historical Association," in *History News,* 23 (May 1968), 92–94, but his later efforts to produce something more substantial were abandoned. This left the task of producing an official history to Dorman H. Winfrey, who combined several earlier accounts to create *Seventy-five Years of Texas History: The Texas State Historical Association, 1897–1972* (Austin, 1975).

The principal sources for the history of the Association remain the *Southwestern Historical Quarterly,* which was first published from 1897 to 1912 as the *Quarterly of the Texas State Historical Association,* and the voluminous archives of the Association, found in the Center for American History at the University of Texas at Austin. In addition to articles on the history of the Association, periodic reports of Association activities have appeared in every volume of the *Quarterly* since its inception. These include remarks on annual meetings, the decisions of the Executive Council, budgets, membership, and occasionally obituaries. There are also useful notices and comments that were regularly published in the *Quarterly* for extended periods of time under such titles as "Historical Notes," "Texas Collection," and "Southwestern Collection."

The archives of the Association at the Center for American History hold everything from annual reports and correspondence to faded check stubs and menus. Among the many treasures to be found here are Lester G. Bugbee's manuscript minutes of the organizational meeting of the Association in 1897. The papers of several former directors can also be found at the Center: George P. Garrison, Eugene C. Barker, Walter P. Webb, and H. Bailey Carroll. The Center also houses the archives of the President's Office for the University of Texas and the papers of persons otherwise involved in the progress of the Association: Samuel E. Asbury, Guy M. Bryan, Lester G. Bugbee, Robert C. Cotner, Merle M. Duncan, Louis W. Kemp, Walter F. McCaleb, Hally B. Perry, and Oran M. Roberts. Frank Brown's papers also contain much about Austin during the years when several efforts were made to start history societies. The Vertical File on the Association at the Center is useful as well. It contains an idiosyncratic mix of materials, including the results of previous research efforts. Finally, among the many newspaper files at the Center, the most useful for information on the Association have proven to be, in alphabetical order, the *Austin American Statesman*, *Daily Texan* (student newspaper for the University of Texas), *Dallas Morning News*, and *Houston Post*.

Much information can be found in archives far away from Austin. The papers of Adele B. Looscan at the Houston Metropolitan Archives provide much insight on the Association during the time that Barker served as director. Two former directors were very kind to allow the use of materials they had gathered for other projects. Ron Tyler provided his copies of a transcript of an interview with geologist Robert T. Hill from the J. Evetts Haley collection at the Haley Memorial Library and History Center in Midland, Texas. L. Tuffly Ellis generously opened boxes of papers he gathered from the Herbert E. Bolton collection at the Bancroft Library at the University of California, Berkeley. He also provided access to his own correspondence as director of the Association.

Several directors of the Association have been the focus of biographical studies or published memoirs. William C. Pool's *Eugene C. Barker, Historian* (Austin, 1971), provides excellent context for Barker's *Speeches, Responses, and Essays Critical and Historical* (Austin, 1954). Walter P. Webb has attracted the most attention. The only full-length published biography is Necah S. Furman, *Walter Prescott Webb: His Life and Impact* (Albuquerque, NM, 1976), but just as intriguing is Wilbur R. Jacobs, John W. Caughey, and Joe B. Frantz, *Turner, Bolton, and Webb: Three Historians of the American Frontier* (Seattle, WA, 1965). Webb himself produced *An Honest Preface and Other Essays* (Boston, 1959). Sadly, Walter Rundell Jr. never did complete his biography of Webb, but he wrote "Walter Prescott Webb and the Texas State Historical Association," *Arizona and the West*, 25 (Spring 1983), 109–136. For more about Barker, Webb, and George P. Garrison, see Tom B. Brewer, "A History of the Department of History of the University of Texas 1883–1951" (M.A. thesis, University of Texas at Austin, 1957), and Joseph N. Heard, "Preservation and Publication of Texana in the Texas State Historical Association" (M.L.S. thesis, University of Texas at Austin, 1951). For Joe B. Frantz, see David G. McComb, *Travels with Joe, 1917–1993* (Austin, 2001), as well as Frantz's own *The Forty Acre Follies* (Austin, 1983), a history of the University of Texas that often reveals more about Frantz than the institution.

Books about other persons involved in the development of the Association proved to be useful as well. Among these, in approximate chronological order as they appear in the text, were Elizabeth Silverthorne, *Ashbel Smith of Texas*

(College Station, 1982); William J. Hughes, *Rebellious Ranger: Rip Ford and the Old Southwest* (Norman, OK, 1964); Emily F. Cutrer, *The Art of the Woman: The Life and Work of Elisabet Ney* (Lincoln, NE, 1988); John F. Bannon, *Herbert Eugene Bolton* (Tempe, AZ, 1978); Don E. Carleton, *Who Shot the Bear?: J. Evetts Haley and the Eugene C. Barker Texas History Center* (Austin, 1984); and Don E. Carleton, *A Breed So Rare: The Life of J. R. Parten, Liberal Texas Oilman, 1896–1992* (published by the Association in 1998). To this list must be added a pair of autobiographies: William P. Zuber, *My Eighty Years in Texas*, edited by Janis B. Mayfield (Austin, 1971); and John S. Ford, *Rip Ford's Texas*, edited by Stephen B. Oates (Austin, 1963). Finally, the *Southwestern Historical Quarterly* contains many articles on prominent members of the Association, such as Eugene C. Barker, "Lester Gladstone Bugbee, Teacher and Historian," *Southwestern Historical Quarterly*, 49 (July 1945), 1–35.

The production of this history of course involved much more than a perusal of written records. In alphabetical order, the following people were gracious enough to write or speak about the history of the Association and their own experiences: Félix D. Almaráz Jr., Roy R. Barkley, Douglas E. Barnett, Alwyn Barr, J. P. Bryan Jr., Paul Gervais Bell, Norman D. Brown, Clifton M. Caldwell, Randolph B.(Mike)Campbell, Donald E. Chipman, Thomas W. Cutrer, Jesús Frank de la Teja, L. Tuffly Ellis, Colleen Kain, Max S. Lale, Al Lowman, Archie P. McDonald, Ben H. Procter, Marilyn M. Sibley, Robert H. Thonhoff, Ron Tyler, George B. Ward, Dorman H. Winfrey, Ralph A. Wooster, and Robert Wooster. Without their contributions, many gaps in this narrative would never have been filled.

Notes

Abbreviations

CAH: Center for American History, The University of Texas at Austin
SHQ: *Southwestern Historical Quarterly*
TSHA: Texas State Historical Association

ACADEMIC ALCHEMY

1. "Affairs of the Association," *SHQ*, 14 (July 1910), 84 (1st quotation); Bride Neill Taylor, "The Beginnings of the State Historical Association," *SHQ*, 33 (July 1929), 1 (2nd quotation), 13 (3rd quotation).

2. Eugene C. Barker, *Speeches, Responses and Essays Critical and Historical* (Austin: Eugene C. Barker Texas History Center, 1954), 40.

3. "Robert T. Hill Interview with J. Evetts Haley, Dallas, January 30, 1936" (transcript, n.d.), J. Evetts Haley Collection (Haley Memorial Library and History Center, Midland, Tex.).

4. David D. Van Tassel, *Recording America's Past: An Interpretation of the Development of Historical Studies in America, 1607–1884* (Chicago: University of Chicago Press, 1960), 171 (1st quotation), 173 (2nd quotation).

5. Van Tassel, *Recording America's Past*, 173 (1st quotation); J. Franklin Jameson, *The History of Historical Writing in America* (1891; reprint, New York: Antiquaries Press, 1961), 147 (2nd quotation).

6. Taylor, "The Beginnings of the State Historical Association," 2.

7. Taylor, "The Beginnings of the State Historical Association," 13.

8. "The Organization and Objects of the Texas State Historical Association," *SHQ*, 1 (July 1897), 71.

9. Thomas F. Harwood, "Review of the Work of the Texas State Historical Association," *SHQ*, 31 (July 1927), 3.

10. Harwood, "Review of the Work of the Texas State Historical Association," 3 (1st quotation); Dudley G. Wooten to George P. Garrison, Feb. 16, 1897 (2nd quotation), TSHA Records (CAH).

11. Garrison to Oran M. Roberts, Feb. 15, 1897 (1st quotation), TSHA Records (CAH); George P. Garrison, "The First Twenty-Five Years of the University of Texas," *SHQ*, 60 (July 1956), 111 (2nd quotation).

12. Garrison to Roberts, Feb. 15, 1897 (quotation), TSHA Records (CAH).

WE WILL NOT FAIL

1. Oran M. Roberts, "The Proper Work of the Association," *SHQ*, 1 (July 1897), 3.

2. Taylor, "The Beginnings of the State Historical Association," 3.

3. Ibid., 3.

4. "The Organization and Objects of the Texas State Historical Association," 72.

5. Taylor, "The Beginnings of the State Historical Association," 4–5.

6. Taylor, "The Beginnings of the State Historical Association," 6.

7. Dudley G. Wooten to Garrison, Feb. 16, 1897, TSHA Records (CAH).

8. Lester G. Bugbee, "Minutes of Organizational Meeting" (manuscript, n.d.), TSHA Records (CAH).

9. Wooten to Garrison, Feb. 16, 1897, TSHA Records (CAH).

10. John H. Reagan to Lester G. Bugbee, Mar. 19, 1897, TSHA Records (CAH).

11. "A Brief Survey of Recent Historical Work," *Atlantic Monthly*, 81 (Feb. 1898), 274 (1st quotation); Garrison to Reagan, Mar. 22, 1897 (2nd quotation), TSHA Records (CAH); Reagan to Bugbee, Mar. 27, 1897 (3rd quotation), ibid.

12. Eldridge G. Littlejohn to Zachary T. Fulmore, Feb. 20, 1897, TSHA Records (CAH).

13. Wooten to Garrison, Mar. 7, 1897, TSHA Records (CAH).

14. Littlejohn to "Secretary, Texas State Historical Society," Nov. 6, 1901, TSHA Records (CAH).

15. "The Organization and Objects of the Texas State Historical Association," 74.

16. Taylor, "The Beginnings of the State Historical Association," 9 (1st quotation); Wooten to Garrison, July 9, 1898 (2nd quotation), TSHA Records (CAH).

17. Emily B. Cooley to Luther E. Widen, Feb. 2, 1906 (1st quotation), TSHA Records (CAH); Widen to Mary C. Butler, Dec. 4, 1905 (2nd quotation).

18. Garrison to Hally B. Perry, May 6, 1907, Hally B. Perry Papers (CAH).

19. "Affairs of the Association," *SHQ*, 1 (Oct. 1897), 130, 131.

20. Widen to Butler, Dec. 4, 1905 (TSHA Records).

21. Herbert E. Bolton to Fulmore, Apr. 6, 1911, Herbert E. Bolton Papers (Bancroft Library, University of California, Berkeley).

22. Wooten to Garrison, June 15, 1897, TSHA Records (CAH).

23. "Affairs of the Association," *SHQ*, 10 (Apr. 1907), 354.

24. Garrison to Bugbee, June 30 (1st quotation), July 28 (2nd quotation), 1898, Lester G. Bugbee Papers (CAH).

25. Julia L. Sinks to Garrison, Dec. 3, 1899, TSHA Records (CAH).

26. Roberts, "The Proper Work of the Association," 3–4, 7.

27. Guy M. Bryan to Bugbee, Aug. 16, 1897, Bugbee Papers (CAH).

28. William P. Zuber to Garrison, Sept. 4, 1900, TSHA Records (CAH).

29. David F. Houston, "The Texas State Historical Association and Its Work," *SHQ*, 11 (Apr. 1908), 246.

THE CHIEF

1. H. Bailey Carroll to Herbert P. Gambrell, Jan. 30, 1961, TSHA Records (CAH).

2. Walter L. Buenger and Robert A. Calvert, "Introduction: The Shelf Life of Truth in Texas," in Walter L. Buenger and Robert A. Calvert (eds.), *Texas through Time: Evolving Interpretations* (College Station: Texas A&M University Press, 1991), xvi.

3. Eugene C. Barker to Herbert E. Bolton, Oct. 27, 1910, Herbert E. Bolton Papers (Bancroft Library, University of California, Berkeley).

4. Barker to Bolton, Sept. 17, 1910, Bolton Papers (Bancroft Library, University of California, Berkeley).

5. Bolton to Adele B. Looscan, Aug. 19, 1918, Adele B. Looscan Papers (Houston Public Library, Houston).

6. Barker to Looscan, Nov. 13, 1912, Looscan Papers (Houston Public Library, Houston).

7. Barker to Looscan, Nov. 13, 1912 (1st quotation), Looscan Papers (Houston Public Library, Houston); Carroll to Christopher McKee, Mar. 11, 1958 (2nd quotation), TSHA Records (CAH); Barker to Samuel E. Asbury, Feb. 4, 1938 (3rd quotation), Samuel E. Asbury Papers (CAH; copy in Eugene C. Barker Papers, CAH); Joe B. Frantz, "Remembering Walter Prescott Webb," *SHQ*, 92 (July 1988), 28 (4th and 5th quotations).

8. Donald E. Chipman, "Spanish Texas," in Buenger and Calvert (eds.), *Texas through Time*, 108.

9. Walter L. Buenger and Robert A. Calvert, *Texas History and the Move into the Twenty-First Century* (Austin: Texas Committee for the Humanities, 1990), 4.

10. Charles W. Ramsdell to Looscan, May 28, 1917, TSHA Records (CAH).

11. Barker to Alexander Dienst, Feb. 20 (1st quotation), Mar. 1, 1918 (2nd and 3rd quotations), TSHA Records (CAH).

12. Barker to Looscan, Jan. 7, 1915, Looscan Papers (Houston Public Library, Houston).

13. Barker to ——— Clark, July 21, 1912, Barker Papers (CAH).

14. Looscan to Barker, Mar. 5, 1915, Barker Papers (CAH).

15. Tom B. Brewer, "A History of the Department of History of the University of Texas, 1883–1951" (M.A. thesis, University of Texas at Austin, 1957), 211.

16. Ramsdell to Looscan, Mar. 25 (1st and 2nd quotations), Nov. 21, 1916 (3rd quotation), Looscan Papers (Houston Public Library, Houston).

17. Barker to Beauregard Bryan, Sept. 17, 1914 (1st quotation), TSHA Records (CAH); Ramsdell to Barker, Oct. 20, 1914 (2nd and 3rd quotations), Barker Papers (CAH).

18. Barker to Looscan, Mar. 8, 1919, Looscan Papers (Houston Public Library, Houston).

19. "Temporary Chairman, Committee on Patrons" (Thomas P. Martin) to William M. W. Splawn, Aug. 19, 1924, TSHA Records (CAH).

20. Martin to Looscan, Dec. 2, 1924 (1st quotation), Mar. 23, 1925 (2nd quotation), TSHA Records (CAH).

21. Zachary T. Fulmore to Looscan, Jan. 26, 1914 (1st and 2nd quotations), Looscan Papers (Houston Public Library, Houston); Barker to Looscan, Feb. 21, 1918 (3rd quotation), ibid. (copy in Barker Papers, CAH).

22. Barker to Looscan, Feb. 4, 1921, Barker Papers (CAH).

23. Alexander Dienst to Coral H. Tullis, Mar. 5, 1929, TSHA Records (CAH).

24. Walter P. Webb to Barker, Feb. 23, 1938, Barker Papers (CAH).

25. Dorman H. Winfrey (comp.), *A History of the Philosophical Society of Texas, 1837–1987* (Austin: Philosophical Society of Texas, 1987), 129 (1st and 2nd quotations); Barker to Asbury, n.d. (3rd quotation), TSHA Records (CAH).

26. Barker to Winnie Allen, Nov. 24, 1937, TSHA Records (CAH).

27. Barker to John Suman, June 9, 1938, TSHA Records (CAH).

28. Webb to Barker, Mar. 2, 1938, Walter P. Webb Papers (CAH).

29. Eugene C. Barker, *Speeches, Responses, and Essays Critical and Historical*, 23 (1st quotation); Barker to David H. Stevens, Sept. 15, 1942 (2nd and 3rd quotations), TSHA Records (CAH).

30. Brewer, "A History of the Department of History," 210.

A BROADER SCOPE AND A BIGGER JOB

1. Lana Ruegamer, *A History of the Indiana Historical Society, 1830–1980* (Indianapolis: Indiana Historical Society, 1980), 84.

2. Walter P. Webb, "History as High Adventure," in Walter P. Webb (ed.), *An Honest Preface and Other Essays* (Boston: Houghton Mifflin Co., 1959), 197.

3. Walter P. Webb to Ralph D. Casey, Sept. 16, 1938 (1st and 2nd quotations), Walter P. Webb Papers (CAH); H. Bailey Carroll to Samuel E. Asbury, Oct. 23, 1942 (3rd quotation), TSHA Records (CAH).

4. Carroll to Louis W. Kemp, Sept. 29, 1942, TSHA Records (CAH).

5. Webb to Harbert Davenport, May 1 (4th quotation), July 31, 1939 (1st and 2nd quotations),

Webb Papers (CAH); Webb to TSHA Executive Council, Oct. 3, 1938 (3rd quotation), TSHA Records (CAH).

6. "Texas Collection," *SHQ*, 42 (Apr. 1939), 390.

7. TSHA Executive Council to Centennial Executive Committee, Dec. 1, 1932, Eugene C. Barker Papers (CAH).

8. Webb to Pat I. Nixon, May 3, 1939 (1st quotation), TSHA Records (CAH); Webb to Ben P. Hunt, May 3, 1939 (3rd–6th quotations), ibid.; Webb to Davenport, May 1, 1939 (2nd quotation), Webb Papers (CAH).

9. Webb to Herbert P. Gambrell, May 8, 1939 (1st quotation), TSHA Records (CAH); Herbert Gambrell to Walter P. Webb, Aug. 7, 1939 (2nd quotation), ibid.; Louis W. Kemp to Walter P. Webb, n.d. (3rd quotation), ibid.; Webb to Davenport, Jan. 12 (4th quotation), May 10 (5th quotation), 1940, Webb Papers (CAH).

10. Webb to Earl Vandale, Oct. 12, 1940, TSHA Records (CAH).

11. H. Bailey Carroll, "Report and Recommendations Concerning the Texas State Historical Association" (transcript, n.d. [1943], TSHA Records (CAH).

12. Webb to William R. Hogan, Aug. 14, 1941 (1st quotation), TSHA Records (CAH); Carroll to Davenport, June 8, 1943 (2nd and 3rd quotations), ibid.

13. Carroll to Willis R. Woolrich, Jan. 18, 1943, TSHA Records (CAH).

14. "Texas Collection," *SHQ*, 42 (Jan. 1939), 263 (1st and 2nd quotations), Webb Papers (CAH); Webb, Eugene C. Barker, and J. Frank Dobie to Kenneth H. Aynesworth, July 8, 1941 (3rd quotation), ibid.

15. Barker to Hally B. Perry, Dec. 20, 1945, Perry Papers (CAH).

16. Webb to George A. Hill, Mar. 13, 1940 (1st and 2nd quotations), TSHA Records (CAH); Webb to McCune Gill, May 16, 1940 (3rd quotation; same in Webb to Watt Marchman, Jan. 29, 1941), TSHA Records (CAH).

17. Webb to Davenport, Jan. 30, 1939, TSHA Records (CAH).

18. "By Amateurs," *Time,* 50 (Aug. 11, 1978), 77 (1st quotation), TSHA Records (CAH); Webb to Donald D. Parker, Apr. 9, 1945 (2nd quotation), ibid.

19. Webb to B. F. Meek, Oct. 6, 1939, TSHA Records (CAH).

20. Necah S. Furman, *Walter Prescott Webb: His Life and Impact* (Albuquerque: University of New Mexico Press, 1976), 135–136.

21. TSHA Executive Council Minutes, April 10, 1942 (1st and 2nd quotations), TSHA Records (CAH); Webb to Davenport, Jan. 15, 1940, Webb Papers (CAH); Dorman H. Winfrey, *Seventy-Five Years of Texas History: The Texas State Historical Association, 1897–1972* (Austin: Jenkins Publishing Co., 1975), 23 (3rd quotation).

22. Davenport to Webb, May 1, 1939, Webb Papers (CAH).

23. Webb to Coral H. Tullis, May 5, 1938 (1st quotation), TSHA Records (CAH); Webb to Davenport, May 1, 1939 (2nd and 3rd quotations), Webb Papers (CAH).

24. Webb to G. P. Hammond, Dec. 3, 1941, TSHA Records (CAH).

25. Webb to Homer P. Rainey, Jan. 15, 1941, University of Texas President's Office Files (CAH).

26. Webb to Davenport, Feb. 27, 1941, Webb Papers (CAH).

27. Carroll to Kemp, Oct. 22, 1943, TSHA Records (CAH).

28. Carroll to Leslie Waggener Jr., Jan. 24, 1945, TSHA Records (CAH).

29. Webb to "Members Texas State Historical Association," Nov. 15, 1939 (1st quotation), TSHA Records (CAH); Webb to Mrs. A. H. Worden, Oct. 14, 1939 (2nd and 3rd quotations), ibid.

30. Winfrey (comp.), *A History of the Philosophical Society of Texas, 1837–1987*, 39.

31. "Texas Collection," *SHQ,* 49 (Apr. 1946), 459 (1st quotation), TSHA Records (CAH); Webb to Gibb Gilchrist, Oct. 22, 1941 (2nd quotation), ibid.; "Texas State Historical Associa-

tion Broadcast No. 4, Feb. 1944" (transcript, n.d., 3rd quotation), TSHA Records (CAH).

32. Webb to Davenport, Aug. 31, 1943, Webb Papers (CAH).

33. Webb to Samuel E. Asbury, Mar. 6, 1944 (1st quotation), Webb Papers (CAH); Webb to John Marshall, July 22, 1943 (2nd quotation), ibid.; Webb to Donald D. Parker, Apr. 9, 1945 (3rd and 4th quotations), TSHA Records (CAH).

34. Joe B. Frantz, *The Forty Acre Follies: An Informal History of the University of Texas* (Austin: Texas Monthly Press, 1983), 173 (1st quotation); Lewis P. Simpson, "Remembering Walter Prescott Webb," *SHQ*, 92 (July 1988), 28 (2nd quotation).

35. Webb to T. R. Havins, Nov. 4, 1939, TSHA Records (CAH).

OLD MAN TEXAS HIMSELF

1. "Texas Collection," *SHQ*, 50 (July 1946), 113.

2. Herbert P. Gambrell, "The Eugene C. Barker Texas History Center," *SHQ*, 54 (July 1950), 2.

3. H. Bailey Carroll to Clement M. Silvestro, Oct. 25, 1960, TSHA Records (CAH).

4. Ibid.

5. Carroll to Edward Crane, July 23, 1953 (1st quotation), TSHA Records (CAH); TSHA Executive Council Minutes, Oct. 20, 1953 (2nd and 3rd quotations), Walter F. McCaleb Papers (CAH).

6. "Texas Collection, *SHQ*, 54 (Apr. 1951), 479.

7. Samuel E. Asbury to TSHA Executive Council, July 29, 1946, Asbury Papers (CAH).

8. "Texas Collection," *SHQ*, 51 (Jan. 1948), 270.

9. Walter M. Whitehill, *Independent Historical Societies* (Boston: Boston Athenaeum, 1962), 330 (1st–3rd quotations), TSHA Records (CAH); Carroll to Ruth I. Mahood, Mar. 3, 1964 (4th quotation), ibid.

10. Carroll to Hally B. Perry, Jan. 9, 1953 (1st quotation), Hally B. Perry Papers (CAH); "Texas Collection," *SHQ*, 57 (July 1953), 112 (2nd quotation); Carroll to Cooper K. Ragan, Oct. 15, 1964 (3rd quotation), TSHA Records (CAH); Walter M. Whitehill, "Local History in the United States," *Times Literary Supplement*, Nov. 13, 1970 (4th quotation).

11. Gambrell, "The Barker Texas History Center," 4.

12. Herbert Fletcher, "Life, Liberty, and the Pursuit of Texiana," *SHQ*, 54 (July 1950), 65.

13. Carroll to Pat I. Nixon, Dec. 16, 1946, TSHA Records (CAH).

14. Carroll to TSHA Executive Council, Apr. 10, 1959, TSHA Records (CAH); Barker, *Speeches, Responses, and Essays Critical and Historical*, 28. (Quotation found in both).

15. Herbert P. Gambrell to Carroll, May 5, 1952 (1st quotation); Carroll to Gambrell, May 13, 1952 (2nd–4th quotations), TSHA Records (CAH); Carroll to Walter F. McCaleb, May 22, 1952 (5th quotation), ibid.

16. *Alcalde*, 8 (May 1920), 918–919 (1st and 2nd quotations); McCaleb to TSHA Executive Council, Dec. 26, 1953 (3rd and 4th quotations), TSHA Records (CAH).

17. J. Evetts Haley to McCaleb, Nov. 27, 1953 (1st–3rd quotations), TSHA Records (CAH); Gambrell to TSHA Executive Council, Dec. 14, 1953 (4th quotation), ibid.

18. McCaleb to Walter P. Webb, Dec. 26, 1953, TSHA Records (CAH).

19. C. P. Boner to Logan R. Wilson, Sept. 11, 1953, University of Texas President's Office Files (CAH).

20. Carroll to R. O'Hara Lanier, Apr. 1, 1953, TSHA Records (CAH).

21. Carroll to Lanier, Apr. 1, 1953 (1st quotation), TSHA Records (CAH); Lanier to Carroll, Apr. 13, 1953 (2nd quotation), ibid.

22. Carroll to Lanier, Apr. 1, 1953 (1st quotation), TSHA Records (CAH); Carroll to TSHA Executive Council, Apr. 14, 1953 (2nd–4th quotations), ibid.

23. Carroll to Merle M. Duncan, May 12, 1953, TSHA Records (CAH).

24. S. H. Burford to Lester G. Bugbee, Aug. 26, 1900, TSHA Records (CAH).

25. "Affairs of the Association," *SHQ*, 59 (July 1955), 76.

26. Carroll to William C. Pool, Mar. 20, 1961 (1st quotation), TSHA Records (CAH); Ragan to Carroll, Nov. 6, 1962 (2nd quotation), ibid.; Carroll to Ragan, Nov. 7, 1962 (3rd quotation), ibid.

27. Joe B. Frantz to Tom Charlton, Feb. 4, 1974, TSHA Records (CAH).

28. John Graves, *Goodbye to a River* (New York: Alfred A. Knopf, 1960), 11.

29. Carroll to Fred R. Cotten, Apr. 21, 1961 (1st quotation), TSHA Records (CAH); Furman, *Walter Prescott Webb*, 139 (2nd quotation).

30. Carroll to Cotten, n.d., TSHA Files (TSHA Offices, University of Texas at Austin).

31. Carroll to Nixon, Dec. 16, 1946, Mar. 19, 1947 (1st quotation), TSHA Records (CAH); Carroll to Herman Lee Crow, Feb. 26, 1962 (2nd quotation), ibid.; Carroll to Floyd C. Shoemaker, Mar. 27, 1962 (3rd and 4th quotations), ibid.

32. "Texas Collection," *SHQ*, 51 (July 1947), 85; James D. Carter to Robert C. Cotner, May 17, 1966, Robert C. Cotner Papers (CAH).

33. Carroll to John B. Shepperd, Aug. 13, 1962 (1st and 2nd quotations), TSHA Records (CAH); George P. Isbell, "Dr. H. Bailey Carroll, 1903–1966," *SHQ*, 70 (July 1966), 6 (3rd quotation).

IN THE SHADOW OF WEBB

1. Joe B. Frantz to J. Alton Burdine, June 20, 1966 (1st quotation), University of Texas President's Office Files (CAH); "TSHA Director's Report, 1966–1967" (transcript, n.d.) (2nd quotation), TSHA Records (CAH).

2. Dorman H. Winfrey, "Mrs. Coral Horton Tullis (1882–1967)," *SHQ*, 71 (Oct. 1967), 281 (1st and 2nd quotations); "TSHA Director's Report, 1966–1967" (3rd quotation), TSHA Files (TSHA Offices, University of Texas at Austin).

3. L. Tuffly Ellis to Archie P. McDonald, Aug. 9, 1985 (copy provided by L. Tuffly Ellis; in author's possession).

4. "TSHA Annual Report, 1969–1970" (transcript, n.d.), TSHA Files (TSHA Offices, University of Texas at Austin).

5. Harbert Davenport to Walter P. Webb, Feb. 1, 1940, Webb Papers (CAH).

6. "TSHA Director's Report, 1966–1967," TSHA Files (TSHA Offices, University of Texas at Austin).

7. David G. McComb, *Travels with Joe, 1917–1993* (Austin: Texas State Historical Association, 2001), 34.

8. Ellis to Robert A. Calvert, Aug. 18, 1972 (1st quotation), TSHA Records (CAH); Ellis to F. L. Rath Jr., Nov. 1, 1968 (2nd quotation), ibid.

9. Winfrey, *Seventy-Five Years of Texas History*, 30.

10. Ellis to F. L. Rath, Nov. 1, 1968, TSHA Records (CAH).

11. "Southwestern Collection," *SHQ*, 78 (July 1974), 79.

12. "TSHA Annual Report, 1972–1973" (transcript, n.d.), TSHA Files (TSHA Offices, University of Texas at Austin).

13. "Affairs of the Association," *SHQ*, 75 (July 1971), 128 (1st quotation); Ellis to Cooper K. Ragan, Jan. 27, 1970 (2nd quotation), TSHA Records (CAH); Ellis to Paul Scheips, Jan. 29, 1970 (3rd quotation), ibid.; Frantz to W. St. John Garwood, Oct. 5, 1971 (4th quotation), TSHA Records (CAH).

14. TSHA Director's Report, 1973–1974 (1st quotation), (transcript, n.d,, copy provided by L. Tuffly Ellis; in author's possession); Joe B. Frantz, "Eleven Years—A Summing Up," *SHQ*, 81 (July 1977), 40 (2nd quotation).

15. "The Handbook of Texas: A Report" (transcript, n.d.), TSHA Records (CAH), 5.

16. Joe B. Frantz, "History Looking Ahead," *SHQ,* 70 (Jan. 1967), 359.

17. Frantz, "History Looking Ahead," 355.

18. Frantz to Norman Hackerman, Apr. 29, 1968 (1st quotation), President's Office Files (CAH); "TSHA Annual Report, 1969–1970" (2nd and 3rd quotations), " (transcript, n.d.), TSHA Files (TSHA Offices, University of Texas at Austin); Ellis to Frantz, Mar. 6, 1969 (4th quotation), (copy provided by L. Tuffly Ellis; in author's possession).

19. L. Tuffly Ellis, "Director's Report," *SHQ,* 89 (July 1985), 109.

20. "TSHA Annual Report, 1972–1973," TSHA Files (TSHA Offices, University of Texas at Austin).

21. "TSHA Director's Report, 1975–1976" (transcript, n.d., TSHA Files, TSHA Offices, University of Texas at Austin).

22. TSHA Executive Council Minutes, June 23, 1979 (transcript, copy provided by L. Tuffly Ellis; in author's possession).

23. "TSHA Director's Report, 1973–1974," TSHA Files (TSHA Offices, University of Texas at Austin).

24. McComb, *Travels with Joe,* 84.

25. Frantz, "History Looking Ahead," 358 (1st quotation); "Southwestern Collection," *SHQ,* 74 (Jan. 1971), 552 (2nd quotation).

26. Frantz, "History Looking Ahead," 355.

27. Ellis to Ragan, Aug. 13, 1970 (1st quotation), TSHA Records (CAH); Ellis to Gene Brack, Aug. 13, 1970 (2nd quotation), ibid.

28. Ellis to Mrs. Paul Brindley, Aug. 26, 1971 (1st quotation), TSHA Records (CAH); Ellis to Billy Mac Jones, Mar. 21, 1977 (2nd quotation), ibid.

29. Ellis to Richard B. McCaslin, n.d. [Mar. 2002] (1st and 2nd quotations), (in author's possession); "TSHA Director's Report, March 1980" (3rd quotation), (transcript), TSHA Files (TSHA Offices, University of Texas at Austin).

30. "TSHA Director's Report, September 3, 1981" (1st quotation), TSHA Files (TSHA Offices, University of Texas at Austin); William S. Livingston to Peter T. Flawn, Jan. 29, 1982 (2nd quotation), TSHA Records (CAH).

31. "TSHA Director's Report, February 12, 1985," TSHA Files (TSHA Offices, University of Texas at Austin).

32. Seymour V. Connor to Frantz, May 6, 1966 (1st and 2nd quotations), TSHA Records (CAH); Frantz to TSHA Executive Council, Aug. 22, 1977 (3rd quotation), ibid.

33. Frantz, *The Forty Acre Follies,* 23.

34. "TSHA Director's Report, 1976–1977" (1st quotation), (transcript, n.d.), TSHA Files (TSHA Offices, University of Texas at Austin); Frantz, "Eleven Years," 37 (2nd quotation).

35. Ellis to Edward H. Phillips, July 17, 1970 (1st quotation), TSHA Records (CAH); Ron Tyler to Dan E. Kilgore, Feb. 18, 1977 (2nd and 3rd quotations), ibid.

36. Ellis to Tyler, Feb. 15, 1977 (1st quotation), TSHA Records (CAH); L. Tuffly Ellis to James A. Chappell, Mar. 31, 1980 (2nd quotation), ibid.

37. Ellis, "Director's Report," 115.

COMPLETING THE FIRST CENTURY

1. "Southwestern Collection," *SHQ,* 90 (Jan. 1987), 302.

2. "Southwestern Collection," *SHQ,* 95 (July 1991), 134.

3. "Southwestern Collection," *SHQ,* 93 (Oct. 1989), 222.

4. "Southwestern Collection," *SHQ,* 88 (July 1984), 84.

5. "TSHA Director's Report, Feb, 29, 1996," TSHA Files (TSHA Offices, University of Texas at Austin).

6. Ron Tyler, et al. (eds.), *The New Handbook of Texas* (6 vols.; Austin: Texas State Historical Association, 1996), I, x.

7. "Southwestern Collection," *SHQ*, 82 (Jan. 1979), 305.

8. *NHOT Online*, http://www.tsha.utexas.edu/handbook/online/.

9. Anders Saustrup to L. Tuffly Ellis, Apr. 23, 1982, TSHA Records (CAH).

10. "Southwestern Collection," *SHQ*, 92 (Jan. 1989), 475.

11. "Southwestern Collection," *SHQ*, 96 (Jan. 1993), 323.

12. "Southwestern Collection," *SHQ*, 101 (Oct. 1997), 242.

13. Stephen L. Hardin to Ron Tyler, Apr. 3, 1997 (quotation), TSHA Files (TSHA Offices, University of Texas at Austin).

14. TSHA Executive Council Minutes, May 31, 1990, TSHA Files (TSHA Offices, University of Texas at Austin).

15. TSHA Executive Council Minutes, Feb. 29, 1996 (1st quotation), TSHA Files (TSHA Offices, University of Texas at Austin); "Southwestern Collection," *SHQ*, 99 (Apr. 1996), 548 (2nd quotation).

16. "Southwestern Collection," *SHQ*, 101 (Jan. 1998), 371.

17. "Southwestern Collection," *SHQ*, 101 (Jan. 1998), 369.

Index

(Illustrations are indicated by **boldfaced** page numbers.)

C

RICHARD B. MCCASLIN, professor of history at the University of North Texas and Fellow of the Texas State Historical Association, won the Tullis Prize from the Association for *Tainted Breeze: The Great Hanging at Gainesville, Texas, October 1862*. He has also written *Lee in the Shadow of Washington*, which was nominated for a Pulitzer and won the Laney Prize from the Austin Civil War Round Table and the Slatten Award from the Virginia Historical Society.

J. P. BRYAN was TSHA president for the year 1982–1983; his father, J. P. Bryan Sr., was president from 1965 to 1967; and another family member, Guy M. Bryan, was a vice president from 1897, when the Association began, until his death in 1901. Bryan's roots in the history of the state go back to Emily Austin Bryan Perry, sister of Stephen F. Austin, the "Father of Texas." His interest in Texas history was instilled by his father and his Aunt Hally Bryan Perry, and encouraged by Association director H. Bailey Carroll.

COLOPHON

The text typeface for this book is Adobe Caslon. William Caslon released his first typefaces in 1722. Caslon's types became popular throughout Europe and the American colonies. The first printings of the American Declaration of Independence and the Constitution were set in Caslon. The display type is Monotype Latin. Sidebars are set in Gill Sans. The book was printed by Sheridan Books, Inc., of Ann Arbor, Michigan, on 55# House Natural paper, in an initial run of 2,500.

TEXANA
AUCTION
1948

Clockwise above, Evetts Haley len[d]
tic Texas touch to the occasion
Gambrell and Roy Bedichek, fre
luncheon confessions on "How-I-V
survey the standing-room-only crov
peers under his spectacles at the it[e]
posite. Bookseller Heartmann is o
many "in the trade" that keeps a p
on the prices reached. On the faci[ng]
same order, auctioneer Timmons
against the five-fifteen deadline
Carroll pulls on his stogie. Dr. Ni[x]
the bidding on neglected items as
suffers through a new design prob[l]
products sell at a premium. Harb
stays on following his pre-auction
the sport.